The Chameleon

*Life-Changing Wisdom for Anyone Who
Has a Personality or Knows Someone Who Does*

The Chameleon:

*Life-Changing Wisdom
for Anyone Who Has a Personality
or Knows Someone Who Does*

By Merrick Rosenberg

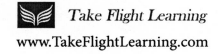

Take Flight Learning
www.TakeFlightLearning.com

Take Flight Learning
TakeFlightLearning.com
ChiefParrot@TakeFlightLearning.com

10 9 8 7 6 5 4 3 2
First Edition 2016
Printed in the United States of America

ISBN-10: 0-9964110-0-3
ISBN-13: 978-0-9964110-0-4
Library of Congress Control Number: 2015957242

Book design by CenterPointe Media
www.CenterPointeMedia.com

Dedication

To my parents, Barbara and Howard Rosenberg,
I am who I am because of you.
Thanks for believing.

To my wife, Traci, you fill my world with light.
Thank you for making my life an incredible adventure.

To my children, Gavin and Ben,
you make me smile every day.
Thanks for being you.

And if you are wondering if there are parts of this book
specifically about you … yes, there are.
Thanks for the inspiration.

Acknowledgments

I want thank all those who made this book possible. I am indebted to the support and insight you shared so willingly.

I am deeply grateful to be surrounded by such an amazing team of committed and hardworking individuals. To Jeff Backal, thanks for joining me on this journey—but get ready, because we've still got a long way to go.

To those who tirelessly introduce the birds to people all around the world, specifically, Andy Kraus, Rick Kauffman, and Jessica Nicols, you lead the way in making a difference in so many lives.

To Dolores Woodington, Cathryn Plum, Elanna Albanese, Nathan Davis, and Laura Williams, thank you for everything you do. This parrot would be lost without you.

To Kerry Bayles, Heather Hafner, and Valerie Vincent, it warms my heart to see the joy, laughter and transformation you bring to everyone you encounter on your travels.

I also want to thank all of those who provided feedback throughout the writing process, including Traci Rosenberg, Aaren Perry, Laura Robinson and Darah Backal.

To Matthew and Joan Greenblatt at CenterPointeMedia, thank you for your wisdom and focused attention to detail in bringing this book to life. I also want to thank Nesta Aharoni and Terrin Irwin for your gift of words and Michael Clarida for illustrating the characters into existence.

Finally, I want express my appreciation to all of the Certified Affiliates and Certified Trainers of Take Flight Learning. Your work sends ripples of positive energy and growth throughout the planet.

Contents

Preface 1

Introduction: The Journey Begins 6

Spring

The New Addition 17

The Sparrow's Nest 29

The Spinning Wind 43

The Crystal Cave.. 55

Hatching Day Surprise.. 69

Summer

A Trip to the Beach 81

The Speech.. 93

The Lost Bird Department 103

The Forbidden Swamp 113

Summer Festival 127

Fall

Spontaneity Day... 141

Squirrel! 151

Observation Week.. 159

Flight of the Groundhog 171

The Storm of all Storms 181

Winter

Mudslide 197

Winter Camp.. 209

The Northern Squirrels.. 221

Lost in Translation... 233

The Magic Rock 245

Epilogue: The Journey Home 262

About the Author 271

Preface

Prior to 1994 I thought I understood people. And why wouldn't I? I had earned an MBA specializing in organizational behavior. I had started one of the first team building companies in the United States, and it was thriving. Each day I taught people about teamwork, trust, communication, and leadership. Of course I understood people.

Then I discovered the DISC model, which described four personality styles that provided a framework for understanding behavior. Through this model I gained deep insight into my own needs, desires, motivators, and fears. I learned how to read people and proactively anticipate their needs. And the more I practiced applying these insights, the more I felt as if I had been living in the dark.

As I developed a new understanding of myself and others, a bright light began to shine on me and everyone else I knew. I never could have imagined something so simple could be so powerful.

For the next fifteen years, I traveled the world helping individuals increase their self-awareness and apply the wisdom of the styles. I watched people improve their relationships, increase their effectiveness at work, enhance their careers, and become better parents and partners. I was living my life's purpose. What more could I ask for?

Then I started to notice a pattern. While I felt gratified when attendees at my sessions shared how much they enjoyed my presentations, many of them added a question afterward that went something like this: "I think I'm a D. Which one is that again?" Or, "If I recall correctly, I'm an S. What does that stand for?"

I became deflated. How could this be? I was spending my days illuminating people's lives with the DISC styles, and the recipients weren't remembering the most basic lessons from those sessions. This revelation cast a shadow of doubt on the value of the training I was providing.

After one such encounter, I sat down to continue writing my new book about the DISC styles. I was excited to be halfway done, even though my enthusiasm had become tempered by an inner voice questioning the effectiveness of the four letters. That was the day I opened myself to the possibility that there must be a better way.

In a mere moment the idea of using four birds revealed itself to me. Perhaps my own parrot, Merlin, worked his magic by appearing in my mind's eye and enthusiastically symbolizing the Interactive I-style. "That's interesting," I thought. "I bet a parrot representing the I-style would be easier for people to remember."

Almost immediately an eagle confidently stepped forward to represent the perfect symbol of the Dominant D-style. Moments later, an owl logically showed himself to be the ideal Conscientious C. Next arrived a dove, who humbly offered to depict the Supportive S. And so it was. The birds were born.

I began introducing the birds into my training programs and speaking events, and I was astounded by the positive reception they received. In nearly every session, someone told me about their previous training and how they had forgotten everything afterwards. But the birds, they said, made the styles easier to remember and apply. During fifteen years as a trainer and speaker, I had been using four letters that provided only a fleeting fascination. The birds, however, were creating lasting change.

As an increasing number of people began sharing stories of the birds' impact, I could not help but wonder what made them so special. At first, I chalked it up to our common impression of each bird's nature, which made them memorable. An owl, for example, instantly conjures up images of logic and precision, making the C-style easy to recall.

But it was more than that. Soon I recognized that people's memory challenges had been rooted in the letters themselves. When the words "Dominant," "Interactive," "Supportive," and "Conscientious" were shortened to D, I, S, and C, they were stripped of their meaning, which made them harder to remember. Unlike the image of an eagle, the letter D meant nothing and, therefore, had no sticking power. The D-I-S-C letters, quite simply, were not brain-friendly.

Applying new insights requires remembering those insights. The birds provide mental models that do just that. In contrast to the DISC acronym, the birds are mnemonic devices or memory aids. Just like "Every Good Boy Does Fine" helps budding musicians remember the lines of the treble clef, the four birds help people remember the four personality styles.

Now, when I meet people long after they have attended a session that incorporated the bird styles, I regularly hear statements such as, "I am a dove" or "I am a parrot with a little bit of eagle." Those pronouncements are often followed by stories about how the styles are playing out in their lives.

When the birds flew into my world, the trajectory of my life changed. I shelved the book in progress about the four letter styles and, instead, coauthored *Taking Flight!* with Daniel Silvert. In that book, the first to include the birds, we taught people about the styles and how to use them in daily interactions ... and how to remember them!

In *The Chameleon*, I take that knowledge and application to the next level. While the characters in the book are birds and chameleons, the content is about you and everyone you know. Does the owl represent your boss? The dove your spouse or parent? Perhaps the parrot is a coworker and the eagle one of your children.

Before we begin this journey, let's review some foundational principles of style. To begin with, each one of us is a combination of all four styles. Nobody is just an eagle, parrot, dove, or owl. We all have a bit of each style within us, and, if we incorporate some flexibility, we can display any of the behaviors ... despite our natural style.

There are no good or bad styles. Each has its own strengths and challenges. And two people who share the same style may display that style to varying degrees.

One person may be a pygmy owl, displaying slight tendencies of the owl style. Another may be the great horned owl, strongly exemplifying owl behaviors in just about everything they do.

We all get caught up in the drama of our life stories, just as the birds get caught up in theirs. Take a page out of this book and become the chameleon. Flexibly adapt to the people you encounter and the situations that unfold around you. As you read each fable, mindfully look inside yourself and consider how the lessons presented apply in your life.

It's time to tap into the wisdom of *The Chameleon*!

Introduction

The Journey Begins

As the sun rose over the Great Lake, Xenia gazed at the dawn of a new era. She adjusted her chameleon skin to match the crimson dawn and then harmonized her coloring with the morning sky as it migrated from orange, gold, and yellow and to soothing daylight blue.

Chameleons have an innate wisdom that allows them to connect to the world and to those around them. Xenia was no exception. She instinctively understood how to handle life's situations with grace and ease. Her intuition, coupled with insight passed down by her father, enabled her to ask the right question at the right moment, and to inspire profound transformation.

Xenia considered herself fortunate to be the daughter of Xavier, a wise and generous master chameleon. She had spent many days shadowing him in the forest, believing he knew nothing of her presence. In retrospect, she now understood that he knew everything of her presence. From a young age, Xavier had taught her to live her life lessons responsibly and to share them with others. Clearly, it was Xenia's duty to pass on her wisdom to the next generation of chameleons as well as to all of the other animals dwelling in the forest she called Home.

Today, Xenia was taking her newest chameleon student, Xander, on his first walk through Home. In time, she would introduce him to the forest's many residents and teach him to sing the song of the birds. She would open his heart to what she had learned when she was young and inexperienced. One day, her student would travel throughout the land and share his lessons—and so the cycle would continue.

Despite her student's young age, Xenia would not treat him as a child. Instead, she would offer him respect and speak to him as if she were awakening a deep knowledge that was sleeping inside him.

Xander arrived early, eager to begin the day, and Xenia did not waste any time. She began, "Everything in life is connected. When one element of the world falls out of balance, waves of discontent ripple throughout the land. I will teach you to anticipate and navigate those ripples. You will learn to appear at the moment you are needed and to nudge life back into balance. You will experience oneness with the forest and all who live here. One day, you will teach those who come after you."

Xenia smiled as she recognized that her words resonated deeply with her student. In his short life, Xander had seen great unease circulate among the creatures of Home, and he wanted to play his part in drawing the forest residents together again.

The teacher continued. "For a while, you will travel with me and observe what I do and how I do it. You will remain unseen at all times and will not reveal yourself unless I announce your presence. Even then, you will remain silent unless a question is directly asked of you. Understood?"

"Understood," the young chameleon affirmed.

"It's time to expand your world in every way," Xenia proclaimed. "To begin, here's a map of the forest. In order to help others find their way, you must first be able to find your own."

Xander reached out to take the map and nodded gratefully.

"Today we will practice the art of invisibility," Xenia said.

"I'm ready," replied Xander with a twinge of excitement. He was elated that a living legend had taken him under her wing.

The pair walked in silence, shifting their coloring to match the varying terrain that evolved beneath them. They walked past bashful blossoms, bulky boulders, and towering pines.

After smoothly crossing a gentle stream, they came upon a family of white doves. Xenia placed a single finger over her mouth, indicating to Xander that they were to stop and observe in silence. The chameleons watched the considerate doves prepare their morning meal and share their bounty with friends. They listened to interested doves ask each other questions about the upcoming day. They noticed supportive doves help a companion who was dealing with a challenging situation. The birds' warm tones and gentle demeanors prompted Xander to smile.

After a few minutes of observation, Xenia advanced Xander onward. "What did you feel emanating from the doves?" Xenia asked her new student.

Xander replied, "Kindness and gentleness. I liked the way they listened to each other. They genuinely care about everyone else's feelings and about the events occurring in each others' lives."

"Very perceptive," replied the teacher. "What do you draw from that?"

Xander glanced once more at the doves and added, "That they are supportive and cooperative, and that they are calm."

"Right again, young sir," Xenia confirmed. "Doves are generally soft spoken and patient. They embody harmony and compassion."

As the chameleons continued on, they transformed from the emerald-olive shades of the vibrant ground cover to the earthy, rich tones of the unassuming stones and twigs. They continued to walk until Xenia spotted a pair of owls nestled in a maple tree. They were planning their day's activities. The observers settled in silence a short distance away.

"We can't get too close to the owls," Xenia advised. "Everything about them is sharp and accurate, including their powers of observation. If we get too close, they will notice us and change their behavior. Let's watch from here."

The owls were busy organizing their belongings and returning various items to their designated places. While one of the owls talked about a problem he was having, the other asked him question after question. The detailed answers and discussions that followed led both owls to explore a series of alternative solutions and then choose a course of action.

After a few minutes, Xenia asked her protégé, "What can you draw from the owls' behavior?"

"They are very structured," Xander said. "They were operating from a checklist while they were organizing their belongings. I'll bet even their checklists have checklists!"

"Perhaps they do," Xenia chuckled.

The chameleons continued to watch quietly as the owls created a plan for the day.

Xander added, "They are very careful and precise."

"Quite accurate, my little friend," Xenia confirmed. "They are analytical by nature and enjoy working through complex problems."

The teacher and student continued onward. They traveled over gently sloping hills and hiked passed the mountainous Xanadu's Peak. Xenia gave a slight bow to the impressive peak, which had been named after the wise chameleon master, Xanadu.

"What was so great about Xanadu?" Xander wondered aloud.

Xenia's bright, yellow eyes grew wider still. "When I was your age, my father, Xavier, taught me Xanadu's guiding principle of the forest: Treat others how they need to be treated. We now call it the Home Rule."

Xander looked puzzled, but he didn't want to challenge his teacher. Xenia noticed his expression and prompted him to speak his mind.

Xander offered, "Well, it's just that my parents taught me that I am supposed to treat others how *I* want to be treated."

"Ah! That is one of the great truths of all forests throughout the land."

"I'm confused. What you just said is opposite of what my parents taught me. Which one is right? Treat others how *I* want to be treated or how *they* want to be treated?"

Xenia laughed. "Sometimes the opposite of great wisdom is more great wisdom. When it comes to virtues such as kindness, respect, and fairness, you should treat others how *you* want to be treated. When you do that, those virtues will be returned to you in abundance. But when you share information, provide instructions, or offer praise, you should treat others how *they* want to be treated. You see, both statements are true."

Xander still looked puzzled as Xenia continued. "In our walks together, keep your eyes open and notice how often the birds impose their style of doing things on others. In the meantime, I hear the parrots up ahead. Let's listen in."

The chameleons did not need to get too close to hear a group of parrots who were telling stories. At times, several stories were circulating at once. When one parrot started a story, another jumped in with her own. Moments later the first parrot continued. None of them seemed to mind the interruptions.

"They sure like to talk!" Xander noted. "And they sound fun."

"Oh, they are," Xenia replied. "What else do you notice?"

Xander laughed. "They seem excited about something. They are bursting with energy!"

"They are not just excited about what they are talking about. They live in a perpetual state of optimism and enthusiasm. Parrots are easy to observe. It's a good thing we can find them everywhere."

"Great! Who's next?" Xander exclaimed, speaking as if he had caught some parrot spirit.

"Look up," the chameleon directed.

They moved to a clearing so they could view the sky above the treetops. Just below the clouds, Xander spotted a lone eagle floating on a current. Her expression was focused and intense. Clearly, she was not flying for the fun of it. She was working. The eagle glided effortlessly until, suddenly, she snapped her head to the right. Without hesitation, she rocketed towards the lake like a meteorite.

"Wow!" Xander exclaimed. "She seems to be on a mission!"

Just then the eagle emerged with a large fish and began to soar to the clouds.

"Once she knows what she wants, there is no stopping her," Xenia replied. "What else did you see?"

"Well, before she dove, she was studying the entire forest."

"Very perceptive," Xenia affirmed. "When you want to watch an eagle, look to the sky. They view the world from a vantage point above the daily details of life. Eagles are direct, decisive, and focused on bottom-line results."

Before the chameleons started their return home, they climbed to the top of the nearest tree and stood on its highest branch. Xenia smiled at her new student and said, "Today you met the four major birds of the forest and learned an important lesson: treat others how *they* need to be treated. Together we will observe the birds and, occasionally, intervene to guide them to greater understanding. By helping them, you will learn the ways of the chameleon. Are you ready to join me on this path of discovery?"

"Absolutely," affirmed her student.

Xenia looked out across the treetops and said, "So it begins. Let us journey together and learn how to take flight."

Spring

The Chameleon

The New Addition

The forest, affectionately known as Home, echoed with the sights and sounds of the cheerful promise of spring. Trees began to reveal traces of a woodland green that had been hibernating all winter. New life sprouted in all directions. A budding kaleidoscope of floral colors signaled a transition was on the way.

The birds were already awake as the forest was emerging from its long winter slumber. Settled high in the swaying trees, they sang excitedly — especially the parrots, whose laughter echoed throughout the land. The eagles soared mightily among fluffy clouds that bid "good morning" to all. The owls were barely visible. Their bark-like feathers obscured them from view, which enabled them to keep a watchful eye on the myriad forms of life that scurried below them.

Walking through Home on this fresh spring morning, the chameleons followed the path of a meandering stream. After passing a grove of wise, old elm trees, they came across a single mighty oak. With his eyes, Xander followed its trunk to its highest point. Thinking he saw something at the top, he squinted, trying to zoom in on the image.

The young chameleon pointed and asked, "Is that an eagle up there?"

"It sure is," Xenia smiled. "That's Sadie. She and her parents have been old friends of mine for a long time. I've known her since the day she first appeared in her parents' lives."

"She looks strong and confident," Xander proclaimed. "I'll bet she was pretty headstrong when she was young."

"Oh, you don't know the half of it," said Xenia. "The day I first met her was a day just like today. My father and I watched from a distance as Samuel and Sarah shook their white dove feathers as if they were releasing the cold winter from their bones. They awoke to the soft cooing sounds of their new little doves, whose tiny white feathers poked outward like miniature stems waiting to bloom."

"As the sun reached the edge of the horizon, the youngsters opened their eyes to the light of the new day. Though they were hungry, they didn't complain. They instinctively knew food was on its way. Sarah stood guard over her brood as Samuel searched for provisions for his expanding family."

"Just as he collected his first catch of the day, Samuel heard a high-pitched squeal from beyond a small stand of trees. He approached cautiously. He peeked behind a mighty oak and was astonished. A baby eagle was staring back at him. The dove looked around for the eagle's parents, but no one was in sight. Samuel yelled out to the forest, but nobody answered."

"Did the parents come to get her?" Xander asked.

"They did not," Xenia answered.

"So what did you do?"

"I watched," Xenia smirked. "Chameleons do not manipulate situations; we adapt to what is. We make small suggestions that can create big impacts. We gently help others see the path that is for the greatest good of everyone involved."

Xenia continued her story. "Samuel shouted to the treetops, 'There's a baby eagle down here! Don't worry, she's all right!' But still no answer. He searched the skies but did not see any adult eagles. He waited and waited, but nobody came for the baby. He couldn't leave the helpless little one alone, so he did what came naturally to him. He scooped up the baby bird and placed her safely under his wing."

"When Samuel returned home, Sarah was upset with him. As Samuel approached her, she called out, 'I've been so worried. What took you so long?' Before Samuel could answer, Sarah noticed the scrawny eagle. Immediately, her heart melted and she wanted to help. As she began to comfort the young one, she directed nearby doves to find food and create a safe shelter for the baby."

"Days later, after an alert had been dispatched throughout Home, the baby eagle's parents still had not been found. The doves searched the forest and talked to everyone they knew, but nobody came forward to claim her. Samuel and Sarah cared for the eagle, and, day by day, grew to love her. They accepted the eagle as their own. They named her Sadie."

"Did you or your father do anything to help the doves?" Xander wondered.

"We did not," Xenia replied. "But I recall my father warning them about turbulent times ahead. Over the years, Sadie grew strong and confident. Soon she grew larger than her adoptive parents. Yet despite her size, she had much to learn. Samuel and Sarah spent a great deal of time teaching Sadie the ways of the doves. As they did with their own children, they conveyed the values and behaviors of contributing members in a community. They taught her how to be kind and thoughtful. They discussed the importance of listening with compassion and putting the needs of others ahead of oneself."

"The eagle gained much from her parents. She learned to speak kindly, although occasionally she offended her dove siblings with her frankness. She loved to play games, but often had to be reminded to be gracious if she lost. Sadie hated losing. She preferred to do things on her own, which Sarah lovingly described as Sadie's 'little independent streak.'"

"As Sadie grew older, she began to feel as if she didn't fit in with her family. When she reached the age nestled between childhood and adulthood, she confided to her dove siblings that she was uncomfortable with many of their ways. Their ways didn't feel natural to her. Her brothers and sisters didn't know how to remedy her unease so they simply offered words of comfort and a promise to always be there for her. Sadie smiled at them and held her tongue, as she had been taught to do."

"A few weeks ago Sadie befriended a fellow eagle. She has been enjoying his company and adopting some of his eagle ways. Lately, Sadie has been confidently speaking her mind and decisively taking charge when things needed to get done. She is losing some of the listening skills that her parents painstakingly instilled in her, but she is gaining other eagle skills."

"Do her parents notice the changes?" Xander asked.

"They do. Sarah and Samuel attribute the changes to her age. However, others in the dove community are dropping hints about what they call 'Sadie's directness,' and I believe they are preparing to talk with her about it."

The chameleons continued walking and enjoying the bright spring morning. Throughout the following week, they observed the dove's large eagle youngster disregarding the values her adoptive parents had instilled in her. At one point, the chameleons overheard Samuel and Sarah debating whether they should talk with Sadie about it. While the two dove parents did not like confrontation, they felt it was important to intervene before their eagle's 'little independent streak' offended someone.

For days, the dove parents agonized over how to best approach Sadie about this growing problem. They didn't want to offend her. The doves decided to prepare a nice meal, then dismiss their other children so they could talk to Sadie over her favorite dessert. Slowly, Samuel and Sarah edged their way into the discussion. Sadie had almost completely finished her treat before they finally got to the point.

The chameleon pair listened as Sarah began. "Sadie, there's something your dad and I want to speak with you about. Is that all right?"

"Okay," shrugged the eagle.

"Your father and I have noticed that since you have been spending time with other eagles, you have been ..." she paused to collect her thoughts. "What I'm trying to say is that when you speak ... how should I say this?"

She looked to Samuel for assistance. "What your mother is

trying to say is that lately you haven't been as nice as usual when you are speaking to others. Is something wrong? Is anything bothering you?"

"Nope. I'm good," replied the eagle.

"Have you noticed how you have been speaking to others recently?" Sarah asked. "It's not as gentle as we taught you."

"I feel great. In fact, I've never felt better."

The doves were unsure about where to go next. Then the eagle added, "I've always had a hard time *softening my words*. Now, I feel like I'm just being me."

Samuel and Sarah didn't know how to respond.

"You don't have to worry about me. I'm fine," concluded the eagle.

With that, Sadie rose to clean up her food. She assumed the conversation was over. Before the doves could say anything more, Sadie leapt from the dove family tree and flew off to spend time with her new friends. The frustrated parents shook their heads as Sarah concluded, "Well, that didn't go as well as I had hoped."

"Is it time to help them out?" Xander squirmed.

"Indeed," replied Xenia.

As the sun's light began to fade and brilliant stars materialized overhead, the parents discussed their dilemma. They had never faced anything like this with their other children, and they did not know what do.

From a nearby branch, Xenia instructed her young apprentice to remain in the shadows. She was going to transform into the color of a bright green leaf that sat beside the dove pair. Suddenly, Xenia burst into the conversation, "Good evening, my friends."

Sarah smiled. "Welcome. It is so nice to see you, Xenia."

The chameleon gave a slight bow of her head and with a gentle smile expressed, "My father sends his regards."

The three old friends spoke at length about the eagle. The chameleon listened with empathy and compassion, just as the doves would have for anyone who shared their problems with them.

When the doves were finished expressing their dilemma, Xenia reminded them of a previous conversation. "I remember the day my father and I were passing by your home. You had just accepted the young eagle into your family and had agreed to become her adoptive parents."

"I remember that discussion," Samuel recalled. He reflected on Xavier's prophetic words: "You will parent with love. You will treat your new addition the only way that you know how, and you will be wonderful parents. But there will come a day when Sadie will appear to change. You will feel as though she has become someone else. She may even become unrecognizable to you. When that day comes, realize that she has not become someone new, but rather, is developing into who she was born to be."

"That didn't make sense to me at the time," Samuel reflected.

"But now I understand," Sarah acknowledged.

"Sometimes it's not that we change," said the chameleon. "It's that we become who we truly are."

Samuel nodded. "I guess we have been trying to turn Sadie into someone she is not. We have been trying to turn her into a dove."

"Oh," Sarah sighed. "I hope we have not been sending a

message that we do not accept her for who she is."

Xenia smiled. "As my father predicted, you have been wonderful parents. Now it is time to let her be who she was born to be."

Samuel and Sarah understood.

Xenia concluded, "Just as my father watched over you and your friends, I will watch over Sadie and hers."

Sarah was about to thank Xenia and tell her how much they appreciated her instinctive ability to adapt to any situation. Before Sarah could tell her chameleon friend that she could see her father's wisdom radiating from her clear eyes, Xenia was gone.

The next morning, Sadie rose with the first light of day. Samuel and Sarah, already awake, joined their daughter for a light breakfast. "Sadie," Samuel said, "we want you to know that we love you for who you are."

"We realize that we have been expecting you to act like a dove, but that is not your true nature," Sarah added.

Sadie smiled, "I appreciate the dove ways, but it's time for me to spread my wings and be an eagle."

They all looked up and saw her new eagle friend standing a few branches above them on an adjacent tree. "Hey, Dee," he called, using the nickname her new friends had given her. "You ready to go?"

The eagle pumped her large wings as she turned back to her parents and said, "You're the best. Thanks!"

Sarah grinned and said, "I guess her little independent streak isn't just a phase."

"I suppose it's not," Samuel agreed. "I suppose it's not."

Chameleon Wisdom

Success means having the courage, the determination, and the will to become the person you believe you were meant to be.
—George Sheehan

The first step to happiness and success is living an authentic life—being yourself. Sometimes we suppress who we are because our natural style is not acceptable to others. The time period we live in creates cultural norms. Our parents tell us how we are supposed to act in social situations. The workplace defines a set of behavioral expectations based on organizational culture. The world around us constantly places pressure on us to fit in.

In *The New Addition*, Sadie (or Dee, as her friends call her) was taught by her parents how she should interact in the world, and she adapted her behavior to harmonize with her adopted dove family. But her eagle nature called to her to act differently. As Sadie struggled to adjust to the dove world, she sacrificed her true self. The resulting inner turmoil left her feeling never quite like herself. In the end, she stepped into her power and became the eagle she was meant to be. In doing so, she did not change her personality. Instead, she embraced it.

If who we are varies from the cultural norm, we often mask our preferences in order to gain approval. We put on social or career facades in our drive to be accepted.

Imagine an individual with a strong parrot nature—energetic, fun, optimistic—who works in a restrictive and restrained work environment. His manager is beginning to lose patience with his frequent interactions with coworkers. In order to maintain his employment, the parrot learns to bury his head in his computer and remain at his desk. He keeps conversations to a minimum and speaks quietly, making certain to minimize his enthusiasm about ideas and experiences. Due to a lack of human interaction, the parrot leaves work feeling more discontented each day. But he wants to keep his job, so he adjusts his behavior.

Eventually, the parrot becomes so dissatisfied at work that he leaves the company to find employment in an organization that allows him to embrace his authentic self. It doesn't take long for him to feel like himself again. A few months later, a former coworker joins his team and can't believe how much he has changed in such a short period time. In reality, he hasn't changed at all. The new environment has simply allowed him to remove his mask and be himself.

We cannot achieve our greatest potential and cultivate deep connections with others unless we live authentically. Acting like someone we are not drains us of valuable energy. Behaving in a way that conflicts with our style creates cognitive dissonance. When we really want to act *this* way, but feel as if we should act *that* way, our thoughts become incongruent. This leads to stress, frustration, anger, and even depression.

Reclaim who you were meant to be. Look inside yourself and identify who you are when you are living mask-free. Recognize when you are out of alignment with your true self, and dare to liberate your true nature. Value your innate gifts, and don't let others define you. Let go of the need for approval, and surround yourself with people who value you for who you are, not who they want you to be. Make a deep personal commitment to be yourself.

Throughout this book, you will discover how to tap into the wisdom of the chameleon. Understand, though, that there's a big difference between flexibly adapting to a temporary situation and changing who you are in order to adapt to a permanent one. Although adaptability takes place in the moment, you need not change who you are and what makes you special. Be honest with yourself, and allow your style to shine through.

- GET TO KNOW YOURSELF. Reflect on what you are doing when you are at your happiest.

- STEP OUT OF YOUR COMFORT ZONE and do what comes naturally.

- PUT YOUR OWN NEEDS FIRST instead of always aiming to please others. You are not good for others if you're not good to yourself.

- DO NOT WORRY about how others see you. Some people may not like who you truly are, but by being your authentic self, you will draw people into your life who do.

The Chameleon

The Sparrow's Nest

The velvety, spring breeze contrasted with the rough, destructive storm that had just passed through the forest. Powerful winds had snapped even the strongest branches, dislodging and destroying many nests. No one had been seriously injured, but the sparrows suffered the greatest loss at the worst time for them. Just as they were about to grow their families, they found themselves homeless.

Fortunately, the sparrows were prepared for such an event. They had stockpiled hundreds of Sparrow Nest Kits, which now could be assembled quickly.

Volunteers came from the four corners of Home to support the nest rebuilding efforts. Helpers were organized in groups of two, and each partnership was tasked with building five nests. After signing in, Carl and Ivory joined forces to assemble their kits.

As an owl, Carl was analytical and renowned for doing things right the first time. He liked to think before acting and had a knack for staying organized. He specialized in accuracy and quality, traits that would serve his nest-building partnership well.

As a parrot, Ivory was brimming with positive energy. She understood how difficult this time was for the sparrows, so she focused on helping rebuild homes that were even better and stronger than before. Her contagious passion and enthusiasm would help her partner stay motivated and upbeat while completing their project.

The owl and the parrot set out to find the perfect tree in which to place their first nest. Ivory excitedly pointed out several locations, but none of them met Carl's precise standards. Eventually, an ideal spot was identified, and the pair felt ready to begin construction. As they laid the nest kits on the ground near the tree, Carl reassured his parrot friend, "Do not worry, Ivory. I will keep us on track."

Ivory wasn't sure what Carl meant by that, but because she was so eager to begin, she let his comment go. Immediately, the parrot started energetically pulling materials out of the first kit. At the same time, Carl was carefully inspecting each item to make sure nothing had been damaged. He inspected the stems, roots, and leaves for cracks. He scrutinized the grass, feathers, string, and papers and compared them with the diagrams decorating the instructions.

Knowing they had five nests to build, Ivory was itching to begin. She made comments such as "These nests aren't going to build themselves," but her commentary did not speed Carl up a bit. So … she waited while the owl focused his attention on the details, tapping her toe impatiently all the while.

Once Carl was certain all parts were in suitable condition, he meticulously lined up the materials and sorted them into precise piles according to their components.

"We are almost ready to begin," Carl announced. "All the parts are in acceptable condition. Now we have to count the pieces to make sure we have the right number of each item."

Ivory gasped. "What do you mean? We just opened a brand new kit. I'm sure it's all here."

"You cannot trust that the kit is right. It is best to count the items and be certain. You may wish to remember this the next time you have to assemble something."

Ivory shook her head incredulously as she watched Carl match the supplies to the checklist. If she had been working alone, she would have had this first nest assembled already. She couldn't imagine having to endure the owl's tedious process four more times!

After confirming that the inventory was accurate, Carl suggested, "Let's read through the instructions before we begin. We do not want any surprises. Would you like to read the directions aloud?"

"Read through the instructions?" the parrot exclaimed. "Are you serious? I think it's pretty obvious how these parts come together. I've seen many sparrow nests. Haven't you?"

Carl was getting frustrated with Ivory's impatience. "Of course I have seen sparrows' nests, but seeing one is not the same as building one. We do not want the nest to fall apart in a storm. There is a right way and a wrong way to assemble a nest. I prefer the right way. Don't you?"

Ivory took a consoling deep breath. She didn't want to spend the day arguing with Carl, so she made a suggestion: "How about this? Let's start assembling the nests, and if we need the instructions, we can refer to them. I've watched many sparrows build nests, and it's always looked pretty easy."

"I am sure it did not *look* difficult, but that is because the sparrows knew what they were doing. You saw sparrows building sparrows' nests, after all. I have watched owls build many things throughout my life. But being an owl does not mean I can create what I observed without careful planning. One day you may be able to apply this particular process to future projects, and you might even discover that being organized serves you well."

Ivory inhaled deeply. In the interest of collaboration, she accepted Carl's terms. Step by step, piece by piece, the sparrow's nest painstakingly took form. At one point Ivory tried to infuse some positive energy into the meticulous process by announcing, "This is looking good. I'm feeling more like a sparrow every minute!"

Carl immediately replied, "This is more complicated than it seems. Let us not develop a false sense of security. We can celebrate when we are finished."

Ivory rolled her eyes, but Carl was too busy securing a twig into the structure to notice. The parrot continued to read through the steps in the instructions … one by one … as she watched her owl partner faultlessly add each element to the nest. After placing a piece, he tested the nest for structural integrity. Each part passed his test, without fail.

After finishing the outer layer of the nest, Carl declared, "We have now completed half the steps. So far this nest is solid."

"Sure is," Ivory replied halfheartedly.

"Before this day is over, you will have developed the building skills of an owl," Carl joked. "What, Ivory, no enthusiastic pronouncements that this is the best nest you have ever seen? No exclamations about how awesome we are for making something so incredible? Where is your parrot spirit?"

Ivory deadpanned, "Yeah. It's great. Very proud."

But Ivory wasn't happy or proud. In fact, she was becoming increasingly upset. The owl's words felt like a personal attack. Ivory reflected on other things she had assembled in her life. She had always seemed to figure it out. She was frustrated that Carl did not trust her to play a more important role than merely reading the instructions. And his snail's pace was maddening to her.

Ivory remained silent during the building of the first nest, but after that she couldn't take it anymore. Before opening the second kit, she decided it was time to speed things up. "How about you read the instructions to me this time?" Ivory requested.

Carl felt less than confident in the role of reader, but he felt compelled to agree. "Uh, sure," he answered.

"Great. What's first?"

Before Carl could even pick up the instructions, Ivory pointed to a nearby tree and declared, "That's the one. We'll put it right there."

The parrot ripped open the second kit, pulled out the directions, tossed them aside, and started to build. As Carl watched her weave seemingly random items together, he recalled the process that he had just followed. He had a bad feeling about this second nest.

Ivory noticed Carl's worried look as she inserted a long twig into the bottom section. She smiled reassuringly and said, "Don't worry, Carl. Sometimes letting go of instructions and following your gut is the best way to work."

Carl didn't know what to say. He could see that Ivory was not going to follow the instructions, so he put them down and helped her as much as he could. Occasionally, he made subtle suggestions, such as "Wouldn't it be best if we put this piece in before that one?"

Carl was open to her ideas, but from his analytical perspective, her way was not the way to assemble a nest … or anything else, for that matter.

Every now and then, Ivory asked Carl to retrieve a part or questioned him about a specific piece. By the time Carl provided all the information she asked for, Ivory was two steps ahead of him. At one point Ivory commented cheerfully, "You see, Carl, sometimes in life you have to forget the rules and just make things happen. Life is meant to be enjoyed, not organized. You need to live more in the moment and not worry so much about the details."

They completed the second nest in half the time it took to build the first. Sure, they had a few parts left over, and Ivory had to redo some pieces and go back a few steps with others, but "that's how it goes when you're building something," enthused Ivory.

The parrot took a step back to marvel at their creation. She concluded, "This is not bad for two non-sparrows."

Carl nodded without saying a word. "What's wrong?" Ivory probed. "You should be proud of this nest. Look at the quality craftsmanship," she beamed.

"I think we each define 'quality craftsmanship' differently," said Carl. But what bothers me most is how you treated me while we were building the second nest."

"What do you mean?" Ivory wondered. "We built the nest quickly, and it looks pretty darn good."

"Yes, it is complete, but I would have gone about it differently,"

Carl explained. "Did you notice how smoothly the first nest went? I respected the process and you played a vital role."

"A vital role?" puzzled the parrot. "I did nothing and the process took forever. That's not how I like to work."

"Are you saying you did not appreciate the focus and methodology we employed in building the first nest?"

"I did not appreciate it, and you made me feel incompetent and unimportant," Ivory explained. "All I did was read the instructions to you."

"I felt similarly while we were building the second nest," Carl acknowledged. "You made me feel like my approach to the project was wrong."

"Seriously?"

"Seriously."

"This conversation reminds me of something that Xenia once taught me," Ivory recalled.

"What's that?" asked the owl.

"Well, one day, I was talking with Simon, who is such a helpful dove. He had just agreed to assist our favorite eagle, Dee, with a river cleanup project, even though he had no time to do it. But you know Simon. He likes to be supportive, and he didn't want to say no."

"I understand that," said Carl.

"I approached Simon after Dee left, and I told him he needs to be more assertive. I explained that there are times we have to stand up for ourselves and that he doesn't always have to put the needs of others ahead of his own. At that moment, Xenia appeared."

"She has a way of doing that," the owl observed.

"Tell me about it!" laughed the parrot. "That chameleon always pops up at just the right moment. Anyway, Xenia said that …"

All of sudden, a cheery voiced inserted itself into their conversation. "Did I hear my name?"

Carl and Ivory nearly fell off of their branch.

"Your timing is impeccable!" Ivory announced. "Can you shed some light on what we're discussing? I'm guessing you heard the whole thing."

Xenia smiled and replied, "I would be glad to."

Carl grabbed a piece of paper so he could capture her wisdom.

"You're going to write Xenia's words down?" Ivory asked.

"Yes, I am," Carl grinned. "Does that bother you?"

"Nope. Not at all," Ivory giggled.

Xenia waited until Carl was ready and then shared. "When you try to change someone's personality, you send a message to them that the way they are is not okay."

Just then a squirrel scurried by holding several nuts she had just unburied. The threesome watched as she zigged and zagged her way through the forest, seemingly unsure of where to go next. As Carl and Ivory stared in amusement, Carl considered the implications of Xenia's words. He rolled up the paper and tucked the scroll away for safekeeping. "I understand," Carl said. "That is what I did to Ivory. I was not just telling her to follow the instructions, I was also expecting her to act like an owl."

"Precisely," Xenia confirmed.

"What I heard from my owl friend was that it was not okay for me to be a parrot," Ivory shared. "Carl was trying to change me into an owl—to not accept me for who I am."

"I never thought about it like that," Carl acknowledged.

"I know that wasn't your intention, but that's how I felt."

"I apologize for my actions," added Carl. "I suppose that is how I felt, too. When you asked me not to follow a process I am accustomed to, I felt as if you were not only discounting my abilities, but also not letting me be an owl. It felt like you were saying that being a parrot is better than being an owl."

"I see that now," Ivory confirmed. "I'm sorry about that."

"How about this," Carl suggested. "We have three more nests to build. Let's put the instructions aside and start working on the next one. What do you think?"

"Can you do that?" Ivory wondered.

"Not sure," Carl admitted. "But I am willing to give it a try."

"Does this mean we're not going to take an inventory of the parts?" Ivory asked with a teasing glint in her eye.

"Let's not get too crazy," Carl replied. "Sparrows need to live in these nests."

"That sounds like a good compromise. How about we just accept that you are an owl and I am a parrot? Together we will find a way to build that works for both of us."

"Sounds like a plan," Carl replied. "Can I hold the instructions for safekeeping?"

Ivory agreed cheerfully.

The pair turned around to thank Xenia for her help. "Hey, where'd she go?" Ivory asked.

"She is gone. She seems to do that a lot," Carl smiled.

The parrot and the owl spent the next few hours constructing the remaining three nests. They worked well together and compromised as they sought to understand one another's style. When they were done with their building project, they were both proud of what they had accomplished ... together.

Chameleon Wisdom

Never try to teach a pig to sing. It wastes your time and it annoys the pig.
—Robert Heinlein

Think about someone close to you who has a habit you have tried to change. Perhaps this person is your partner, child, or coworker. How much energy have you applied to trying to change this individual's behavior? Did your effort make a difference? If they did make the change, did the change stick, or did they eventually revert back to their old ways, leaving you even more frustrated than before?

Now consider the emotional impact on you and on the person you tried to change. What effect did your efforts have on you, and what underlying message were you sending to the other person?

In *The Sparrow's Nest*, Carl and Ivory imposed their styles on each other. By insisting on following their own methodology for building nests, they unwittingly devalued the approach of the other. This ultimately led to frustration and conflict.

Imagine a family in which a father with an intense eagle style is constantly telling his humble and soft-spoken dove child to act more assertively. Picture that parent at a soccer game yelling from the sidelines, "Stop smiling and focus! Attack the ball! Don't wait for him to come to you!"

The eagle father thinks he is helping his child improve his skills and get better results. However, the message received by the dove child is, "I am bad at soccer, and I am not the person my father wants me to be."

The child who was previously enjoying a soccer game with his friends now feels badly about himself and no longer wants to play. In addition, his self-esteem has taken a hit.

When you judge the way others act, you send the message that who they are is not okay. In contrast, when you accept someone fully, you validate that person's worth. Accepting others for who they are, rather than for who you want them to be, replaces judgment with acceptance. This acceptance creates the foundation for a meaningful connection.

However, acceptance of others does not preclude the importance of giving constructive feedback. In fact, it is the role of a parent or a manager to help those under their wings to learn, grow, and prosper. Balance constructive feedback with positive reinforcement that highlights strengths.

Finally, there's a big difference between addressing a single action and addressing a pattern of behavior that is rooted in someone's personality. When you try to change an overarching behavioral trait, recognize that you are not just asking that person to adjust what they do, you are also asking them to change their core nature. Be careful and compassionate.

- CONSIDER HOW YOU WOULD FEEL if someone tried to change you.

- PAY ATTENTION TO YOUR THOUGHTS. Do you judge what others do as good or bad, right or wrong? Accept that there may be more than one way to approach issues.

- ESTABLISH REALISTIC EXPECTATIONS of others. Determine whether your expectations are based on your approach to the world and whether you are imposing your style on others.

- FOCUS ON THE POSITIVES. Rather than trying to fix others, put your energy into identifying what you appreciate.

- FOCUS ON YOURSELF. Instead of trying to change something out of your control, focus your energy on what you can control ... *yourself.*

- ACCEPT YOURSELF FULLY, so that you create the space to accept others.

The Chameleon

The Spinning Wind

A cool spring breeze ruffled the feathers of the birds who gathered in the Great Field. Gentle swirls of air harkened them back to what brought them together on this day. Xenia, the wise and all-knowing chameleon, scanned the pasture for familiar faces. Ahead of her, sitting quietly on a sizeable boulder, was Simon, a dove whom Xenia had taken under her care.

As Simon's soft, white dove feathers lifted gently in the wind, he smiled at Xenia and her student, Xander, as they approached him. He was happy to see familiar faces during this somber time.

Simon, Xenia, and Xander were three of the many who had gathered to commemorate the tenth anniversary of the Spinning Wind. On that day, a twister tore a path of destruction through the northwest corner of Home and took the lives of two of the land's most beloved parrots.

In a few minutes, the sun would touch the horizon and signal two-minutes of silence in honor of the heroic parrots who lost their lives. Many conversations punctuated the wait. Most were recollections about where someone was and what they were doing when the tragedy occurred.

Xenia made a request. "Xander was not yet born when the

Spinning Wind rushed through the forest. Can you tell him about your experiences that day?"

"I'd be glad to," responded Simon, the gentle dove. As he took in a deep breath, a tender breeze stroked him and slightly lifted his wings. Seeing Simon's white feathers standing at attention served to remind his friends of the catastrophe that had destroyed so much of the forest and taken the lives of his friends.

Simon began. "After a long summer vacation, I was back in school. I had just returned home from my third day at Flight School, and I was telling my parents about my new parrot friend, Ivory. I described how different she was from me. She was comical, outgoing, and fun to be with. I had asked my parents if I could play with her, and they agreed. A group of parrots was gathering near the Great Lake, and I went to join them."

"Sounds like a pretty typical day," Xenia said.

"It started out that way," Simon replied. "I was quiet and shy when I was young, so my parents were happy I had made a new friend. They already knew many of the parrots and often called on them. After we arrived at the lake, my parents visited for a time with their adult friends. They told me they were going back home and would come back to pick me up before dinner. With friendly waves and warm glances over their shoulders, my parents left me with Ivory."

"At first, the parrots sounded so noisy. I heard conversations from the adult parrots and cheers from the young parrots, who were joyfully engaged in a crazy game. I was astounded as I watched the youngsters energetically dive-bombing the lake with pine cones. It was pretty funny," Simon smiled in remembrance.

"The parrots sure know how to have fun," Xenia agreed.

"It didn't take long for us to realize that something was wrong. Suddenly, the sky turned dark—very dark. It transformed from a promising blue into an ominous greenish-black shade unlike any I had ever seen before."

"I recall that sky as well," Xenia added. "Then what happened?"

"Unexpectedly, we were pelted with giant balls of solid ice falling from the sky. We all flew for cover. When one of the pieces of ice hit me, it hurt. I was smaller than the parrots, so that one ice ball knocked me right over. When I tried to stand up again, I felt dizzy, and everything in my view went blurry."

"The next thing I remember, I was being sheltered somewhere dark and enclosed. At first, I thought I was dreaming, but when I felt the bump on my head, I realized someone had carried me into a tree hollow. My friend Ivory was with me, and we huddled together. That's when the forest grew as silent as a void. There was a great emptiness. I did not even hear the constant and familiar rustle of leaves. But the stillness was short-lived. That temporary quiet space was merely the forest inhaling deeply in preparation of the devastating wind about to rip through Home.

"Then the forest began to roar. At first it sounded like a few growling bears. But it grew louder and louder until the low rumble turned into a mighty howl. We were puzzled. We didn't know what the sound was. The reverberation increased in intensity until it resembled the bellow of a long, loud waterfall, but that didn't make sense to either of us. Was it a massive swarm of angry bees? That didn't seem right either."

"In those initial moments we were all confused," the chameleon confirmed. "None of us had ever experienced anything like this phenomenon, so we had no frame of reference to work from."

"It was scary," the dove admitted. "But it soon got even scarier. A wall of dirt mixed with dry, dead leaves barreled through the forest. We could hardly see anything. We didn't know where our parents were, and we felt alone. Next, a massive spiral wind began twisting its way through the forest. We heard some trees crashing as they were ripped from the earth. Others were tossed throughout the forest like twigs. Small branches were torn from big trunks, and they slammed into the trees surrounding us. There was so much noise and so much flying debris that we just covered our heads and waited for it to pass. Even though the storm lasted only a few minutes, it felt to us that it would go on forever."

"Fortunately, you were inside a strong tree," Xenia said.

"We were. One of the parrots who did not survive the Spinning Wind had the foresight to place us there. We owe her our lives," said the dove.

"It all sounds so frightening," Xenia said.

"Very," Simon acknowledged. "When the storm passed and I poked my head out of the tree, I saw dark, low-flying clouds overhead. Again, we suffered through an uneasy silence. No one dared make a sound. Even the trees appeared frozen in place. I had never felt anything like what we experienced that day. After a few minutes of stillness, the sun broke through the murky clouds and the branches once again swayed lightly in the breeze. It was as if nothing distressing had happened. Everyone shouted to everyone else, trying to confirm that friends and relatives were all right."

"You survived," affirmed Xenia.

"I did. But Home lost two great friends that day."

"Yes, we did."

"I was amazed at how the surviving parrots responded to the tragedy," Simon stated. "At the same time they were mourning the loss of their loved ones, they were radiating with the optimism that Home would recover soon."

"Hopefulness is a gift the parrots bring to the world," Xenia affirmed.

"Yes. I wish I had some of that," Simon said softly. "The eagles impressed me too."

"How so?" asked the chameleon.

"As soon as the wind died down, the eagles took charge. They rose above the chaos that ensued and immediately jumped into action to make sure everyone was safe."

Xenia smiled. "Eagles handle crises well. In fact, they shine brightest when things are turned upside down."

"I'm not good at that," Simon added.

"Everyone played a role in the aftermath of the Spinning Wind," Xenia noted.

"They did," said Simon. I remember watching in awe as the owls organized everything with peak efficiency. They thrived on figuring out the complex steps required to return Home to order."

"It was a marvel to behold," Xenia stated.

"I don't know how they do that," said Simon.

"We each have unique gifts," responded Xenia.

"I get that," said the dove. "I just don't understand how something that is so easy for someone else is so difficult for me."

"The reverse is also true. What is easy for you may be difficult for others. I remember watching you in action after the Spinning Wind. You and your family provided comfort to those who had lost their homes. Even though you were young, you listened empathetically to your friends who were impacted by the damage. You selflessly offered your time and energy to help clean up the mess left by the wind. You added stability and consistency at a time when nothing was certain. Others could not have given what you shared so effortlessly."

"But what I did was easy. What they did took skill," Simon replied.

"What they did was easy for them because they were using their natural gifts. What you did was easy for you because you were using yours. Just because what you did was easy for you, doesn't mean that it was less important. Do not devalue your gifts simply because they come easily to you."

Simon took a moment to consider Xenia's words. He had never thought of what he contributed as being special or unique.

Xenia continued. "Did the eagles find it difficult to kick into action and take charge?"

"I don't think so," Simon answered.

"Did the owls find it challenging to create a detailed plan out of nothing?"

"No. In fact, they seemed to enjoy it," answered Simon.

"Precisely!" Xenia declared.

"Do you think it was grueling for the parrots to look on the bright side following the crisis?"

"No. Parrots are eternal optimists. They always find the bright side," said Simon.

"You see," the chameleon explained, "our gifts are easy for us to express. We assume that if they are easy for us, they will be easy for others as well. But that is not the case."

Before beginning the moment of silence designed to honor their lost friends, Xenia offered Simon one final thought: "Value who you are instead of dwelling on what you are not. Self-acceptance is the first step toward releasing the power of your special gifts."

As the forest fell silent, Simon pondered, "When my time in this forest is over, I want to be remembered for how I shared my gifts. I guess the first step is to identify what they are."

Chameleon Wisdom

Wanting to be someone else is a waste of the person you are.
—MARILYN MONROE

In *The Spinning Wind,* Simon admires how the eagles, parrots, and owls responded to the crisis. At the same time, he downplays his own contribution. He does not understand the role he plays in the community and fails to acknowledge his own gifts and contributions.

It is easy for us to look at others and wish we could do what they do. It is more difficult to look at ourselves and appreciate our own abilities.

Before we can get to a place where we accept ourselves fully, we must know ourselves. To know yourself is a lifelong journey of self-exploration. By reading this book, you are already walking down that path.

Getting to know yourself means looking inside and examining your strengths and weaknesses, your likes and dislikes, your habits and idiosyncrasies. Self-knowledge means recognizing your fears and motivations, your feelings and thoughts, your passions and moods.

Once you deepen your understanding of your nature, it is time to accept yourself unconditionally. Self-acceptance is about looking inside, avoiding external distractions, living in the present moment, and owning your failures and successes. When you unconditionally accept who you are, you create the space for growth and joy.

Conversely, self-acceptance does not mean resigning yourself to the hand that has been dealt you. It does not mean ceasing to strive for personal development. It's not about what you did or did not do, or what you wish you were capable of doing.

When a talent is a natural expression of who we are, we think anyone can do it because for us it is easy. We all have abilities that require minimal effort, and these represent our strengths. However, we place more value on the things we work harder to accomplish. We think, "If I don't work for it, it's not valuable." Think about how rewarding your life would be if you valued your natural abilities. The higher the level of self-acceptance you achieve, the more happiness and abundance you can manifest.

Consider a scenario in which an office owl is presented with an exciting new opportunity by a parrot coworker. The parrot is enthusiastic about the possibilities, but all the analytical owl can see are potential obstacles and challenges. A series of worst-case scenarios flood the owl's mind, which causes him to launch a barrage of concerns at the parrot. The parrot leaves the conversation with a list of questions she has been tasked to answer. She is feeling deflated by her interaction with the owl.

Meanwhile, the owl feels better now that the idea will be carefully evaluated. He feels bad, though, that he had to burst the parrot's bubble, and he judges himself disapprovingly for having done so. Further, he wishes that he could be as happy as the parrot and not have to worry about all the things that could go wrong.

Unconditional self-acceptance means embracing the things

you like about yourself and the things you do not. In the previous paragraph, the owl made a great contribution to the process, but rather than valuing his own input, he became envious of abilities he did not have. When we embrace ourselves fully, we free ourselves from the need to be accepted by others. This allows our gifts to shine through as we aspire to be the best we can be.

Your worth is not based on a degree that you hold, your performance at work, what your children have accomplished, awards you have won, a title you have earned, the things you own, the money you make, or anything else outside of you. Your self-worth is based on your level of self-acceptance. Self-acceptance is a verb. It is something you do.

The challenges you face are not character defects. There is no such thing as a character defect. Celebrate your strengths and avoid making comparisons with others.

Who you think you are creates your identity. Who you think you are not creates your limitations.

- CONSIDER SELF-ACCEPTANCE as a skill that can be nurtured.

- FORGIVE YOURSELF for not being able to do what others can do. You have strengths that others wish they had.

- SILENCE THE INNER CRITIC. Identify and challenge negative thoughts by replacing them with positive ones.

- LET GO OF PAST REGRETS about things you wish you had done.

- IF YOU WISH TO DEVELOP A CERTAIN SKILL, imagine already having the skill.

- DON'T FOCUS ON WHAT YOU CANNOT DO. Celebrate what you can do.

The Chameleon

The Crystal Cave

Two longtime friends, Simon, the dove, and Carl, the owl, sat together enjoying the melodious sounds and dazzling sights of spring. They were delighted by the antics of a group of lively chipmunks who were scurrying back and forth across the forest floor. As the two friends watched the chipmunks invent game after playful game, they were impressed by their neighbors' natural creativity.

Spring, the season of inspiration and expression, was evident in the new life blossoming all around them. Myriad flowers added a variety of vivid colors and fragrant scents to the forest. The trees gave birth to budding leaves, which transformed the warming woodlands from neutral browns into artful greens. The air echoed with the sounds of countless newborns. Simon and Carl felt happy as they sat basking in nature's glory.

Simon and Carl met every Friday morning to enjoy each other's company and talk about life's events. Sometimes, their parrot friend, Ivory, joined them, but she could not make it today. Simon shared how the doves were decorating their family tree with rich and seasonal yellows, reds, and violets. Carl described with precision an invention that he and some other owls were working on, a new weather device that would measure wind speed and provide data on the severity of oncoming storms.

After a few more minutes of enjoying the scene provided by the scampering chipmunks, Simon said, "Ivory would love watching these guys. They are so funny."

"Yes, she would," Carl replied. "Now that I think about it, I have not seen her in days."

"Me neither. I wonder what she's been up to."

The chipmunks scattered hastily as Dee, the eagle, landed in the center of the clearing where the chipmunks had just been playing.

"I'm beginning to think they don't like me," Dee laughed, as she looked up at her two friends.

"I am not sure I blame them," Carl yelled down to Dee. "Eagles and chipmunks are not typically the best of friends."

"I heard what you two were both talking about as I was approaching. Are you looking for Ivory?" the eagle asked directly.

"Yes, we are," Carl replied.

Dee's head turned quickly to the right when she thought she saw a chipmunk run by. "I spotted Ivory flying southeast this morning. She was heading toward Crystal Falls."

"My, that's so far away," Simon gasped. "Was she alone?"

"I didn't see anyone else with her," Dee answered.

"This is quite puzzling," the owl said.

Dee became distracted by a chipmunk who had poked his head out of a hole at the base of a nearby tree. The eagle walked over to the tree and peeked her head into the hole, but she didn't see anything. She looked back to where the little creature had just been, but once again was at a loss. After a few moments of searching, Dee looked up and said, "Hey, I'm going in that direction. Want to join me? We'll see if together we can find Ivory."

"I, for one, would like to find some clues and solve this mystery," Carl stated.

"I don't want to intrude on her private business," Simon added, "but I don't suppose it would hurt anyone to fly out there and see what's happening."

With a powerful thrust of her wings, Dee was airborne. She glanced back over her shoulder with a look that said "follow me."

It took a minute for the dove and the owl to catch up with the eagle, who had slowed down to wait for her friends. Soon the three birds were flying high above Home. Dee was in front. She was followed by Carl, who was flying just off of the eagle's right wing tip. He was trying to find a way to reduce the wind resistance for his friend, Simon, like the geese do, but he couldn't quite get the hang of it. Simon flew right behind Carl.

The trio followed the river below as it snaked its way through the fresh vegetation. The thick smell of spring filled the air as the birds scanned the trees for Ivory. If she were sitting in a tree, she would be easy to spot because of her bright red, yellow, and green feathers. But if she were sitting on the ground, finding her would be more challenging.

Suddenly, Carl was struck by a bright light that bounced off of something below him. At first, he thought it was a reflection of the sun shining on the cascading waters of Crystals Falls, so he didn't mention it. Then, he saw it again. "I see something. Look over there," he pointed.

"I don't see anything," Simon said.

"Me neither," Dee concurred.

All of a sudden, a blinding, bright yellow ray of light caught their eyes. This time they all saw what it was.

"Let's go," Dee instructed, as she took a sharp turn and dove to the right. She was heading directly for the light, and Carl was right behind her.

Simon's eyes grew wide. "We don't know what's down there. Are you sure we should ..."

As the eagle and the owl bolted straight to the flash, Simon turned to join his friends. He landed on a branch high above the river, which was being fed by the waters of the tumbling waterfall. The dove recognized this place; his parents had brought him here when he was just a little bird. Simon remembered the wisdom his father had imparted to him long ago. "These falls hide a great secret," his father had said. "Behind that rushing waterfall is the Crystal Cave. It is filled with gems of all shapes and sizes—red rubies, purple amethysts, green emeralds, yellow citrine, orange sunstone, clear quartz, and more." Then he said something about a magic egg-shaped rock.

As Simon approached his friends, he noticed they were gazing at the ground beside the falls. From up high, the dove could only see waterfall mist blowing in the wind. But when he landed, he could not believe his eyes. Simon looked at Carl who was looking at Dee who was looking at Simon.

"What on earth?" Carl asked.

"How stunning!" Simon exclaimed.

"I've never seen anything so creative," added Dee.

The trio stared in amazement at the exquisite work of art that adorned the land below them.

A burst of color erupted out of the center of the falls. It was Ivory! She was carrying a long piece of orange citrine, and its vivid gold form was reflecting off the water. The parrot didn't seem to notice her friends as she set herself down next to an elaborate maze of twinkling, multicolored gems. She studied her artwork a bit before deciding to move some items around.

First, she picked up a dozen small, red stones and used them to encircle a long, clear piece of quartz. Next, she took three quartz crystals, each slightly bigger than her parrot frame, and stood them vertically in a line. She then shifted her attention to a royal-purple amethyst. She moved it onto a large slab of white selenite, where it rested peacefully. Her rearrangement had made room for her to place her new specimen, the citrine.

"Wonderful, isn't it?" said a soft, low voice from just behind the trio.

The three friends immediately recognized the voice. "Over here," called their mentor, Xenia. The birds turned toward the voice, but the chameleon had already slithered across a long branch to rest just above them.

"Quite astonishing, is it not?" the chameleon asked.

"It's so lively and colorful," Carl said, "but it is so … um … well …"

"Abstract?" the chameleon offered.

"Exactly!" the owl replied. "It is quite creative. I could never do anything like that. But there is no order to it."

"Yet it is still beautiful," the chameleon affirmed.

The structured owl tried to make sense of what he was seeing. "I am not saying it is not beautiful. I just do not understand how she could have conceived of something like that, let alone constructed it without a plan. Does she have an objective for this project?"

Xenia smiled.

Simon interjected, "I think Carl is saying that Ivory is so imaginative, and the rest of us just don't think like that."

"So you are not creative either?" Xenia asked.

"Not really," Simon conceded. "I'd like to be, but I never have been."

"Fascinating," replied Xenia. She then shifted her perceptive eyes to Dee. "And how about you, my eagle friend? Are you creative?"

"Well, I do have a lot of ideas, but I'm too busy to explore them. So I guess not."

"If I understand the three of you correctly, Ivory is the only creative one among you?" Xenia probed.

"Seems that way," Dee confirmed.

Xenia looked down at the glowing mandala of gems. She then glanced back at the trio and stated, "Everyone is creative, but each of us expresses creativity differently."

"But look at that," Carl suggested. "I could never do that."

Xenia replied, "If you judge your creativity based on the works of others, you will inevitably perceive yourself as inadequate."

Carl looked down at the glowing gems, then back at Xenia. "I have never considered myself to be creative because I am such a perfectionist. It is hard to be original when I am always caught up in details."

"Carl, that is precisely what makes you so inventive," answered Xenia. "You examine the world around you from so many perspectives, and that skill enables you to embrace complex problems. Take a look at your crafting hobbies. You can focus for hours on solving an issue when others would have given up long before you. And when you create something, you make sure it is precisely the way you want it. I remember the intricate welcome sign you crafted. You used materials in ways I had never imagined before. It must have taken you weeks to prepare each component of the sign before you began construction."

"Actually, it took months," Carl said.

"I have no idea how you managed to curve the outer branches on the frame of that the sign. That was so inventive," complimented Xenia.

"I used steam from the hot springs. It took a while," explained Carl.

"The sign is so ornate. I marvel at your creation," Xenia said.

"If I am being honest," Carl admitted, "it has a few mistakes in it."

"When I look at it," Xenia said, "I see how much time and attention you put into every aspect of the sign. And those 'mistakes' aren't mistakes. They are, instead, part of the sign's charm."

"Well, thank you," Carl responded.

Ivory popped out of the falls again. This time she was carrying a dark-burgundy garnet. The group watched as she shifted a few other stones to make room for the new arrival.

The chameleon looked deeply into Simon's eyes and shared, "You display creativity as well. Have you ever noticed how you bring harmony to the world around you? You always know how to bring others together and make them feel comfortable. You figure out how to say things in just the right way."

"But that's not me being creative. That's just me being me," Simon suggested, downplaying Xenia's compliment.

Xenia laughed. "Simon, my friend, when you express yourself creatively, it feels easy because it's natural for you. Look how you decorated your home. You have created an inviting place for everyone who visits. You make meals that delight your guests, and you are a warm and wonderful host. When you see others engaged in a conflict, you find a creative way to bring those who were estranged back together again."

"I never thought of that as creativity," Simon acknowledged.

"Well, it is," Xenia affirmed. "Remember the day you put yourself right in the middle of that battle between two rabbits? They were talking too quickly and not listening to each other. I will never forget what you did."

"You saw that?" Simon asked.

"I watched you feed one of the rabbits a mixture of carrots and maple sap. While he was eating, you asked the other rabbit to share what was bothering her. Since the first couldn't talk while he was eating, he was finally able to hear what was upsetting the other. You then offered the second rabbit your sticky mixture, and while she was eating, the first one shared his concerns. Within a few minutes, you mediated a battle that had been raging for days. You figured out how to get the two rabbits to listen to each other and resolve their differences. It was brilliant! Pure creativity in action!"

"Thank you, Xenia," said Simon. "You're very kind."

Dee straightened up a little because she knew she was going to be next. "Before you say anything about me," stated Dee, "I'd like to retract my previous statement that I am not creative."

"So you now see yourself as creative?" Xenia asked.

"Not exactly, but I think you are about to tell me that I am creative, and I don't like being wrong," Dee laughed.

"You are never wrong!" Xenia jested. "But sometimes you aren't always completely right."

"I'll accept that," the eagle chuckled. "So how do you see my creativity?"

"You can create something out of nothing. You see the world from 10,000 feet above, and you don't get caught up in the minutiae. You challenge yourself to achieve new heights. And when you offer solutions, you decisively break free of old patterns and ways of thinking."

Dee immediately understood what Xenia was saying, even though she, too, had not previously considered herself to be creative. She just thought that how she acted was how it should be done.

The group silently watched Ivory as she continued to reorganize the gems. The parrot picked up one stone and moved it. She took a few steps back to review the design and then moved that same stone again. Ivory disappeared into the cave for a few minutes and emerged with something new. She didn't seem to have a plan, yet she worked quickly and with purpose.

After watching Ivory repeat her pattern several times, Xenia noted, "Ivory is in *the zone*. She has no sense of time while she is creating. Her inspiration flows from her intuition, and even though she can get quite excited about her ideas, she has no attachment to them."

"I guess I've been thinking about creativity all wrong," Simon said contemplatively. "It's not a question of whether or not we are creative. It's a question of how we express our creativity. We are all creative."

Xenia grinned and said, "My work here is done." And with that, she harmonized her coloring with the branch she was sitting on and faded into the assorted shades of the forest.

The three friends watched Ivory's artistic efforts for a while longer and then decided to leave her to her work. As they headed home, they talked about the unique and interesting ways they each expressed themselves.

Chameleon Wisdom

Everybody is talented because everybody who is human has something to express.
—BRENDA UELAND

We were all born creative. Along the way, however, many of us have convinced ourselves that we were not. Think back to your childhood. It's a safe bet that you built sand castles, played with Legos, created Popsicle-stick art, served plastic food to imaginary people, and invented new games.

When you hand crayons to children, they start drawing. They don't say, "I'm not creative." Some children draw a sun surrounded by alternating short and long yellow rays. Other children's suns wear a face. Still others are colored purple. Yet all are created freely, without judgment.

As we get older, people buy into the societal belief that creativity must be spontaneous, bold, and original. We have been taught that creativeness resides exclusively in the domain of artists, crafters, writers, musicians, and performers. If you don't fall into one of those categories, you probably have assumed, by default, you are not creative. It's as if someone has told you along the way that you are not creative, and you have accepted the idea as reality.

In *The Crystal Cave*, Dee, Simon, and Carl were impressed by Ivory's creativity. They marveled at what she was capable of doing while, simultaneously, downplaying their own creative abilities. They defined "creativity" in a way that did not match their own gifts. They believed that only someone with a different style than theirs could be creative.

We all live in a constant state of creativity, but because it is not conscious, we discount it. How we think, react, solve problems, and approach the world defines our creative expression. Yet many of us are not in touch with our creative gifts, so we don't see ourselves in that light.

Creativity can take many forms. Each is driven by our personality style. When we are "in the zone," we display originality and inventiveness because the comfort of using our style-driven strengths frees us to take risks and express freely. Consider the creative power of each of the four styles:

Eagles: These paradigm shifters think out of the box, reject existing assumptions, and display revolutionary thinking. Eagles see possibilities where others see obstacles. They see rules as a problem, and they do not feel bound by artificial constraints. Eagles prefer working on challenges at their inception, where boundary-breaking thinking takes place, rather than at the more structured implementation phases of ideas. They tend to be independent problem solvers and do not need consensus to move forward. In fact, others not recognizing the merits of their ideas spur them to push even harder. Eagles are creative at figuring out ways to make things happen and get results.

Parrots: The parrots are idea factories; they solve problems intuitively. They create innovative ideas out of nothingness. They represent what many people typically define as a "creative" person. Parrots find new uses for existing objects and combine things in ways that others do not consider. Since they generate a lot of ideas that aren't always based on a significant amount of thought, they are not overly vested in their ideas. And why should they be? To parrots, there's always another idea on the way. Parrots tend to have proverbial "Eureka" moments. Like eagles, they prefer not to focus on the details required to bring an idea to life.

Doves: Doves are stabilizers who transform disorder into harmony. Instead of developing completely new systems, they work creatively within existing frameworks and systems. Novelty is not a requirement for the creativity doves share with the world. They tap into the knowledge, skills, and abilities of others; utilize structures; and convert them into something new. Doves are comfortable with solutions in which everyone agrees with the process and result. Doves enjoy hobbies like scrapbooking or fashioning family photo albums. They enjoy working with others during the creative process and do not tend to recognize themselves as creative, despite the deeply personal innovative style they express.

Owls: Owls bring structure and order to the world around them. Their creations can be highly complex, requiring patience and an eye for detail. Sometimes their creativity evolves from asking such questions as "why" and "what if." Their ideas come from a deep examination of the possibilities based on data and knowledge. They consider many options before acting. Owls have insight into highly specialized areas, and they do not share their ideas until they have been properly vetted and can be well-articulated. Owls can become consumed by analyzing ideas and producing perfection, but they sometimes get stuck when it comes to implementing these ideas.

When we appreciate the differences in creative approaches, we can recognize and tap into our own natural talent. The only difference between creative people and uncreative people is that creative people understand how to express their creativity.

- KNOW THAT YOU ARE CREATIVE. Even if you feel you haven't created anything in a while, you are more imaginative than you think you are. The capacity for creativity resides within you.

- DON'T LET OTHERS DEFINE WHAT CREATIVITY means to you. Define it for yourself.

- RECOGNIZE HOW YOU CHANNEL your creative energy.

- IDENTIFY AND ALTER disempowering beliefs about your creativity.

- DO THINGS THAT INSPIRE YOU, and share your creativity with the world.

Hatching Day Surprise

Spring was the time to revel in all of life's glory. Almost daily the birds celebrated Hatching Day parties for the older residents of Home who were being acknowledged for the first day they felt the warmth of the sun.

When Ivory stopped by to visit her friend Carl, she was hiding something—but Carl was none the wiser. Ivory and the rest of her parrot friends were organizing a Surprise Hatching Day party for the owl, and it was Ivory's job to keep him busy and nowhere near the location of the big event.

After convincing Carl to join her on some errands, the two birds made their way to the Lost Bird Department, where Ivory dropped off a job application. When they arrived, Carl asked, "Isn't today the deadline?"

"Yes, it is," Ivory answered.

"You waited until the day it was due to submit it?" questioned Carl.

"It's not late" Ivory answered, a bit confused. "What's the problem?"

Carl shook his head. He couldn't imagine waiting until the due date to drop off an application.

The two friends traveled north to the amphitheater at the base of Xanadu's peak. Ivory delivered several scrolls that contained costume designs for the upcoming play. Carl wondered what play they were going to put on, but Ivory only would reveal something about a groundhog and some wings. "You're going to love it!" she promised the owl.

The pair then made their way to the Great Field, where Ivory dropped off vines and twigs that she had been gathering on their journey. When Ivory handed the bundle to a blue-and-yellow parrot, she said with a big grin, "My *hat* comes off to you, dear sir. It is an *honor* to bring these sticks to you."

When Carl asked what she was talking about, Ivory avoided the question by pretending to be distracted. The owl didn't give Ivory's diverted attention another thought because her focus was often pulled in different directions.

The friends spent a pleasant day together wandering throughout Home. They stopped to visit a few eagles, shared some information with several parrots, and picked up some food that had been prepared by a family of doves. Ivory kept Carl busy while their party friends got ready for the big gathering. The plan had worked perfectly.

As the sun neared the horizon, Ivory informed Carl they had to make one last stop.

"Where are we headed this time?" Carl questioned. He was getting tired of covering so much distance. He thought they could have been much more efficient. He would have mapped out all of the stops before they began.

"My father asked me to go to the Council Tree to deliver a

message. It won't take long," Ivory assured him.

By this point, Carl had resigned himself to the fact that Ivory was not going to provide specifics, and even though it went against his nature, he went along for the ride. When they landed on an outstretched branch at the far end of the Council Tree, nobody else was there.

"This is odd," Carl observed. "Where is everyone? There's always someone ..."

Ivory interrupted her friend. "I've got something to tell you."

Without warning, more than fifty of Carl's friends burst forth from behind the trunks of the trees and shouted, "SURPRISE!"

Carl jumped. His heart skipped a beat. It took a moment for him to regain his breath. He was not a fan of the unexpected. He looked around and noticed that all eyes were aimed on him, and he didn't know what to say. He hesitated then stuttered, "Uh ... um ... what are all of you doing here?"

He turned to Ivory and whispered, "You shouldn't have."

"Oh, get out," Ivory laughed. "Of course I should have. You're a great friend and you deserve this celebration."

"I deserve this?" Carl mumbled to himself. "What did I do to deserve this?"

From a higher branch, the blue-and-yellow parrot they met earlier bestowed Carl with what he called "The Hatching Day Hat of Honor." The parrot was so excited to place the hat on Carl's head. He had worked hard to weave thick, brown vines together to form a ring. From the center of the hat rose a large, colorful arrow pointing straight down to Carl. The owl couldn't have felt more ridiculous.

One by one, Carl's friends approached to wish him a Happy Hatching Day. Carl felt trapped. This was *not* his idea of fun.

A little while later, a large purple-and-red parrot rapidly approached Carl and said, "Come with me. I want to show you something!"

The owl could not imagine what new horror awaited him. The pair flew to a neighboring tree and Carl saw a mouse-shaped cake topped with candles. *Things are shaping up*, Carl thought.

Then another parrot rushed over and said, "I found your hat. It must have fallen off."

"Oh, great," Carl replied through a forced smile, as he placed the hat back on his head. The group then sang a rousing rendition of "You Got that Right, You're My Favorite Owl."

The song transitioned the party to the highlight of the evening, at least from the parrots' perspective. The entire group of birds was summoned to a high branch overlooking Home. One of the parrots introduced what she called "Canyon Karaoke." This involved singing a song as loudly as possible so that it echoed off the canyon wall in the distance.

When nobody was looking, Carl quietly escaped to talk privately with Simon, his longtime dove friend. For the first time since the party began, Carl felt comfortable.

Later that evening, after most of the guests had cleared out, Carl and Ivory sat quietly on a large branch away from the center of the action. "Can I take this off now?" Carl asked, looking up toward his hat.

"Sure. It's yours. You can do anything you want with it," Ivory replied.

Carl removed the hat and looked thoughtfully into the distance. Ivory broke the silence. "I'll bet you were surprised."

"Oh, you can say that again," Carl stammered.

Sensing some hesitation in his voice, Ivory asked, "Didn't you like the party?"

With practiced diplomacy, Carl replied, "It was a nice gesture."

"But didn't you enjoy it?" Ivory asked with astonishment.

"Well, I am not accustomed to being the center of attention."

"Why not?" she asked. "It's your special day."

"I do not know how to react. It is uncomfortable for me."

Ivory felt bad. "I didn't mean to make you feel uncomfortable. I love parties, and, I must admit, I enjoy the attention. I figured you would, too."

"I know you meant well. And it was nice to see everyone." Carl stated as he looked off into the distance. "This reminds me of something that Xenia once shared with us. She told me that we often expect others to like what we like and want what we want."

"I remember that day," Ivory said. "And if I recall correctly, Xenia also said that if we only consider our own desires when we try to please others, we honor who *we* are, not who *they* are."

Ivory looked down at the hat. "I guess what we're saying here is that if it were me, I would have enjoyed a surprise party to celebrate my Hatching Day. I assumed you would, too."

"That is not an unreasonable assumption," Carl acknowledged. "Truth be told, I would never have thrown a party for you because I would not have wanted one myself."

"So you're not throwing me a party for my next Hatching Day?" Ivory joked.

"Well, now that I realize that I need to consider what you like as opposed to what I like, one never knows what lies ahead."

"Oh, a mystery. I like that!" Ivory grinned. "And for the record, I wouldn't mind a Hatching Day Hat of Honor."

Chameleon Wisdom

Do not do unto others as you expect they should do unto you. Their tastes may not be the same.

—GEORGE BERNARD SHAW

We've all heard the Golden Rule, also known as the Ethic of Reciprocity, "Treat others how you want to be treated." This guideline for how we should treat other people exists in many religions and cultures throughout history and across the globe.

This moral truth is most notably applied to virtues such as kindness, respect, and honesty. For example, if I want you to be kind to me, I should be kind to you. If I want you to respect me, I should respect you. And if I want you to be honest with me, I should be honest with you. It's hard to argue with such a time-tested principle that is so universally accepted. The Golden Rule puts your own needs in the spotlight, and this is perfectly acceptable when applied to virtues.

However, this maxim does not work in every situation, especially those in which we have needs that are based on our own style. What if someone has a different style than you do and their needs are not the same as yours? If you treat others how *you* want to be treated, you will be honoring your style, not theirs.

There is another principle that takes the style of others into account, and it is based on the notion that the opposite of profound wisdom is often more profound wisdom. In this case, the inverse of the Golden Rule—referred to in *Taking Flight!* as the Home Rule—states, "Treat others how *they* need to be treated, not how *you* need to be treated." The Home Rule is based on the premise that we all have different needs. Therefore, the Home Rule requires energy, empathy, and insight.

Overall, we tend to treat others how *we* like to be treated, not how *they* like to be treated. We saw this play out in *Hatching Day Surprise* when Ivory mistakenly assumed that Carl would enjoy a surprise party because she would have enjoyed a surprise party. By inadvertently applying the Golden Rule, the parrot treated the owl how *she* would like to be treated. Had Ivory taken a moment to consider Carl's personality style and needs, she would never have arranged such an event.

Imagine an owl and a parrot as a married couple. The owl spouse has a lot of systems that need to be followed in the household. These systems relate to everything from where shoes should be stored to how the dishwasher should be stacked and the towels should be folded. Now imagine the owl's parrot spouse. The parrot feels that a home should be comfortable and free of constraints. As a result, the parrot feels overwhelmed trying to keep everything in predefined locations all the time.

The owl becomes frustrated with the parrot and proceeds to annoy him with constant nagging. The couple gets stuck in an endless loop of conflict. If we can rise above the discord, it is easy to see what is taking place. The spouses are imposing their own style-driven needs on each other. They are creating an environment that makes themselves feel comfortable without taking into consideration the needs of the other.

This tendency to consider our needs ahead of the needs of others also plays out in the workplace. Consider an eagle manager who leads a group of dove employees. The eagle creates a new process that changes all of their procedures. He informs the doves of the new set of guidelines but provides little information and almost no warning before they take effect. The eagle is excited about the results he expects from the new system, and he assumes the doves will be as well.

After announcing the change, the eagle asks the doves if they have any questions. They do not speak up because they need time to consider the new information. The eagle interprets their silence as acceptance. When it comes time to implement the latest procedures, the doves move slowly to adapt and support them. This frustrates the eagle, who cannot understand their resistance. The eagle treated the doves as if they had eagle-like preferences, and the results will not be optimal for either party.

When you treat others based on your own needs, you convey that you do not care enough about the others to figure out what they want. Applying the Home Rule requires effort. First, you have to recognize your own style and not impose it on others. Second, you have to consider the styles of others so you can meet their needs.

When you make conscious decisions based on who you are *and* who others are, you create the basis for deep and lasting relationships. You are also more likely to get what you want when others get what they want.

- PAY ATTENTION TO HOW OTHERS TREAT YOU. Since we tend to treat others how we need to be treated, the way others treat you is a window into their needs.

- DISPLAY EMPATHY AND COMPASSION. Tune in to the unstated needs of others.

- PRACTICE ACTIVE LISTENING. When you pay attention, you may hear others telling you what they want.

- ASK OTHERS WHAT THEIR NEEDS ARE. The easiest way to identify someone's needs is to ask what they want.

Summer

The Chameleon

A Trip to the Beach

For weeks, Ivory had been asking Dee to join her for a weekend adventure at the beach. Ivory planned to kick off the summer with an exciting bang. The journey required nearly half a day's travel, so Dee wasn't sure the strategy of taking a short trip, with only one overnight, would give them enough time to see all the sights. Nevertheless, in order to stop her enthusiastic parrot friend's constant pestering, Dee agreed.

On the morning of their departure, Dee waited for Ivory in her large eagle nest settled high above Home. As the blushing dawn had already transitioned into a stunning blue, Dee was becoming increasingly annoyed. They were supposed to have taken off a while ago, but Ivory was nowhere in sight.

Finally, the parrot's bright colors flashed across the horizon as she leisurely approached Dee's nest. The eagle was tapping her talon impatiently when Ivory swooped in for a landing.

"Sorry I'm late," the parrot apologized.

The eagle sighed. "I thought we were supposed to meet at dawn. We need to get started so we have enough time to explore the beach today."

"I'm ready to go," Ivory announced excitedly. "I would have

gotten here sooner, but I saw the most amazing sight—the sun rising over the Great Lake. It was incredible. You should have seen it. The mist was floating on the water, and a bunch of shiny fish were jumping so high they were penetrating the fog. It looked as if they were sailing through clouds. You should have been there."

"Actually, you should have been *here*," Dee stated. "Well, you are here now. Let's get going."

The two birds leapt from the nest and set a course for Sea Turtle Cove. They flew south, over hills that rolled like giant turtle shells and fields filled with salmon and indigo wildflowers. The landscape was stunning, and Ivory was overwhelmed. Once they left their familiar surroundings, Ivory commented on almost everything she saw. "Look at that!" she often exclaimed. "Check that out! Do you see it? Isn't that incredible?"

Ivory's animated commentary continued nonstop for hours. Dee was amazed at how she could carry on a conversation by herself. When Ivory passed a rocky stream, she shared a funny story about something that had happened to her in a rocky stream. When they passed a fallen tree, she shared a story about a fallen tree. It was as if Ivory had an endless reservoir of experiences to call upon. Dee tried hard to listen to the details of Ivory's stories, but often found herself tuning them out.

At one point they came to a towering waterfall, even bigger than Crystal Falls. "Oh, my!" the parrot declared. "We *have* to go see it. It is humongous! I've never seen a waterfall this big before! Have you?"

Before the eagle could answer, Ivory banked right, beelining toward the falls. "Well, I guess we're taking a detour," Dee mumbled.

"Do you believe this?" Ivory asked. "That must be a 1,000-foot drop! This is remarkable!"

"It is *impressive*," Dee agreed.

"I'm going in!" the parrot proclaimed.

"Going in?" the eagle asked. "What do you mean by ..." but it was too late. Ivory was heading directly toward the falls. Just as she reached the water, she turned a hard left and coasted through the iridescent spray that was the byproduct of the tumbling water.

"Isn't this fantastic?" Ivory yelled.

"Uh, yeah. It's fantastic," Dee replied. "But we've a got a lot of distance to cover, and there are a lot of things to see at the beach. We've got to get going."

After the parrot made a few more passes through the mist, they continued on their way. The next hour or so was filled with waterfall talk. Well, actually, it was filled with Ivory gushing about the waterfall and Dee listening. Somehow, the falls were growing bigger and the danger was becoming more pronounced with each telling of the story.

Next they flew over a dense area of Home filled with mangrove trees that ranged as far as their eyes could see. The groves were framed by a steep cliff rising high into the air. As the two friends increased their altitude to soar above the rock face, Ivory spotted something new.

"What is that?" the parrot inquired as she directed Dee's sharp eagle vision to the center of a rock formation jutting out from the cliff.

"It's a mountain goat," Dee answered. "There are several of them there."

"I've only heard about mountain goats," Ivory said with delight. "We've got to check them out."

Without hesitation, Ivory aimed straight toward the strange and unfamiliar creatures. She landed at the top of a tall pine and shouted to Dee, "Let's watch from here."

Dee settled onto a tree that was not far from their original flight path.

"These guys are hilarious!" Ivory yelled to her friend. "Look how they jump from rock to rock. And if you listen closely, they sound like laughter. It must be fun to be a mountain goat! Isn't it entertaining to watch them butt heads?"

"Butting heads, huh? Don't know what that's like," Dee thought sarcastically. "Now I know why eagles are bald. This parrot is driving me so crazy, I'm going to lose all my feathers by the time this trip is over."

"What was that?" Ivory shouted. "I can't hear you over all the head butting!"

"Nothing!" Dee grimaced. She squirmed for a few minutes until finally stating, "We need to go. We still have a long flight ahead of us, and we don't want to miss anything at the beach."

Ivory stayed for a few more minutes before turning to her friend. "I'm having such a great time on our trip. A sunrise over the lake. Giant waterfalls. Funny mountain goats. Who could ask for anything more?"

The pair continued on as Ivory reflected on her experience with the goats and talked about what she wanted to do when they arrived at Sea Turtle Cove.

After one more detour into a foggy swamp where Ivory

thought she spied a double-rainbow, they finally arrived at their destination.

"We're here," Dee declared.

They landed on the dry sand, just out of reach of the ocean waves. Ivory looked out at the red-wine sky stretching across the horizon and asked, "Isn't this beautiful?"

"It is. I just wish we would have gotten here earlier," Dee replied with a hint of annoyance.

"Is something wrong?" Ivory asked. "It sounds like something is bothering you."

"It's just that we took too much time to get here. We should have ..."

Just then, a large sea turtle floated in on a wave and walked patiently onto the shore. Both birds were both surprised to see it heading their way. When the turtle reached them, she spoke softly and deliberately. "Welcome to Sea Turtle Cove. Consider our beach to be your home away from Home."

The turtle then turned and walked leisurely back to the surf.

"Can you believe it?" Ivory beamed. "That was the oldest sea turtle I've ever seen! She must be a 100 years old!"

"Yes, she must be quite old," Dee replied.

"So what's wrong?" Ivory asked. "Aren't you excited to be here?"

"Yes, I am, but it's already dusk," Dee replied. "We planned to get here earlier, but you kept taking us off course."

Ivory was about to respond when they noticed the turtle making her way back to them. Neither bird said a word. The turtle asked them, "Would you indulge an old turtle such as me to share a few observations?"

Surprised by the turtle's reemergence, they both nodded.

The sea turtle took a slow, deep breath before saying, "Many creatures have crossed my path throughout my lifetime. From the assertive seagull to the playful dolphin … from the industrious beaver to the patient snail … I have met them all. And if there is one thing I have noticed, it is this: There are many ways to reach a destination, and we usually choose the path that reflects who we are."

The turtle turned to Dee and continued, "As an eagle, you keep your eye on your goal and do not get distracted by what is around you."

"Absolutely," Dee affirmed. "That's how I get things done."

"And your path mirrored your desire to get here quickly," said the sea turtle.

The turtle then turned to Ivory and said, "As a parrot, you enjoy life to its fullest. You take every opportunity to experience whatever presents itself to you. It does not matter if it takes you off course for a little while."

"You got that right," Ivory agreed. "Life is meant to be lived."

"And your journey here reflected the essence of who you are." The old turtle hinted at a smile and asked, "So which way is the right way?"

After pausing to watch a seagull dive into the water and emerge with a fish, the turtle added, "Or should I ask, is there a right way?"

Both birds started to answer in unison, but the turtle interjected. "The answers are not for me. They are for you. I will leave you with this: We tend to stay in our natural style until someone or something pulls us out of it. When that happens, we feel uncomfortable. But make no mistake, that uncomfortable zone is where growth occurs. It is also where adventure resides."

The laid-back sea turtle bowed her head respectfully to the visitors and eased herself into a large incoming wave. As she drifted gently out to sea, she bellowed, "Learn from others, and add these new ways to your own. One day they will serve you well. And say hello to Xenia for me." They watched the sea turtle float effortlessly away, drifting wherever the waves took her.

The pair spent the rest of the day enjoying beach sites. Dee was excited to watch an albatross diving for squid. The eagle was particularly impressed by the albatross's hunting technique. They also got to see a hidden cove that very few before them had explored. Dee and Ivory bravely navigated the tunnel's twists and turns, and they exited feeling exhilarated.

Dee said, "On our trip here, I noticed a cave that might be filled with bats. Want to check it out on our way home tomorrow?"

Ivory grinned, "Sure. But let's not spend too much time there. We don't want to return too late."

Chameleon Wisdom

Growth demands a temporary surrender of security.
—Gail Sheehy

We all have behaviors that are natural and comfortable. These behaviors represent a relaxed *and* energizing place that is based on the bird style that most resembles us. We call our natural state our "style zone."

Working outside of our style zone can feel awkward and exhausting because we are internally battling to return to a place of comfort and security. After being out of our zone for a while, we feel the need to go home, rest, and recharge. We feel as if we need to reset ourselves back to our original factory settings. Our brains are creatures of habit; they prefer to follow well-known and well-worn neural connections. When we move outside of our default approach to solving problems or interacting with others, we feel uneasy. We have no hardwiring for the new behaviors.

The human brain is like a human muscle. When we stretch it, it gets stronger. Each time we try something new, we create fresh neural connections and synapses. When we repeat the process, the new actions become ingrained. This progression expands the outer edges of our range by challenging habits that limit performance.

We spend a good portion of our lives on autopilot, mindlessly living our days without thought or intention. On the positive side, our habits help us successfully engage in familiar tasks without wasting too much brain power or energy. On the negative side, the boundaries of our natural tendencies require a great expenditure of energy in order to expand. Because we often fear that the challenge of acting in new ways will lead to failure, judgment, or rejection, we fall back on a state of complacency.

We all seek to remain in our style zone until someone or something pulls us out of it. In *A Trip to the Beach*, Dee is annoyed that Ivory continually stops to enjoy the sights on the way to their destination. As a parrot, Ivory lives in the moment and thrills at experiencing the many wonders of the forest. As an eagle, Dee is goal directed. She wants to get where they are going and feel as if they have accomplished their goal. Dee becomes frustrated when Ivory pulls her out of her natural style. However, when Dee does open up to new ways of behaving, she creates the potential for deeper and richer experiences. Likewise, Ivory learns from Dee that it's important to remain focused.

When you expand the perimeter of your natural state, you gain confidence and fresh perspectives. You acquire new skills and grow stronger and wiser. You may even inspire those around you to leave the safety of their preset factory settings.

Let's take a look at the typical style zones for each of the birds:

Eagles are willing to try new things if the risk will create a big reward. Eagles are all about the outcome. They will put themselves in a position of discomfort if it is likely to yield a big payoff.

After all, you have to be willing to try something new if you want to go where nobody has gone before. Eagles find it frustrating to slow down and pay attention to the feelings of others when a task needs to be accomplished.

Parrots often seek new and varied activities. They will leave their style zone for the exhilaration of a new experience. Parrots revel in new adventures. And why not? Whatever happens will make a good story to tell. Parrots find it more difficult to spend time creating detailed systems than to simply wing it.

Doves will step out of their safe approach to the world to defend friends or family members who are being treated disrespectfully. While doves dislike confrontation, they will push their boundaries to come to the aid of others. However, doves may have difficulty being assertive and standing up to fight for their own needs.

Owls will leave the clearly defined scope of their style only if it makes logical sense to do so. Before they do, they typically engage in a thorough analysis. When owls finally take the risk of leaving their well-practiced behaviors, hazards are often minimized by careful planning. Owls are uncomfortable when they are placed in the spotlight or in situations that require a significant outward display of emotion.

Recall a moment in your life when you stepped out of your style zone. You may have felt pride in your willingness to do so. Or you may have felt apprehension or fear. Either way, the experience was likely memorable, leaving you with a sense of fulfillment and accomplishment, regardless of the outcome.

Your style zone makes life easier because it gives you a place to comfortably operate from. But, every now and again, try pushing the boundaries of your self-imposed limitations. You may discover a whole new world is waiting for you just outside your natural style.

- BREAK YOUR ROUTINE. Do things differently.

- TAKE SMALL STEPS in order to leap out of your comfort zone into something manageable.

- CELEBRATE THE SMALL STEPS you take out of your comfort zone.

- LET GO OF PERFECTIONISM and give yourself permission to fail.

- BE COURAGEOUS. Feel the fear and do it anyway.

The Chameleon

The Speech

The Council Tree's mighty limbs stretched in every direction from a massive trunk. Many of its branches were as long as some of the forest's tallest trees, which, on this special day, made it the perfect venue for the big event.

Eagles flew in from all parts of Home and capped the top of the tree. Just below them, the parrots presented a band of blues, reds, yellows, and greens that brightened the forest scenery. The owls arrived early and positioned themselves in the center of the tree directly in front of the stage. Their location afforded them the perfect angle from which to watch the speakers address the crowd. Small groups of doves were scattered throughout the tree in pairs and small groups, filling in the gaps made by the other birds. The entire community gathered for the celebration, except for the squirrels. They seemed to have wandered off.

Simon's white dove feathers blended into the sea of birds that perched around him. He stood on a log to the right of the stage, which gave him easy access to center stage when it was his time.

Everyone had been looking forward to this day ... well, almost everyone. Simon was gratified to have been the leader of the Pasture Project, which was formed to clean up the swamp and return it to a thriving pasture. After months of work, the project was complete. But this was the day he was dreading. In fact, this day almost stopped him from taking on a leadership role in the first place.

Simon watched the Council President, a short, round owl, explain the details of the project. She described the entire process, complete with charts, statistics, and before-and-after drawings. The speaker took special care to provide a full account of the various challenges they had encountered and how Simon had pulled everyone together to fix them.

Simon stood reluctantly, watching as if he were in a fog. "This is an honor?" he reflected. "I have to stand here in front of everyone and talk about what a great job I did? I succeeded in transforming the swamp and this … *this* is my reward. It feels more like a punishment." He sighed in resignation of his fate.

Two parrots watched from a perch high in the Council Tree. They spoke with each other throughout the president's talk. "Simon is up next," a small, green parrot whispered.

"I know. He's not going to like this," responded a large red parrot. "This is a really big crowd. Doves don't like to speak in front of large groups."

"You got that right! He must be freaking out!" said the green parrot.

"I feel bad for him. He'll never be able to pull this off. They should have asked someone else to deliver the speech for him," added the red parrot.

"That would have been the kinder thing," the green parrot agreed.

The longer the Council President spoke, the more nervous Simon became. The idea of making a speech to a small group was scary enough. But this was a large group. Everybody was here.

For days Simon had obsessed about this moment. What if he doesn't remember what he is supposed to say? What if he forgets to mention someone? What if he offends someone by introducing one volunteer before another volunteer who played a bigger role on the project? As Simon's time approached, so did the butterflies in his stomach. He felt physically ill at the thought of looking out at all those eyes staring back at him. Now, his speech was just moments away. The owl was winding down her talk and beginning to introduce him. "Oh, my gosh," the dove thought. "Here it is. I really have to do this."

The owl continued. "And so it is both my honor and privilege to introduce to you the individual who made this all possible. Without his hard work and dedication, we would not be here today. Without further ado, I would like you to give a warm Home welcome to our guest of honor, Simon."

"Here we go," said the red parrot.

"I can't watch," replied the green parrot as he partially covered his eyes with his wing.

The group welcomed Simon with rousing applause and cheers, especially the parrots, who sounded louder than anyone else. Simon took a long … slow … deep breath and walked deliberately to the podium. The parrots continued to cheer.

"I can do this," Simon told himself.

"Thank you," the dove said, as he gestured for the group to settle down.

Simon took his time to scan the audience, as if he were making eye contact with each individual separately. "Today is not about me," he began. "Today is about the selfless effort put forth by so many. I am humbled by the commitment of those who gave so much of themselves for the benefit of all."

"Hey, he's off to a good start," the green parrot observed.

"Yes, he is," the surprised red parrot agreed.

"I'd like to take a moment to share some of the special things that were done to get us where we are today. First, I'd like to tell you about ..."

Simon spoke for nearly twenty minutes. He pointed out contributions both great and small. He remembered everyone who had done anything to help with the project, and his speech was met with raucous applause.

"Well, I'll be darned," said the red parrot.

"I can't believe it either," added the green parrot. "That was really good! I didn't know he had it in him."

Just then, a small voice radiated from a branch next to the two parrots. Xenia and her young apprentice, Xander, had overheard the parrots' conversation. Xenia looked at them and said, "When you believe that others are only capable of what their personality might predict, you limit what they can do and who they can become."

The parrots looked at each other and winced. By the time they turned to thank the chameleon, she and her young friend were gone.

"I guess we underestimated Simon's ability," the red parrot acknowledged.

"The chameleon did raise a good point. Just because he's a dove doesn't mean that he can't talk effectively in front of a large group. I suppose we can do anything we want to if we put our minds to it — even if it's something uncomfortable," said the green parrot.

The parrot pals looked at each other, feeling a bit guilty that they had ever doubted Simon.

As the event came to an end, the two parrots approached Simon to congratulate him, both on the work he had done in beautifying the pasture and on his wonderful speech. But when they reached the dove, he looked exhausted. This surprised the parrots, as they were usually brimming with energy after being in the spotlight.

While the parrots told Simon he had done a great job, the dove downplayed his role and gave all the credit to the rest of his team. This, too, surprised the parrots, but they dismissed it quickly and invited Simon to join them at an after-party.

"Thank you so much," Simon replied, "but I really need to get home and recover from all this."

The parrots wondered why Simon needed to recover, but as they flew off to their post-meeting celebration, they recalled what Xenia had taught them.

Chameleon Wisdom

If we treat people as they ought to be, we help them become what they are capable of becoming.
— JOHANN WOLFGANG VON GOETHE

While we tend to anticipate specific strengths and weaknesses in others based on their natural style, we can all benefit by learning behaviors that are not typically associated with our primary style. These learned behaviors can be just as strong as our innate ones. When we only consider natural strengths and discount learned behaviors, we stifle the development of new skills. Furthermore, when we hold limiting beliefs about what others are capable of achieving, we restrict their potential.

When the red-and-green parrots in *The Speech* were discussing Simon's probability of success, they did not believe that he was capable of talking in front of so many onlookers. They assumed that public speaking skills did not reside in the domain of a dove. Fortunately for Simon, they kept their comments to themselves. If Simon had learned about their lack of confidence in him, he could have lost some of his own confidence.

Consider what would have happened if one of those parrots was Simon's manager in the workplace. It is unlikely he would have been given the opportunity to make that speech. The parrots would have deprived him of the chance to develop new skills, build confidence, and expand the boundaries of his style zone.

When we believe that others are not capable of expanding their style zone, we do not offer them opportunities to stretch themselves beyond their style zone. This lack of opportunity holds them down—limits them to where they are. Ironically, the intentions of those who hold limiting beliefs may not be negative. In fact, they may very well be perceived to be compassionate.

An owl might try to protect someone from providing poor quality work. A dove or parrot might not wish to make someone feel socially uncomfortable. And an eagle might not want to put someone in a position that limits results. In the end, however, the intention does not matter because the impact is the same: high expectations lead to opportunity and high performance, while low expectations lead to limitations and poor results.

While there is little doubt that our short-term success is driven by our strengths, our long-term development is based on our ability to transcend our existing skills. Growth comes when we extend beyond the edges of our past experiences.

Consider an office owl who is not given the opportunity to make a big presentation to a high-profile client. Making the presentation could make the owl temporarily uncomfortable, but taking on the challenge will enable her to grow and expand her capacity. So the next time a similar opportunity arises, she would not feel as anxious. New, learned behaviors may never create excitement, but the negative, draining effects can be minimized with practice ... if given the opportunity.

Consider a parrot whose owl spouse takes care of all of their financial matters. The owl does not trust the parrot to track things properly, so she never teaches him how to manage their money.

And why would she trust him? From her perspective, managing finances is not a natural parrot skill. When the owl unexpectedly passes away, the parrot has no idea what do and is left without any financial skills. While the parrot may not have enjoyed dealing with the checkbook and the bills (and possibly despised every minute of it), he surely could have learned how to do it. His owl wife failed to activate his potential because she thought it was outside of his style zone.

Visualize an eagle with a group of his close college friends. Whenever someone needs advice about how to handle a crisis, they immediately call upon him to swoop in and save the day. But when an upset friend needs comforting or an empathetic ear, they never ask the eagle to help. When the eagle marries, his spouse is constantly disappointed by his lack of support and validation. No surprise there, since the skill of being emotionally available during difficult times had never been developed by him. The eagle's college friends had never given him the chance to try new behaviors. If they had, they might have been surprised.

Picture a young dove child whose father declined to place him in the awkward position of approaching his teacher about a problem with a grade. To protect his son, the dove parent made the call himself. And why shouldn't he? When he was young, he hated it when his mother made him do things that made him feel uncomfortable. He had vowed long ago that he would never do that to his own child. But now, his son lacks the confidence to stand in his own power and find his own voice.

We communicate expectations to the people around us in conscious ways through our words and in unconscious ways through our tone and body language. A smile to a child walking to the plate in their first little league game builds their confidence. Likewise, the wince you make when you ask someone if he or she is comfortable trying something new conveys volumes.

All of us stay in our comfortable style zones until the world nudges us out of them. When you set high expectations that stretch people out of their zones, they will rise to meet those challenges. When you believe in someone more than they believe in themselves, you build their confidence and increase their potential. You also strengthen your relationship with them.

When you set low expectations for others, they are likely to do only as much as you think they can, especially if you are in a leadership position (manager, coach, parent, or teacher). When we limit others, we limit our relationship with them.

Give others the chance to step out of their style zones, and be there to support them when they do. Recognize their discomfort and honor their courage. Be supportive and accept that the quality or the results may not be perfect the first time through … but that is how we learn. Provide positive recognition for their effort, and know that you have helped others to be the best they can be.

- ENCOURAGE POSITIVE THINKING in others.

- EMBRACE FAILURE as a learning opportunity.

- BELIEVE IN OTHERS and they will believe in themselves.

- SET THE BAR HIGH. Expectations can affect reality and create self-fulfilling prophecies.

The Lost Bird Department

This was the day Ivory had been looking forward to. The clear blue sky set the stage for the world of possibilities that awaited her. She was about to start a new phase of her life. She was beginning her first job as a contributing member of Home.

This year the Lost Bird Department was in desperate need of assistance, and numerous recruits had committed to help. Many of the tasks assigned to the birds in this department had been arranged long ago. Dee, for example, like the eagles before her, was destined to become a scout. Dee would spend her days scouring the skies above the forest. Her keen eyesight would help her locate lost birds who entered the airspace above Home. While Dee worked as an apprentice to an experienced scout, she would gain the skills necessary to identify flight patterns typical of lost birds. Dee stretched her wings in preparation for her big day.

As a young dove, Simon knew he would be a host for the Lost Bird Department. He was perfectly suited to nurture lost birds with words of support and to provide them with food and a nice tree to sleep in. Simon prepared for his new job by gathering snacks for those in need.

While Ivory was excited to play her part in supporting the

community, the role she would take was a mystery to all. After her parrot parents had died suddenly during the Spinning Wind a decade ago, Carl's parents took her in and raised her as their own. Day after day, she watched her new owl family return from work and discuss everything that happened during their day. As mappers, Carl's parents created detailed maps that guided lost birds on their way. They regularly talked about how their work was making a difference. They loved their jobs.

Before they passed away, Ivory's parents were prominent greeters for the Department. When a scout located a lost bird, the hapless fellow was brought directly to a greeter. It was the greeter's responsibility to give the newcomers a tour of Home and make them feel welcome until a host had gathered suitable food for them and located a place for them to rest. Ivory liked the idea of becoming a greeter and thought she would make an excellent tour guide.

Would Ivory follow in the footsteps of her parrot parents and become a greeter, or would she take on the mapper role of her adopted owl parents? Maybe she would surprise everyone and choose to become a scout or a host. Nobody wanted to pressure her. The selection of a job was a personal choice, and the owls wanted her to decide for herself.

For weeks Ivory wrestled with the decision. She recalled her days as a young parrot, listening to her parents share stories about the interesting cast of characters they met as greeters. She also spent the past ten years listening to the owls clearly describe their jobs as mappers. She hoped she could be as inspired by her work as they were with theirs.

The day had come for Ivory to declare her choice. She arrived at the Lost Bird Department ready to announce her decision. In honor of the owls who had taken her in, she selected the role of mapper. She had taken Map Making 101 in Flight School and had done pretty well. It wasn't one of her favorite classes because she found the detailed work to be a bit tiring, but she told herself that training for a job was probably much different than performing the job on a daily basis. Practicing in school to make maps didn't feel rewarding, but maybe that was because she wasn't helping anyone during her practice. She was just trying to get good grades.

After sharing her decision with the Bird Resources Director, Ivory was assigned to shadow Clark, the greatest mapper of his generation. Her first day was exhausting, but she attributed that to having to learn all the steps she would have to follow in her new role. The next day drained her as well ... as did the next day and the one after that. Each day, her feathers seemed a bit more ruffled, but she was getting through it.

Over the coming weeks, the work grew harder, not easier. She slowly gained mapmaking skills, and, in fact, became quite proficient at it. But she was not excited to go to work, and she didn't understand why not. Carl's parents loved being mappers.

After several weeks, Clark approached Ivory to tell her that she had learned the key skills of mapping. He said she would improve further over time, but that she was proficient enough now to take on her first charge. Her apprenticeship had come to end.

"Maybe," she hoped, "I'll enjoy my job now that I have the freedom to do it on my own."

A few hours later, Ivory met her first lost bird. For the first time in quite a while, she was eager to be a mapper. She was excited at the prospect of helping someone on their travels.

Ivory retrieved her clipboard with the Lost Bird Tracking Form she used to document the process, just as she was taught. She methodically started at Step 1: "Conduct intake interview to determine starting point and destination."

The parrot understood that the data she gathered in Step 1 was critical for tracking patterns. She recognized that every detail was significant. Once Step 1 was complete, she moved on to Step 2: "Consult the Map Catalog." She proceeded to the Map Room and began to scour diagrams created by previous mappers.

It was tedious work that required intense focus and concentration. Ivory spent the entire day measuring, drawing, calculating, checking, and rechecking. In the end, she was proud of her creation, but she felt drained.

The next morning, Ivory repeated the process she had performed the day before—interview the lost bird, analyze the extensive catalog, create a map, and confirm the plan's accuracy.

Before long, Ivory was dreading going to work.

One day a scout brought Ivory two quiet little birds who, while traveling together, had lost their way. "Ivory, let's talk," the eagle said.

"Sure thing," answered the parrot. "What can I do for ya'?"

"Do you recognize these guys?" the eagle asked.

The two small birds looked at Ivory with big, sad eyes.

"Hey, you were just here two days ago," Ivory said to the pair. "Are you lost again?"

The birds nodded.

"Didn't you follow the directions I gave you?" Ivory probed.

They didn't know how to respond. Evidently, they followed Ivory's directions, but Ivory had sent them off to fly in circles, and they had never left Home.

The small birds handed Ivory the map she had created, and she immediately understood why they had gotten lost. Even though the map wasn't accurate, she was impressed by her drawing.

The eagle called to a nearby host to take the lost pair aside. The imposing eagle looked directly into Ivory's eyes and said, "Look, this is the third time I've found a lost bird who remained lost after you had helped them. It seems as though your maps, your instructions, or both are not clear enough. I didn't want to mention this before because I recognized that you were new to the job, but your work has not been acceptable."

Ivory felt terrible and apologized to the eagle for creating extra work for him.

"Hey, I don't mind the work. It's what I do. I love my job," the eagle replied.

The parrot grimaced.

"Ivory, I'm sensing that you don't like being a mapper. What's going on?"

Ivory exploded with weeks' worth of frustration. "I can't take it!" she declared. "I thought I would love being a mapper. I listened to Carl's parents rave about this job, and I don't get it."

"It sounds like you're the one who is lost," the eagle observed. "Is there another job you think you'd like better?"

"Now that you ask, I've been watching the greeters taking our lost visitors on tours of Home, and it looks as if they are having a blast!" Ivory said. "In that job, I'd get to meet fascinating travelers and show off our awesome forest. And the best part is, I wouldn't have to draw any maps!"

They both laughed.

"My father once told me," the eagle said, "that if I find a job based on my strengths, my spirit will soar."

"I wish I was doing that," Ivory sighed. "I'm experiencing the opposite. I'm not using my strengths, and my job feels like drudgery."

"Your job should feed your spirit, not drain it," the eagle explained. "What you are experiencing is not good for you or anyone else."

"Especially these little lost fellows," the parrot acknowledged. "It's time for me to stop making maps and start making conversations as a greeter."

"I think everyone would appreciate that," the eagle agreed with a smile.

"I think you're right," Ivory responded. "Now where did those little guys go? One more map couldn't hurt anyone."

The eagle looked at Ivory in disbelief until he noticed the teasing smirk on her face. "Oh, I think it could," the eagle laughed. "How about we leave the maps to those who enjoy making them?"

Chameleon Wisdom

The only way to do great work is to love what you do.
—STEVE JOBS

During our careers we spend about a third of our waking lives at work. One would hope that those hours are being spent doing something that feeds our spirit.

Unfortunately, for most people work is just that … *work*. Sometimes it is the environment that does not resonate with us. Other times it is the job itself. There are many variables that impact job satisfaction, but one thing is clear — if our style matches the job and the organization's culture, the work will feed us. If not, it will drain us.

Each style has different career needs. *Eagles*, for example, prefer to work in an environment that allows them to spread their wings and operate freely. They don't like routine work. They prefer a wide range of responsibilities. Eagles favor an environment that values candor and offers opportunity for advancement based on performance.

Like eagles, *parrots* get frustrated when they feel constrained. They need a high degree of interaction with others and thrive when they can socialize and connect with people. They prefer to work for a motivating and empowering manager who provides positive feedback and the freedom to express ideas.

Doves seek a calm and stable work environment that

has predictable routines and defined standards. They prefer incremental, rather than revolutionary, change. Doves like to work in a small, tight-knit group that enjoys minimal conflict and a high degree of trust and respect. They value sincere appreciation for a job well done.

Owls like to work within clearly defined expectations and procedures. Because they focus on details, they prefer a private workspace with little interruption. Owls value a business-like environment that offers opportunities to demonstrate their expertise, and they require sufficient time to ensure that they can produce quality results.

In *The Lost Bird Department*, Ivory was in a job that did not match her style. Playing the role of mapper drained her energy. She tried to make it work, but there was no way for her to create long-term success at a job that did not resonate with her social parrot style. Ultimately, she was destined to become a mediocre mapper because her true talents were being underutilized. When she changes her role to greeter, her gifts will be employed, she will become successful, and she will feel fulfilled.

Imagine a young parrot personality whose persuasiveness and verbal adeptness have inspired many people to encourage her to become a lawyer. As she grows older, she internalizes the idea that she would enjoy being an attorney, so off she goes to law school. However, once she begins working as a practicing attorney, she discovers that being is lawyer is far from the dramatic television images she has seen of legal battles in courtrooms. She discovers the job entails more research and writing than she had ever conceived. This doesn't mean that a parrot cannot be a talented attorney or enjoy being an attorney. But this parrot's personality style did not match what was required of her at work.

Not liking parts of your job description does not necessarily mean you should be dusting off your resume and looking for a new job. Everyone has responsibilities they find distasteful. The question is this: How much of your energy is being zapped by a job or work environment that does not match your style?

If the energy drain is small, look for ways to minimize its impact. Perhaps you can find a coworker with whom you can trade unwanted tasks. Maybe you can talk with your manager about having unpleasant responsibilities removed from your plate.

Take an energy audit of your job. Does the organization's culture feel like a good fit or does it feel out of sync with who you are? Does your job nourish your soul or eat away at your spirit?

Remember, your job should feed you, not drain you.

- **SPEND TIME WITH OTHERS** who love their jobs. Let their joy inspire you to re-imagine your career.

- **DON'T SETTLE FOR TASKS** that drain you. Ask for what you want.

- **MAKE SURE THAT EVERY DAY** has an element in it of what you love to do.

- **CREATE OPPORTUNITIES** to engage your hardwiring.

- **DO SOMETHING THAT FEEDS YOU.** Choose to do what you love.

The Forbidden Swamp

A cheerful sun warmed a summer breeze as it wafted through the air. It was the perfect day to take a meditative stroll through the outer reaches of Home. Xenia enjoyed her alone time. She had discovered the perfect place to connect with the spirit of the forest. Not many creatures ventured this far west of the Great Lake. Her secret spot afforded her the opportunity to sink deeply into the silence of the woods.

The chameleon took pleasure in her oneness with the land. As she walked, she matched her color to the teals, violets, golds, and reds of the flowers nearby. Xenia ambled by a small stream and approached a pungent marshy area. Vines hung above the soggy land, and trees grew out of the water. Cattails and water lilies decorated the landscape, and mosquitoes and dragonflies filled the air.

As she approached the dreaded Forbidden Swamp, she was surprised to hear two voices in the distance. Because of the many spooky stories that had circulated about the dangers of the swamp, it was rarely frequented by the birds or any other forest creatures. Some said that the swamp emitted a powerful gas that could drive you instantly mad. Others said it had the power to change your form into one of a horrible being. Everyone in the forest seemed to know someone who knew someone who had never been heard from again after inhaling the swamp's powerful vapors.

Xenia walked peacefully towards the swamp as if she were impervious to its effects. As she drew closer to the voices, she could see the shadows of an eagle and dove. When she got even closer, she saw they belonged to Dee and Simon.

Though she couldn't make out their words just yet, the tone of their voices indicated that they both seemed troubled. Once Xenia got within earshot, she discovered that Dee was troubled that the other birds thought she was bossy and overbearing, and Simon was upset that they viewed him as passive and weak.

Xenia continued to approach the pair as they continued to express their concerns. Simon felt that if he were female, the others would feel differently about him. "I don't understand why the others view the female doves as friendly and considerate, yet I'm considered a pushover."

Dee echoed Simon's sentiment. She believed that if she were male, others would not criticize her as being bossy. She described one dominating and demanding male eagle who was considered to be a great leader. "I don't get it," complained Dee.

"Me neither," replied Simon.

Xenia chose this moment to appear. "Perhaps I can shed some light on the subject."

The two birds jumped, and Xenia smirked. She always relished the reactions to her surprise visits. "I couldn't help but overhear your conversation, and it sounds like you are both bothered by how others see you."

"You got that right," Dee snapped. "It's not fair that others judge me by my gender."

Xenia turned to Simon, "And you feel judged because you're male?"

"I guess I do," the dove responded.

"It might be helpful for you to see how the other half lives," the chameleon shared.

The eagle and dove looked puzzled.

"Allow me to explain. Simon, would you like to experience how others would see you if you were more like an eagle — full of strength, conviction, and power?"

"Sure," he nodded tentatively.

"And Dee, would you like to see what it would be like if others perceived you as if you were a dove — considerate, thoughtful, and kind?"

"That would be nice for a change," Dee said. "But how ..."

"Then follow me," Xenia said as she walked towards the Forbidden Swamp. When they reached the edge of the mucky water, she instructed them. "I need you to do exactly what I say and nothing more. Do you understand?"

The two birds looked at each other, not certain of what they had gotten themselves into. However, they trusted Xenia and cautiously agreed to the chameleon's conditions.

"Sit beside me and relax," she guided.

The chameleon nestled her small frame onto a large, dry leaf. She crossed her legs and placed her hands upon her knees. The birds tried to follow suit, but they could not quite get their legs in the same position, so they squatted down on the wet ground.

Xenia continued. "I know that the swamp does not smell good, but do not fear. It will not harm you. Let go of all thought and simply be here in this place at this time. I want you to take three long, slow breaths, each time drawing the air deep into your belly."

Sitting silently, the pair focused on their breathing. "Dee, visualize yourself as soft-spoken, helpful, and caring. See yourself exactly as you would like others to perceive you. Simon, visualize yourself as being strong, confident, and in command of every situation. Feel with every aspect of your being what that would be like. Breathe deeply and think of nothing else."

For the next few minutes, the birds focused intently on seeing themselves as they would like to be seen. Gradually, a strange sensation began to wash over them. Xenia noticed that Simon was sitting up a little straighter. His expression became more serious and resolute. Dee, in contrast, softened her features. She seemed content and peaceful.

"It is done," Xenia announced. "Open your eyes. You are not to speak to each other until the sun disappears below the horizon. Return now to your familiar surroundings. At dusk I will meet you on the large boulder in the center of the field beside the Great Lake. Now go. I will see both of you later."

The two looked at each other, pressed their weight into the ground, and took off into the sky in opposite directions.

Xenia smiled and thought, "This is becoming an interesting day."

Simon soared over the forest. He flew higher and higher until he was looking down on Home from the bottom of the clouds. As he drifted over the forest, he spied two doves, one gray and one white. The gray dove was crying. Simon landed firmly next to the pair and barked, "What's wrong?"

The gray dove was too shaken to answer, so her friend replied. "She lost a heart-shaped gem that her grandmother gave her. She's afraid it is gone forever."

"That's it?" Simon replied.

"Well, yeah," the white dove said. "It means a lot to her."

There are lots of heart-shaped gems in the Crystal Cave," Simon stated. "Just go there and get another one. In fact, I believe a group of parrots are heading there tomorrow. Would you like me to ask them to get one for you?"

Both doves looked at Simon in disbelief. "You don't understand," said the sobbing dove. "That stone has sentimental value and cannot be replaced. You can't just …"

Simon interrupted. "I understand. You're grandmother gave it to you. But it's gone. I'm just trying to help you to replace it."

Neither dove knew how to respond to Simon's callousness, so the white dove leaned in and suggested, "Maybe it would be best if I comforted her alone."

"Suit yourself," Simon replied as he flew off to see what else was happening in Home.

Across the forest, Dee was aiming toward the treetops, but they seemed higher than usual. The eagle slowed herself down and decided to fly a little closer to the ground. As she dipped downward, she heard shouts coming from a group of nearby owls. She made her way there and was stunned by what she saw. A newborn groundhog was wedged in a tree hollow, and several owls were debating how to resolve the situation. They had suggested a few options and were now evaluating each one. In the meantime, the groundhog was becoming increasingly agitated. Someone had to do something.

"Thank goodness," one of the owls declared. "Dee is here. She will know what do."

Another owl asked, "Dee, can you help us out? We need to make a decision, and we cannot seem to agree on a course of action. We need someone to make the call."

Dee's gaze was fixed on the groundhog. She uneasily watched him squirm. He looked as if he had an itch on his hind quarters that could not be scratched. She felt his frustration as deeply as if it were happening to her.

"Well, Dee?" another owl pressed.

"So?" inquired yet another.

"Well, I'm not sure," replied the eagle. "Can you hold on for a moment? I'd like to talk with our furry friend. He seems rather upset."

For the next few minutes, Dee chatted supportively with the groundhog. The owls watched in surprise. Dee's words were comforting and helped to calm him.

"Excuse me, Dee," one of the owls interrupted. "We already spoke to the groundhog, determined the cause of his predicament, and discussed his physical condition. He has no injuries. He's just stuck, and we need to get him out of there."

"I'm not sure what to do," Dee said. "But he seems a lot more relaxed now."

"Dee," one of the owls cracked. "If you are not going to help, you are just in the way."

Dee shrugged and decided that she was distracting the owls from making a decision. She wished the groundhog well and offered a few more supportive words to the owls before she left them to sift through their options and determine a course of action.

The setting sun began to creep toward the horizon as Dee and Simon headed to the designated meeting place. Simon arrived first and Dee shortly thereafter.

Xenia had blended so flawlessly into the rock she was on that only the bright yellow glow of her eyes was visible. Beside her, a set of smaller orbs appeared. They belonged to her protégé, Xander. Xenia introduced the young chameleon to the birds, who were beginning to feel more like themselves again.

Dee spoke first. "What did you do to us?"

Xenia smiled. "Oh, don't worry about that. Tell me about your day."

"Before I tell you what happened, you've got to tell me what you did," the eagle insisted.

"I did not do anything," Xenia answered. "The swamp emits an invisible gas that magnifies your thoughts. The effects are only temporary, but they can be intense."

"Intense? That's one way to describe it," Dee snarled.

"So how was your day?" the chameleon asked again.

"How was my day?" Dee replied. "Well, let's see. I discovered that trees are really tall and the forest can be dangerous. I came across a groundhog who got stuck in a tree hollow, and the owls had no idea how to help him."

"Did you help them?" Xenia asked.

Dee hesitated before saying, "Not exactly."

Dee explained that she wasn't quite herself and that her initial impulse was to ease the groundhog's stress. The owls, on the other hand, just wanted her to make a decision.

"Did you tell them what to do?" the chameleon probed.

"Not exactly," the eagle repeated. "I didn't feel comfortable telling them what to do. I just wanted to ease the groundhog's distress."

Xenia squinted her eyes and said, "Fascinating."

Dee replied, "As I said, I wasn't exactly myself."

"It appears that being someone else is not as great as it may seem," the chameleon said.

Dee nodded in agreement.

Xenia then turned her gaze to the dove. "And you, Simon, tell me about your day."

Simon looked away when he admitted, "I'm a little ashamed."

"Why is that?"

"I came across a dove who was very upset. I tried to fix the problem, but instead I should have consoled her. I did not act very nice."

Xenia stood up straight, looked intently into Simon's eyes, and said, "It appears that the same behavior can be perceived differently depending upon your gender."

"But that's not fair," Dee asserted angrily. "I should be allowed to do what male eagles do without being called bossy."

"Indeed," Xenia confirmed. "I guess you have an important decision to make. What matters more to you, how you see yourself or how others see you?"

Simon reflected, "You're saying that male doves can act the same as female doves, but that those actions may not be interpreted the same way."

"Precisely!" Xenia exclaimed. "Simon, I know you do not want those around you to see you as weak. However, your peers do not see you as weak. They see you as a compassionate friend. And Dee, you do not want to be thought of as bossy. While sometimes you may be viewed as being bossy, your peers also view you as a confident leader. You each have wonderful traits that you can be proud of."

Dee and Simon were beginning to feel a lot better about themselves.

The chameleon took a moment to allow her words to resonate and then said, "Your personality is your own. Do not let others define it for you. You were gifted with a specific set of strengths, but those strengths come with a related set of weaknesses. If you trade away your gifts for a new set you consider to be better, you will lose the essence of what makes you special. And, you would not only be acquiring new strengths, you would also be gaining a whole new set of challenges."

Xenia's granite gray color transformed into a rich crimson that matched the evening sky. Xander followed his teacher's lead and shifted his color. Just before the two chameleons departed, Xenia asked her student to share what he had learned. He cleared his throat and said, "Accept yourself fully and you will be free of the need to be accepted by others."

Dee and Simon could see that Xenia was beaming with pride at her student's response. The teacher looked back, gave the birds a wink, and faded into the sunset. The eagle and dove watched as the sky turned a deeper shade of red. Simon said, "I kinda like who you are, Dee. You don't need to act like a dove."

Dee responded, "Yeah. I like who you are, too. Besides, there's only room for one eagle."

They both laughed and, together, enjoyed the spectacle of the setting sun.

Chameleon Wisdom

To be successful, you don't have to change who you are. You have to become more of who you are.
—SALLY HOGSHEAD

While gender roles have certainly changed over the past fifty years, gender stereotypes still exist. These labels impact both men and women. They can inhibit well-being and limit a person's full potential. As we unconsciously conform to cultural views of femininity and masculinity, we may be ignoring our innate personality style.

The notion that all men display more eagle characteristics — being direct, daring, and risk-taking — and women more dove-like qualities — soft-spoken, sensitive, and good listeners — is not grounded in reality. Of course we know that men can be good listeners and women can be assertive. Female eagles are just as confident and candid as their male counterparts, and male doves are just as empathetic and compassionate as female doves.

But due to cultural norms, we may perceive the same action differently, depending upon which gender displays it. In *The Forbidden Swamp*, Simon and Dee felt as if they would have been treated differently if they were the opposite gender. The eagle felt as if her behaviors would have been more socially acceptable if she were male. The dove felt as if his actions would have been more acceptable if he were female. As such, they sought to change their style to conform to societal expectations. In so doing, they discovered that changing who they were resulted in detrimental consequences. By giving up their strengths, they lost the essence of their true nature.

Whether we seek to change ourselves because of societal pressure, cultural expectations, or any other reason, understand that every strength is paired with a corresponding weakness. While our strengths and weaknesses may seem contradictory, they are actually interdependent. One cannot exist without the other. And when we exchange one strength for a new strength, we also pick up its related weakness.

Consider how each style listens to others. *Eagles* are bottom-line listeners. They do not want to be bothered with minute details or long explanations. If you do not get to the point quickly, eagles will either cut you off or tune you out. *Parrots* are responsive listeners who like to share personal stories about topics at hand. Like the eagles, they do not tune into details. *Doves* are empathetic listeners who pick up on the emotion of others as they tune into tone and body language. *Owls* are analytical listeners who focus on facts and logic. They compare what is said by others to what they know or think should be said. If there is a match, the owls have no problem. However, if the information received does not coincide with their previously held knowledge, the owls will ask a lot of questions.

What would happen if someone tried to change his listening style? Imagine a parrot salesperson who is going on sales calls and bringing high energy and passion to his prospects. He spends little time describing his product, but his excitement is so contagious, the finer points of what he is selling do not seem to matter.

At home his wife often tells him that he is not a good listener. She cites his inability to pay attention to details and complains that when he is speaking, he talks excessively about himself. After years of hearing he is a poor listener, he begins to think his wife may be correct, and he internalizes the notion that this behavior may be impacting his effectiveness at work. As a result, he decides it is time to become a better listener and communicator in every aspect of his life.

Now, when he heads out on sales calls, he focuses on providing details about the features and benefits of his products. He asks many questions and tries to listen without interrupting to share personal anecdotes. While this new approach takes a tremendous amount of energy to sustain, he acknowledges he has become a more attentive and analytical listener. At home, his wife is ecstatic. But at work, he is surprised to see that his sales have gone down … not up.

While the parrot salesman gave up talking about himself, which his wife had considered a weakness, he picked up a new weakness — not connecting with his sales prospects. He traded his stories and enthusiasm for attention to the details. As he did so, he lost the essence of what made him successful.

Pressure to conform to the world around us comes from many places. Society imposes unstated expectations on us. Organizational cultures encourage us to fit in if we want to be successful. Even parents and spouses place pressure on us to act how *they* think we should act. But in the end, we are not good for others if we are not good for ourselves.

Don't trade away your true self just to fit in. If you do, be aware that you will pick up a whole new set of weaknesses, and you will never feel like you are who you were meant to be. Developing new skills is a good thing, but do not give up what makes you special.

- BE INDEPENDENT OF THE FEELINGS OF OTHERS. Be yourself … everyone else is already taken.

- WORK ON AREAS that you would like to improve, but don't try to be someone else.

- THE BEST WAY TO SHOW LOVE is to accept others, not try to improve them.

- DON'T CHANGE FOR OTHERS. If people do not like you for who you are, decide if they are people you want in your life.

- DON'T TRY TO CHANGE OTHERS to satisfy your needs. They will ultimately resent it.

The Summer Festival

With the last remnants of summer fading away, the residents of Home were preparing for the cooler days of fall. From the smallest dove to the largest eagle, the forest dwellers were eager to spread their wings and breathe in the sun's warmth one last time.

The last weekend of summer was a time to honor everything the season had bestowed upon them. And for as long as anyone could remember, the community bid goodbye to this special time of year with a festival. Since summer embodied light, heat, freedom, and joy, the Summer Festival had to capture that sense of playfulness.

Each year, one owl and one parrot were selected to coordinate, plan, and run the festivities. Carl and Ivory were chosen to lead this year's event.

Carl prepared to apply the owl wisdom his mother, Crystal, had passed down to him when she advised, "Aim twice, strike once." He was tasked with supervising food and logistics and was looking forward to organizing an efficiently managed event.

Ivory's red, yellow, and green parrot feathers symbolized the energy she planned to infuse into this year's festivities — or "The

Ultimate Extravaganza," as she liked to call it. She was in charge of the activities and entertainment.

With just two days to go before the celebration took place, Carl reviewed the scrolls containing his detailed plans, charts, and timelines. He arranged the food for the different species, taking all dietary restrictions into consideration. He designed an overall map of the grounds and established a system for the doves to watch over their increasing number of little ones. He even prepared a rain plan in case of inclement weather.

Ivory selected a few of her favorite games and made up a couple new ones. She even procured a few Venus flytraps for an activity that she named "Snapper." The last time she ran an activity using these plants, it didn't go so well, but the parrot was certain she worked out the kinks. This time it was going to be hilarious, or so she hoped. "What's the worst thing that could happen?" she wondered.

The big day arrived. As the sun's first rays began to sweep across Home, the two leaders met in the Great Field that bordered the Great Lake. When Carl arrived, he saw Ivory circling speedily above the water, rising and lowering as she went. He had never seen a parrot fly so fast.

"Oh, just wonderful," the owl thought sarcastically. "We've got work to do, and Ivory is already playing games."

Carl hopped onto a branch that hung over the water and called to his partner. "If it is not too much trouble, can you come over here so we can get started? We have much to do."

"Sure thing," Ivory bellowed as she made one more quick lap around the field.

Carl had barely glanced up from his scrolls before Ivory landed with a thump beside him. The owl immediately began dictating instructions. "I have prioritized our morning and would like to start by establishing a perimeter to contain the day's events. After that, I will prepare the day care area for the young ones. Once that is complete, I will ..."

The list went on and on. Although Ivory didn't hear much of what he was saying, she let him talk. When Carl was done, the parrot asked, "Since you seem to have everything under control, how about I go set up the games?"

"That is acceptable," Carl replied. "When you are done, please return to me so we can determine what needs to happen next."

"Will do," Ivory said, as she flitted off for the area that Carl designated as "Games" on one of the tracking scrolls he had created.

Carl was happy to be left alone so he could focus on his work. Before long, the sun would be overhead and everyone would be arriving. Carl felt burdened by how much was still left to do.

By the time Ivory made her way back to Carl, the owl hadn't even left to perform his first project. He was still reviewing his tasks on paper to ensure everything was in the proper order and that no critical steps were missed.

Ivory could immediately see the concern on Carl's face, and she wanted to help. "The games are ready," Ivory announced. "Gimme something. Anything at all. Whadya got for me?"

Carl frowned because he worried that Ivory would not follow the plan exactly and that her actions would thrust the entire event into disarray. But he needed the help, so he hesitantly said,

"I suppose you can set up the food for the eagles. It is right over there. Now, listen carefully. When you place the food down, there are a few things I would like to review with you. First, as you ..."

"Don't worry, I've got it," Ivory exclaimed.

She zigged and zagged her way toward the spot marked, "Eagle — Food." Carl returned to his scrolls. Everything looked in order.

A few minutes later, the parrot returned to Carl, proud to have fulfilled her assignment. "Now what?" she asked eagerly.

"You are finished?" asked Carl.

"Yup. That wasn't hard. What's next?"

"How is that possible?" he thought. His desire to get everything accomplished overwhelmed his need to question her thoroughness. So he gave her the next assignment and continued his work.

Carl tried to focus, but all he could do was speculate on how Ivory had set up the eagle's food. There was, after all, a very specific way he wanted the food arranged. His concerns about Ivory not following his guidelines gnawed at him until he couldn't take it anymore. He had to see what she had done.

Carl marched quickly across the field to the eagle's food area and gasped. "What the ...? This is not right," he protested. "I provided her with a clear diagram of how the eagles prefer their food to be arranged, or at least how they *should* want their food to be arranged, and this is not even close. I suppose if I want something done right, I have to do it myself."

As Carl reorganized just about everything Ivory had prepared, he berated himself for his carelessness. "I should have known better. That parrot is just getting in the way."

A few minutes later, Ivory flew by the eagle's food. Her smile turned to a confused pout. "Wait a minute. What happened here? Did someone rearrange this?"

And then it struck her. "Carl did this! He didn't like the way I set the food out, so he took it upon himself to redo it! Why did he ask me to do it in the first place if he was going to rearrange it? Well, I'll be darned if I'm going to waste any more of my time doing things that are going to be redone."

Ten minutes passed before Carl realized that Ivory was nowhere to be found. He scanned the sky above the Great Field and couldn't find her. He looked above the Great Lake, but she wasn't there either. When he looked over the grounds to the western tip of the pasture, he spotted her. "What on earth is she doing?"

The owl shook off his stunned disbelief and charged toward Ivory. With each step, he got angrier. When he got about ten feet away from her, he launched into a tirade. "Why are you playing with the Venus flytraps? Don't you know how much we have to do? We were selected for this job, and we are tasked with doing it right. This festival is not going to set itself up!"

Ivory shrugged, "That may be true, but it doesn't get *reset* by itself, either."

Carl didn't know what to say. He wanted to point out that he wouldn't have changed her food arrangement if she had done it right the first time, but he knew that would not help the situation. He just sighed in frustration.

Ivory then added, "How about you organize things how you want them, and I'll just stay out of your way. I'd rather get snapped at by a Venus flytrap than get poked by your lack of confidence."

Carl felt conflicted. While it was true he did not trust the parrot, it was only because she displayed disregard for the process. Carl never intended to hurt Ivory's feelings, but he could see he had done just that. As they walked across the Great Field together, Carl apologized to Ivory. The parrot reluctantly agreed to set up the welcome area, with one condition.

Carl stopped in his tracks to focus on what Ivory had to say next. The parrot looked directly into his big owl eyes and stated, "If your way is the only way to do something right, you will end up being the only one who is going to do it."

Carl knew that Ivory was right, and he nodded in agreement. The owl considered his words carefully before he replied. "I appreciate your help, and I will try to be open to other ways of doing things."

"That's all I'm asking," the parrot returned as she clapped him on the back a bit too enthusiastically. "Now let's get this extravaganza started!"

Chameleon Wisdom

Everyone driving slower than you is an idiot. Everyone driving faster than you is a maniac.
—GEORGE CARLIN

Have you ever seen two parents in the same household, two managers in the same department, or two people with the same job perform their roles differently while being equally effective? Yet, if you were to ask one of those folks to describe the optimal way to play that role, they would inevitably describe their own approach.

It is not unreasonable to think that our way is the best way. Because our achievements have proved to us that our way works, we hold them as concrete evidence to support our assumption.

We solve problems and live our lives in a way that is consistent with our personality. While style is not a predictor of success, it is a predictor of how we are likely to go about achieving it.

Consider the approach of the four bird styles: *Eagles* drive results by taking bold risks to accomplish big things that have never been done before. *Parrots'* eternal optimism and faith in others drive them to try out new ideas and trust others to help them along the way. *Doves* achieve success by cultivating long-term relationships and creating a supportive and nurturing environment. *Owls* maintain efficient systems to ensure consistency and attain quality results.

In *The Summer Festival*, Carl's owl style compelled him to follow his own high standards of excellence. He had a specific way he wanted things done, and he forced those expectations on Ivory. This served to alienate and discourage his friend. To the owl, the adage "If you want something done right, you have to do it yourself" became "If I want something done *my* way, I have to do it *myself*."

Like Carl, we each unknowingly impose this perspective on others more than we might think. However, while our perspectives are based on our own experiences, they do not represent the *only* way to achieve objectives.

Whether we are at home, work, or with friends, the "My Way" attitude creates hierarchy and inhibits trust. Since strong relationships are built on a foundation that allows *both* individuals to get their needs met, compromise is sometimes necessary. If one spouse, partner, or coworker is subordinated to following the rules and methods of the other, resentment and animosity can undermine their foundation.

Imagine two parents who have different views on how to deal with a child who has disrespected a friend. The eagle parent simply wants to explain to the child how her behavior has made her friend feel. Afterward, the eagle is willing to drop the issue entirely. The dove parent wants the child to call her friend and apologize so they can get back on good terms. Both parents think their way is the right way to handle the situation, and each is closed to the other's approach. When they entrench themselves in their own perspectives, they invalidate their partner's solution, and they also invalidate who their partner is as an individual.

Parents who hyper-control every aspect of a child's life are referred to as "helicopter parents." These mothers and fathers swoop in and hover over everything their children do. While they believe they are being helpful, they are actually decreasing their children's confidence and increasing their anxiety. Hovering parents send messages to their children that they are not capable of figuring things out for themselves. This, in turn, creates a self-fulfilling prophecy — the children stop trying to identify solutions to their own problems and become even more dependent. This cycle then boomerangs back to reinforce the parents' notion that they need to be more involved.

Imagine an owl/dove child who enjoys spending time with his one and only friend. The two companions are inseparable. The mother, a parrot, is dismayed that her child is not part of a larger social group. She is constantly telling her child that he should try to make additional friends. The more the child resists, the harder the mother pushes. The mother is inadvertently conveying to her child that his approach to friendship is wrong. By imposing her style on her child, the mother is sending a message to him that he is inadequate.

While the mother is trying to be helpful, she is actually being harmful. Her actions are driven by her own experience that happiness is derived by having many friends. She incorrectly assumes that if having many friends makes her happy, it will also make her son happy. Unfortunately for her offspring, the mother's actions have the inverse effect of decreasing her child's self-esteem.

At work, managers who have a "My Way" attitude are referred to as micromanagers. Like helicopter parents, they impose their methodology and, in turn, their style on others. Imagine an eagle who has been successful in his role for many years. He gets a new owl-like manager and, suddenly, it seems as if he cannot do anything right. His manager is critical of the processes he uses. The eagle's quality seems to be constantly under fire. He feels like his initiative and creativity are being stifled by a boss who criticizes everything he does.

Over time, the manager starts taking over some of the eagle's responsibilities. This leaves the eagle feeling disempowered and the owl overwhelmed. The manager's inability to realize that there is more than one way to drive success has a detrimental impact on both the employee and the manager.

This urge to control the way things are done is ultimately based in fear. We may have a fear of failure, which is common to eagles, or a fear of making mistakes, which is typical of owls. We may fear looking bad, which is characteristic of parrots, or fear not being accepted by others, which often defines doves.

The next time you find you are imposing your way on others, ask yourself, "What do I fear?" Then consider the possibility that the negative outcome of using the other individual's methodology may not be as real or significant as you believe it to be. Entertain the possibility that your need for control may actually create a worse outcome.

Remember, someone with a style unlike your own may approach a situation differently from you, but their way may be equally valid and, maybe, even better.

- ASK PROBING QUESTIONS to gain a deeper understanding of different perspectives.

- LISTEN TO AND EMPATHIZE with the needs of others.

- RECOGNIZE THAT LEARNING AND GROWTH OCCUR when we are open to alternative ways of doing things.

- SEEK EXCELLENCE NOT PERFECTION and allow for the possibility of mistakes.

- RELEASE BLACK-AND-WHITE THINKING and consider the gray areas where alternative options live.

The Chameleon

Fall

The Chameleon

Spontaneity Day

A sweet, gentle mist hovered in the air as the autumn leaves began to turn. The parrots loved this time of year. The trees began to add touches of splendor to the forest, complementing the parrots' multihued contributions. The harvest moon, a stirring sight, was set to rise just after sunset. Tonight the moon is going to be bigger and brighter than usual, emitting an orange glow that will favorably highlight the forest's complete palette of fall colors.

The parrots were looking forward with great anticipation to an event that always took place on this day of the year. But not Carl. He was hoping for rain or, at the very least, a cloudy evening. Every year the weather had been perfect for this occasion, as if the parrots' optimism willed it to be so. "It never rains on a parrot," Ivory and her friends liked to say.

Tonight was the night that many migratory birds, including the geese and ducks, began their long journey to a warmer climate. Everyone in the forest supported the "migrators" by gathering together and cheering them on.

A brief afternoon shower gave Carl hope, but, predictably, the sky cleared up. The event would go on as planned. The forest dwellers gathered in the Great Field to get a clear view of the sky.

Everyone was there, including eagles, parrots, doves, and owls. The squirrels made an appearance, too, but concentrated mostly on the food.

As the sun began its descent, the parrots were the first to arrive at the field. They were excited to see their friends and wanted to spend as much time socializing with them as possible. Meanwhile, Carl braced for another evening of pointless small talk. To him, there was nothing worse than spending hours engaged in superficial conversation. He preferred having long, meaningful discussions, but this was not the place for that. Small talk was the agenda for the night.

As the first migrators took wing across the golden sky, the parrots' cheers could be heard across the land. The soaring geese honked in appreciation.

When Carl arrived at the Great Field, Simon was the first one to greet him. The owl was happy to see a familiar face and to have someone to talk with. After they chatted a few minutes, Dee joined the pair. The eagle asked them both what they had been up to lately, shared what she had been working on, and took off. The owl and the dove continued talking until Ivory popped into their conversation.

The parrot shared story after story, effortlessly flowing from one topic to the next. It was a marvel to behold. Ivory was a storytelling tour de force!

Loud cheers erupted from the crowd as another V-shaped gaggle crossed the path of the moon. Every time a bird crossed the moon, the onlookers shouted "Moooooon!" and then took a sip of their drink. Nobody knew at what point this ritual began, but most feel certain it was started by a parrot.

Carl, Simon, and Ivory continued their conversation until Ivory had them both laughing hysterically. She then spied an old friend, promised to catch up with them later, and was gone.

Carl and Simon stood there dumbfounded. "Wow," the dove said. "That was impressive."

"You are telling me," Carl replied. "She seems to have an infinite number of stories, and they all sound funny or unprecedented."

Simon smiled, "No matter what topic comes up, Ivory always has stories, and they are usually quite entertaining."

"I wish I could do that," Carl admitted.

"Yeah, me too," Simon replied.

"I really dread these events. I never know what to say," the owl continued.

"I know what you mean."

Their conversation was briefly interrupted by loud cheers, then an even louder chorus of, "Moooooon!" The two friends each took a sip of their drinks.

"That does it," Carl resolved. "I am going to be more like a parrot. Look at them. They never worry about anything. Everything is either working out as planned or on the way to working out. They live carefree lives and don't stress the small stuff. From now on, it's all parrot all the time for me."

"Are you sure about that?" Simon questioned. "Parrots are quite impulsive. Are you ready for that?"

"How about this?" asked Carl. "I will start by being spontaneous one day a week. That will ease me into the change. Starting tomorrow, Sunday will officially be known as Spontaneity Day."

"That's great!" Simon replied, as he pondered the irony of planning for spontaneity.

The next day the sun rose bright and hot over Home. Carl woke up early, ate a light breakfast, and prepared for his first adventure. He placed his lunch into a satchel while at the same time acknowledging that his meal could have been part of his unscripted day, but ... there was no need to be reckless. Carl was ready to launch himself into the blue unknown.

For the first time in his life, Carl was winging it. He did not know where he was going. Without a specific destination in mind, he wondered how he would know when to stop. "I'll figure it out on the way," he thought. From the beginning he flew like a bird on a mission.

As he rushed passed a family of doves, he waved a quick hello. He zipped by some parrot friends who were lost in conversation, but he kept going. He crossed the southern tip of the Great Lake and continued on.

"I get it," he realized. "I am in the moment. Of course, now that I am thinking about the moment, am I really still in it or just thinking about it?"

He pondered that thought until he realized not only had he lost track of time, he had also lost track of his whereabouts. Had he turned north at the lake or headed south? Was his course east toward Crystal Cave or west toward the Forbidden Swamp?

That's when panic began to settle in. "What is wrong with me?" Carl thought. "How does anyone live like this? I am an owl, not a parrot. I have no idea what I am doing."

In an attempt to gain his bearings, Carl stopped flying. He

looked around but nothing seemed familiar. A group of squirrels carrying an inordinate amount of nuts rushed by. "Look at that," he thought. "Even the squirrels are planning ahead."

After a long, steady exhale, he tried to convince himself that everything was okay. "This is really no big deal. Someone will come along and find me before it gets dark, and if not, I will be able to figure this out on my own."

He reflected on the conversation he had had with Simon, the one that had initiated Spontaneity Day, and that's when he remembered. "Oh, no! I told Simon I would spend time with him today. I never miss the commitments I make to others. This is a disaster!"

Carl decided to reverse his course and see if he could find his way back to familiar territory. He crossed a recognizable stream and looked around. He noticed a few rotted branches, which triggered another realization. "I cannot believe this! Today I planned to remove the dead branches above the entrance to my hollow. There is no way that is going to happen now!"

He couldn't believe he had gotten himself into this confusing mess. Suddenly he strained to pinpoint a small voice he heard ahead of him. He stopped and looked around, but saw nothing. He was about to continue onward when he heard it again. "Carl," the voice called. "Over here."

If it weren't for Carl's keen owl hearing, the voice would have gone unnoticed. Because of the anxious and heightened state he was in, Carl heard every sound as if it were bouncing off of a canyon wall and echoing back to him. "Carl, this way," the voice instructed.

That's when his sharp eyesight kicked in. Just ahead of him — sitting on a small, gray boulder — sat Xenia and her young friend Xander. The chameleons had shifted their color to neon yellow so they could be seen. Carl swooped from his branch and landed with a *thud* beside them.

"What's wrong?" Xenia asked. "You look distraught."

After releasing an expressive sigh, Carl explained in detailed glory how he was seeking to add a measure of spontaneity to his life so he could be more like the parrots. He described how the experiment had caused him to get lost and how he had failed to meet commitments to himself and others. After he had finished explaining his predicament, he asked, "Xenia, can you point me in the right direction?"

"I'd be happy to," she grinned. "Pointing others in the right direction is my specialty."

Carl relaxed a bit as Xenia looked deeply into his bright owl eyes and said, "It looks as if you were being spontaneous today."

"I was trying to experience some parrot energy," the owl answered. "I thought that if I practiced the parrots' ways, I could master them and learn to let go of my need to control, well, pretty much everything."

Xenia smiled and said, "Carl, you can get comfortable with what's hard for you to do, but that doesn't mean you have to try to turn your weaknesses into strengths."

"But sometimes I feel as if my need to plan everything hurts me," Carl said.

"So work on being a little more spontaneous," Xenia suggested. "Let go of some control when it benefits you to do so. But don't put so much energy into mastering that new skill because it's not who you are. As long as you can be spontaneous when you need to, you'll be fine."

Carl understood what she meant. He had not felt like himself all day and could not imagine acting like this on a daily basis. He also knew that it would take a tremendous amount of work to change the controlling part of him. No matter how hard he tried, he would never be a parrot. He acknowledged there would be times when he could ease up on his need for control, and he vowed to work on that.

"And so you are headed in the right direction," Xenia concluded. The chameleon and her young apprentice spun around to continue on their way.

"Wait a second!" Carl called to them. "I still do not know how to get home."

"You're already there," Xenia grinned. She looked to Xander to point Carl in the right direction. The young chameleon proudly said, "Just ahead you will find a stream. Follow it until you see the Council Tree. I assume you know where to go from there."

The group heard a chorus of "Moooooon!" in the distance. The parrots were continuing to cheer on the migrators. As the chameleons disappeared into the landscape, the owl found his way home. And he laughed a bit at himself as he wondered if it wasn't too late to get productive and trim the branches on his tree.

Chameleon Wisdom

Weakness fixing is damage control, but it is not development. And damage control can prevent failure, but it will never elevate you to excellence.
—MARCUS BUCKINGHAM AND
DONALD O. CLIFTON

We can spend three things in life: money, time, and energy. When we invest our money, we seek to maximize our return. When we spend our time and energy working on personal growth, shouldn't we expect the same? Developing our strengths provides the best return on that investment.

Why do we expend so much time and energy trying to fix weaknesses that will have the least impact on our success? Perhaps it is because somewhere along the line it became politically correct to reframe weaknesses as challenges that need to be fixed or overcome. This idea prompts people to place their developmental efforts into turning liabilities into assets — a bad investment. It is more effective, instead, to focus on building our strengths.

This does not mean that we should completely ignore our weaknesses. In fact, we should expend some energy into developing our weaknesses so they do not hinder our future success. If something inhibits our ability to do our job or creates conflict with others, we should fix it. Acknowledge your weaknesses, but do not obsess over perfecting them.

In *Spontaneity Day,* Carl sought to let go of all controls and fly wherever the winds took him. He quickly discovered that his focus on his weaknesses inhibited his effectiveness. Whatever we focus on expands, so focusing on his weakness increased a feeling of incompetence. If Carl had concentrated on developing his strengths, he would have increased his self-esteem because confidence is grounded in our natural gifts. With Xenia's assistance, Carl realized he does not have to master being spontaneous. Instead, he has to get comfortable with being so when necessary.

Consider a dove in an office setting. He is reserved and does not like to speak in front of a group of people. During a meeting, a decision has to be made that would significantly affect his role. If he can endure the discomfort of sharing his concerns with the group, his needs will be met. But if he cannot, the team could make a decision that would make his job more difficult. The dove does not need to work on becoming a highly assertive person who lives his entire life candidly expressing his concerns openly to everyone he meets. However, it would serve him well to get comfortable enough with speaking up in meetings when it is critical to his job to do so.

Putting energy into developing our natural gifts empowers us because we are targeting behaviors that feed us. In turn, we reach higher levels of performance and accomplishment.

Greatness is not based on the absence of weakness, but rather, on living from one's strengths. Invest your time and energy in that which produces the greatest return on investment.

- ACCEPT THAT EVERYONE HAS WEAKNESSES. We are human.

- DEVELOP SKILLS based on your existing style rather than trying to develop a new style.

- LOOK FOR WAYS TO IMPROVE your weaker areas, but don't obsess on them.

- FIND OTHERS who have strengths in your weaker areas and either delegate to them or ask for their assistance.

- FOCUS ON YOUR TALENTS, not your faults.

- BE FLEXIBLE ENOUGH to display other styles when needed, but don't try to change who you are.

Squirrel!

"Ivory, focus!" Dee commanded with eagle directness. "The committee meeting is almost over. Can you please pay attention for a few more minutes so we can get out of here?"

"Sorry 'bout that," Ivory laughed. She pointed her multicolored wing toward the ground and explained, "Those two squirrels are cracking me up."

Carl rolled his large eyes in aggravation.

"That big, gray squirrel just pulled a nut out of the ground, the same nut that the small, brown squirrel just buried. Then the brown one ran back and discovered an empty hole where his nut used be."

Dee just shook her head.

Ivory continued. "The brown one looked pretty angry. He spiraled up that tree until he reached the big branch over there. He then he made a leap to another branch located above the gray squirrel. The gray one didn't like that one bit, so she just puffed out her belly. Now they're arguing."

"So they're arguing," Dee stated. "Let's finish our meeting so we can leave. I have other things to do."

"I feel bad for the little guy," Simon said compassionately. "I'm sure he worked hard to find that nut, and then it was taken away from him in an instant. That's not nice."

"It has nothing to do with being nice," Carl declared. "Your statement offends my owl sensibility. The gray squirrel clearly violated the Squirrel Code of Conduct, which states that one squirrel cannot remove a nut buried by another, even if the original squirrel forgot where he or she had buried it."

"How do you know the Squirrel Code?" Ivory asked.

"Doesn't everybody know all of the rules of the forest?" the owl replied.

"I guess not," Ivory shrugged. "Any way, I think of rules as suggested guidelines."

Carl's jaw dropped.

Dee interjected, "At least the brown squirrel is standing up for himself. That's important. You can't let others walk all over you, or they'll just keep doing it."

"I think he should just let it go," Simon said. "There are a lot more nuts out there."

"Let it go! You would just let it go? That's madness!" Dee declared.

"I don't feel that one nut is worth arguing over," Simon responded.

Even though Ivory originally laughed at the mayhem, she was becoming increasingly uncomfortable with how the squirrels were treating each other. "As I watch the brown squirrel trying to get his nut back, I feel as though the gray squirrel took advantage of him, and that's not fair. I'm going down there to talk with that nut thief! What she did was wrong, and I'm going to tell her."

"Nooooooo!" Carl and Dee shouted simultaneously.

"They'll stop arguing in a minute, and they'll forget about the whole thing before our meeting is even finished," the eagle said.

"I can't imagine that the brown squirrel will just let this go," Simon worried. "It would take a long time for me to forget something like this."

"That makes no sense," Carl announced. "First you said the brown squirrel should not stand up for himself. Now you are saying he will likely hold on to his anger for quite a while. Those two things are contradictory."

"You got that right!" Dee proclaimed. "Simon has it all backwards. You should stand up for yourself, and then you should let it go."

Ivory was puzzled by what she was hearing. "This isn't about deciding whether or not to fight or how long you will hold a grudge. This is about social justice. When someone has been wronged, the right thing to do is insert yourself into the situation and stand up for them."

"But you don't even know this squirrel. That makes no sense," Carl protested. "It is better to look at the facts and determine who is right. *Then* act accordingly based on the data. According to my observations, the gray squirrel violated the Squirrel Code. Therefore, the brown squirrel should enforce the established rules."

"Let's all take a deep breath," Simon requested.

"I agree," Ivory said. "You know what real madness is? We are arguing about arguing!"

"I think it's good that we have different perspectives," Simon said. "None of them are right and none of them are wrong. They are just different because we are different."

"I see what you're saying," Dee confirmed.

The two squirrels were winding down their disagreement when Simon concluded. "I remember Xenia once telling me that we see the world through our own eyes, and what we see creates our reality."

Ivory asked, "So we can all see the same situation and each respond differently?"

"I believe that is right," Carl stated. "We see the world and react to it based upon who we are."

"I've always expected everyone else to see things how I see them," Dee acknowledged. "Maybe that's why you guys annoy me so much," she said with a grin.

Everyone laughed.

"That makes sense. I think you each have a valid viewpoint about the squirrels," the eagle announced with smile. "But we have a meeting to get back to, if that's okay with you."

As the meeting resumed, Dee noticed Ivory watching several bees pushing each other out of the way in order to claim a bright yellow flower as their own.

"Ivory, focus!" Dee directed.

Chameleon Wisdom

We don't see things as they are,
we see them as we are.
—ANAIS NIN

We view the world through many lenses, such as culture, beliefs, experiences, and personality. They all impact how we perceive what happens around us. Just as a goldfish does not realize its view is distorted by the curve of the fishbowl's glass, we do not realize we are looking through our own lenses, which both create and distort our reality.

Our style shapes our perception of ourselves, others, and the world. It gives meaning to every conversation and event. The lens of our personality guides how we interpret what happens, why it happens, and how we think and feel about what has happened. Something that upsets one person can be no big deal to another. What thrills one individual can terrify someone else.

If we look through the eyes of a parrot, going on an unplanned adventure is exciting. That same experience may produce anxiety in an owl.

Without realizing it, we assume others see the world as we do, and we are surprised when they respond to circumstances differently. In *Squirrel!*, each bird was puzzled by how the others interpreted what they were watching.

What was offensive to one bird was a non-issue to another. Because the birds interpreted the situation through their own eyes, they did not understand each other's reactions.

We often misinterpret people's behavior because we use our own lens to understand their desires, expectations, motivators, and fears. Since we believe that we see the world as it is, unfiltered by own interpretation, we tend to overestimate the degree to which people will be aligned with our perspectives. Therefore, we expect the people in our lives to like what we like, want what we want, and react how we react.

Imagine a parrot eager to purchase a new car. He is excited to test drive a few vehicles and figures he can make a decision by the end of the day. His owl wife sees the situation differently. She would like him to conduct significant research before visiting various dealers. The parrot does not feel that level of preparation is necessary. The couple ends up arguing, not about which car to purchase, but rather how to make the decision. They see the situation differently and impose their views on each other.

Sometimes our lenses act like magnifying glasses that amplify the differences between ourselves and others. Blowing these differences out of proportion leads to personality clashes. People do things *for* themselves, not *against* us, so when others act in ways that push our buttons, we need to consider what needs they are attempting to satisfy. In most cases, their needs are *not* based on pushing our buttons.

With a little empathy, we can see the world through the eyes of others and increase our understanding and acceptance of them.

- RECOGNIZE THAT YOU HAVE A LENS through which you see the world, and that others have a different but equally valid lens.

- ASK YOURSELF, "What is the other person's motivation and desired outcome?"

- EMBRACE OTHER POINTS OF VIEW and ways of doing things.

- LET GO OF EXPECTATIONS, and be open to the needs of others.

- ASSUME OTHERS HAVE POSITIVE INTENTIONS to meet their own needs, not invalidate yours.

The Chameleon

Observation Week

The autumn-tinted leaves blended effortlessly with the morning light. Fall was shining in all its glory, which meant that humans were on their way. With the heat of the summer behind them, people would soon invade the forest armed with binoculars, cameras, and backpacks.

Soon they would scatter throughout Home, though they usually congregated near the Great Lake and its adjoining pasture. The people came to observe the birds, but for the birds, it was an opportunity to observe the people. The birds liked to watch the human behavior up close and listen in on their conversations. Observation Week, as it had come to be known, allowed the birds to learn more about these elusive and unusual creatures.

On the first morning of Observation Week, the birds watched the foreign visitors spraying all sorts of substances on their bodies. The humans seemed to be inexplicably afraid of the sun and of bugs. Ironically, the sprays made them smell bad, which made them easier to locate and track.

The birds worked in pairs. Each couple contained two different types of birds. This allowed for diverse interpretations of human interaction.

On one team, Carl and Ivory joined forces for the day. Carl was pleased to be with such a vibrant companion. He thought that her vibrant colors would attract the attention of the humans and, as a result, afford the two birds greater opportunities to observe the people in action. Ivory was happy because she didn't have to take any notes. She knew that Carl would play that role.

Shortly after sunrise, the owl and parrot partners spotted their first human. Carl reviewed the three rules of Observation Week: "Be heard, but only occasionally. Be seen, but not too often. Be watched, but not for long. Most of all, do not do anything too unusual."

Their first quarry included one man and one woman. The owl and parrot maintained their distance. They didn't want to be discovered too soon. "We want them to get excited when they spot us. So let's not make it too easy," Ivory suggested.

As their prey approached, the birds could see that the man was carrying a small human on his back. The people spoke in hushed tones, but the baby squealed periodically, to the man's dismay. Carl's keen hearing picked up everything.

"What are they saying?" Ivory asked.

"The woman just told the man that she appreciates how well he organized their trip to the forest. I like him," Carl joked.

"Sure, you like him because he's an owl in human clothing!" Ivory smiled.

"Perhaps," Carl acknowledged. "In any case, the man is saying that he appreciates how she has entertained the child for the entire trip, singing songs and playing games."

"I like her," Ivory laughed.

"Of course you do. She is a parrot in human clothing," the owl concluded.

"And what beautiful clothing it is."

"Let me focus," Carl requested, as he tried to tune in again to their conversation.

The people continued walking through the woods, and Carl noticed how methodical the man was in his search for birds. When he periodically stopped to write in his journal, the woman entertained the child on his back.

Carl and Ivory did a good job of staying out of sight. They hid behind patches of leaves and large tree trunks. Occasionally, they would fly away and return, making certain to keep track of the visitors. The first time the woman spotted Ivory, she pointed loudly in the parrot's direction. This caused the child to squeal with excitement and the man to scold both of them.

The two birds occasionally allowed themselves to be seen, which kept the people interested. This gave Carl and Ivory a lot of time to watch the couple.

As the man took notes and photographs, Carl continued to be impressed by his attention to detail.

Ivory kept pointing out how funny the woman was. "Look at those faces she makes!" announced the parrot. "She's hilarious!" Her funny faces were making the child laugh in loud squeals of joy. This seemed to bother the man, but he did not say anything to her because he was too busy documenting their experience.

"Shhhhhh. They will see us," Carl cautioned. "And once they have seen enough of us, they will move on to find different birds."

After more than an hour of playing hide-and-seek with the

humans, Ivory noticed that the male was becoming increasingly frustrated. As he kept trying to hush the woman, she kept trying to exclaim what a wonderful day she was having. She tried to encourage the man to relax and enjoy the surrounding nature, but he was too busy cataloging his experience.

Before long, the couple's banter turned into heated conflict. He was annoyed with her. She was annoyed with him. And they both seemed to be annoyed with the child.

"This is turning out to be a productive Observation Day," Carl noted. "But I must admit, I do not understand how these two humans joined together in the first place."

"I hear ya!" Ivory agreed. "They seem wholly incompatible."

"She must drive him crazy!" the owl exclaimed.

"I'll bet she has to do things exactly how he wants them done or he gets annoyed," the parrot hypothesized. "And he probably likes things done the same way every time."

"What is so bad about that?" Carl wondered. "That is how things get done properly."

Ivory huffed, "That's how things get done boringly."

Just then, a small voice emerged from the branch beside them. The owl and parrot were startled to discover Xenia and her newest student.

"Hey, Xenia and Xander," Ivory said. "Check it out — arguing humans!"

"Oh, is that what is happening here?" the wise chameleon grinned. "I thought I saw arguing birds."

"It must be contagious. We caught it from the humans," Ivory laughed.

Xenia smiled softly and turned her gaze to the owl. "Carl, you look puzzled."

"I am fascinated by these humans. I do not understand how this couple chose to pair."

"What do you mean?" the chameleon inquired.

"They are opposites, just like Ivory and me," the owl noted. "I cannot imagine why they did not select someone more like themselves to partner with. Wouldn't that help them get along better?"

"That's not always the case with humans," Xenia explained. "They are often attracted to their opposite. In fact, I regularly see parrot people paired with owl people."

"That makes no sense," Ivory declared.

"I also see human eagles matched with human doves," the chameleon added.

"That makes even less sense!" the parrot concluded. "How does that work?"

"Think about it like this," Xenia began. "When humans first meet, they appreciate gifts that are different from their own. In fact, it's those very differences that often create the initial attraction."

"I can see that," Ivory said. "I suppose that's why Carl and I are friends. I appreciate that he likes to do things that I find challenging ... like track all the stuff we are supposed to record during Observation Week."

"I can see how two very different people can complement each other," acknowledged Carl. "Truth be told, I do appreciate how Ivory adds serendipity to my world. Her spontaneity impresses me."

"If you listen carefully," suggested the older chameleon, "you can hear humans say things like, 'He completes me' or 'She's my other half.'"

"But if they are so perfect for each other, why were these two humans arguing?" Ivory asked as she pointed to the couple down below.

"Did they get along better when they first arrived?" Xenia probed, as if she already knew the answer.

"Correct," Carl answered.

"As the day has worn on, they have grown tired and frustrated," Xenia said. "Their differences are causing conflict. In a relationship, when times are easy and simple, such as when two people first meet, opposites attract."

"Or like when this couple's day first began," added Carl.

"Precisely," Xenia confirmed. "But during more complicated or stressful times, opposites repel."

"That must be inconvenient!" Ivory declared.

"Oh, it is," the chameleon replied. "When everything is going smoothly, they appreciate their differences. But when they need each other most, their differences can create friction."

"Um, we have a bit of a problem," Xander interrupted.

The young chameleon pointed towards to the humans below, "They're, uh, watching us."

"Well that must be quite an intriguing sight — an owl, a parrot, and two chameleons talking with each other on a branch," Xenia chuckled.

"It's time for us to go," Xenia stated. "You two enjoy the rest of your day. And try not to get caught chatting with anyone else. I believe that falls under the category of 'not doing anything that is too unusual.'"

"Now what do we do?" Ivory asked Xenia. But she asked too late. The chameleons had vanished. The humans below were still looking up toward Ivory and Carl.

Just then, the bushes behind the humans started to shake. The man grabbed the woman's hand, and they quietly fled the area. Ivory and Carl looked down toward the bushes to see what had scared the humans away.

Xenia and Xander jumped out of the bushes and landed on the ground. Xenia looked up toward the birds and gave them a thumbs-up and a smile. "I recommend you move on to another tree before they come back."

Carl and Ivory agreed. They flew away to find another human couple to watch on this year's first day of Observation Week.

Chameleon Wisdom

We are sun and moon, dear friend; we are sea and land. It is not our purpose to become each other; it is to recognize each other, to learn to see the other and honor him for what he is: each the other's opposite and complement.
—HERMANN HESSE

Do birds of a feather flock together, or do opposites really attract? The answer depends on what we mean by "opposites." If we are referring to physical attractiveness, values, class, religion, race, and intelligence, more often than not, like attracts like. But when we are talking about personality styles or traits, quite often opposites attract.

In terms of the bird styles, the first pair of opposites is the eagles and doves. Eagles tend to be fast-paced, assertive, and independent risk-takers. Meanwhile, doves are deliberate, reserved, and group-oriented. They like to plan before taking risks. The second pair of opposites is the parrots and owls. Parrots are outgoing, social, big-picture oriented, and intuitive. Owls are reserved, private, detail-oriented, and logical.

It is important to note that any combination of styles can enjoy a joyful and lasting relationship. Opposites are not necessarily happier; they just tend to be drawn to each other.

So why is it common to hear people describe a partner as "my other half" or say that a spouse "completes me"?

Perhaps, if we tweak our language and think of opposites as complements, it would make more sense. Someone who complements our style provides us with the opportunity to experience a type of energy that we typically would not seek. Eagles, for example, might add intensity to a relationship, and parrots might add adventure. Doves might introduce compassion, and owls might offer precision. Our complement expands our horizons, enables us to see things differently, and transports us from familiar territory to unchartered waters.

A complementary partner may have qualities that we admire or wish we had. They help us learn, grow, and heal as their natural strengths subconsciously force us to deal with our deficiencies. An outgoing parrot, for example, can help an introverted owl in social situations. In return, the owl can help teach an impulsive parrot to stay organized so that life's responsibilities do not spiral out of control. A daring eagle might encourage a habitual and consistent dove to attempt new and varied activities. Meanwhile, a compassionate dove can teach a forthright eagle how to deal with situations that require a sensitive touch.

While connecting with our complement may have its perks, it can also have its challenges. When times are easy and comfortable, a partner with a complementary style can be endlessly fascinating, rich, and diverse. However, during stressful times, we are repelled by those who have a perspective different from our own. When times are tough, we do not have the time, energy, or patience to deal with someone who varies from our approach. When we are stressed, opposites don't just repel, they attack!

Perhaps that is why people of different styles often push our buttons in the workplace. At work there is constant pressure to perform. We are regularly faced with competing deadlines and ongoing changes in technology, procedures, and regulations. High-volume periods or busy seasons inevitably increase tension. In the office, we actually anticipate that there will be stress, which causes us to seek out people who think and act like we do. We want to get things done and wish people would see things the way we do.

Complementary styles can also repel each other at home. When couples have to deal with challenging situations or make significant decisions, they can enter into conflict and push each other away. Imagine an owl and a parrot trying to buy a new home. The owl wants to think through all of the pluses and minuses, while the parrot intuitively feels "this is the one!"

Imagine an eagle and a dove trying to coordinate their wedding. The eagle wants an unconventional event that reflects who they are as a couple, while the dove wants to satisfy the needs of everyone in attendance and wishes to adhere to a host of family and wedding traditions.

In *Observation Week*, Ivory and Carl watched an owl and parrot couple. In the early part of the day, when the pair was relaxed and eager to see the birds of the forest, their styles complemented each other. However, as the day wore on, the humans grew tired and frustrated. As their stress increased, their style differences created conflict.

While complementary styles often attract each other, individuals of the same style can be attracted as well. These like-minded individuals may validate each other's perspectives, and, therefore, have fewer disagreements. On the other hand, their similarities can get heated up and create friction. Two eagles may appreciate each other's candor, but each may vie to take the lead and dominate the other. Two parrots may appreciate each other's sense of adventure, but they may also compete for airtime during conversations. Two doves may value each other's support and compassion, but they might end up patiently waiting for the other one to take action when decisions need to made. Two owls might respect the other's attention to quality, but they may have competing ways of getting things done.

In the end, successful relationships depend less on what the differences are and more on how the differences are handled. The styles of two partners will not predict the couple's level of happiness or how long their relationship will last, but if the partners value their differences, they can create a well-rounded pair capable of achieving things that neither one could accomplish alone.

- EMBRACE DIFFERENCES as a way of having new experiences.

- MEET YOUR PARTNER HALFWAY by being willing to compromise.

- CAPITALIZE ON THE SKILLS that your partner has that you find difficult.

- DON'T JUDGE DIFFERENCES AS BAD, but rather, appreciate the benefits of what they offer.

Flight of the Groundhog

After a long journey, Ivory and Simon had almost reached Xandadu's Peak. Since the mountain rose so high above Home that it nearly touched the clouds, they had been able to see their destination for hours. With each passing minute, the peak grew larger and more imposing.

Xanadu was named after the wise chameleon teacher widely considered to be the greatest storyteller and wisdom-giver ever to grace their land. To this day, it is said that Xanadu watches Home from the top of the mountain, waiting to appear at just the right moment to teach another important lesson.

The Xanadu Theater sits at the base of the mountain. It is used to enact plays that embody the many lessons taught by Xanadu and his chameleon followers.

On this day hundreds of birds have huddled together, waiting for the amphitheater gates to open. They flew in from all over Home to watch one of the most ambitious performances ever attempted: *Flight of the Groundhog.*

Ivory and Simon circled the clearing beside the mountain and flew over the large crowd below. As the parrot and dove landed at the back of the crowd, Simon turned to Ivory and commented, "I wish we could have arrived a little earlier. I guess we'll be pretty far from the stage."

"Well, what can you do?" Ivory replied. "Sometimes ya gotta' stop along the way if something catches your eye."

"It's okay. We'll sit wherever there's a seat," said Simon.

After a long wait, they made it through the entrance and then inched their way to the back of the seating area. As they moved through the crowd, Ivory exchanged greetings with what seemed to be half of the audience. The dove could not believe how many birds his parrot friend knew.

Ivory was especially excited about this play because she had had a role in creating the costumes. Even though she had never had a chance to watch a performance, she had been told it was hilarious and had crazy special effects. Simon was looking forward to it as well. He had heard that the play was very touching.

As the show was about to begin, darkness fell upon the amphitheater. The crowd grew quiet as thousands of fireflies surrounded the stage. Then, in one mighty pulse of electricity, the theater exploded with light. The audience erupted in applause. The illumination revealed a stage set that resembled a three-dimensional map of the entire forest.

In the center was the Great Lake represented by a pool of water contained by a low, stone wall. At the back, a peak, formed out of a hill of dirt and some baby trees. In the front, the beach, created from a generous amount of silky sand. To the left, the ominous Forbidden Swamp, fashioned from vines and muddy water. And to the right, the beautiful Crystal Cave, crafted from a variety of colorful crystals.

A small, gray dove dressed as a groundhog ambled onto the stage and stood between the sandy beach and the Great Lake. She looked at the sky and then glanced around the staged forest as if she were looking for something or someone. After she failed to find what she was seeking, she slumped down next to a tree, expressing profound sadness and solitude. Simon joined many others in the crowd who were voicing a sentimental, "Awwwww."

Ivory glanced at her dove friend as if to say, "You already feel bad for the groundhog? You don't know anything about her yet."

"She's upset," Simon said sadly.

As a bright yellow sign rose from the bottom of the stage, the fireflies increased the intensity of the lighting. The groundhog began to wander woefully around the forest. She was soon joined by a hilarious duo of eagles dressed as chipmunks. It was quite a sight. The chipmunks danced their way to the stage, wiggling their backsides as they performed what they called, "The Acorn Dance."

Ivory burst into hysterics.

Simon turned to gaze at the parrot.

"What? That's awesome! Just look at them," Ivory said.

"Yeah, it's funny," Simon replied blankly.

When the groundhog and the chipmunks began talking, the audience discovered that the young groundhog had been separated from her parents and was traveling the land, hoping to find them. Simon wiped a tear from his eye. "Oh, come on, Ivory. How are you not crying?" Simon asked.

"It's touching," the parrot conceded.

"But how are you not *feeling* anything?"

"I'm crying on the inside," Ivory responded.

Simon shook his head in disbelief.

The groundhog traveled throughout the land, meeting a collection of interesting characters, from owls dressed as bears to parrots dressed as chameleons. As the groundhog sought help to keep going, she received a gift of food here and a place to stay there.

Simon felt every act of compassion as if he were receiving it directly. As the play progressed, the groundhog gained strength. Soon the groundhog became the helper and not the one in need. She gradually transformed into a confident hero, providing support to whoever required assistance.

When the play reached the grand finale, the young groundhog slapped on a pair of wings and soared through the air. Ivory nearly exploded with laughter ... and she couldn't stop. Even after the groundhog landed, she was still laughing. "It keeps getting funnier!" she giggled. "What is wrong with you, Simon? Isn't this the funniest thing you have ever seen?"

"I do find it funny," Simon responded. "I'm laughing on the inside."

Ivory, who was already having a hard time containing her giggles, found Simon's words to be utterly hysterical. "Well, if you think it's so funny," she said, "you should tell your face. Because you don't look like you think it's funny."

Behind the parrot and dove sat two owls, one white and the other brown. Both owls were listening to Ivory and Simon's running commentary. The owls were puzzled by what they had been hearing. The white owl noted, "I find it fascinating that they cannot read each other's emotions."

"Indeed," the brown owl said. "Listening to them is more interesting than watching the play. They seem to completely misinterpret each other's feelings."

"Why do you think that is?" asked the white owl.

"They are making assumptions based upon their own reactions and then drawing faulty conclusions," explained the brown owl.

"Tell me more," the white owl requested.

"Well, the parrot thinks, 'If it is funny, I laugh. So if you do not laugh, you do not find it funny.'"

"I see," the white owl affirmed. "And to continue that logic, the dove thinks, 'If it is touching, I cry. So if you do not cry, you do not find it touching.'"

"Exactly." Their conversation was interrupted briefly by raucus laughter. When it died down, the brown owl added, "I see your point, but it is not unreasonable to make assumptions based upon the data that is available."

"Ah! But that is when we introduce error into the equation," said the white owl, who had paused to look up at the towering peak above them. "If I recall correctly, it was the great Xanadu who once said, 'Do not project your emotions onto someone else's reactions.'"

"He was truly wise," the brown owl declared.

When the play came to an end, everyone stood in appreciation. Ivory turned to Simon and asked, "So what do you think?"

"I loved it," Simon replied. "The story was so moving."

Ivory concurred. "I loved it too. It was so funny!"

As everyone was exiting the theater, the brown owl turned to the white owl and concluded, "For the record, this play was funny, but I'm not sure it was as funny as the parrot thinks it is."

"I concur. The play was touching," the white owl noted. "But not as touching as the dove feels it was."

Chameleon Wisdom

Real magic in relationships means an absence of judgment of others.
—WAYNE DYER

In our objective world, emotional reactions have clearly defined meaning. Laughing indicates something is funny. Crying indicates it is sad or touching. In *Flight of the Groundhog*, Ivory's laughter meant the play was funny. When Simon did not laugh, she *obviously* thought he did not find it humorous. At the same time, since Ivory didn't cry, Simon *clearly* construed that she did not find the play moving.

We interpret people's reactions based upon what we see. We also judge their reactions based upon what they would mean if we had that same reaction. We are the standard by which behaviors are defined and construed. We expect others to match our emotional intensity, and when they do not, we assume they do not feel that emotion as deeply as we do.

When eagles get aggravated, we see the strength of their conviction. If we do not match their intensity, eagles perceive that we are not as annoyed as they are. When parrots are excited and we do not match their level of enthusiasm, they assume we do not understand or appreciate how good something is. If doves become upset because someone has hurt their feelings, they presume we are insensitive if we are not as offended as they are. And if owls worry about something and we do not display the same level of concern, they suppose we must not be as committed to dealing with the issue as they are.

When someone else's emotional intensity does not match our own, we may assume that they are not aligned with our perspective. In the above examples, eagles expect a passionate display of emotion, while parrots expect enthusiasm. Doves expect empathy with their emotional needs, while owls expect us to join them in thoroughly assessing situations. If we do not meet the needs of others, they may not feel supported by us or believe that we care as much as they do.

Since all disappointment comes from expectations not being met, we set ourselves up for discontent when we expect the reactions of others to match our own level of intensity.

Consider a married couple consisting of an eagle and a dove, who are upset with each other. The eagle has a massive outburst. The dove remains silent but feels deeply hurt. Since the dove does not raise any concerns, the eagle assumes the dove is not bothered. Meanwhile the dove assumes the eagle is holding onto anger because she knows that if she had unleashed that much emotion, her anger would have lingered for quite a while. In reality, though, the eagle simply raised the issue and let it go.

It is very easy to project our interpretation of what a certain reaction means onto someone else's reaction. How we interpret other people's actions reveals more about who we are than who they are.

Consider a parrot who has a great idea while driving to work. He believes his idea will fix an issue that has plagued the organization for months. The parrot is brimming with excitement.

As soon as he arrives at work, he heads directly to his manager's office. His owl manager is engrossed in a project. She looks up from her desk with an expression that reads, *I am busy so make it quick.* The parrot does not waste any time sharing his idea. The owl listens intently as the animated parrot speaks enthusiastically and makes such optimistic claims as, *This will change everything!*

The owl manager takes a moment to consider the idea and then requests, "That could work, but there are a lot of questions that need to be answered before we move forward. Why don't you look into it and get back to me with what you discover."

The parrot leaves the office feeling utterly deflated. He was hoping for a level of reaction that matched his own. Instead, he received an assignment with a business-like acknowledgment that his idea was worth investigating. If the parrot had heard, instead, that his idea was an amazing one that could transform the company, he would have been energized beyond words. Since the owl did not convey what the parrot judged to be any measure of exuberance, he felt she must not have loved the idea. In fact, the parrot was not even sure that she liked it.

The parrot did something we all do all the time. He filtered his interpretation of another individual's response through the screen of his own personality style. It is hard for us to imagine that a reaction can mean something different when it is displayed by someone else, but it is important for us to consider the personality style of the source of the reaction.

The next time you feel concerned, hurt, or bothered by someone else's reaction, do not ask yourself, "What would I be feeling in order to elicit such a reaction?" Rather, ask yourself this: "Given the nature of this individual, regardless of his or her outward behavior, what is he or she likely feeling?" If you are uncertain, you can always ask.

- DON'T MAKE ASSUMPTIONS about how someone is feeling based on how you would be feeling if you had that same reaction. Always consider the source.

- CONSIDER PERSONALITY STYLE when making sense of others' behaviors.

- RECOGNIZE THAT EXPECTATIONS ARE THE SOURCE of disappointment.

- LET GO OF THE NEED FOR OTHERS to match your intensity of emotion. Someone might be feeling something deeply despite their non-reaction.

The Storm of All Storms

The wind howled throughout the day, and the late autumn leaves twisted wildly. As lightning flashed in the distance, booming thunder echoed throughout the land. Dead branches fell to the ground. Sharp *snaps* and dull *thuds* kept everyone's heads spinning.

Carl poked his head out of his tree hollow to assess the damage caused by a nearby crash when he heard the sound everyone dreaded. The Forest Alert System had been activated. A bird from the Westlands, the area west of Home, was the last bird in what had been a series of messengers. Her warning: The current storm was worsening, and more powerful winds were on their way.

As Carl watched the trees forcefully sway, often bending to the point of breaking, he wondered what else lay ahead of them on this ominous day. Through the relentless rain, he noticed something dark and large moving at a high speed … and it was coming his way. He stared at the brown blur until it came into focus. It was an eagle. No, wait. It was Dee, and she was battling strong winds as she struggled to navigate through the trees. Carl was accustomed to watching her surf the thermals high above the treetops, but these winds were impossible to ride.

When the eagle landed on a branch near Carl, the bough dipped under her weight. Skipping the usual pleasantries, Dee immediately dove into the crisis at hand. "From what I hear, the incoming storm is a monster. The Westlands are being pounded with rain. Floods are washing away the topsoil, and mudslides are ripping trees from their roots. Everyone is scrambling for cover. We need to prepare."

"Sounds like it's going to be a bad one," the owl replied.

"I just came from the Council Tree, and I have been appointed to coordinate the preparations. I selected you to be my assistant. Congratulations."

"Uh, thank you," the owl stuttered. "I am glad to help."

"Good. Let's begin. First, I need you to contact the parrots. They are responsible for communicating the strategy, once we determine what that will be. Second, talk to the other owls and have them draw up a plan. On second thought, scratch that. The owls will take too long. I'll create the plan."

Carl was a bit offended that Dee insulted his fellow owls, but he put that aside for now because there was much work to be done.

"Should I contact the doves?" Carl asked. "I can ask them to prepare to support anyone who gets displaced during the storm."

"No time for that. We'll worry about damage control later," the eagle said as she flapped her mighty wings and disappeared.

"Okay, then," Carl replied to the empty space where Dee had just stood. "I guess I will go talk to the parrots. Though I am not quite sure what I am supposed to tell them."

The wind was pushing and pulling Carl in every direction as he made his way to his colorful friends. On arriving, he could only tell them that it was their job to convey the storm strategy to everyone else, and that they should stand by. The parrots were eager to play their part.

As trees twirled beneath the dark gray sky, and violent winds tore leaves off branches and sent them swirling through the air. A wall of rain pelted Carl as he fought his way back to his tree. He felt responsible for keeping everyone safe, and uncomfortable at not understanding the plan.

Shortly after Carl returned to his tree, Dee arrived. Before she even touched down, the eagle began dictating orders. "Here's what we are going to do. First, we will move everyone further south, where the storm is not as severe. The base of the large falls, just north of the pine forest, will be our meeting place. When we get there, we'll take attendance and determine if we need to move further south. If we do, we will identify someone who has the energy and speed to fly ahead and identify trees with large leaves that can act as a canopy for the smaller birds. I don't know if we have enough food to weather this event, but we'll figure that out when …"

"Hold on. I have a question," Carl interrupted. He was feeling uneasy about Dee's strategy. "How do you know that the storm will not be as bad in the south? When we were hit with a big storm two years ago, the south received more rain than the north did, and they had terrible flash flooding and landslides. Have you received additional information about what is coming?"

"No," said Dee, "but in a crisis you sometimes have to make assumptions. My experience tells me that I am right. Besides, this is not a good time to doubt leadership. This is a time for action."

"Whoa. Wait a second," the owl requested. "I am not challenging your leadership. I just want to make sure we have thought this through. Is that your entire plan, or is it an overview?"

"That's all of it," Dee declared. "What more do you need? Head south and I'll see you there."

Carl was dumbfounded. Surely there had to be more. He stared at Dee in stunned silence.

Dee took Carl's lack of response as acceptance of the plan, so she continued. "I will be part of the advance team. I'll head south and establish a base. You make sure the parrots tell everyone where to go."

And she was off.

Carl shook his head in disbelief. With great effort he made his way back to the parrots. He tasked them with announcing the plan, such as it was.

As Carl made his way to the pine forest, he thought about the storm and their options. He visualized their destination, and he had an epiphany. "We are heading south to seek cover in the pine forest, but pine trees do not have leaves! Where does Dee think we are going to get protection from the wind and rain? This will not do. This will not do at all."

As he continued to fly, the owl watched the approaching black sky spread like a blanket across the forest. The rain had softened slightly. When he arrived at the meeting place, Dee seemed a bit smug that her plan was working. Carl approached the eagle and asked, "Now what?"

"The storm is still coming this way. We need to head further south."

Dee turned away from the owl and hopped up to a higher branch. She called for everyone's attention, and the group quickly grew silent. "We can't stay here. We need to keep moving. Ivory, you fly ahead and scout out a safe place for us to shelter from the storm."

"Got it," Ivory confirmed as she leapt into the shadowy sky.

"Now, follow me!" Dee shouted over the growing wind.

No, not again, Carl thought. *We need to think this through.*

Without another moment's hesitation, the owl summoned his courage and let loose a mighty shout. "Deeeeeeeeeeeeee!"

To the owl's surprise, the eagle heard him and wheeled quickly around to return. When Dee arrived, she snapped a quick, "What?"

Everyone froze.

"Dee, can I speak with you for a moment?"

The eagle stared intensely into Carl's eyes without saying a word. The owl quickly began, "Your plan is not complete. Think like an owl for a moment. We need more details that include step-by-step instructions for each of us to follow. We need to carefully consider our strategy and determine precisely where we are going. I'd also recommend that we assign group leaders who will be responsible for …"

"Carl, you think like an owl, but I'm an eagle, and that's not what I do. I was chosen to lead everyone through the storm, and so we're going to do it my way."

"But I just want to discuss …"

Lightning cracked nearby, followed by an immediate *boom*. The raindrops grew bigger and began to hit harder. The storm was worsening.

"I already gave you clear instructions. Head south and find cover. As for assigning roles, here's one for you. Get behind the group and bring up the rear."

Before Carl could utter another word, Dee commanded, "We can talk about this when we get further south. I know what I'm doing." Once again Dee announced, "Let's go!" With a powerful pump of her wings, she launched herself into the threatening darkness.

The owl sheltered his eyes with his wing so he could better see through the pummeling rain, but all he could make out was the eagle's fuzzy outline traveling away from him. As he watched all of the other birds get airborne, he remained on a branch thinking about what to do next. Watching his bird friends dodge leaves and falling branches prompted his decision to talk with Dee.

Carl was accustomed to making sharp, quick turns in the forest. Dee was not. Though it would take all his skill to navigate the deep woods and catch up with the eagle, he had to try. As Carl pressed against the wind, he thought about what he would say to Dee when he reached her. He acknowledged how much he appreciated her ability to handle a crisis without panicking, and he reflected on how he valued her willingness to take charge and make tough choices. Logic told him that she was the right one for this job, but her strengths seemed to be working against her. The eagle's desire to be in control had closed her off to the ideas of others. Her decisiveness could potentially make her reckless.

The wind whistled through the trees as bursts of lightning illuminated the forest. Dee's large wings slowed her down, which gave Carl the opportunity to catch up. As he watched the eagle repeatedly adjust her path based on ever-changing airstreams, he realized that he needed to shift his approach to her.

In a flash of insight, Carl recognized that he was treating Dee like an owl, not an eagle. He was trying to change how she acted when, in reality, the only thing he could truly change was how he dealt with her. Talking about plans and clarifying roles wasn't going to get him anywhere with Dee. Those were his strengths. He needed to adapt his message so it made sense to Dee, and encourage her to maximize her own abilities. This wasn't going to be easy, but so much was at stake.

When Carl approached Dee's right wing tip, she whipped her head around to see who was there. As thunder boomed around them, Carl tried to talk to Dee, but there was too much noise for her to hear him. The owl pointed to a nearby tree and signaled the eagle with his eyes to set down there. Dee could not imagine what Carl wanted, but she assumed that if he was motioning her to stop, it must be important. Dee gestured to everyone that they were going to take a quick break. Even though the group had not traveled far since their last stop, most of the birds were happy to rest their tired wings.

Carl landed first, and Dee slammed down beside him. The owl heard a sharp crack from the branch he settled on, but he disregarded it as the least of his problems. "Why did we stop?" Dee snapped.

The owl stood tall to address her as another eagle would. He confidently looked into her eyes and said, "Dee, I know you are on a mission to get us all to safety."

"That's right," she affirmed.

"You are driven to achieve success, and I appreciate that. But I'd like to share a concern that I think may prevent you from accomplishing your goal. Are you open to hearing it?"

"Yes, but make it fast. We've got to get moving."

So far, so good, Carl thought.

The owl continued, "Xenia once explained to me that I was overusing my strengths, which turned them into weaknesses. In my case, my desire for accuracy paralyzed me from making an important decision."

"Well, I don't have *that* problem," Dee observed proudly.

"Decisiveness is not your issue," Carl agreed. "But we both overuse our strengths, thus turning our greatest assets into our greatest liabilities. My perfectionism made me stuck. Your desire for action is making you closed and potentially careless."

Dee softened her tone. "So you're saying I am not listening to you and by not hearing what you have to say, I may be preventing our success?"

"Exactly!" Carl declared.

Dee spoke a little quieter and slower. "I am just trying to accomplish this goal as quickly as possible. I guess all the excitement about the storm has turned me into a super eagle." She paused for a second and then clarified, "And I don't mean that in a good way."

Carl's smile was followed by a brief silence. He was pleased that he had found a way to convey his concerns to Dee. The eagle summarized, "So to recap, I should not overuse my strengths. Got it. I'd love to talk more about this, but that lightning is getting close, and we've gotta go."

"If I may be so bold," Carl interjected before Dee could tell the group it was time to depart. "You just did it again. We need to act decisively, but before we do, can we take a couple of minutes to consider a few elements of the plan before we implement it?"

The eagle took a deep breath to slow herself down. "This is going to take some practice. Okay. What are your concerns?"

It didn't take long for the pair to assess the plan. After two minutes, they set off toward a nearby cave that Carl once visited.

They waited out the tempest from within the safety of the cave. When the clouds and the danger had passed, the eagle and owl were elated that the "Storm of All Storms," as it had come to be known, did not take anyone's life, even though it had caused a lot of damage. Dee and Carl were treated as heroes who acted quickly and thoughtfully to save the day.

As Dee and Carl returned north, they could see the tremendous destruction that had been caused by the storm. What had once beautified the forest as towering trees lay smashed on the ground in pieces. Branches were strewn across the forest floor, and rivers of mud flowed throughout the land. As the two friends passed over the Great Lake, Dee glanced down and saw their reflections on the water. She thought about everything that had happened and said, "That was pretty exciting, huh?"

Carl chuckled. "I think we define 'exciting' a bit differently. For owls, solving a challenging puzzle is exciting. Dealing with an unpredictable storm bearing down on us and feeling like we do not have a plan is anxiety provoking!"

"You like challenging puzzles? It sounds like figuring out how to handle me as I overused my strengths was a challenging puzzle," Dee acknowledged.

"I guess it was," Carl replied.

"And you solved it. You slowed down an overzealous eagle and got her to listen."

Carl nodded slowly.

"You can thank me later for making your life exciting," Dee smiled.

"But ... you ... oh, forget it," Carl grinned sarcastically. "Thanks."

Chameleon Wisdom

Everyone thinks of changing the world,
but no one thinks of changing himself.
—LEO TOLSTOY

Think about a personal habit you would like to change. If one does not come immediately to mind, reflect on a previous New Year's resolution. Most people put effort into changing a habit for a few days or maybe even a week or two … only to revert back to the previous behavior afterward.

Now identify someone else — a spouse, child, or coworker — who has a habit that you would like to change. If you have put forth any effort to encourage them to alter that habit, you have discovered how difficult it is to change someone else. One of life's hardest lessons to learn is this: It is challenging enough to change ourselves, but it is practically impossible to change someone else.

You cannot change your child's annoying taste in music. You cannot change your spouse's neatness or lack thereof. And most of all, you cannot change someone else's personality style. We can lecture them, scold them, and highlight their shortcomings, but those tactics only lead to *our* disappointment and *their* resentment.

While we cannot push others into a different personality style, we can pull them in the direction of their own. Rather than trying to change other people, we can draw the best out of them by helping them capitalize on their natural strengths while, at the same time, not overusing their innate gifts.

In *The Storm of All Storms,* Carl tried to change Dee's behavior by attempting to get her to act more like an owl. He failed miserably until he realized he needed to honor Dee's style and help her to become the best eagle she could be. When Carl adapted how he spoke to Dee, she became more effective and he became less anxious. Dee was overusing her innate strengths. Carl brought her back into balance. He helped turn her into a great eagle rather than a mediocre owl.

When strengths are overused, they become weaknesses. An *eagle's* natural assertiveness turns into aggression. Directness hardens into bluntness and insensitivity, and their ability to take charge becomes domineering. A *parrot's* optimism turns into unrealistic expectations and impracticality. As parrots overuse spontaneity, they become scattered, and their abundance of enthusiasm appears superficial and over-the-top. *Doves* become passive. Their need for consistency creates resistance to change, and their desire for harmony causes them to become too lenient and permissive. *Owls* overuse their analytical skills and become indecisive. Their need for perfection causes them to become too critical. Their focus on the task drives them to detach from people.

When we overuse our own strengths, the stress eventually passes, and ultimately, we return comfortably to our successful style. However, when others overuse their style, we sometimes try to change them.

Imagine a dove who wants to give feedback to her owl spouse. The dove is unhappy that the owl is inflexible with the rules they have imposed on their children. One day, their child arrives home late, and the owl immediately applies strict consequences. The dove feels that, in this instance, there were extenuating circumstances, and they should have been more lenient.

The dove approaches the owl with an impassioned plea to reduce the child's punishment, but the owl simply reiterates the rules. The dove speaks to the owl in the language of the dove, making statements like, "You need to be more sensitive and compassionate." She also says things that run counter to the language of the owl, such as, "Not everything is so black and white."

The dove would have had more success changing the owl's behavior if she had honored his innate owl style while she was trying to get him to tone down his overuse. Instead, she tried to get him to exhibit dove behavior. She would have accomplished more if she had said, "I understand that we have rules and they need to be followed. I also recognize that it is important for parents to enforce the rules. However, if we impose consequences without considering all the facts, we may trigger our child to rebel against what he feels is unfair treatment, which could prompt him to violate more rules in the future. Perhaps we can look at the specifics of this incident and determine an appropriate response."

We may not be able to change others, but we can change the way we deal with them. When we try to alter someone's fundamental nature, we are rarely effective. And worse, the attempt can damage the relationship. But when we help others become the best version of themselves, our efforts can build a stronger connection and help them to shine.

- NOTICE YOUR JUDGMENTAL THOUGHTS about others. Instead of thinking about how you would like to change them, think about how you can positively impact them.

- YOU WOULD NOT WANT PEOPLE TO TRY to change you, so consider how others feel when you to try to change them.

- CHANNEL YOUR ENERGY into altering your approach rather than trying to change someone's style.

- SEEK TO TONE DOWN OVERUSE rather than change someone completely.

- HELP OTHERS TO BE THE BEST they can be, but don't try to change them to be more like you.

Winter

The Chameleon

Mudslide

Because of a heavy rainstorm, Dee, Ivory, Simon, and Carl had rescheduled their Council committee meeting. After working through several issues, they were happy their gathering was finally coming to a close. With all their business now completed, Ivory announced it was time to celebrate.

As she flew to a nearby tree to retrieve something, Carl asked, "What are we celebrating?"

Ivory shouted over her shoulder, "Life!"

When she returned to the Council Tree, she placed a container filled with a pungent, bluish-yellow mixture in the center of the group.

The parrot explained that she had flown for hours to a secret location in order to find an ancient exotic plant. From the roots of that plant, she had brewed this special concoction for her friends. Ivory was eager to share her creation.

The parrot carefully poured some of the liquid for each of her friends. She sensed their hesitation to taste it, so she encouraged, "Don't worry. It won't hurt you. Enjoy!"

They all picked up their drinks and, in an act of solidarity, simultaneously sipped their drinks. The birds' eyes grew wide.

With the compassion of a dove, Simon spoke first. "Ivory, this is very good. Thank you for taking the time to prepare this for us."

Dee, the feisty eagle, looked as if she was about to say something to the contrary when Simon shot her a look. Dee thought better of her plan and just smiled.

As soon as Ivory turned to Carl to get his opinion, the forest received another urgent warning. For the second time in a few days, The Forest Alert System had been activated. The message was being transmitted to the Council members by an out-of-breath dove who had come down from the north. "Mudslide … on … Xanadu's … Peak."

Carl was about to ask the dove if she knew anything else about the mudslide when he remembered that, according to the System rules he amended last year, all messages had to be five words or fewer in order to increase accuracy. He was now beginning to regret that requirement.

The mudslide was personal to the owl. Last year he had studied Xanadu's Peak with highly sensitive equipment and determined there was a low mudslide threat in that area. While the Council had previously recommended to the ground and tree dwellers in the area that they should relocate, Carl's report encouraged many to stay. He hoped that no one had been hurt today because of his report. He had to go check it out.

Dee stood tall, as eagles tend to do in the face of danger, and announced that she would join her owl friend. After Carl quickly packed a few measuring tools, the two friends flew swiftly to the unfolding disaster.

Meanwhile, Simon and Ivory remained back at the Council

Tree so they could coordinate a rescue effort, if one was needed. Simon was worried about his friends, but he was even more concerned about injuries to those who lived at the base of the mountain. Ivory called on her innate optimism to reassure Simon that everything would be fine, but Simon was not convinced.

When the owl and the eagle arrived on the scene, they couldn't believe the extent of the devastation. Though the rainstorm had passed, a large mass of gooey muck was barreling down the southern slope of Xanadu's Peak. Large boulders were being sucked into a giant mud river overflowing with rocks, vegetation, and water. Piles of rubble were left in the mud's wake, and a mass of toppled trees created a new stripped and swerving path. The mud was moving straight to the Xanadu Amphitheater.

Calls for help echoed throughout the valley. Carl and Dee didn't know where to go first. Survivors caked in mud emerged from the forest. Dee flew to the top of the mountain for a bird's-eye view of the situation. That's when she saw it. A young weasel was being swept away in the mudflow. Dee gasped. When she was a young eagle, she had been caught in such a flow and had nearly drowned. Had it not been for a resourceful dove who had used a large vine to save her, Dee would not be here today.

The eagle summoned her courage and rapidly descended toward the weasel. Her heart raced as she got closer and closer to the unfortunate critter. She circled him for a bit, but she kept making larger and larger circles instead of banking in to make smaller ones. The weasel reached up for help, but Dee kept circling. Something inside her was pushing her away.

A nearby parrot saw what was happening and swooped in to

save the day. With the mud-covered weasel secured to his chest, he made a jubilant victory lap before gently touching down beside the frightened weasel's relieved parents. As the reunited family hugged, everyone along the mud bank cheered ... except for Dee.

When the eagle returned to her owl friend, she saw him surveying the extent of the damage. He was busy checking and rechecking his findings. Perhaps he didn't even notice what had happened.

Carl had just concluded that the unprecedented amount of rain must have saturated the earth. That caused loose dirt to mix with water to form mud, and all of this happened too quickly. Gravity kicked in and pulled the masses of wet soil down the slope.

"How could I have missed this?" Carl wondered aloud.

"Hey, we all make mistakes," Dee replied, happy to discuss anything but what had just transpired.

The owl reached into his bag and pulled out a measuring instrument. It only took a moment for him to realize that the equipment had been calibrated incorrectly, thereby causing all of his previous data to be wrong. It was hard for Carl to imagine that he made an error of such great magnitude, but he could not deny what he was looking at.

Carl explained the problem to Dee, who was still so embarrassed by her failure to save the weasel that she didn't tell Carl what she was really thinking. If Carl had checked his equipment, none of this would have happened.

Carl, too, was at a loss for words. He had been stunned when he noticed Dee's attempt to rescue the weasel, and now he was ashamed of his own actions. As the owl packed up his gear, Dee said quietly, "The wind was rough down there. A parrot with a wingspan smaller than mine was able to rescue a weasel from the mud. His diminutive wings allowed him to make the tight turn needed to grab the little fellow. You do know that I would have done it if I could have, right?"

Carl just nodded.

The pair headed back to the Council Tree without saying another word. When they arrived, Carl explained to Simon and Ivory how faulty equipment had created inaccurate measurements in last year's study. Ivory didn't seem to need all the details. She was just happy they had returned and relieved that everyone was okay.

However, the longer Carl spoke, the more agitated Dee became. She kept thinking that she would never have been placed in the awkward position of trying to rescue the weasel by herself if Carl had not made such a critical mistake in the first place. Ultimately, the eagle couldn't take it any longer. "You know, Carl, if you had carefully checked your equipment before you made your measurements, the Council would not have declared 'minimal danger' in this community and none of this would have happened."

"Excuse me, Dee," Carl snapped. "But I did not make a mistake. The equipment was not set correctly."

"And who had used the equipment?" the eagle shot back.

"I think you are upset because you were too afraid to fly close enough to the mudslide," accused Carl, as he abruptly changed the subject. "I believe you could have saved that weasel and that your version of the facts lacks a factual basis."

"Are you saying that I am lying?" Dee glared.

"Hold on everyone," Simon interjected. "Let's all calm down. None of this is anyone's fault. And nobody is calling anybody a liar. I'm sure that both of you did your best today, and that's all we can ask of anyone."

It was only then that Dee and Carl noticed it was no longer just the four of them standing on the branch on the Council Tree. Between Simon and Carl stood their old friend, Xenia. The chameleon's apprentice, Xander, watched silently from a nearby tree.

After some quick pleasantries, the chameleon cleared her throat and offered, "May I shed some light on the matter?"

"By all means," Simon requested.

"Can I be completely honest?" she questioned.

A chorus of "of course," "yes," "absolutely," and "sure" gave her permission to proceed.

"Very well, then," she continued. "I sense that a bit of deception has taken place here today. But we all engage in deception every now and then."

"So you agree that I lied?" the eagle snapped.

"Dee, we all stretch the truth at one time or another," the chameleon explained.

"Well, I wouldn't blame equipment for my inadequacy," Dee insisted.

"Perhaps," Xenia acknowledged, "but that's because your personality is different from Carl's. Who we are drives why we deceive others."

A group of fast-moving squirrels whizzed by the birds carrying an abundance of nuts. The friends froze in wonder until the squirrels passed, and then they turned their attention back to the chameleon. Recognizing that the group needed more information, Simon asked Xenia to explain.

Xenia continued. "Xander and I couldn't help but overhear your conversation earlier today when Ivory offered each of you a bit of her special drink. Xander is right over there, by the way. Don't try to look for him. He's practicing blending into the colors of a beehive, so I don't think we should call attention to him."

Ivory smiled as she tried to catch a glimpse of the beehive-colored chameleon. "Hey, if I knew you two were there when I was pouring the drinks, I would have offered you some."

"Oh, that's quite all right, Ivory," the chameleon grinned. "But thank you for thinking of us. Besides, I'm not so sure that everyone enjoyed it as much as you did."

"What do you mean?" the parrot asked. "They all loved it!"

Xenia caught Simon's eyes before speaking. "Simon, did you enjoy it?"

Simon didn't know what to say. He tried to speak but couldn't seem to summon the right words.

"That's all right," Xenia said, letting him off the hook. "You see, like the rest of us, doves tell what we like to call 'white lies.' They sometimes obscure the truth so they don't hurt others' feelings."

Simon gave a subtle nod to acknowledge the truth spoken by Xenia.

Ivory then turned to Simon and said, "Don't worry about it, Simon. Honestly, this batch wasn't my best."

Xenia shifted her gaze to the parrot. "Ivory, as for this mysterious root you gathered, I am quite familiar with it. If I am correct, it's easily obtained not too far from here."

For once, Ivory didn't know what to say. Simon broke the uneasy silence. "But the distance did make it seem more mysterious."

"Parrots often embellish or exaggerate the facts," Xenia explained. "And as Simon just said, the distance does make for a better story."

Ivory nodded. "I suppose that's true."

"Now then, let's get to the bottom of this mudslide situation," the chameleon stated. "Dee, you do not like to appear weak, do you?"

"Heck no!" the eagle confirmed.

"And you don't want anyone to think that you lack courage, do you?"

"Absolutely not," Dee replied reflexively.

"So could it be that you were not completely forthright about what happened when you were trying to save that weasel?"

"Well, maybe not," conceded Dee.

Carl shot the group a judging glance. "I, for one, am very concerned about all of this deception. I would never ..."

Xenia raised her right palm to silence Carl before he dug himself into a hole. "Carl, are you upset with yourself that you did not properly calibrate your equipment before surveying the mountain?"

"I suppose I am," admitted the owl. "I don't like providing faulty data."

"Is it uncomfortable for you to admit that you have made a mistake?"

"It is. I want others to be able to rely on me," Carl said.

Simon turned to the owl and said, "But we would never think that you are unreliable."

Carl returned a thank-you nod and stated, "I appreciate that. Nevertheless, my first step to regaining your trust will be to support the cleanup efforts."

Xenia summarized, "We are all practiced at the art of deception. And who we are determines why and how we deceive ourselves and others."

The chameleon motioned Xander to move away from the bees before they noticed him. She then walked over to Ivory's strange brew and inhaled a whiff of the substance. She poured several droplets onto a leaf and tasted it with her tongue. She gave the group a big smile. Just before she faded into the tree, she said, "Delicious!"

Chameleon Wisdom

*I've tried to do away with lying in my life
in the last few years, but it's hard.*
—Louis C.K.

Let's set one thing straight right from the start: Everyone lies. In fact, the average person lies several times a day. But before you get defensive, this statement refers to white lies typically borne out of kindness, not lies intended to deceive or harm. In fact, people often tell white lies to be polite or to protect the feelings of others.

White lies may be told to maintain privacy or foster positive relationships. We may tell these untruths to entertain, embellish, or exaggerate. Sometimes white lies are even told to boost the self-esteem of others or maintain our own self-confidence. While each of us tells white lies for different reasons, fear is the common underlying driver. Some people may fear looking bad, while others may fear upsetting someone or damaging a relationship.

We all have a self-image that we strive to maintain, and we want others to see us as we see ourselves. We tell white lies to protect our image, and we guard against projecting anything that runs counter to the way we wish to be seen. The particular fear that drives a white lie is based, in part, on our personality style.

In *Mudslide*, Dee sees herself as a strong and confident eagle. She does not want to project that she has fear or weakness of any kind. This self-image drives her to tell a white lie so that she is not seen as someone who lacks courage or experiences failure. Eagles like to cut their own path and take ownership of their destiny. Sometimes they stretch the truth to get what they want. To them, the ends often justify the means. If they fail, they may shift the blame to factors they could not control. Imagine a workplace eagle who says, "I would have achieved my goal if only that other department would have gotten me the information sooner."

Like Dee, Carl also told a white lie in *Mudslide*. As an owl, his self-image is based on his ability to do things accurately. He sees himself as careful, compliant, and consistent. As such, he lied to protect the perception that he can be trusted to do things properly. From his owl perspective, others rely on him for quality results. Therefore, he feels compelled to guard against his friends seeing him as inefficient or substandard. Owls are often driven to cover up their mistakes so they do not look incapable or inaccurate in the eyes of others.

Doves tell white lies for a different reason. They fear being seen as harsh, selfish, or unsympathetic. Thus, doves might stretch the truth to project kindness and thoughtfulness. You might hear them say, "That's a beautiful sweater you're wearing," even though they dislike it. Or "The dinner you made was delicious," despite the fact that they did not enjoy it. Doves tell white lies to protect the feelings of others. Ironically, doves value sincerity, but their white lies embody insincerity.

Parrots, who like to impress others, are known to embellish the truth. If a story is good but not great, they might embellish the facts to make it more exciting. Parrots like to project that everything works out well for them because their self-image is based on that reality. At the same time, they like to be seen as fun-loving optimists. So if something bad happens, they may describe the event as if it were an incredible adventure instead of a traumatic experience. Parrots like to be liked, and they may exaggerate the facts so they don't look bad and, therefore, become less likable.

The next time you judge others for telling white lies, consider that their style is driving their behavior. And remember, everyone tells white lies based on their personality style ... even you.

- AVOID JUDGING OTHERS for telling white lies. We all tell them.

- NOTE THAT A WHITE LIE IS SERVING a deeper personality-driven need.

- CONSIDER THE IMPACT of being completely truthful and how that could positively impact the relationship.

- CONSIDER THE WHITE LIES YOU TELL and ask yourself whether your perceived negative impact of telling the truth is real or imagined.

- RECOGNIZE THAT THE BETTER you know and accept yourself, the more truthful you will become.

Winter Camp

Three days ago, winter camp had begun for the children of Home, and Simon and Ivory were ready for the challenge. The camp provided a place where little ones could go when their parents were taking a winter vacation. The adults took turns volunteering at the camp, and today Simon and Ivory were tasked with keeping the children safe and entertained.

The campers were usually excited to be together at camp, but on rainy days many of the fun activities were cancelled. When Simon arrived, he did not have a good feeling about the weather. The sun was nowhere to be seen, and the clouds threatened a torrential downpour. The dove worried that the children would not enjoy themselves with a rainy day activity schedule. He was also concerned about his ability to engage the campers because he was not accustomed to taking the lead.

By the time the children arrived, the cold winter rain was falling down hard. The youngsters gathered below an assemblage of large leaves that had been woven together to protect them. Twenty of the youngest looked at Simon excitedly, anticipating the fun that awaited them.

Simon hopped up on a branch and called everyone to attention.

"Hello campers," he said invitingly. It took a few moments before the kids looked his way. "I'm sorry you won't be able to participate in your normal activities today, but the rain … Well, don't worry. We will make do."

Simon was not surprised to hear a loud groan emanate from the group. "I know. I know. I'm sorry. Since we are implementing the rain plan today, I need you to listen carefully so you all know what to do."

The campers let out another loud groan.

"Let's make the best of it everyone," the dove requested. "The first activity today is leaf origami."

"Are you kidding?" a young eagle complained.

"Seriously?" a young parrot squawked. "That's not going to be fun at all!"

One owl whispered to another, "He had weeks to create a rain plan, and all he could come up with is a game for babies?"

"Don't worry. It will be fun. Let's begin."

As the group begrudgingly played with their leaves, Simon heard Ivory and her campers, who were gathered nearby. Ivory had a loud parrot voice, and he could hear everything she was saying. She was running a little behind schedule and was only now announcing her group's first activity.

"Are you ready for some crazy rainy day fun?" Ivory called to her campers.

"Good luck with that," Simon reflected, as he picked up a leaf with the hope of turning it into the shape of a dragonfly.

A few of the oldest campers returned a halfhearted "yes" to Ivory.

The parrot repeated louder, "*I said*, are you ready for some crazy rainy day fun?!"

"YES!" the group returned.

"So who thinks they've got what it takes to be The Origami Champion?" Ivory challenged.

A loud "meeeeee!" echoed through the forest.

"I can't hear you," she replied. "Who here can make something awesome from their leaf? Something so cool that all the other leaves in the forest will be calling your name and asking you to fold them into something amazing?"

"Meeeeee!" shouted the chorus of campers.

Ivory hopped down from her branch and began weaving in and out of the members of her group. She lowered her voice as if she were sharing a great secret. "Here's what we are going to do. First, each of you will select a leaf from my Big Basket of Fun. Then, I'll be looking for the craziest, wackiest, funniest, silliest leaf you can muster. Who thinks they can win the Rainy Day Crazy Leaf Origami Challenge?"

Again, a loud choir of "meeeeee" reverberated throughout the land.

"Let's do it!!!" Ivory cheered. "Grab a leaf and let the games begin!"

Simon just shook his head. "I do not get it. My campers are doing the same thing as her campers, yet her kids are looking forward to it and mine are dreading it. How does she do that?"

"I think I can help," offered a quiet voice that resonated beside him. "Oh!" Simon jumped. "I didn't see you there Xenia and Xander. You startled me."

The pair emerged from beneath a large piece of foliage that was being propped up with two twigs. Xenia was holding a leaf that she had turned into a stunning replica of a chipmunk. The detail was astonishing, right down to its joyful facial expression. Xander held a leaf that looked as if it had been simply folded a few times.

Simon smiled politely at Xander as he held up his creation and said, "It's a turtle. See, here's the head. These are his feet. It's a turtle."

Xenia winked at Simon. "It seems like you've got a tough group of campers," the chameleon noted.

"Oh, I don't think so," conceded Simon. "I think it's me."

Xenia revealed the hint of smile. "It sounds like Ivory has everything under control."

"I know. That's what makes me think it's me," the dove said.

Xenia turned to her young student and asked, "Xander, what do you do when you're not sure how to handle a situation?"

"That's easy," Xander answered. "I just ask myself, 'What would Xenia do?'"

"Hum. That's interesting," Xenia replied.

"Well, the rain seems to be picking up. I need to get Xander home to his parents. You have a great day," Xenia said, as she and her protégé shifted their coloring to match the fertile-brown earth below them.

The noise from Ivory's campers drowned out the near silence of Simon's group. "That was an odd interaction," the dove thought. "Xenia usually helps me. But this time, she didn't say anything."

When it was time to introduce the next exercise, Simon was still thinking about what Xander had said, and that's when it struck him. Though he may not naturally *think* like a parrot, that doesn't mean he can't *act* like one for a little while. So Simon relaxed, closed his eyes and thought, "What would Ivory do?"

"I need to turn up my energy. If I am not having fun, they will not have fun. I need to get excited to get them excited. Well, here goes nothing."

The dove glanced down at his list and saw that his second activity was called Council Elder.

"Attention everyone," he called. "Can I have your attention, please?"

Simon knew that they preferred sunny day activities to rainy day ones, but he was on a mission to make this day fun. After a few more requests for silence, the group became quiet. He took a deep breath and thought, *Be like Ivory. That is all I have to do. Be like Ivory.*

With a burst of energy, Simon cheered, "Who thinks you can outsmart the rest of your fellow campers?"

A few wings tentatively raised into the air. "That's it?" he questioned. "Let us try that again." With even more energy, Simon added, "Who among you can out-think, out-logic, out-reason your fellow campers?"

This time, many of the campers lifted their wings into the air. He even noticed a few smiles as well.

"Very good, then," Simon commented. He pointed to Dean, a young eagle who seemed rather confident that he was up for the challenge. Simon directed the youngster to hide behind a nearby tree and then informed him that he would retrieve him soon and give him instructions.

Simon then turned to face the group, crouched down real low, and whispered, "Come closer everyone. I will tell you what we are going to do."

Simon selected one of the doves and instructed, "You are going to be the Council Elder. You are free to move however you like. The rest of us will repeat everything you do. If you smile, we will all smile. If you tap your foot, we will all tap our feet. If you stick out your tongue and try to touch the tip of your beak, we will all stick out our tongues."

Simon stuck out his tongue and crossed his eyes. Everyone laughed.

"Now, everyone else, in addition to following everything the dove does, you can also do anything you like, but nobody else will be copying you. When Dean returns, he has to figure out who the Council Elder is. Can you fake him out?"

"Yes," the group responded.

"I can't hear you," Simon said as he widened his eyes and placed his left wing beside his head.

"*Yessssss!*" returned the cheerful campers.

Dean returned and the group began laughing from start. Simon could not believe his eyes. He had done it. He had turned his unhappy campers into a joyful bunch of children.

Simon took out his pencil so that he would not forget what he just learned. "Whenever I need to do something that is not natural for me," he wrote, "identify someone who would do it well and ask myself what that individual would do … then do it."

Simon smiled as he looked at the day's third activity. He could already hear the laughter from Ivory's group and he was confident that he would make it fun for his campers as well ... just like Ivory would do.

As Xenia and Xander secretly observed Simon from behind a tree, a large box turtle slowly walked by the chameleons. Xander thrust his origami art forward and said, "See, it's a turtle! It looks just like him."

Chameleon Wisdom

Act the part and you will become the part.
—WILLIAM JAMES

Throughout our lives there are times when our natural style is perfectly suited for the situation we are in. However, there are also occasions in which we need to display behaviors that are not typically associated with our innate approach to the world. Imagine a strong parrot speaking with a software Help Desk. The rep requests, "Tell me what's happening." The parrot replies, "I don't know. The thingy just stopped working."

This parrot is faced with the everyday experience of needing to tap into behaviors that are not natural.

In this situation, the parrot needed to be highly specific, despite his tendency to speak in generalities. The ability to flexibly display behaviors that are not native to our style is critical to our success. Yet, sometimes the required actions are so foreign to us that we have no idea what to do.

Fortunately, there are masters of each style, and they are all around us. They are our coworkers and our family members. They are on television, in books and movies, and scattered throughout human history. These experts are the people who strongly embody the characteristics of the bird styles.

The next time you get stuck and do not know what to do, ask yourself, "Who would be great at handling this situation?" Then imagine yourself acting like they would act. Visualize yourself adopting their body language, posture, facial expressions, wording, tone, and pace.

When we act as if we are a certain type of person, we can become that person, even if it is just for a little while. Holding the body language of someone we would like to emulate creates an emotional readiness to display the behaviors we want to exhibit.

As we watch someone display a behavior, or simply picture that action in our mind's eye, our brains activate the same neurons as if we were enacting that behavior ourselves. Amazingly, just thinking about a behavior creates the hardwiring for it. So when it comes time to engage in the action, it is easier for us to do so because our brains have been prewired.

In *Winter Camp*, Simon watched Ivory and replicated her behaviors. His positive self-talk empowered him to act like a parrot. When it came time to energize the kids, the dove became more animated and spoke with greater enthusiasm. He did not change who he was, but rather, for a short time *acted as if* he were a parrot.

As our inner voice tells us how to respond to challenges, our thoughts create our reality. When we imagine ourselves easily resolving difficult issues and then putting new behaviors into practice, we gain inner strength. Over time, we will be able to spontaneously display formerly uncomfortable behaviors and turn obstacles into opportunity.

Imagine an eagle who has to deal with a frustrated dove customer or, perhaps, an upset dove spouse. The natural tendency of an eagle is to charge forward and try to fix the problem.

However, doves need emotional validation. They want to know that we understand and feel their pain. Only then, are they ready to look forward to a solution.

But this eagle does not know what to say or how to display empathy. In addition to directly asking how to act, the eagle has several viable options. First, the eagle could ask another dove what to do. If another dove is available, this a simple way to understand a dove's needs.

Second, the eagle could reflect back on how this particular dove has handled other upset people in the past. Since we treat others how we ourselves like to be treated, looking at how this dove has treated others in a similar situation provides a window into the dove's needs.

Third, the eagle has been presented with the opportunity to develop new hardwiring that can be used in this and similar occasions in the future. The eagle might identify a dove who would naturally handle this situation effectively. This could be a person that the eagle knows, a famous person, or a fictitious character. The eagle could visualize this individual responding to the dove, while paying attention to the body language and words that are employed.

With new hardwiring in place, the eagle can embody that person's energy and implement new actions. While these behaviors may not feel natural, the attempt is likely to yield better results than if the eagle responded in eagle mode. In fact, if the dove is the eagle's spouse, the eagle is likely to gain points for making an attempt to be empathetic.

As we engage new behaviors, we create a mental script that

guides future actions. We stretch ourselves and gain comfort with a greater range of responses. And while these new behaviors may never become core strengths, at least they will not inhibit our effectiveness.

While *acting as if* can be scary, it can also be fun to approach problems with a new state of mind.

- PAY ATTENTION TO OTHER PEOPLE who effortlessly act in ways that are challenging for you.

- COMMIT TO TRYING out new behaviors; eventually they will flow spontaneously.

- VISUALIZE YOURSELF AS THE PERSON you wish to emulate. Take on every aspect of their style and let go of inhibitions.

- LET GO OF HOW WELL YOU PERFORM when you try new behaviors.

- RECOGNIZE THAT acting as if you are someone else does not mean that you are trying to change who you are. Rather, you are simply doing what needs to be done in a situation because those behaviors are the ones that are needed.

The Chameleon

The Northern Squirrels

When Simon awoke, a soft coating of snow mirrored the whiteness of his dove feathers. He always enjoyed the winter season, when crystal snowflakes made the forest sparkle. But this year was a challenging one for him and for many of the other forest dwellers. For the past few weeks, Simon and many of his dove friends and family members were having a hard time locating seeds. With each passing day, the birds grew more concerned about their winter stockpiles.

Simon headed out early to see if he could find some food to bring back to his loved ones, but he was having no luck. He searched the weeds and grasses where seeds were typically found, but the seeds — all of them — were gone. Someone had taken them. The dove stared helplessly at the snow-covered forest, wondering what to do next.

Dee, circling above the treetops, noticed her dove friend and approached to see what he was doing. Simon explained the lack of food and shared his fears about making it through the frosty winter. He worried especially about the youngest and oldest in the dove community. How could they survive the season without enough nourishment?

Dee looked at Simon curiously. "I just heard that the doves in the Northern Territory are having the same problem. I also heard that the squirrels up north are enjoying an abundance of food this winter."

"That's interesting," Simon commented. "For the past few weeks, I've seen lots of northern squirrels carrying food throughout the forest. You don't think the squirrels planned this, do you?" He shivered at the thought.

"I think it's clear what has happened. They took your food, and I'm going to help you fix it. Let's head north and ask the squirrels to return some of the food. If they are unwilling, we will take it."

"Whoa," Simon protested. "I am sure they will understand our situation. If we go there and express our concerns, certainly they will be willing to help."

"Help? What are you talking about? They took your food. Returning it isn't being helpful. It is doing what must be done," said Dee.

"I'm sure that they don't realize what they did," Simon responded. "If we just talk with them ..."

"Okay. Let's get one thing straight. They know exactly what they did. You are not a bear who can sleep your way through winter, and neither are the other doves, who must be hungry by now. I'm thinking that you are going to want to eat sometime before spring."

They spoke for a few more minutes but found it hard to find common ground. In fact, the more they talked, the farther apart they became. Simon requested they spend the rest of the day thinking about each other's perspectives before actually doing anything. They planned to meet again the next morning to formulate a strategy.

Later that evening, as the chatter of the frogs gradually replaced the conversations of the birds, Simon sat alone looking out at the Great Lake. As the sky reflected the sunset's radiant red onto the pale ice, his dove feathers blended effortlessly into the dusting of snow decorating his branch.

Simon felt depleted from the day. However, what drained him most was not the content of their discussion, but rather, its tone. The dove was not thinking about the squirrels right now. Instead, he was reflecting on how Dee had communicated with him. While he appreciated her help, he felt as if Dee was condescending in her manner. "She didn't have to be so harsh," he thought. "I would never speak to someone like that."

As the snow continued to fall, Simon shook his head in frustration.

On the other side of the lake, Dee majestically gazed out over the great expanse of the wilderness. She, too, was thinking about her talk with Simon. *What a colossal waste of time that was*, she thought. *Simon is unwilling to take bold steps to fix the problem.*

Dee believed that they should have been able to solve this problem hours ago, but until now they hadn't settled a thing. Now they would have to continue the conversation when, instead, they should be investing their energy into fixing the problem. As Dee watched the snow blanket the forest, she knew the urgency of the situation was becoming more pronounced every day.

After a long, cold night, the dove and eagle met again in the morning. Dee arrived early, eager to resolve the issue. Simon arrived late. The dove was withdrawn and could barely make eye contact with the eagle.

Simon answered questions with one word answers such as "fine" and "whatever," which only irritated Dee even more. In turn, she became more blunt and aggressive, which further aggravated the situation.

That was it. Dee had had enough. "I don't see how we are going to figure this thing out with you acting like this."

Simon was stunned. "Me acting like what?" For the life of him, he couldn't figure out what she was talking about. He felt Dee's tone was getting in the way of finding a reasonable solution.

Dee could not believe what she was hearing. All she was trying to do was help, and Simon was getting in the way of progress. "This is crazy!" Dee snapped.

Simon sighed in frustration.

Just then, a puff of snow fell from the branch above them. They both looked up and noticed a white tail sliding down the trunk of the tree and heading towards them. "May I join you?" Xenia requested politely.

"Please do," Simon answered with relief.

"I guess so," Dee shrugged.

"I couldn't help but overhear your conversation. It sounds like you are at an impasse," the chameleon observed.

"You can say that again," the eagle snarled.

Lowering his head, Simon agreed.

"You are pushing each other's buttons and frustrating each other," the chameleon explained.

"I don't see how I am doing anything wrong," Dee proclaimed

adamantly. "I am willing to do whatever it takes to fix the problem. A problem, I might add, that Simon asked me to help him solve. I'm just being candid in expressing what we must do. Simon is avoiding the issues and isn't willing to take definitive action."

"And that bothers you?" Xenia asked.

"You're darn right!" the eagle declared.

The chameleon then turned to Simon. "And you're upset with Dee?"

"Well, yes, I am," the dove said hesitantly. "She's not being respectful."

"Talk with me," Xenia prompted. "Tell me more about how she is not being respectful."

Dee was about to snap back at Simon, but Xenia lifted her hand to stop her so that Simon could respond. "Simon, continue," she instructed.

"She's not listening, and she speaks to me in a harsh and pushy way. I don't want to seem ungrateful because I truly appreciate her help, but I would never treat her like that."

"So she is pushing your buttons, too?" Xenia asked.

"I guess so."

"It has been my experience that if someone is pushing my hot buttons, it is possible that I am also pushing theirs," Xenia advised.

Dee thought about that for a moment, and then replied. "So you're saying that every time someone is annoying me, I am probably annoying them, too?"

"Yes," Xenia acknowledged with a nod.

"Oh, that is not good," Dee chuckled. "If that's really the case, I must bother a lot of folks."

Simon and Xenia laughed as well.

"That makes sense," Simon acknowledged. "It upset me that Dee was being too blunt, and now I sense that I frustrated her because I was not being assertive enough."

"I'd agree with that," confirmed the eagle.

Xenia continued, "The fact that you push each other's buttons means that you have something to learn from each other."

The chameleon flicked her tail, shooting a wisp of snow into the air. Just before she leapt to an adjacent branch and disappeared into the snow, she whispered, "Those who bother us most can often teach us best."

Before they could thank the chameleon, she was gone.

"You do kinda push my buttons," Simon smiled.

"And you definitely push mine," Dee grinned. "But we've got work to do. How about this? Why don't we go talk to the northern squirrels? We'll start off with your plan. I won't say a word. But if they are not receptive to giving us back some food, I will become a little more assertive."

"Sounds good to me," Simon said. "But remember, they're not bears, either. They need to eat, too."

Chameleon Wisdom

If we learn to open our hearts, anyone,
including the people who drive us crazy,
can be our teacher.
—Pema Chödrön

When two people enter each other's lives, each has something to gain from the other. While at times the relationship may seem lopsided, no two people come together to benefit just one of them.

Sometimes we come across people who we find difficult to deal with. Perhaps those closest to us have habits that annoy or confound us. These people are not in our lives to be conquered. They are there to be understood so we can better understand ourselves. In fact, our greatest teachers are often those who evoke deep emotional responses as they provide us with opportunities to learn.

While these teachers may generate stress or adversity, the situations they trigger help us to stretch ourselves and grow. So instead of blaming them for their shortcomings, thank them for providing the opportunity to practice tolerance and acceptance. Appreciate that they give us the chance to practice useful conflict management and negotiation skills that we will surely need in the future as we struggle to meet our own needs. These people help us see ourselves differently and, thus, increase our own self-awareness. And if we are feeling particularly open and gracious, we can thank them for reflecting our own issues back to us.

While it is hard to feel appreciative of someone who seems to be making our lives more difficult, try to look inside and understand the hot button they are pressing, instead of reacting with defensiveness or anger.

People push our buttons for many reasons. Sometimes individuals upset us because they are reflecting back to us our own shortcomings or the parts of ourselves we do not like. They may reflect fears, unresolved issues, or disliked behaviors that we subconsciously adopted from someone else. These people act like mirrors, revealing a part of ourselves that we try to hide from others. They can also reflect a former version of ourselves that we do not want to revert to.

Those individuals whose personalities and actions push our hot buttons are often our greatest teachers. They help us to see, to heal, and to gain balance. In *The Northern Squirrels*, Dee and Simon had different approaches to the squirrel problem. If they had been willing, Dee could have learned how to approach others with an open heart, while Simon could have learned how to be more assertive. Simon reflected Dee's impatience and insensitivity. Dee reflected Simon's inability to stand in his own power.

As Dee and Simon have taught us, when someone pushes our hot buttons, it is likely that we are pushing theirs. Imagine a parrot and owl couple who need to pick up a few things at the grocery store. The owl usually does the shopping, but, in this instance, the parrot is coming along. The owl, wanting only to help the parrot, provides concise directions on where items are located in the store. The owl draws a map and highlights the pathway that the parrot should follow. Instead of feeling appreciative, however, the parrot feels micromanaged and starts tuning out the owl's instructions. The owl has pushed one of the parrot's buttons. The owl then gets annoyed because the parrot is not listening, which means she will be more likely to be inefficient or forget something. The parrot has pushed one of the owl's buttons.

Our emotions are triggered when our desires are not met. When our core needs are not honored, we can get frustrated, angry, or resentful. And yet, in those times when we do not understand someone else, chances are, they do not understand us, either. In other words, you may be just as difficult a person in the eyes of the person you find difficult.

Consider two young eagle and owl siblings. To their parents' dismay, they are constantly bickering. The eagle annoys the owl because the eagle does not follow the rules. The pair agreed on specific shower times before school, but the eagle often stays in the shower too long. In addition, the eagle invites friends over while their parents are not home, which is a clear violation of their parents' rules. The owl resents that the eagle is breaking the rules while he is following them.

Meanwhile, the owl annoys the eagle because the owl is slow. One house rule is that the entire family must remain at the dinner table until everyone has finished eating. Each night, the owl takes much longer to complete his dinner, which frustrates the eagle, who eats much faster. The eagle is also bothered that the owl takes too long to finish his homework because another rule is that the house must remain quiet until everyone's homework is complete.

Both the eagle and the owl are annoying each other because their style-driven needs are not being met. Eagles move at a fast pace and are frustrated by slowness. Owls adhere to rules and are dismayed by those who view them as loose guidelines. While they are each having their own hot buttons pressed, they fail to realize that they are also pushing the other's buttons.

We are all here to help each other grow. Take a step back and accept that we push the buttons of the person who is pushing ours. This realization puts us on equal footing with the other person.

It is said that when the student is ready, the teacher will appear. We are all students and we are all teachers, each of us doing the best we can by being who we are. Along the way, we may push a few buttons and have a few of our own pushed, as well. But when we open ourselves to the gifts that others give us when they create adversity in our lives, we learn the lessons that we need to learn most.

- RECOGNIZE THAT PEOPLE do not do things against you, but rather, for themselves.

- MANAGE YOUR EMOTIONS when dealing with button-pushers who are different from you.

- STOP TAKING THINGS PERSONALLY and gain control of your emotions.

- DO NOT TRY TO CHANGE OTHERS. Look inside and see which one of your thoughts needs to be adjusted.

- LET GO OF JUDGMENT and accept others for who they are.

The Chameleon

Lost in Translation

After enduring a particularly relentless winter, Ivory was more than ready to escape the cold. Though it took significant prodding, she finally convinced her friends — Dee, Simon, and Carl — to head southeast for some sun and excitement.

The parrot agreed to map out the journey, while Carl took on the responsibility of coordinating their meals. Arranging four different diets in a foreign land would be no easy task, but the owl was up for the challenge.

Simon was a little worried because the residents of the Eastern Tidelands spoke a different language, but Dee's confidence assured the dove that everything would be alright.

The four companions met just after sunrise at the Council Tree. They hoped to get an early start on their adventure. As they leaped into the blue unknown, Ivory knew exactly where she was headed — the Eastern Tidelands.

They were supposed to follow the river to the Crystal Cave and then to the edge of Home. From there, she was certain she could figure it out. After all, many of Home's residents visited this popular vacation spot, and they always found their way. *How hard can it be to get there*, Ivory thought.

A few hours into the journey, Dee asked, "How are we doing with time?"

"Great!" Ivory proclaimed. "We're right on track."

"Excellent," the eagle replied.

"And you're positive that we are on the right path?" Carl questioned.

"We're always on the right path," Ivory affirmed. This didn't completely satisfy the owl, but it would have to do for now.

When they stopped to eat, Carl removed four individually-packed meals from his satchel. In preparation for the trip, he had carefully selected some of his friends' favorite meals. For Simon, a beautiful array of nuts, including his beloved sunflower seeds. For Ivory, an assortment of fresh fruit, including her favorite, star fruit. For Dee and himself, well, let's just say there are fewer chipmunks in the forest.

A few hours later, Ivory informed the group that it was time to make camp for the evening. "This looks like as good a place as any to tuck in for the night."

When they awoke, they enjoyed another thoughtful meal prepared by Carl before they continued onward. To Ivory's delight, they arrived a few hours later, just minutes after the time she had expected to arrive. Ivory was eager to get closer to the water. She had never seen giant waves like these before. They were huge compared to the waves she and Dee had seen at a smaller beach last summer.

The four friends stood on the hot sand and listened to the beautiful seaside sounds. They were fascinated by the hypnotic rumbling of the waves rolling out to sea and back again with mighty crashes. The peculiar squeals of seagulls filled the air above them. The forest had no seagulls, so the four friends couldn't understand a word the seagulls were saying. It simply sounded like pure chatter, without any meaning.

The friends stood for quite a while, enjoying the salty air and listening to the unfamiliar sounds. They were delighted to see a pod of dolphins swimming near the shore and to hear their distinctive clicks and squeaks. They wished they understood dolphin dialogue. After a while, a pair of owls flew by and landed on a nearby palm tree. Even with noisy seagulls squawking all around them, the friends were able to tune in and understand the owls' conversation about the rhythmic timing of the waves.

The friends spent the next few days thoroughly enjoying their adventure away from Home. They tried unusual foods, slept in new kinds of trees, and even attempted surfing on strips of palm bark. By the time they were ready to leave, three of the friends were quite good at surfing. Simon chose not to try. He preferred to encourage the others from the safety of the beach. Simon enjoyed building sand castles and writing words of encouragement in the sand, such as "Way to go!" His words lasted most of the day, until the tide finally came in and washed them away.

When they got home, the four friends were famished. They had opted to skip one of Carl's planned rest breaks so they could return by sundown. They decided to share one last meal together before returning to their respective trees.

After setting out the final vacation dinner, Carl noted, "I want to thank Ivory for making this trip happen. When she first approached me, I was a bit hesitant. But Ivory did a wonderful job of organizing the experience. She looked at maps and plotted our course. She timed out the trip with precision. She did a great job coordinating where we were going to sleep each night. Ivory, you are quite an efficient event planner."

"Actually," Ivory shrugged, "I just figured if we headed mostly southeast we'd eventually run into it. And we really lucked out finding good places to stay. I wasn't quite sure how that would work out, but I liked where we made camp. I love it when a plan comes together!"

"Hold on a moment," the owl stated. "Are you telling me that you didn't map out the ..."

"Oh, don't worry about it, Carl. We made it, didn't we?"

"Yes, but ..." Carl began.

"Great!" Ivory interjected. "Carl, did you enjoy the trip?"

"Of course I enjoyed it," the owl replied. "That's what I just said."

The parrot raised an eyebrow, "You did?"

"Of course. I was just telling you what a great job you did and how well-planned it was."

"Well, thanks then," the parrot said hesitantly. "And I absolutely loved what I ate. Everything was delicious. In fact, I had some of the best meals I've ever eaten. You're the man!"

"Uh, thanks, I suppose," Carl uttered.

"What do you mean by 'I suppose'? The food totally rocked!"

"Specifically, what did you like about it? Just in case I am arranging meals for you again, I'd like to know exactly what you liked and didn't like. Is there anything you would do differently?"

"All of it was fantastic! I'm not sure what you mean," Ivory said.

Carl needed greater clarification. "Not to sound ungrateful, but how am I supposed to replicate the success of selecting the meals without knowing exactly what you found so enjoyable?"

Xenia and Xander were watching the entire conversation from a nearby branch. Xenia whispered to her apprentice, "Xander, this is the moment you've been waiting for. I know you are ready. Do you feel you are?"

"I am," he whispered confidently.

"Okay," Xenia said. "When you appear to the birds, you do not have to cautiously edge yourself into the conversation from afar. Get as close as you can, and when they least expect it, *bam*! Pop in with your greeting."

"Got it," Xander smiled.

"Hey, we have to have some fun, too," laughed the teacher. "I'll wait over here. This one is all yours."

As Xander turned to make his way toward the birds, Xenia whispered from a short distance away, "Remember, don't share too much."

With a single nod, the young chameleon made his way to his first assignment. Nobody saw him coming, so he nestled in right between Simon and Dee. With his arms wide open, he announced, "Good evening, everyone!"

All four of them swiveled their heads around in surprise. Simon put his wing on his chest to catch his breath. Dee looked as if she were about to pounce.

"Welcome," Ivory said, while Dee took on a more relaxed posture.

"Thank you," Xander replied. "I couldn't help but overhear

your conversation. It sounds like both of you did a great job in planning the trip."

"They did," Simon agreed.

"It also sounds as if you are each saying that you appreciate each other's work in making the trip happen, but your appreciation is not registering," the young chameleon offered.

"Ya know, he's right," Dee stated. "I like this chameleon."

The eagle turned to Xander and asked, "What else can you tell us?"

Xander continued. "Xenia recently taught me that when we compliment someone, we need to think about who we are praising. Otherwise, it's as if we are speaking a foreign language that makes no sense to them."

"So you're saying my feedback to Carl didn't even count?" Ivory asked.

"Interesting question," Xander answered. "I need to get going, but you might wish to ask Carl that."

All eyes turned to the owl. "I didn't get any feedback. I just heard that Ivory liked the food. I do not mean to sound unappreciative, but that does not help me."

"Help you? I couldn't have been more enthusiastic," Ivory exclaimed.

"I think that's the point," Carl replied. "I do not need energetic praise. I want the details."

"But how do the details inspire you? Details don't make you feel good."

"Feedback isn't meant to inspire," the owl explained. "It is meant to drive future behavior."

"Well, for future reference, if you gave me upbeat encouragement like I just gave you, I'd put it on a repeating loop for the whole flight home."

"But how does that serve you?" the owl puzzled. "You will not be able to improve next time without receiving specifics from this time."

Simon softly inserted himself into the conversation. "I think what we're discovering here is that praise must match the needs of the individual who is getting it or it doesn't register as feedback."

Ivory and Carl understood.

Dee, watching the conversation from the sidelines, added, "This reminds me of when we were on the Eastern Tidelands and the seagulls were speaking a different language. Then the pair of owls appeared. The owls spoke our language, so I was able to tune in to what they were saying. I felt like I was eavesdropping, but I couldn't help but listen."

"Exactly," Simon confirmed. "When those around us speak our language, we pay attention. When they do not, we don't even hear them."

Ivory cleared her throat. "So, Carl, I want to tell you that I found your selection of food to be flawless. I specifically appreciate that you considered each of our dietary restrictions. You selected the right meal for each time of day, and each of the meals was well-suited for what we were doing. You prepared light meals for our travels and more substantial meals in the evening. I personally liked the selection of entrées you chose for me. I enjoyed every one of them and wouldn't change a thing."

"Why, thank you," Carl smiled. "And your mapping out of the

trip totally rocked! I had a blast!"

"Excellent!" Ivory grinned. "Ya know, I'm not 100 percent sure you mean that, but it feels good anyway. I'll be hearing that over and over in my head as I fly home."

They all laughed as they reminisced about their adventure and wondered where their next joint vacation would take them.

The young apprentice returned to his wise master. "Nicely done," Xenia praised. "I have one suggestion for you, however. It is best not to sneak up on eagles," she smirked.

"Now you tell me," Xander smiled. His heart raced as he glanced back at Dee.

Chameleon Wisdom

We believe we do a better job at giving feedback than we really do.
—Rick Maurer

Here are two universal truths: We all need feedback. And we do not get enough.

Most of us fail to give as much feedback as we ourselves desire, despite its many benefits and the fact that it costs absolutely nothing. Feedback helps us grow. It reinforces our self-esteem and makes us feel good. The most basic psychological principle tells us that behaviors that are rewarded tend to be repeated.

In the workplace, positive feedback can enhance our sense of achievement, increase motivation, heighten accountability, and lead to greater results. Yet workers regularly cite lack of feedback and recognition as one of their biggest complaints. It is one of the primary reasons people leave organizations.

In our personal relationships, positive feedback builds trust and strengthens connections. Expressing a positive sentiment toward another offers us the opportunity to show our appreciation for their valued contributions and greatest gifts.

When we receive positive feedback, the reward center in our brain becomes stimulated. So whether we are at home or in the workplace, positive feedback creates feelings of being valued and appreciated. This boosts our self-esteem and leaves us open to new and greater possibilities.

Even though positive feedback offers us many benefits, people still do not seem to provide that much of it. Or do they? We may be receiving more feedback than we realize, but since it is given in the wrong style, it does not trigger our hardwiring. As a result, it is discounted, or it does not register as feedback at all.

The standard advice for providing positive feedback does not take personality style into account. Experts typically suggest that positive feedback should be specific, timely, encouraging, sincere, impactful, and regular. It is hard to argue with that advice. However, the true power of positive feedback occurs when people receive praise that triggers their natural hardwiring.

In *Lost in Translation*, the birds screened out the sounds of the seagulls who spoke a different language. But when the owls were nearby, the birds became attentive and tuned in to every word. The owls spoke the language of the forest birds, and they listened. This is exactly how it works with feedback. We tune in to feedback provided in our language — our style. Conversely, we tune out feedback that is offered in a different style, despite its good intentions.

The most effective feedback is tailored to the recipient; it resonates with what is important to that person. Consider each of the four bird styles. *Eagles* value bottom-line results. Therefore, when providing feedback to eagles, focus on what they have accomplished and the impact they have had. Say something like, "You helped us achieve our objective. That allowed us to increase *this* or decrease *that*. Thank you."

Parrots are motivated by enthusiastic praise. Turn up the volume when praising them. Tell them, "You were fantastic!

When you *did this*, you really exceeded my expectations. I totally appreciate everything you did! Great effort and enthusiasm. Thank you so much!"

Contrary to the parrots, *owls* need details. They want to know exactly what they did right and what they can improve next time. Take the time to walk through their project from beginning to end. Be certain to highlight specifics. Your attention to detail will show them that you truly understand the quality of their work.

Doves value genuine and sincere appreciation. They want to know that they made a difference for their coworkers and the people they serve. Share with them, "You truly impacted all of us in a positive way. I appreciate everything you have done. Your role in this project allowed us to support our customers, and I want to thank you for your hard work and dedication."

Imagine giving an eagle feedback as if she were an owl. Or giving an owl feedback as if he were a dove. The words and effort are likely to fall on deaf ears. We all need feedback, but it needs to be given in the right style. Praise given in the wrong language is like white noise. We hear it, but it has no value or meaning.

Be the person who makes someone else's day by providing the recognition they so deeply crave, and personalize the feedback so they receive the full power of the message.

- DON'T LET GOOD WORK GO unnoticed.

- RECOGNIZE THAT ONE-SIZE-FITS-ALL feedback does not work.

- CONSIDER THE STYLE OF THE PERSON to whom you are giving feedback, and provide it to them the way they like it, not the way you like it.

- ACTIVELY LOOK FOR PEOPLE DOING THINGS WELL, then tell them! You may be surprised how many great things you discover.

The Magic Rock

Ivory and Carl watched the sun trace its familiar path across the morning sky. Ivory had found some snow-frozen blueberries, and she shared them with her owl friend. The parrot loved how the berries burst with sweetness in her mouth, as if each one had a joyful surprise in its center. Soon their conversation wound its way to comments about Xenia, their teacher and mentor. They talked about how much the chameleon had helped them over the years and decided to thank her for the impact she had made on their lives. Xenia had a special way of appearing exactly when her friends needed her most, and the pair wanted to give her a gift of appreciation. Now they had to figure out what that would be.

Together they ran through options, but nothing seemed quite right. A caricature drawing of Ivory, Carl, Dee, and Simon from their trip to the Eastern Tidelands? A box of maple-smoked crickets? A framed quotation from Xanadu? They rejected one idea after another until Carl remembered a story that Xenia had shared with them earlier in the year. The chameleon had described an egg-shaped rock that could be found only in the Crystal Cave. She talked about its "magic" powers.

"That's it!" Ivory declared.

"That's what?" Carl asked.

"Let's go to the Crystal Cave, find an egg-shaped rock, and bring it back to her as a gift."

"The cave is far and there's no guarantee we will find it. The unknown variables lower the probability of us locating an egg-shaped rock," the owl hypothesized. "We do not know how big it is, what it looks like, or even where to look once we get there."

"I'm sure we'll find one," the parrot affirmed. "She said they're in the cave."

After some careful consideration, and some prodding by Ivory, Carl reluctantly agreed.

"We will need to prepare for the trip," Carl advised. "We have to consider the tools that we will need to locate the rock and how we will transport it back here. Plus, it will take us a good part of the day to get there, so we need to determine how long the journey will take so we can figure out how much time we can spend at the cave. I would like to make it back before dark."

Ivory said, "It's really not a big deal. Even if we have to stay overnight, we will be home before the sun reaches the midday sky. And I know lots of folks who have traveled to the Crystal Cave for the day and made it back while it was still light. Trust me, we'll be fine."

"So when do you want to go?" Carl asked.

"No better time than the present. Let's go now!"

Given that Ivory knew many others who had traveled to the Crystal Cave and returned in a single day, Carl agreed to leave right away.

They flew past the Great Lake and followed the river as it

twisted its way through the forest. After several hours of flying, Carl grew concerned that the cave was still quite a distance away. The sun had passed the overhead position a few hours ago.

"Don't worry," Ivory reassured him. "It's not far at all. In fact, I believe it's just over these hills."

Carl breathed a sigh of relief. According to his calculations, if they arrived at the cave within the next few minutes, they would have about two hours to explore, find an egg-shaped rock, and make it back before it got dark.

After traveling for another half hour or so, Carl caught sight of a familiar rock formation. He was simultaneously comforted and annoyed. "Ivory," Carl said sternly. "Do you know where we are?"

"Yup. We're almost there," the parrot smiled knowingly.

"Actually, I recognize those rocks from our trip to the Eastern Tidelands. We are still about an hour away."

"That's what I said. We're almost there."

"In what forest does 'almost there' equal an hour?" the owl queried.

"Uh … this one?" Ivory stammered.

Carl was flabbergasted. "I trusted you. You told me you knew where we were going. You told me that this would be a day-trip!"

"Well, I'm mostly right," Ivory suggested. "We will get there today, and we'll have time to look for the rock. We just won't have time to get back by dark. That's pretty close to a win - especially if we find the magic rock."

"I don't want to argue. Let's just get there and find what we are looking for," Carl sighed.

"Hasn't that been the plan all along?" Ivory wondered.

After an hour of flying in silence, the pair followed the winding river to the cave. When they arrived, Ivory was concerned. "I've been in that cave before, and I've never seen a rock that looked like an egg. I think you should try to find it."

Just before Carl headed to the falls, Ivory advised, "Make sure you hit the water right beside that jutting rock." She pointed to a stone protruding from the cliff wall. "If you don't enter at exactly the right spot, you'll slam into a really hard rock," she advised, as she rubbed the top of her head in recollection.

"Got it," Carl replied before he took what felt like a leap of faith. The owl headed precisely where Ivory had instructed. After passing through the ice cold water, he found himself inside the cave. He could not believe his eyes. All around him were shimmering crystals of diverse and spectacular colors and sizes, just like the ones he had seen when he and Simon had watched Ivory create a mandala a few months earlier.

In the meantime, Ivory pushed aside underbrush, checked under stones, and inspected tall grass. She lifted smaller rocks to see if they were hiding anything beneath. All she yielded was a treasure trove of beetles and one very startled snake.

With the owl's ability to see in near darkness, Carl headed deeper into a long tunnel. He saw many rocks, and some sharp looking spikes that hung like cones from the ceiling or grew up from the ground like beams. The owl spotted stones that were long and flat, sharp and pointy, and round and irregular. But he didn't find anything that was remotely egg-shaped.

Carl had nearly given up when he decided to forge onward through a bend in the cave where he suspected few had ventured before him. As he picked up some long, flat slabs of rock, something caught his eye. The brown and muddy tip of a rock stuck out like a dome. He used his claws to wipe away the dirt and discovered a rock shaped like an egg, just as Xenia described it. When he tried to pick it up, he realized it was too heavy for him to move by himself. He called Ivory to provide assistance, and when she arrived, she found Carl staring at the ground.

The parrot had a difficult time seeing in the near darkness, so she bent down to feel the stone. "This is great!" Ivory proclaimed. "We found it!"

"Yes, we found it," Carl confirmed, "but now we need to get it out of here."

They tried lifting it but it was too heavy. Instead, they decided to roll the stone out of the cave so they could look at it in the sunlight. As they rolled the stone across the cave floor, Carl and Ivory got muddier and muddier. Pushing an egg-shaped rock through a cave was hard work for the two birds, and they knew they couldn't roll it all the way home.

Ivory washed the stone with water from the pool at the bottom of the falls, then she and Carl rinsed themselves off in the cool waters.

"This is it?" Carl asked. "It doesn't look like anything special.

Ivory smiled as she shook her body to dry herself. "Xenia said that the magic is inside."

The pair stood quietly staring at the rock as they tried to figure out how to get it home. Ivory broke the silence. "There is no way we are going to leave this thing here. There's gotta be a way to take it with us."

"I understand your desire to give this rock to Xenia, but we need to think this through."

"How about we just take turns carrying it?" Ivory suggested.

"That would be fine, but neither of us can lift it by ourselves," Carl replied. "We need to do this together."

"Okay. How about we grab hold of it and carry it as a team?"

"That does fix the carrying it alone problem, but we won't be able to fly like that," Carl stated.

"Maybe we need to get a flying start and grab it at full speed."

"Here, watch!" Ivory announced confidently.

Ivory backed up and gave herself some room to reach maximum velocity. As she rocketed towards the stone, Carl watched with a disapproving stare. To Ivory's credit, she managed to move the stone — about a stone's length from where it originally sat. She then tumbled in a whirlwind of precious reds, blues, and greens. When she came to a stop, she shook her head and said, "Well, now we know one way that *won't* work!"

The two gazed blankly at the egg-shaped rock for another minute until Ivory offered, "How about we tie a vine around it and we each hold one end of the vine? That oughta do it."

"Nope. That won't work either," Carl replied. "It will just slip out."

"Carl, all you do is cut down my ideas. You're like an idea beaver!"

"I have not yet heard a suggestion that will work. When I hear one, I will be quite complimentary."

"So what do you recommend, oh wise one?" Ivory sniped.

"Let's take this problem apart. One of us can't carry the rock alone. Yet to carry it together, we need to be some distance apart so that we can spread our wings. Utilizing vines sounds appealing, though the rock can slip out." Carl's eyes suddenly got big with inspiration. "How about we wrap the rock in large leaves and then tie long vines around the leaves? That will ensure that the rock stays secure, and it will give us the space to fly. This method will double our lifting power. And if we grab the vines after we already have some speed, the momentum will help us get it off the ground."

Ivory shook her head in disbelief. "So, basically, you've added a few leaves to all of my ideas, and now you want me to celebrate your brilliance?" the parrot protested.

"I am not looking for a celebration. I am looking for a methodology that works," replied the owl.

"You were clearly intent on cutting down all of my ideas, and then you go ahead and use them," Ivory huffed.

"That is not it at all. I was simply seeking a solution. Your ideas were not fully formed. Between the two of us, we have created a workable plan."

"Is that your way of giving me credit?" Ivory said.

"Let me get this straight. You spent an entire day misleading me, and now you want me to revel in your genius?"

"What are you talking about?" Ivory asked. "I didn't mislead you."

"From the beginning of our trip, you continually deceived me about how long it would take to get here. I would never have come today if I knew the real facts about this trip."

"I didn't lie," Ivory snapped defensively. "I believed we could make it."

"You must have said, 'We are almost there' a dozen times," the owl said.

"I wasn't lying. I was being optimistic. If I were to fly here thinking that we might get lost or not find the rock or not be able to make it back today, I would have been discouraged the entire way here. What's the point of that? My intention was simply to be positive."

"You didn't just hold positive thoughts," Carl complained. "You deceived me with your false optimism, and I made decisions on faulty data."

"I like to think positive thoughts, and I like to share what I think," Ivory said.

"But you had no facts to support your belief. I trusted you, and now we are not going to make it home tonight."

After a few more minutes of bickering, they decided to put their differences aside and attempt to carry the rock out of there. Carl wanted to cover as much distance as possible before it got dark so they wouldn't have as far to travel the next day. So off they went, once again, flying in silence as they carried the rock.

Flying with the extra weight was difficult, but neither one complained. When it became too dark to fly any farther, they agreed to make camp for the evening. Their muscles ached, but both birds sulked privately. Ivory made an occasional moaning sound as she cleared a place to sleep.

The next morning, they got up early with a goal of reaching home by noon. The long, quiet flight seemed to take forever.

When they finally got back, they had one last task to complete together. The pair arranged a dinner with some close friends for the next night. Xenia would be the guest of honor, and they would present her with the egg-shaped rock to thank her for sharing all of her wisdom. Ivory wrapped the stone in a beautiful array of flowers, and she and Carl were excited to present it to their chameleon teacher.

At the celebration, Dee and Simon sat between their owl and parrot friends. Simon could sense that something was wrong, but he didn't want to address the issue during this special evening. When Xenia arrived, she was escorted by Xander, who managed to get her there without revealing the true purpose of the event. After welcoming the chameleons to the festivities, Carl retrieved his Hatching Day Hat of Honor from beneath the table and presented it to Xenia. It didn't quite fit her, though she appreciated the sentiment. And Carl was happy to get rid of it.

After a delicious dinner, many of the guests spoke about Xenia and gave examples of how she often abruptly appeared out of nowhere and scared the living begeebers out of them. They talked about the many lessons she had taught them and thanked her for improving their lives.

After listening to the many tales told about the master chameleon, it was time to unveil their gift. With a great flourish, Ivory and Carl lifted the present into the air and spun it around so everyone could see it. Together, they placed it in front of their teacher, friend, and mentor.

Xenia was overwhelmed. While she gently removed the flowers and carefully placed them beside the stone, she thanked everyone for their kind words. After the rock was fully revealed, she slowly rolled it forward and backward with a beaming smile.

"This is one of my favorite wonders in the forest," she told the group. "Inside this stone are beautiful crystals that hold a secret message."

"What's the message?" Ivory shouted.

"I'm glad you asked," Xenia said with a grin. "The message is that we only see what's on the outside and make assumptions about what's on the inside. When you look at this rock and its dull brown-and-gray shell, you might assume that it is nothing special. *So what?* you might wonder. It's a brown-and-gray stone. But I can assure you there is much more to this rock on the inside. It is filled with sparkling crystals, and the only way to know what it looks like inside is to crack it open."

The group promptly gathered around the magical rock. Calls to crack it open rang throughout the group.

Xenia smiled and informed everyone that she would be right back. When she returned, she held a strange looking device she called "The Revealer." She walked over to the stone, glanced at Carl and Ivory, and said, "This reminds me of an important lesson."

Everyone cheered. After all, Xenia was being honored today for having shared so many lessons to those in attendance. The chameleon grinned and said, "Come now. You didn't expect to invite a chameleon to a gathering and not share a lesson, did you?"

"We were hoping you would," Ivory bantered, almost daring her to share just one more nugget of wisdom with all of them.

The group cheered even louder this time. When the chameleon turned her gaze to the stone, a hush fell over the forest. "Look at this amazing rock," she began. "You don't know what's inside. You only know what you see. But if you dig a little deeper, you may be surprised by the beauty you discover."

Everyone hung on her every word. Since she rarely had an opportunity to speak with so many of her followers at one time, she decided to delve a bit deeper. "And so it is with all of you. We see what's on the outside. We see what others do, but we do not know why they do it. In other words, we see actions but not intentions."

Xenia glanced at Carl and said, "Let me give you an example. For some, optimism creates the belief that everything will just work out. These folks tend to make gut decisions and truly believe everything will be okay. For others, decisions are better made based on data and analysis. For the more fact-based among us, optimism can be perceived as unrealistic. And when this optimism is imposed on others, it might even be interpreted as misguided or deceptive."

Carl understood. He was looking at Ivory's behavior as misleading, but really, Ivory was just being hopeful, which is not a bad thing.

Ivory felt vindicated. She knew she was not trying to trick Carl, but he judged her behavior to be deceptive.

Xenia then turned her attention to the parrot and asked, "Would another example be helpful?"

"Uh, sure," the parrot replied, secretly wishing that one example would be sufficient.

"Excellent," smiled Xenia with a subtle wink that only Ivory caught. "Sometimes, when others shoot down ideas, it's not because they are being critical of you. It's because they are analyzing the facts in order to make the right decision. For them, until the problem is completely resolved, there is no cause for celebration."

Ivory understood now that Carl was not being critical. He really just wanted a workable solution.

Xenia lifted The Revealer high into the air above the rock and offered one last piece of advice, "We judge ourselves based on intention, but we judge others based on behavior. Don't just look at what's on the outside. Consider what's on the inside as well. When you understand someone's style, you can determine their intention. And when you do, you shatter all judgment and discover the radiant center that lies at the core of each of us."

Xenia slowly and carefully positioned the device around the egg-shaped stone and, with a mighty crunch, split it in half to reveal …

Chameleon Wisdom

We judge ourselves by our intentions and others by their impact.
— JOHN WALLEN

We are well aware of our own intentions. We understand what motivates us. We are familiar with our deepest fears, hopes, and desires. When things do not go as we have planned or goals are not achieved, we cut ourselves some slack because we judge ourselves on our intention.

We have no access to the intentions others, and, accordingly, do not afford them the same leniency. We only know what we see. Therefore, we judge others based on their observable behaviors and results.

When we wish to gain a deeper understanding of why people behave as they do, we look to the only intentions that we are sure of — *our own*. Subconsciously, we superimpose our intentions on others by looking to what *our* intentions would be if we acted as they did.

Consider a dove watching an eagle confidently and vehemently make her point during a staff meeting. The dove perceives that the issue must be very important to the eagle. The dove knew that he, himself, would only have displayed that level of intensity if it were an issue of utmost importance to him. The dove judged the eagle's behavior based on what would prompt him, as a dove, to act in such an assertive manner. When it came time to make a decision, the dove backed down. The eagle's passion convinced him that the eagle must be right. He assumed the issue was critical to the eagle, and the dove did not want to deny her something of such importance to her. In reality, the eagle was simply expressing her views and had little attachment to her ideas or the issue.

In this scenario, the dove filtered the eagle's actions through the lens of his own intentions. This created an inaccurate interpretation of the eagle's needs and perspective. This demonstrates that we have it backwards. When it comes to ourselves, we should look at what we *do* rather than what we *intend*. For others, instead of considering only behaviors, we should look to what drives particular actions.

Making a shift to consider the intentions of others does not mean we should dismiss dysfunctional behaviors because someone "meant well." Positive intentions should not be used to justify disrespect, poor quality, or failed results. Harmful behaviors should be addressed and people should be held accountable for their actions, in spite of their intentions.

An owl cannot excuse his inability to meet a deadline with the justification that she wanted the project to be perfect before submitting it. Nor can a parrot excuse ignoring critical facts because he likes to make gut decisions based on intuition. Intention should not be used as an excuse.

While brainstorming solutions in *The Magic Rock*, Ivory and Carl each had positive intentions that negatively impacted the other. If they had considered each other's intentions, their conflict would have been minimized — or even avoided.

By understanding each other's internal motivators, we can

look more accurately at the intentions of others. Consider what motivates parrots and owls. *Parrots* are energized by interacting with others. They desire freedom of expression, and they capitalize on opportunities to experience all that life has to offer. They are social, outgoing, and optimistic, and they thirst for adventure. When trying to interpret a parrot's actions, recognize that parrots are guided by the intention to enjoy life, not to avoid responsibility.

Owls seek precision, logic, structure, and clarity. They may ask a lot of questions, but do not take this as a sign of mistrust. They simply intend to do things right the first time. They will take every possible step to ensure quality outcomes. For the owl, if it is not going to be done right, then why do it? Understand that the intention behind the owl's behavior is to ensure reliable, consistent, and accurate results.

Imagine a parrot and owl couple on their day off from work. The parrot wants to have fun and then deal with their chores. The owl would prefer to complete their responsibilities first and then relax. The parrot needs to appreciate that the owl's thinking does not mean he does not intend to have fun. He just wants to finish the work first so it does not weigh him down. Conversely, the owl needs to grasp that it is not the parrot's intention to shirk responsibility. Rather, the parrot lives in the moment and wants to have fun for as long as she can before having to carry out chores.

Now consider what motivates eagles and doves. *Eagles* value autonomy, power, action, and candor. They are driven by an intention to get results, and they push back when something interferes with the achievement of their objectives. Eagles can be blunt and direct if they believe something is getting in the way of their productivity. Their intention is simply to achieve their goal.

Doves crave harmony, stability, comfort, and loyalty. They actively seek to minimize conflict, establish collaboration, and ensure trust and emotional safety. This may cause them to avoid confrontation or ignore glaring issues. Doves simply want everyone to get along. Their intentions are often infused with their need for peace and sensitivity.

Picture an eagle and dove couple. The eagle candidly points out the flaws in their child's school project, while the dove offers unconditional positive support. The eagle is irritated by the dove's lack of honesty, and the dove is offended by the eagle's forthrightness. By understanding the intentions behind their actions, the eagle and the dove can shift from judging each other's behaviors to valuing each other's contributions.

We prefer to be judged by intentions rather than actions or outcomes because we perceive our intentions to be well-meaning. Perhaps it is time to offer that same courtesy to others.

- REFRAME YOUR PERSPECTIVE and seek to understand the positive intentions of others.

- CONSIDER INTENTION prior to making judgments.

- DON'T IMPOSE YOUR INTENTIONS on others. Consider your own style as well as the style of the person with whom you are interacting.

- DON'T JUSTIFY POOR RESULTS or negative treatment of others with your positive intention.

Epilogue

The Journey Home

It was the first day of spring, and the sun had just risen over Home. A light fog floated on the forest floor as Xander stretched his neck to see above the hovering mist. Xenia and her apprentice were out for a morning walk. They saw new life piercing through the nurturing earth around them. The neighborhood trees bared hints of green, and the air smelled fresh and sweet.

As the chameleons walked side by side on the forest floor, Xenia shared stories of her younger days when she was learning how to adapt her appearance to the scenery. She told Xander of the time she attempted to match a raccoon and how, for two days, she looked as if she was wearing a mask.

Although Xander had improved on his ability to shift his color over the past year, he was still having a little difficulty matching rocky terrain.

"You're trying too hard," Xenia noted. "You're attempting to get the stones to adapt to you when, instead, you need to adapt to them."

"Well, it would be a lot easier if they just adapted to me," Xander said with the hint of a smile.

"If only it were that easy," Xenia replied.

"I know," Xander said. "The only thing I can truly change is myself."

They walked together up a slight incline and came across a family of unfamiliar doves enjoying their breakfast. Xander made eye contact with the mother dove, who immediately waved them up. The two chameleons scurried up the tree to join the group.

"Welcome, friends," the father dove said.

"Thank you for inviting us into your home," Xenia replied. "What a lovely crew you have here."

"Oh, thank you. We're quite proud of our little ones," the mother dove responded. "We've got plenty of food. You're welcome to stay for breakfast."

"Thank you so much," Xenia replied, "but don't worry about us. We're fine."

"Really, it's no trouble at all," the father dove said. "It would be our pleasure."

"I'd love to stay," Xenia acknowledged, "but I promised Xander's parents I wouldn't keep him out too long today. We really must be moving on."

"It won't take too long. And what kind of hosts would we be if we didn't feed you? Let me fix you both a little something," the mother dove insisted.

Xenia smiled and respectfully took the meal she was offered. She finished everything she was given. Xander, on the other hand, had recently eaten a large breakfast at home, and he wasn't hungry.

"Don't you like it?" the mother dove asked. "It's good for you. It will help you grow to become a big, strong chameleon like your teacher."

"I'm just not that hungry."

"How about one bite?" the dove encouraged.

Xander complied, and soon the two chameleons continued on their way with a satchel full of food in case they got hungry on their walk. The chameleons made their way past a field of large boulders when a young owl couple spotted them. The male called out, "Where are you going?"

"We're heading to the Great Lake to bring a message to my father," Xenia replied.

"Please tell him we send our regards," the female requested.

"Will do. How's your new tree hollow coming along?"

"Very well," replied the male owl.

"Not so good," countered his wife with a glare.

"Anything I can help you with?" the chameleon offered.

"No, thank you," said the husband. "We just cannot seem to agree on how to arrange the items in the hollow."

"That is because you are not following the plan," she replied.

"That is because your plan is not right," he retorted. "My plan is based on what I have been doing since I was Xander's age."

"Well, my parents taught me the right way to do this, and your way is not it," said the wife.

Xenia waved to the owls, who seemed lost in their conversation. She and Xander continued toward the lake. As they walked on, they could hear the owls continuing their debate until their voices faded into the distance.

As the chameleons approached the Great Lake, Xander spotted a blue flash out of the corner of his eye. A moment later, a green bolt of color whizzed by them so close that they could feel the wind from it on their faces. They quickly realized that the parrots were dive bombing the lake, trying to drop pine cones into a circle of twigs in the center of the water.

"Twenty points," the bright green parrot taunted. "Beat that!"

Just then a blue-and-yellow blur flew by, and another pine cone plummeted towards its target.

"Oh, so close," the green parrot announced.

"Hey, it's Xenia and her new little buddy," the blue parrot noted. "What's shakin'?"

"I'm looking for my father, Xavier. Have you seen him?" Xenia asked.

"Nope," replied the two parrots at the same time. "But hey," added the blue parrot, "we could use your help. We need someone to judge the competition. What do you say?"

"I'd love to help," the chameleon replied, "but I've got a message to deliver, and I need to get Xander back to his parents."

"It'll just take a few minutes," the green parrot pleaded. "We could sure use your help. And I bet that Xander will enjoy watching this."

The young chameleon glanced at his teacher. Seeing his eager eyes, she couldn't say no. "Alright, but just for a few minutes."

After several rounds of judging the target competition, Xenia and Xander thanked the parrots for letting them take part in their game and continued on their way. The pair was circling the outskirts of the lake when they noticed Xavier meditating on a large palm leaf set on a large boulder. His legs were crossed, and his palms rested peacefully on his lap. Without opening his eyes, he warmly greeted his visitors. After catching up for a few minutes,

Xenia delivered her message to her father. She didn't have much time to spend with the master chameleon because the doves, owls, and parrots had eaten up most of their extra time.

Father and daughter shared a few words, stared deeply into each other's eyes for a long moment, hugged, and parted. Then Xenia and Xander began retracing their steps back to Xander's parents. They were almost at Xander's home when he spotted an eagle circling high above. In a flash, the eagle swooped down and landed with a thud in front of the chameleons.

"Hello," the large eagle said.

"Good morning," Xenia replied.

"I noticed that you walked to the Great Lake and are now returning home," he noted.

"That's correct," Xenia confirmed.

"You didn't take the fastest route," the eagle commented.

"You are very observant," the chameleon acknowledged.

"Next time, take the lower pasture and head towards the Great Boulder. From there pass the Council Tree and head south to the Great Lake. That's the best route."

"Thank you so much," said the chameleon. "Your advice is much appreciated."

"You're welcome," the eagle stated. And with that, he was gone.

Xander turned towards the elder chameleon and said, "He seems to have a pretty strong idea about which is the best path to follow."

"Everyone does," Xenia replied.

"But it's more than that, isn't it?" Xander asked.

"Go on," Xenia requested.

"Since you've been teaching me, I have noticed that everyone imposes who they are on others. We saw that several times today."

"Even the doves?" Xenia asked knowingly.

"Even the doves," Xander smirked. "They offered us food that we didn't really want."

"Very observant. But it goes deeper than just imposing food. They imposed kindness. You see, they appreciate kindness from others, so they imposed kindness on us, even when we didn't want it."

"That makes a lot of sense," Xander said.

"Then, we saw the owls. What did they impose on us?"

"They didn't impose anything on us. They imposed on each other their ideas on how the tree hollow should be organized."

"Ah, the owls," Xenia reflected. "They often have such a clearly defined view of how things should be done that they impose their way on others."

Xander hopped over a small branch and said, "And you gotta love the parrots."

"What did they impose?"

"Well, they were just having fun, but they imposed that on us, too," Xander explained.

"You're right," Xenia confirmed. "They imposed on us their desire to play when we had a job to do."

Xander turned to watch several chipmunks scurrying up a tree, and then concluded, "And that brings us back to the eagle. He imposed his path on us. But I'm guessing it goes beyond that."

"Yes, it does," Xenia agreed. "Eagles often speak with such confidence and conviction that it's hard to say no to them, even if they are just sharing an opinion. They impose their ideas on others."

The two chameleons made their way back to Xander's home. Just before Xenia left him, she advised her young friend, "Remember, Xander, the secret to being a great chameleon is to adapt to others and not impose who you are on them."

He nodded a quick thank you.

Xenia smiled. Just before she faded into the lush green grass, she said, "You have returned home to where you began. But now you see with new eyes. You have grown much over this past year, and it is time for you to live what you have learned. Share what has been entrusted to you. It is time for you to take flight in every aspect of your life."

- The End -

The Chameleon

About the Author

MERRICK ROSENBERG is the CEO of Take Flight Learning. He is an accomplished entrepreneur, keynote speaker, facilitator and author. In 1991, he co-founded Team Builders Plus, which paved the way for team building as we know it. In addition to innovating more than a dozen team building programs, he led DISC personality styles training for more than 20,000 people. In 2012, Merrick went on to found Take Flight Learning to bring the four styles to the world in a more meaningful and impactful way.

Merrick is an engaging speaker who has shared his insights with many organizations such as TEDx, Association for Talent Development, Society for Human Resource Management, Project Management Institute and Vistage International.

Merrick has worked with small and mid-sized businesses as well as more than half of the Fortune 100 companies. Over the years, Merrick has shared his wisdom with organizations such as AAA, Adidas, Aramark, Bank of America, Blue Cross Blue Shield, Campbell Soup Company, Chase, Colgate Palmolive,

Comcast, ExxonMobil, Ford Motor Company, General Electric, GlaxoSmithKline, Hewlett-Packard, InterContinental Hotels Group, Johnson & Johnson, L'Oreal, Lockheed Martin, Lufthansa, Nabisco, National Institute of Health, NBCUniversal, Nestle Purina, Novartis, PECO Energy, Pepsi, Philadelphia Eagles, QVC, Roche, Samaritan Hospice, Temple University, UnitedHealthcare, Verizon and many more. Merrick has also led sessions for government agencies such as the Environmental Protection Agency, Homeland Security, Interpol, and the Social Security Administration, as well as the US Army, Navy, Air Force and Marines.

Merrick received his MBA from Drexel University, who selected him as their Alumni Entrepreneur of the Year. Under Merrick's leadership, his companies have received numerous awards including New Jersey Business of the Year by NJ Biz magazine, one of the Fastest Growing Companies in the U.S. by Inc. magazine, and on numerous occasions, one of the *Fastest Growing Companies* and *Best Places to Work* in the Philadelphia region by the Philadelphia Business Journal.

His first book, *Taking Flight!*, changed the way people think about personality styles.

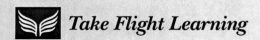 *Take Flight Learning*

Take Flight Learning reimagined the age-old DISC model by linking the four letters to visually appealing birds and providing a more brain-friendly and engaging approach to learning.

Take Flight Learning offers a variety of DISC training programs, products and services. The Taking Flight with DISC profile and workshop provide the foundation for understanding yourself and others. This groundbreaking session takes DISC training to new heights, as people learn to flexibly adapt to the people and situations in their lives. The Chameleon Leader and Chameleon Selling programs build on the Taking Flight with DISC session to transform leadership and selling skills.

Through a growing network of affiliates around the world, Take Flight Learning offers consultants the opportunity to grow their practice like never before. DISC certifications are available for consultants and in-house trainers who want to reinvent how to teach people about the styles.

Merrick Rosenberg is available as a keynote speaker to enliven conferences with DISC wit and wisdom.

Praise for The Chameleon

The lessons in this engaging book pack a powerful punch. With Rosenberg's remarkably perceptive insights, we can finally understand the particular forces that drive our behavior and interact with others more successfully than ever!
— **Marshall Goldsmith**, author of the *New York Times* and *Wallstreet Journal* #1 Best Seller *Triggers*

The Chameleon breathes life into the DISC behavioral styles by giving you characters and stories that you will see yourself in. More importantly it provides wisdom that you will hold onto, internalize and implement more than you ever could with your DISC profile alone.
— **Mark Goulston**, author *"Just Listen" Discover the Secret to Getting Through to Absolutely Anyone*

This book is filled with practical ways to build strong relationships and winning teams. Merrick Rosenberg has shown he's not just a great speaker, he's a great writer as well.
— **Ron Jaworski**, ESPN Analyst

Some will remember the fables; others will remember the lessons. But everyone will feel the impact of these powerful truths that can transform even the most challenging relationships. Every boss, every parent, every coach, every friend — read this!
— **Michael Wilkinson**, author of *The Secrets of Facilitation*

Through a series of cleverly written and relatable fables, *The Chameleon* brilliantly conveys the complexities and deepest truths of what it means to be human — living an authentic life, honoring and embracing the differences in others, and staying true to who we are yet learning how to adapt and change. Rosenberg masterfully combines his gift for storytelling with the depth of who he is as a teacher, business consultant and expert in human behavior.
— **Patricia Leuchten**, President and CEO, The Avoca Group

Merrick Rosenberg's collection of fables share timeless principles that challenge the way you think and act. *The Chameleon* is thought-provoking and transformational. This book should be required reading for anyone who pursues happiness and prosperity.
— **Vince Stango**, Chief Operating Officer, National Constitution Center

The Chameleon provides great insight into how to build prosperous relationships in business and in life. It will open your eyes to understanding different personalities and why it's important to treat others like they need to be treated vs. how you want to be treated.
— **Paul Muse**, President and Chief Executive Officer, 1st Advantage Federal Credit Union

If it's true that the most self-aware people are the most successful, those who read *The Chameleon* are destined for greatness. Rosenberg firmly establishes himself as a thought leader as he makes learning about yourself easy and enjoyable.
— **Sue Schick**, Chief Growth Officer, UnitedHealthcare

The chameleon wisdom contained in this book should serve as a valuable addition to any educator's collection — a true gem for teachers to understand themselves, their students and the dynamics in the classroom. Rosenberg captures the essence of how and why people get along and how they can create harmony, not just in school, but in any setting.
— **Salvatore J. Illuzzi**, Ph.D., Superintendent of Schools, Cinnaminson Township Public Schools

This book provides practical wisdom through captivating storytelling that is applicable and influential throughout the many aspects of your life. *The Chameleon* provides deep understanding of how the styles interact and how to get the most out of working together to fulfill your mission. Merrick's books continue to make me a better CEO, husband, and parent.
— **Kevin Havens**, CEO, Allied Health Media

When Merrick Rosenberg introduced the four bird styles to the world, I could never have imagined the impact they would have. *The Chameleon* teaches lessons about personality that help us to be the best we can be as we build enduring relationships and drive results. This is a book you should read, share and live.
— **Neil Aaron**, Senior Vice President, News Corporation

We have all learned the truism that "perception is reality." Merrick's engaging stories about eagles, parrots, doves, and owls teach us how our personality shapes our perceptions and how other peoples' personalities shape theirs. With this knowledge we can navigate past inaccurate perceptions and towards real communication and understanding. A great, instructive read.
— **Steve Johnson**, Rear Admiral, U.S. Navy (retired), Vistage Chair and Executive Coach

The Chameleon is a modern day Aesop's fables for people who deal with people, not only at work but in their personal lives as well. In each and every scenario, I was able to pick out the personality traits of co-workers, friends, family and myself. A great follow-up to Taking Flight with DISC and is now on my must read list for Leadership Development.
— **Terri Fanz-Falzone**, Sr. Human Resources Manager, TE Connectivity

Merrick Rosenberg has done it again. A few years ago, I discovered I was a strong eagle personality. That enabled me to adjust my behavior when interacting with doves, parrots and owls. Now, I am finding new insight as to how to be a chameleon. Powerful, practical and informative.
— **Gail Ruopp**, Executive Director, Flaster/Greenberg PC

As a CEO, I am always looking for ways to break down barriers to misunderstanding and improve communication throughout my organization. The fables in *The Chameleon* illustrate how understanding communication styles can help people connect more effectively. I strongly encourage business leaders to introduce this book to their entire staff and tag along on an interesting journey through the forest.
— **Bob Rosania**, CEO, Ehmke Manufacturing Company

Merrick Rosenberg soars again with *The Chameleon* as his fables and bird styles teach us real-world applications helpful in both our personal and professional lives. This book is filled with sound advice for life-long learners of any age.
— **Michael Toscani**, Research Professor/Fellowship Director, Rutgers, The State University of New Jersey

In *The Chameleon*, Merrick Rosenberg uses his bird take on the DISC personality styles to teach readers about the different ways people work and communicate. His stories demonstrate how different personality types can go beyond just getting along to thriving together. Big props to Merrick!
— **Jay Scott**, Executive Director, Alex's Lemonade Stand Foundation

The Chameleon was a quick and easy read. I found it interesting how I related to different characters in different situations, which as a leader in my organization, reinforced my belief about inclusion and adaptation — getting the right people in the right seats and playing to people's strengths. This is not just a business book as its lessons apply in all aspects of our lives!
— **Rob Curley**, South Jersey President, TD Bank

Merrick Rosenberg's style is engaging and *The Chameleon* is a quick and easy read. The fables are practical and filled with real life situations you can relate to both personally and professionally. It's one of those books you can read over and over with a new takeaway each time. I highly recommend it.
— **Kristie Pappal**, Vice President of Human Resources, Philadelphia Eagles

CPSIA information can be obtained
at www.ICGtesting.com
Printed in the USA
LVOW10s2317141116

512983LV00001B/89/P

ABOUT THE AUTHOR

Joanne Koenig Coste is a recognized expert on Alzheimer's disease. She developed her approach after her middle-aged husband was diagnosed with progressive dementia and has practised as a family therapist for over thirty years. During that time she has written and lectured widely on the illness and has also appeared on numerous television shows, including the *NBC Nightly News with Tom Brokaw*.

PRAISE FOR
Learning to Speak Alzheimer's

'I know of virtually no one who can match Joanne Koenig Coste's knowledge and commitment in the area of Alzheimer caregiving. She is unswerving in her dedication to the patient and family. No one is more well suited to "speak Alzheimer's" than Joanne Koenig Coste.'

– Dennis J. Selkoe, M.D., Harvard Medical School

Learning to Speak
Alzheimer's

The New Approach to Living
Positively with Alzheimer's Disease

■ ■ ■

Joanne Koenig Coste

Vermilion
LONDON

To TEDDIE, my beloved husband,
who provided the structural and emotional space
to pen these pages, along with reams of computer
paper, Massenet and Mozart in the background,
silence when necessary, breakfast in bed, lectures as
needed, and love.

And to PAUL RAIA, a.k.a. "Dr. Know,"
who for more than two decades has led thousands
of families to more positive and productive places
with his witty style, habilitative wisdom, and
compassionate advice.

12

Copyright © 2003 by Joanne Koenig Coste
Forewordcopyright © Robert N. Butler, M.D.

Joanne Koenig Coste has asserted her right to be identified as the author of this
work in accordancewith the Copyright, Designs and Patents Act, 1988.

First published in 2003 by Houghton Mufflin Company.
Published in 2003 by Vermilion,
an imprint of Ebury Press, Random House,
20 Vauxhall Bridge Road, LondonSW1V 2SA

www.randomhouse.co.uk

Addresses for companies within The Random House Group Limited can be found at:
www.randomhouse.co.uk/offices.htm

The Random House Group Limited Reg. No. 954009

Book design by Victoria Hartman

A CIP catalogue record is available for this book from the British Library

ISBN 9780091886721

This book gives **non-specific,** general advice and should not be relied on as
a substitute for proper medical consultation. The author and publisher
cannot accept responsibility for illness arising out of the
failure to seek medical advice from a doctor.

Penguin Random House is committed to a sustainable future for
our business, our readers and our planet. This book is made from
Forest Stewardship Council® certified paper.

Printed and bound in Great Britain by Clays Ltd, Elcograf S.p.A.

Acknowledgments

This book has taken a very long time to research and write. My ideas for living through the process of Alzheimer's disease, and doing so with an occasional smile, have been enriched by the feelings expressed by the patients and care partners I have worked with over the past three decades. My suggestions have been validated by a multitude of professionals who daily make life kinder for this very special fellowship of memory-impaired adults and those who love them.

I've designed the book to underscore my philosophy of living in the patients' world — of reaching them through their remaining emotions, and, when words fail, "listening" to their eyes. I have attempted to capture the feelings of those whose verbal language is failing in my poems at the opening of each chapter. I hope this will assist the reader in comprehending the emotion and the remaining cognition behind the loss of memories.

I am deeply grateful to my children, Scott, Wendy, Kristen, and Jason, who have always been the root of my strength and dearly loved. Many thanks also to Mimi and Grampy, who said, "Of course you can"; to Todd, for his hugs and warm words; to Garrett, who learned to say "Just a minute and I'll get her" as part of his daily routine; and to my precious darlings, Shay, GG, Jamie, Ty, and Hunter, whose faces beam at me from a desktop photo and keep me centered.

From deep within my heart I thank Nancy Stone Hindlian and Linda Gibson, who have taught me a deeper and more profound meaning of the word "sister." To Carrie Jochelson, Dr. Dilar Acar, Dr. Jeanne

Richard, and Cheryl Weinstein—thank you for teaching me how to listen to myself. I offer this book up to heaven as well—to Helen Stone and Paul Wilson for snapshots of life reflected through loving eyes.

I joyfully acknowledge Muriel Baum, Dick Blinn, Jerry Flaherty, Paul McCarty, Walter Ohanian, Dan O'Leary, Dr. Harold Schiff, Dr. Dennis Selkoe, Mike Splaine, Dr. Marrott Sinex, Marilyn Stasonis, and a myriad of other health care professionals who were there beside me in the earliest days of pioneering compassionate best-practice efforts for those with Alzheimer's disease. Thanks also to Mark Ailinger and Kate Salmon, who continue to help.

For my friends Lois Pecora, Paul Raia, and Elaine Silverio, who have sat beside me as facilitators of early-stage patient groups for many years, thanks for the sharing, the laughter, the untamed joy, and the tears. You have given unconditionally and helped thousands—how lucky I have been to share this journey with you.I must thank Laura van Dam, editor extraordinaire, for believing in this book from the beginning—her sense of what's right and her compassion go hand in hand; Erica Avery, who has made this process much smoother; Janet Silver, publisher and editor-in-chief, for standing so firmly behind this endeavor; Bridget Marmion, director of marketing, and Lori Glazer, executive director of publicity, whose support for this book has been gratifying and exhilarating; Suzanne Cope and Gracie Doyle, whose thoughts and energy in the marketing and publicity for this book have already been extraordinary; Peg Anderson, manuscript editor, who showed me wonderful new ways to be a writer; and all the other great people at Houghton Mifflin.

Thanks to Bill Patrick, who initially edited my words into a book that I'm proud to have written. To my agent, Jeff Kleinman, of Graybill and English, I offer much gratitude for sharing many joyous accomplishments and for pushing, applauding, and being there at all hours to write with me, guide me, chastise gently, and lead me on this journey into myself. You are the greatest, Jeff.

Above all, this book would not have been possible without countless patients and the care partners who have helped them. I am grateful to everyone who shared anecdotes, joys, fears, tears, and laughter with me. Each person is a part of my memory bank, and each has made my heart fuller. Thank you.

Contents

Foreword by Robert N. Butler, M.D.   ix

PART ONE
Learning about Alzheimer's

1. The Ticking Meter   3
2. Seeking a Correct Diagnosis   13
3. What to Expect: Making the First Decisions   20
4. Habilitation, the New Approach   32
5. Seeing the World from the Patient's Perspective   48

PART TWO
The Five Tenets of Habilitation

6. Tenet #1: Make the Physical Environment Work   61
7. Tenet #2: Know That Communication
   Remains Possible   77

8. Tenet #3: Focus on Remaining Skills   85

9. Tenet #4: Live in the Patient's World:
   Behavioral Changes   108

10. Tenet #5: Enrich the Patient's Life   127

PART THREE

Beyond Habilitation

11. Caring for the Care Partner   149

12. Receiving Home Care   163

13. Receiving Care Outside of a Family Home   176

14. Inspiration   193

Glossary   203

Appendix: Good Food for People with Alzheimer's   206

Further Resources   212

Index   233

Publisher's Note

We believe that *Learning to Speak Alzheimer's* is destined to be an essential text throughout the world for those suffering from Alzheimer's disease and their families, friends and carers. Nevertheless, you may find that some of the information provided, particularly in Part Three, is very specific to the United States of America. If in those instances you would like information more pertinent to the United Kingdom, we recommend that you contact the Alzheimer's Society (see Further Resources on page 212).

Foreword

Alzheimer's disease is one of the great scourges of old age in the twenty-first century. Devastating, irreversible, and progressive, it robs millions of older Americans of their use of language, reasoning, memory, and judgment. Alzheimer's destroys a lifetime of memories and whittles away at the core of a person's identity. It irrevocably alters the lives of families who have a member with Alzheimer's, often necessitating a painful redefinition of the primary relationship between parents and children, between husband and wife. Alzheimer's disease exacts an enormous emotional, physical, and psychological toll upon caregiving family members.

The third most costly disease after heart disease and cancer, Alzheimer's places an enormous burden on the U.S. health care system. Experts estimate that the dollar cost to the nation of caring for people with Alzheimer's was more than $100 billion in 2002, with neither Medicare nor most private health insurance providers covering the long-term care that most patients eventually need. The cost to American businesses in 2000 was more than $61 billion, with the costs of absenteeism, productivity loss, and employee replacement as a result of family caregiving consuming $36.5 billion.

In 2002, 45 percent of the National Institute on Aging (NIA) research budget was earmarked for research on Alzheimer's disease. That percentage represents a major advance over the funding level in 1975, when I became the founding director of the NIA and identified the study of Alzheimer's and other dementias as a key priority. From 1955 to 1962 I had worked at the National Institute of Mental Health, studying healthy aging and dementias full-time, and I continued to do so part-time thereafter. When I began to prioritize the research agenda at the NIA, my clinical and scientific interest in dementia contributed to the decision to promote research in Alzheimer's.

Up to that time "senility" was the popular term used to describe all the dementias. Patients, doctors, and scientists alike viewed a diagnosis of dementia with a sense of hopelessness. Their pessimism stemmed from the false belief that senility — the dementias — was an inevitable result of aging. Dementias were often presumed to be the result of cerebral arteriosclerosis (colloquially known as "hardening of the arteries"); researchers didn't recognize preventive measures for that condition until the 1970s. In that era, doctors assumed that Alzheimer's disease was a rare form of senility that began before age sixty.

The image of the senile man or woman, the traditional stereotype of old age in Western society, was translated into hesitancy on the part of social and scientific policymakers to invest in research into the basic biology of aging. The rationale was that money spent on aging research was money wasted on the decrepit and incompetent.

In 1975 the government funded only twelve grants for the study of "brain aging," totaling $700,000. But concern was building about Alzheimer's, eventually resulting in the successful mobilization of federal and private philanthropic resources. In 1979, twelve independent groups for Alzheimer's disease existed in the United States and Canada. Dr. Donald Tower, director of what was then known as the National Institute of Neurological and Communicative Disorders and Stroke, and I brought together representatives of those groups and urged them to unite. Their consolidation constituted the beginnings of the present-day Alzheimer's Association.

Around the same time, the public began to learn about the disease through the media. Princess Yasmin Aga Khan appeared on *20/20* with Hugh Downs and spoke compassionately about her mother, the former movie actress Rita Hayworth, who was afflicted with the disease. Abigail Van Buren, of "Dear Abby" fame, also helped develop awareness of the disease through her column. And the National Institute on Aging in conjunction with the Neurology and Mental Health Institutes sponsored a symposium led by neurologists Robert Katzman and Robert Terry, along with Kathryn Bick of the Neurology Institute, that focused on Alzheimer's disease. The book that resulted from the symposium, *Alzheimer's Disease: Senile Dementia and Related Disorders* (New York: Raven Press, 1978), stimulated research in the field.

Senator Thomas Eagleton and Congressman Joseph Early supported the initial efforts to make Alzheimer's a national research priority. Today the federal government, voluntary organizations, and private industry provide support for research, public education, and critical services to people with Alzheimer's and their families. This funding has enabled scientists to make valuable progress in understanding the genetic, molecular, and cellular aspects of the basic biology and neurobiology of aging. And clinical trials are now under way to test potentially useful drugs for Alzheimer's. But until effective treatments are found, we must continue to work on behalf of the growing number of people who deal with the disease.

First we must redesign and expand Medicare to finance long-term-care services at home, in the community, and, when necessary, in nursing homes. And we need to ensure proper care at home, where 75 percent of the care for people with Alzheimer's takes place. An Alzheimer's patient requires constant care and vigilance, often for many years.

As *Learning to Speak Alzheimer's* makes clear, family members and others intimately involved in caring for patients need support in finding constructive ways to handle the inevitable stress, tension, and frustration of dealing with this extraordinarily challenging disease. Supportive professional advice is essential in the day-to-day struggles of caregivers, who constantly have to overcome their sense of helplessness as they observe the ongoing mental and physical erosion of a loved one.

Finding ways to provide such advice is in the best interest of both the government and employers. Caregivers often have to juggle home, child care, and adult caregiving responsibilities with paid employment, necessitating that they take off many hours and days from work to fulfill their obligations. The Alzheimer's Association estimates that each full-time employed caregiver of a patient with Alzheimer's loses, on average, about twenty-four days a year.

With the aging of the baby boomers, government experts estimate that the number of people diagnosed with Alzheimer's disease will dramatically increase, and costs will become unsustainable. Clearly, it is critically important to accelerate drug research and find more effective means of prevention and treatment. Our society must rise to this scientific and cultural challenge. The search for a cure has expanded in recent years through research to determine genetic and environmental factors that cause Alzheimer's. Neuroscience is making great advances, propelled by cell biology, chemistry, genomics, and imaging technology, and in the past ten years, some exciting findings have provided clues to the causes of the disease. But private as well as public investment in research must be accelerated, with more funding for drug discovery and development by academic laboratories and biotechnology companies.

As people live longer, their susceptibility to Alzheimer's disease increases. Today, for every five-year group beyond age sixty-five, the percentage of people with the disease doubles. Until a solution is found, that statistic will not change. One quarter of the population over seventy-five will continue to be stricken, and attitudes toward old age will continue to be shaped by the fear of cognitive decline.

Old age without dementia will be the medical triumph of the twenty-first century.

— Robert N. Butler, M.D.,
    president and chief executive officer,
    International Longevity Center — U.S.A.,
    and professor of geriatrics and adult development,
    Mount Sinai School of Medicine

PART ONE

Learning about Alzheimer's

1

The Ticking Meter

My head feels like an old depot,
worn by time and tears.
No more locomotives passing through,
café filled with tales and baggage.
The old depot's barren now.
There has been a great brain robbery.

ONE COOL SPRING DAY in 1971, the kind that makes New Englanders smile at each other, I was driving with my husband down the main street of a small coastal town south of Boston. I spotted a parking space in front of our destination, a café where we dined frequently, sharing chowder, fried clams, gigantic iced teas, and dreams of the future.

I told my husband, "Look, there's a parking space. Not only that — there's money in the meter."

"I'm glad," he murmured, seeking my eyes through his sunglasses. "But I think my meter is running out."

His metaphor fell on deaf ears. With a new life growing inside me — our fourth child — I may have been unwilling to accept his meaning.

At the time my husband's lapses in memory seemed innocuous. He might forget a neighbor's name or neglect to stop at the store or forget where the ignition was in the car, but I was clever at disregarding the hints of medical illness. After all, he frequently drove different cars as part of his advertising business, and he was so busy; keeping up with minor details was too much to expect. *The situation will improve when we move into a new house,* I told myself, or *when the children are older,* or *when someone in the medical community will listen to what I am saying.*

We moved, the children grew, and the improvement never happened. We were near financial ruin. Customers weren't calling us back; new jobs weren't coming our way. He had ever greater difficulty focusing and organizing his thoughts, sometimes rewriting ad copy he had finished the day before. Once so gentle, docile, and fun to be around, he became frustrated and angry. My mantra continued whenever I was awake: "Things will be so much better when —" When?

Our journey into the world of dementia began in 1971, when no guideposts, advocates, manuals, or support groups were available to help us. The National Alzheimer's Association would not be organized for another decade. My husband was only in his forties, and I did not believe that his forgetfulness was a natural part of aging. The children chided their father occasionally about his "absent-mindedness" but seemed to see nothing deeper. The prescription for Valium to treat his supposed "depression" was refilled many times. And sometimes my husband unwittingly doubled the dose or forgot to take it at all.

Always well dressed in the past, my handsome, athletic husband began to need help matching his suit, tie, and shirt. I started to lay out his clothes for the next day before we went to bed at night. I made sure to tell him what fun I had selecting the outfits, but I was embarrassed to be doing this task. I never mentioned it to others.

Then in 1973, a major stroke paralyzed him on one side, and I replaced the Brooks Brothers suits with sweatsuits, which he soon stained with food. The stroke took away his language ability, transforming a man who had made his living through eloquent writing into someone who had to rely entirely on words of one syllable. Neurologists and physical therapists told me not to expect any improvements in his speech though he did learn to walk again, ever so slowly, with a leg brace and a walker. Life was very hard for all of us, but it was especially horrible for my husband. He became frustrated beyond comprehension.

At times he did not seem to recognize our children or me. Sometimes he appeared thoroughly perplexed about our home. I remember him angrily rattling the doorknob in an effort to go outside but not being able to open the door. And yet I also recall his having enough of his former self that when he looked at our young baby, tears would run down his face.

His abilities continued to decline. As soon as I became the least bit comfortable with his current condition, he would take another step in the downhill progression of dementia. I felt completely overwhelmed. At times I was diapering both our youngest child and my husband. *There's no way I can do this,* I would think to myself.

Finally things came to a head. My husband kept opening the door to go outside — as if to escape from what was happening to him — and my toddler would follow him out. Soon our son started trying to open the door and walk out on his own (this was before safety devices were so readily available). I realized I had to act — proactively, positively, and immediately, before my husband and son left home and got lost. I installed a new handle higher on the door, leaving the old knob intact but disabled. My son could no longer reach the door. More incredibly to me, my husband didn't understand the concept of the new handle: he would repeatedly go over to the door, try the old knob, and think that the door was broken.

This tiny event made me realize that I could make some changes in the way we were living. I could stop walking on eggshells, in fear of what would happen next, and start making a positive difference in our surroundings and in my approach to his illness. I'm a very competitive person, and I started thinking of the entire situation as a game — a brand-new game I wanted to win. I knew I had to get suited up and be ready to play. Each daily task — eating, dressing, toileting, everything — was a new inning, a new round in this game.

I stopped making excuses for the changes in his behavior and the decline in his cognitive functions. The neurologist had told me that my husband's disease was progressive and would be fatal — and in an odd way, that knowledge helped me. It gave me the energy I needed to cope with what he and I both faced, because I knew that the situation would not go on forever.

I vowed to learn to live with this person who was inhabiting the body of the man I cherished. I had to detach myself emotionally from the man my husband used to be and live now with the man he had become. The task at hand — this minute, and every minute of every day — was to ensure my family's survival; I couldn't waste time focusing on my lot in life. I had to deal with the reality of today.

I decided not to heed the hospital social workers who told me that my husband would be "fine" if he went to live at an institution for the mentally ill or at a nursing home for the elderly, where he would be with others suffering from dementia. In that era, I did not trust that hospital and nursing-home workers would try to connect with him. And I knew that if he stayed at home, I could still reach parts of this man. A great deal of the time, his emotions seemed akin to mine. If I can reach him on an emotional level, I thought, instead of on a verbal or cognitive one, maybe life can be less threatening and frustrating for him.

I started a two-part list of issues related to his illness. Those elements that I thought could be changed, ameliorated, or implemented I put in part one. The elements that no amount of concentrated effort could ever change I listed in part two. I wrote "improved mobility" on the first list, while I relegated "return of speech" to the second. I placed "daily laughter" on the list of goals that could be implemented and "planting the garden" on the list of those that could not. Eventually my lists filled a spiral-bound notebook, with several hundred entries.

After putting into practice the ideas and goals on the first list, I found that a smile from my husband, calmness in our household, meant a win for all of us. I wanted to laugh at the end of the day, not curl up in a corner or break down in despair.

From the items in my notebook I developed five simple tenets, which I now teach to people who care for patients with Alzheimer's disease or related forms of progressive dementia such as vascular dementia, Pick's disease, and Lewybody disease. These ideas are the basis for the humanistic approach to caring that I call "habilitation." The literal meaning of habilitate is "to clothe or dress," but I use it in the sense of "to make capable," which is actually an older meaning of the word. A habilitated person with dementia can live using his or her upper limits of function, intellect, emotion, and spirit. Using the tenets of habilitation, both patients and care partners can feel successful at what they do, rather than feeling constantly weighted down. (I prefer the terms "care partner" or "habilitator" to "caregiver," which assumes less involvement on the part of the patient.)

The following are the tenets that I developed, first for my own use at home and later for the use of other patients with dementias.

1. *Make the Physical Environment Work.* Simplify the environment. Accommodate perceptual loss by eliminating distractions.
2. *Know That Communication Remains Possible.* Remember that the emotion behind failing words is far more important than the words themselves and needs to be validated. Although many losses occur with this disease, assume that the patient can still register feelings that matter.
3. *Focus Only on Remaining Skills.* Value what abilities remain. Help the patient compensate for any lost abilities without bringing them to his or her attention.

4. *Live in the Patient's World.* Never question, chastise, or try to reason with the patient. Join her in her current "place" or time, wherever that may be, and find joy with her there.

5. *Enrich the Patient's Life.* Create moments for success; eliminate possible moments of failure, and praise frequently and with sincerity. Attempt to find humor wherever possible.

These tenets require continuous examination of how the patient thinks, feels, communicates, compensates, and responds to change, emotion, and love. Improving understanding in these areas can lead to the biggest successes in treatment.

Along with my direct experience, my decades of work with professional and family care partners have shown that the habilitation approach *works.* Having worked with thousands of patients and care partners over the years, I have come to know that even people with fatal neurological illnesses still possess the innate drive to maximize their potential. After observing the success of the habilitation approach, colleagues and friends began to study and implement the tenets themselves, easing the burden of care partners, developing activities for Alzheimer's patients, studying those in long-term care, and addressing their special architectural and interior design needs. All of these researchers from varying disciplines have long believed in and studied the innate drive that remains in people with neurological diseases such as Alzheimer's. This shared belief has led to a clearer understanding of why we should continue to focus on patients' positive aspects and remaining skills.

During the years I care partnered with my husband, I clarified the tenets, and both he and I were able to succeed at living under our changed circumstances. When he died in 1976, I moved back to my parents' home with our four children, whose ages ranged from four to sixteen. I had told my parents that I wanted to stay with them just for a few weeks to figure out what I should do with the rest of my life; instead I stayed for fifteen years. The children grew up, and I bandaged cut fingers and injured spirits. They participated in Pop Warner football, Little League baseball, high school soccer, track, and championship swimming. They found friendship and love and went on to colleges and careers. Now that they are enriching the lives of others, I often wonder how they would have matured without the years of turmoil and distress, fear of the unknown, and terror of the known that they endured. Perhaps support and love for all of our family — my husband included — offset family tragedy.

After moving in with my parents, I immediately began working as a nursing assistant in a nursing home run by a local hospital. I soon became director of restorative services, which let me initiate a program to try to help several residents who had progressive dementias — and who at that time bore such lofty diagnoses as "organic" and "chronic" brain syndrome. Before long, newly admitted people wanted to be included in the program, which was based on the habilitative tenets described above. I led daily sessions with the patients, worked with the care partners at the facility, and developed a support group for spouses. I have been leading such groups continually since 1978, and this work remains a great joy in my life.

The nursing home developed a special-care unit for the patients in the program, and soon we recognized that they were doing much better cognitively than they had done before and were participating more fully in daily living activities, such as dressing and bathing. All of the patients appeared calmer, which meant that their medications could be reduced. In this unit, restraints were removed; hugs were instituted.

After successfully mentoring the staff and performing daily cognitive and supportive interactions with a population that grew to comprise more than half of the patient roster at the facility, I attempted to have this new kind of care — the habilitative approach — recognized by state and national regulatory agencies concerned with confidentiality and the right to a private diagnosis. But in the 1970s, civil libertarians and others were loath to have specific beds set aside for patients with dementias. They were concerned that such groupings would reveal the patients' diagnoses, which would be an invasion of privacy.

I was very lonely during that time. I had no one to talk to about changing the scene for cognitively impaired adults. Alzheimer's was beginning to be given as a diagnosis, even though it was treated as a brand-new discovery; but except for a few colleagues at the nursing home, no one was willing to listen to my ideas. I was so elated when I discovered John Panella at Cornell University, who was studying the impact of special programming on patients with Alzheimer's disease at a day care facility in White Plains, New York. At last I had discovered someone else who believed that we could make a difference in the lives of Alzheimer's patients.

The establishment in 1980 of the National Alzheimer's Association gave me and the growing number of concerned individuals and organizations renewed courage to fight for specialized housing and programming. By 1981 the program at the nursing home where I worked became an officially sanctioned special unit. As attempts to duplicate it popped up all over the Northeast, I became happily busy teaching and mentoring.

During the next two decades, the National Alzheimer's Association grew, with branches in every state offering family support and patient care, professional education, research opportunities, and advocacy. And as other professionals became interested in the care of people with Alzheimer's, the effort to institute habilitative settings became easier. Advocates traveled to state houses and government agencies to describe the major differences that specialized care made in the lives of Alzheimer's patients, their families, and the staff of institutions caring for them. Special-care units now exist in every region of the United States, and specific programming for people with Alzheimer's disease and the related disorders are common in adult day health, assisted-living, and retirement centers.

Still, families need to be wary of institutions that claim to offer specialized care but do little more than secure the doors. Without trained staff, ongoing education, and a habilitative philosophy of care adopted by the whole staff, the unit is not "special." Both the National Alzheimer's Association and its state chapters can help sort through the differences.

For people seeking care for patients outside the home, as well as those planning to provide care themselves, this book teaches both the habilitation philosophy and the practical techniques that make care partnering effective and enriching. It focuses primarily on the early and middle stages of Alzheimer's and other progressive dementias, when habilitative care can be most effective.

This book is divided into three parts. In Part One, to foster an understanding of Alzheimer's disease and to underscore how altered behavior relates to the changes in the brain, I present an overview of the disease in lay terms. I then discuss some of the most common issues immediately affecting people with Alzheimer's.

Part Two moves into the core idea of habilitation — creating a positive milieu in which the patient can enjoy feelings of success. I focus on basic, simple suggestions for use of leisure time and offer practical solutions for bathing, dressing, toileting, and eating independently. I include tips for communication and for dealing with negative behaviors.

Part Three discusses the need for care partners to take care of themselves and provides a summary of short- and long-term-care options most conducive to the habilitation principles.

At the end of the book, the Appendix and Further Resources provide the most practical, useful information I've been able to compile — from simple finger food suggestions to books and other reference materials to companies and dealers who specialize in materials I use in my habilitation work.

Most of the anecdotes used throughout the book are composites based on stories I have heard through the years or incidents in which I was a participant. While the dialogue is often based only on my impressionistic memory, the deeper truth contained in each vignette is real. I selected the anecdotes to show what remains in the heart and soul of the person with Alzheimer's disease or other progressive dementia, and to help care partners move into the patient's world and focus not on what is missing but on what is still there.

If you are a care partner, remember to be kind to yourself as you read through the ideas presented here. Do not try to implement all the ideas at once, since that would be overwhelming. After all, the goal of habilitation is to create a positive emotional and physical environment for the care partner as well as for the patient. Figuring out what most needs to be done at any moment makes achieving the overall goal far more manageable. Congratulate yourself on what you can do.

2

Seeking a Correct Diagnosis

I am not here anymore.
Somewhere else is where I am.
A place so hard to find,
you cannot see me here
or visit me there
or wish me out of this anywhere.
If this is where I am supposed to be,
why can't I find me?

BETH ARRIVED for her doctor's appointment two hours late — and terrified. "I can't remember the day, or month, or sometimes even the year," she sputtered. "What's happening to me? Am I losing my mind? Am I crazy?"

Her physician, trying to offer reassurance, said, "You're seventy, Beth. What do you expect? You can't perform like a twenty-year-old anymore."

Like all of us, Beth wanted to perform as she always had, regardless of her age. A serious decline in mood, cognition, or functional behavior is *not* a normal part of aging; it indicates an underlying medical problem.

According to the National Alzheimer's Association, Alzheimer's disease has ten warning signs:

- Loss of memory
- Difficulty performing familiar tasks
- Problems with language
- Disorientation to time and place
- Poor or declining judgment
- Problems with abstract thinking
- Misplacing things
- Changes in mood and behavior
- Changes in personality
- Loss of initiative

An impairment in or loss of mental powers is called dementia, but dementia is a symptom, not a diagnosis. A finding of dementia cries out for more precise medical evaluation to rule out illnesses that may be not only treatable but curable. Larger metropolitan hospitals usually perform such an evaluation, called an Alzheimer's disease workup or AD workup, but residents of small communities may be able to find several different doctors who can collectively conduct the necessary tests. Call your nearest Alzheimer's Association chapter for specific information on where to find help in getting a diagnosis.

The evaluation includes a physical examination, psychological and neurological exams, and a complete medical history (including hospitalizations, serious illnesses, family members' illnesses and causes of death, and so forth), and a social history (education, military service, organizations joined, and so forth). Neurologists look for possible changes in the brain through magnetic resonance imaging (MRI) and possibly other scanning techniques. Other clinicians investigate medications used, nutrition, alcohol intake, metabolic disturbances, depression, and other possible causes of dementia.

Not only will the workup confirm Alzheimer's disease if it is present, but the exams should be able to identify whether the apparent problem has another cause.

Other conditions that can appear to be Alzheimer's disease include the following:

- Alcohol abuse
- Drug interactions
- Emotional problems/depression
- Endocrine imbalance
- Infection
- Metabolic disorder
- Poor nutrition or dehydration
- Trauma (emotional or physical)

Left untreated, many of these conditions can lead to irreparable physical or mental damage or even death. Unlike Alzheimer's, some of them can be cured.

Carrie joined an Alzheimer's support group and, at her first meeting, described how her family had "diagnosed" their mother, Therese. "It didn't take a medical degree," she told the other members. She and her brothers had not wanted to subject their mother to a lot of poking and prodding. "She's seventy-nine years old and the family doctor has known her for years," Carrie explained. "He told us that her forgetfulness and language problems are typical of Alzheimer's."

The other members tried to persuade Carrie to seek a more complete neurological evaluation. After three more meetings, Carrie gave in, if only "to prove to you all that Mother really does have Alzheimer's." She scheduled a visit with a memory-disorder clinic at a local teaching hospital, and with the help of a CAT (computerized axial tomography) scan, the doctors there discovered a small tumor growing in Therese's brain. She received the appropriate treatment and slowly returned to her old self, free of dementia and free of Alzheimer's.

Until recently, a diagnosis of Alzheimer's was quite difficult to prove; it could only be done definitively after death. The German neurologist Alois Alzheimer first identified the disease just about a century ago, in 1906, when he examined the brain of a deceased fifty-one-year-old woman whose "early-onset dementia" he had been following for many years. During the autopsy he discovered that nerve-cell fibers in her brain were entwined in what he called "neurofibrillary tangles." He named the areas of marked deterioration "plaques." Tangles and plaques remain the markers of Alzheimer's disease at autopsy. (We now know that plaques consist of a protein that goes awry, a malfunction that some scientists attribute to a genetic defect. As the plaques accumulate, brain function deteriorates.)

Some Early Tests for Alzheimer's

In recent years, doctors have become better able to identify Alzheimer's disease in living people. I do not give detailed or cutting-edge medical advice in this book — my expertise is in care partnering — but here are some tests that you may want to discuss with your physician.

- A lumbar puncture in the later stages of the disease that looks for amyloid and tau protein deposits, which are hallmarks of Alzheimer's
- An examination of tissue from the nasal passages
- A bone marrow test
- A commercial "sniff" test that can indicate certain types of dementia, which is readily available in drugstores
- A "Seven-Minute Screen" (contact your local Alzheimer's Association for details) that indicates whether further diagnostic tests are advisable
- A saliva test, given to people whose parents or siblings have developed Alzheimer's at an early age, that looks for genetic markers or hereditary factors.

As researchers try these tests on more patients, medical journals, the media, and the National Alzheimer's Association and its local chapters will alert the public and health care providers to the diagnostic value of each test. At present, too little is known about their efficacy for me to recommend any of them unequivocally.

Scientists have now determined that in people with Alzheimer's, nerve cells in the brain may start dying long before intellectual functioning changes noticeably, so the sooner a diagnosis is made and treatment begins, the better the chances are that the treatments will make a difference.

If you feel you are showing some early signs of the disease and you have a family history of Alzheimer's, consult with your physician to help you decide if you want to be tested. Evidence shows that if a parent, brother, or sister — first-degree relatives — develops Alzheimer's disease at an early age, you have a greater probability of developing the disease. If a family history of symptoms that we now recognize as Alzheimer's disease can be traced back for several generations, the incidence in future generations rises considerably. The genetic marker ApoE4 now helps detect familial Alzheimer's in families with a history of the disease.

More than a decade ago, my friend Charlie Pierce began wondering if he might develop Alzheimer's disease, since his father and siblings had had it. Charlie's book, *Hard to Forget,* about familial Alzheimer's, has given us all a more concrete and humane understanding of people like Charlie, still symptom free, who live each day knowing they may be the next one in the family to show signs of Alzheimer's.

A host of scientists are now using state-of-the-art technology to examine all potential causes of Alzheimer's, including genetic, viral, biochemical, and environmental problems, hoping to better understand the disease and find new treatments and, if possible, ways to halt or cure it. Genetic engineers and genomic researchers continue to delve into the recesses of the brain and the uncharted pathways of the body to find answers before people like Charlie have to deal, one more time, with familial Alzheimer's. This book cannot address all of the cutting-edge research that is being done, but certainly, if you have a family history of Alzheimer's, consult with your physician to determine the best course of action.

Products That May Alleviate Symptoms

A number of products — herbs, vitamins, and medicines — have been tested and found to provide some relief from certain early symptoms of Alzheimer's. None can be considered a cure, although they have shown some promise in reducing brain-cell damage. *These products should never be taken without consulting a physician, since any of them might be dangerous for a particular person.* The herbal products and vitamins include green-tea extract, selenium, grapeseed extract, and antioxidants such as vitamins A, C, and E. Researchers have not yet determined whether extract of *Ginkgo biloba* improves memory in people with Alzheimer's; studies show differing results. Also, because ginkgo is a blood thinner, it may cause more problems than improvements.

Some federally approved medications show varying amounts of success in reducing symptoms of Alzheimer's disease in some people and in keeping symptoms in others from getting worse. Each patient differs in the degree of responsiveness to the drugs and in the length of time they must be used before having any effect. Aricept, Exelon, and Reminyl work by increasing the amount of a bodily compound that is diminished in Alzheimer's patients, resulting in short-term memory loss. Anti-inflammatory medicines, including Celebrex and naproxen, may help by reducing swelling of the brain tissue associated with plaque formation. These drugs may slow the progression of the disease or protect people from exhibiting any symptoms. In clinical trials, Axura, or memantine, has shown some promise in slowing deterioration in the middle to late stage of Alzheimer's, though it has not yet been approved by the U.S. Food and Drug Administration.

Some compounds may even reduce one's chances of getting Alzheimer's. Certain researchers have shown that cholesterol-lowering drugs (statins) can block the toxic effects of cellular processes associated with Alzheimer's. Eating fish such as mackerel, sardines, and other cold-water fish whose oils contain omega-3 fatty acids can also promote brain health.

The medications and supplements mentioned above are generally most useful during the early and middle stages of Alzheimer's — a period that generally lasts between five and ten years.

Anyone who receives a positive diagnosis of Alzheimer's needs to deal with a host of social matters immediately. A man named Bill summed up this situation for me. "I need to get on with living," he told me. "There are so many things I want to do while I still can." Like most people, he had long dreamed of taking a trip to Europe with his wife, taking his grandchildren to Disney World. Now he wasn't going to wait any longer to put those plans into action. "Getting this news is not fun, and it does not make me happy, but it sure as hell beats getting run over by a car without being prepared. Now I can get on with living for whatever time is left. I have all this really great stuff in my head."

Every newly diagnosed Alzheimer's patient should learn that he or she is not simply "going crazy," that any changes in functioning are rooted in a physical disease. Certainly knowing that one has a neurological disorder is far better than silently worrying about a vague and menacing fear. Although it's completely normal to want to avoid the hard, bright line of a diagnosis of Alzheimer's, once the patient receives a competent, correct diagnosis, it is possible to take some concrete, positive steps that can significantly improve his quality of life.

Once the diagnosis is clear, the time is right for the care partner to tell the afflicted person, "No matter what happens, I will be here for you."

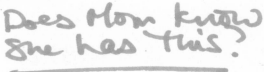

3

What to Expect:
Making the First Decisions

*I wish there
were Cliff Notes
to help cheat my way
through this disease.*

GARY WAS a sixty-one-year-old high school math teacher who chose early retirement when his forgetfulness began to be an issue in class. Over the course of a year, although he had remained kind and caring, he had neglected to correct midterm exams, unknowingly missed a teachers' meeting, continually forgot where he parked his car in the staff parking lot, and had growing difficulties with a curriculum he had used successfully for nineteen years. At home a burnt teapot, a microwave explosion, and several small kitchen fires had forced him to exist on a diet of cold foods.

Some faculty members began to talk about how slovenly Gary had become. Some wondered if he had developed a drinking problem. Others thought he might be depressed. "Whatever it is," one colleague said, "he's just not the same Gary. And I feel as if I've failed as his close friend. He always says he's 'just getting old' and abruptly changes the subject. I know something more is wrong, but he just won't discuss it." Gary was encountering the early stage of Alzheimer's.

Sherry, too, was in the first stage of the disease but, unlike Gary, she had long been a domineering person. For five decades as a homemaker she had invested her energies in her three sons and her husband, Howard, and had felt in control of her life. Unfortunately, as the boys matured, married, and began raising families of their own, she had tried to stay in control by becoming more demanding, and her sons and their wives had begun to see her as a busybody much too involved in their affairs.

Then the family noted that getting along with Sherry had become even more challenging. If she made a mistake and someone corrected her, she would leave the room, banging the door behind her. When she repeated a story, as she often did, and the boys reminded her, she would raise her voice and tell them to "get out now." Then her daughters-in-law noticed a large purple bruise that covered most of Howard's lower arm. He explained that Sherry had hit him on the arm with a croquet mallet. He brought up other worries, too. "She won't stop driving," Howard said. "Every time she goes out in the car I feel sure she'll kill someone. But I can't stop her."

Sherry's domineering behavior did not diminish as her cognitive abilities began to decline. Quite the contrary: as she became aware of "losing control," she was far more likely to try to control those around her, and she did so by angry outbursts. She was essentially saying, in the only way she could, "I am still the boss and don't you forget it."

As was the case with Sherry and Gary, it is often a colleague, friend, family member, or outside helper who is the first person to notice changes in mood or behavior that suggest progressive dementia. The person experiencing the mood variations probably is aware of them but cannot face what they may mean. He hopes that the idiosyncrasies are temporary matters that can be explained away — "I need a good long vacation" — although he may begin to take stock and shift his priorities.

The Progression of Alzheimer's Disease

Clinicians typically refer to three stages of Alzheimer's disease — early, middle, and late. Each stage may be as brief as one year or as long as ten years, and there are wide variations from individual to individual. The first changes that Alzheimer's patients tend to go through are listed in the table below, followed by changes that occur in the later stages. Recognize that the intensity of a change — sometimes subtle, sometimes profound — varies widely from case to case. For good reason the constant refrain of care partners is "The most predictable part of Alzheimer's disease is the unpredictability."

Behavioral Change	Probable Stage
Not remembering appointments	Early
Not recognizing once familiar faces	
Losing track of time	
Not storing recent information or events	
Getting lost	
Having difficulty finding words	
Misplacing needed items	
Being unable to make decisions or choices	Middle Early
Finding it hard to concentrate	
Acting accusatory or paranoid	
Being unable to separate fact from fiction	
Being unable to translate thoughts into actions	
Misunderstanding what is being said	
Making mistakes in judgment	
Withdrawing, being frustrated and/or angry	Late Early
Losing ability to sequence tasks	
Speaking in rambling sentences	
Misusing familiar words	
Having difficulty writing	
Requiring supervision for "activities of daily living"*	
Showing impaired computing abilities	
Reacting less quickly	

Behavioral Change	Probable Stage
Losing fine motor skills (such as buttoning a shirt)	Early Middle
Having more serious difficulties with ADL	
Not recognizing objects for what they are	
Being unable to understand written words	
Possibly displaying more sexual interests	
Engaging in repetitive speech and action	Middle Middle
Having hallucinations and delusions	
Having problems with social appropriateness	
Experiencing altered visual perception	
Showing frequent changes of emotion	
Having minimal attention span	
Reacting catastrophically (overreacting, having outbursts)	
Needing assistance with all ADL	
Exhibiting frustration, anger, or withdrawal	
Walking with a shuffling gait	
Being incontinent	Late Middle
Being mostly unintelligible	
Exhibiting a downward gaze	
Being unable to separate or recognize sounds	
Losing all language	Late or Final
Losing gross motor skills (sitting, walking)	
Having swallowing difficulties	
Needing total care	

*Activities of daily living, or ADL, include bathing, dressing, grooming, eating, toileting.

After a diagnosis of Alzheimer's disease is made, the afflicted person (or her family or friends) should quickly start to look into some important matters concerning her care. Because many aspects of the Alzheimer's patient's daily care will not be performed at home, and because the patient may at some time need professional care, thoughtful financial planning from the start is important.

No matter how small the patient's resources are, a financial planner or elder-care attorney may provide compelling, unexpected reasons why someone else should manage the finances.

Keep in mind that not all nursing facilities will accept a patient who has no personal funds and who therefore must rely on Medicaid (state-provided medical assistance). The care partner needs to be sure that funds will be available when they are most needed — and that the question of who controls those funds has been decided. Addressing financial issues in depth is beyond the scope of this book (see Further Resources, page 212). At the first opportunity, contact a financial planner you can trust, and make the necessary arrangements.

The person with Alzheimer's should authorize someone trustworthy to make financial and medical decisions when she becomes unable to do so by a power of attorney or other appropriate documents. The patient might also create a living will, which may dispose of no-longer-needed assets and items while she is still alive. The Five Wishes Living Will (see Further Resources, page 225), which is valid under the laws of most states, also takes into consideration the person's emotional and spiritual needs. It provides specific instructions for the time of death, such as levels of comfort, life support, and other important factors. A health care proxy (which may be associated with either a power of attorney or a living will) allows the person to name someone she knows and trusts to make medical decisions. Of course, the legal needs of individuals vary, and each patient should consult a legal adviser on these matters.

At no time does an Alzheimer's patient feel more threatened than when facing the decision to stop driving — particularly when he either has not recognized or has denied that there's even a problem. When the habilitator confronts him, the subject generally becomes a battle — the patient will counter with verbal flare-ups and statements like "I've never had an accident before" or "I'm a much better driver than you are." Try not to argue with these kinds of statements. The issue now is not previous driving history, but what the future holds. The nature of the disease, which is hallmarked by problems with reflexes, judgment, way-finding, reaction time, decision-making, and other cognitive functions, will at some point make driving impossible.

Many people diagnosed with early-stage Alzheimer's decide to stop driving before they are in danger of getting lost or having an accident. But for many others, the issue is clouded by the overriding fear of losing independence and control over their life. The care partner must often find creative ways to keep the Alzheimer's patient from driving, perhaps by keeping the keys out of sight, getting into the driver's seat first, disabling the car by disconnecting the distributor cap, or by finding a trustworthy scapegoat such as a physician who will write a "prescription" to stop driving. If she has her own vehicle and the family has another car, take hers away as soon as possible — getting it out of sight will help dissipate her longings to drive. "It's at the garage" buys time; "It's having a tune-up" buys patience. These stratagems are all ways to deal with the problem until such time as the person no longer expresses a desire to drive — and this will happen.

Drivers Fifty and Older: Self-Rating Form*

This is a great quiz to help determine whether you should stop driving.

Instructions
For each of the following fifteen questions, check the symbol of the one answer that most applies to you.

Question	Always or Almost Always	Sometimes	Never or Almost Never
1. I signal and check to the rear when I change lanes.	○	□	□
2. I wear a seatbelt.	○	□	□
3. I try to stay informed about changes in driving and highway regulations.	○	△	□

Question	Always or Almost Always	Sometimes	Never or Almost Never
4. Intersections bother me because there is so much to watch from all directions.	○	△	○
5. I find it difficult to decide when to join traffic on a busy interstate highway.	□	△	○
6. I think I am slower than I used to be in reacting to dangerous driving situations.	□	□	○
7. When I am really upset, I show it in my driving.	□	□	○
8. My thoughts wander when I am driving.	□	△	○
9. Traffic situations make me angry.	□	△	○
10. I get regular eyesight checks to be sure my vision is sharp.	○	□	□
11. I check with my doctor or pharmacist about the effects of my medications on my driving ability. (*If you do not take any medication, skip this question.*)	○	□	□
12. I try to stay abreast of current information on health practices and habits.	○	△	□
13. My children, other family members, or friends are concerned about my driving ability.	□	△	○

Question	None	One or Two	Three or More
14. How many traffic tickets, warnings, or "discussions" with officers have you had in the past two years?	○	△	□

Question	None	One or Two	Three or More
15. How many accidents have you had during the past two years?	○	□	□

Self-Scoring

Count the number of check marks in the squares and record the total in the square below. Follow the same procedure for the triangles and circles.

□ △ ○ These are your check-mark totals. For score and interpretation, see the next section.

Step 1: In the square to the right, write the check-mark total recorded in the previous square.

□ × **5** = ____

Step 2: In the triangle to the right, write the check-mark total recorded in the triangle above.

△ × **3** = ____

Step 3: Multiply the number in the square by 5.

Step 4: Multiply the number in the triangle by 3.

Step 5: Add the results of Steps 3 and 4.   **YOUR SCORE IS** ____

Interpretation of Your Score

The *lower* your score, the safer you are as a driver. The *higher* the score, the more dangerous you are to yourself and others.

Score	Meaning
0 to 15	GO! You are aware of what is important to safe driving and are practicing what you know.
16 to 34	CAUTION! You are engaging in some practices that need improvement to ensure safety.
35 and over	STOP! You are engaging in too many unsafe driving practices. You are a potential or actual hazard to yourself and others.

These scores are based on what drivers fifty-five years old and over have told the Foundation for Traffic Safety about their driving practices and habits. Your score is based on your answers to a limited number of important questions. A complete evaluation of your driving ability would require many more questions, along with medical, physical, and licensing examinations. Nevertheless, your answers and score give some indication of how well you are doing and how you can become a safer driver.

In general, a checked square for an item reflects an unsafe practice or situation that should be changed immediately. A checked triangle means a practice or situation that is unsafe or becoming unsafe. Checked circles are signs that you are doing what you should to be (and remain) a safe driver.

*This quiz is adapted from the quiz used by the Automobile Association of America (AAA)'s Foundation for Traffic Safety and is used with permission.

Formulating a Plan of Care

No matter what situation the care partner or family members find themselves in — caring for the person with Alzheimer's at home, in an assisted-living situation, or in a nursing home or similar facility — it is important to develop a plan of care. Care partners can use the plan to make sure that the patient's physical, social, emotional, and spiritual needs are being met *over a specific period of time.* Because the behaviors and needs of people with Alzheimer's change constantly as the disease and symptoms progress, the plan must be reviewed and updated on a regular basis — this is its primary purpose.

In the beginning, it may not be necessary to write out the plan of care — it can emerge from discussions with others involved in the caregiving process. If you do put the plan in writing, it could be as simple as "Continue with day care three times a week — no other changes."

Think of the plan of care as the routine you want the person with Alzheimer's to have. Initially, the routine should be close to whatever routine the person followed before the diagnosis. As the disease progresses, certain symptoms become apparent and certain behaviors become more problematic; for example, the patient may begin "sundowning" (becoming more aggressive in the evening). At this point you'll want to vary the routine to incorporate the change — by not inviting friends to visit during that time, for instance.

To develop a plan of care, consider the following needs:

- Physical: Is the person with Alzheimer's doing all right physically? Is she clean? Clothed? Eating regularly? Sleeping well? Having regular sexual intercourse, if desired?
- Social: Does the person with Alzheimer's have adequate social contacts? Does he seem withdrawn? Unhappy? Overly aggressive? Would modifying his social interactions positively change the behavior?
- Emotional: Is the person with Alzheimer's all right emotionally? Some of the questions here are the same as those concerning social needs; what is at stake here is whether the person's needs for love, intimacy, comfort, independence, easing of paranoid feelings, and so forth are being met.
- Spiritual: Does the person with Alzheimer's have adequate opportunities to fulfill spiritual needs? This aspect of the plan of care may be hard to quantify. Spiritual needs may range from attending religious services to feeding the birds: whatever spiritual sustenance maintained her before the disease began.

On a regular basis, assess the plan of care and modify it as necessary. For example, in January Corinne was taking care of her father, Rick. She kept him clean and fed (meeting his physical needs), regularly walked with him and some friends in a nearby park, took him to his favorite restaurant once a week (meeting his social and emotional needs), and allowed him time to putter

around in his workshop/den (meeting his spiritual needs). In February, when Corinne assessed her plan of care, she noticed that her father had been acting more aggressive and more disoriented at the restaurant. She decided to go there only once every two weeks and substitute a take-out order at home for the second restaurant excursion. In March she realized that the two visits to the restaurant had become too difficult, so she removed them from her plan of care altogether.

The assessment of the plan of care will vary from care partner to care partner, and situation to situation. If the patient is being cared for at home, the habilitator should revisit the plan of care once a month. Assisted-living facilities and nursing homes generally use the plan of care as the basis for the patient's daily life, determining the patient's participation in recreational programs, menus, medications, and so forth. The usual policy is to review the plan of care once every three months.

For home care, the monthly assessment of the plan provides an ideal occasion to discuss the situation with others who may be helping out — the teen who comes once a week to take Grandfather on a walk in the park, for example, or the sister who arrives every Tuesday to watch Dad for a few hours. This once-a-month casual meeting can allow the care partner and helper to recommit to the process for the next month — "Would you like to come Tuesdays between three P.M. and six P.M. this month?" The helper can plan on this time to change the status, if necessary; and if the helper is used to this regular schedule of assessment, any changes of schedule will be easier for everyone.

The care partner has to continually assess what skills the patient has lost and what skills remain. For instance, you should check to see whether the oven has been left on, if burn marks have appeared on the bottom of the teapot, if the refrigerator contains spoiled food, and if the home is no longer as clean as it used to be. Deterioration in any of these instrumental aspects of daily life should not cause panic, but they do signal potential safety problems that should be considered seriously. Such findings may mark the time to ask others to help out or to bring in a professional support system. The chart showing the progression of Alzheimer's on pages 22–23 can be used as a checklist of sorts to determine the need for reassessment and evaluation of the patient's current abilities.

Habilitation, the New Approach

Take away my license,
but don't steal my independence.
I will let you drive.
But let me tell you
where I want to go.

THE STAFF was busily opening draperies, letting the first beams of morning light into the rooms inhabited by the forty-five residents on floor two of the nursing center.

"I want to see my mother," Mary said softly to no one in particular as she shuffled from her room, holding on to the wall.

Claire, a young nurse's aide who happened to pass by at that moment, took Mary's hand. Then she said, sympathetically, "Mary, your mother has been dead a long time."

"Don't be so fresh," Mary said, pulling her hand away. "You don't know what you're talking about."

"Try to remember, Mary. You haven't seen your mother in years. She died when you were in your forties. You're eighty-seven now."

Mary shoved Claire out of her path. "My mother was right

here this morning. We had breakfast together like always. Now, get out of my way."

Gently, Claire took Mary's arm and began to guide her to the large-print calendar hanging in the nurses' station.

"No. I'm not going with you."

Claire tightened her grip. "I want to show you the date. Your mother died a long time ago."

Mary sputtered, "You — you — you — *hussy!*" Then, swinging her free arm, Mary caught the aide with a backhand slap to the face.

Claire called for help. Her colleagues responded and quickly subdued Mary, injecting her with an antipsychotic medication. For the rest of the morning, the staff kept Mary restrained to a chair in front of the nurses' station, where they could see her.

Until recently, this kind of scene occurred often in nursing homes where, in dealing with residents who might harm themselves or others, staff followed a protocol known euphemistically as "appropriate care." Claire's part of the dialogue with Mary followed a theory called "reality orientation." Staff members were taught to enforce a sense of the here and now. The idea was to make sure that all residents knew where they were, what food they had had for breakfast, the date, the day of the week, the year, and the name of the president of the United States.

"Your mother has been dead for years" is a prime example of reality orientation, although the person being addressed is far beyond being able to process the information. Sadly, the primary effect of forcing Mary to "face the truth" of her mother's long-ago death led to an escalation in her negative behavior. Her outburst was a way of defending herself against what she saw as a lie. Guided by emotion, her words failing, she reacted physically. In her internal reality, her mother was alive and they had enjoyed breakfast together earlier that morning.

Reality orientation is the antithesis of habilitation. Habilitation teaches care partners to place themselves in the patient's world, no matter where that world is. This teaching — live in the patient's world — is the fourth tenet of habilitation, as discussed in Chapter 1. The habilitative approach also acknowledges that reasoning with someone who has lost the power to reason only ensures confrontation.

Now imagine the same scene with staff members trained in the habilitation model of care.

When Mary expressed her wish to see her mother, the nursing aide said simply, "Tell me about her."

"She's a great cook," Mary said.

"What does she make that you especially like?"

"Oh, her pies are the best," Mary recalled. "I can never match 'em. Oh, dear, now I'm getting hungry."

Claire took Mary's hand and guided her toward the dining room. "Me too," she said. "You have a cup of coffee while I go get your friend Pat — we'll be right back."

Dignity intact, free from medical or chemical restraint, Mary sat back with her coffee and awaited her friend's arrival. Thoughts of her mother faded, replaced by the positive experience of Claire's smiling face and extended hand.

Following the tenets of habilitation, Claire made no attempt to "correct" Mary's sense of time and place or to reason with someone who no longer had that ability. At the same time, though, the aide validated Mary's emotional responses — her feeling of loneliness and her need for nurturing. Claire also bypassed a situation in which Mary could have felt a sense of failure. In taking this approach, the aide heeded the second, fourth, and fifth habilitation tenets: know that communication remains possible, live in the patient's world, and enrich the patient's life.

It is important to note as well that Mary required less time and fewer staff resources with the habilitation model — a compelling advantage in an era when the people who run nursing homes and other care facilities complain that there is never enough time or enough staff to practice new methods. Habilitation is by far the most effective approach for people in the early stages of the disease, when they are struggling to maintain their independence.

The habilitative method is significantly helpful when the patient's daily activities involve engagement with the rest of the world. Although such tasks as shopping, banking, doing the laundry, and driving will become increasingly more difficult as Alzheimer's progresses, by integrating the help of others and providing some simple cues, the care person can make daily tasks easier.

For example, one late afternoon Judy and Paul were preparing for visitors. The sun was shining in as Judy settled herself on the sofa across from the window while Paul made tea. The visitors arrived, and everyone sat down and began to talk, sipping tea and eating cookies.

Suddenly Judy rose and walked directly across the room to where one of the visitors was seated and shoved him squarely on the forehead, yelling, "Stop it! Stop it!"

Paul led her out of the room. The visitors excused themselves and graciously left the house, accepting Paul's apologies. Once, Paul would have seen Judy's behavior as "part of the disease" — but now, after several months of support group meetings, he knew how to look for what had triggered her outburst. When he returned to the living room, he sat where Judy had been seated on the sofa and immediately noticed that the sun shone directly in his eyes from the spot where the visitor had been sitting. Judy's way of ridding herself of the discomfort of the sun in her eyes was to try to beat it away. Paul's solution was to close the shade. By doing so, he successfully minimized both Judy's stress and his own.

As you'll see in later chapters, the patient may be able to live independently for longer and feel more in control if the care person modifies the environment in useful ways. For example, consider how you can help an afflicted person continue to do laundry, a task that can help make him feel like a helpful, important part of the housekeeping effort. Here are some suggestions:

- Keep laundry detergent in plain sight near the washing machine.
- Number the different boxes and bottles to be used; detergent, for example would be labeled #1, and softener would be #2.
- Write out a simple, clear list of steps for doing the laundry, and place the list near the washer and dryer.
- Mark the most frequently used washer and dryer settings with red nail polish or paint.
- Stick to a routine, doing the laundry on the same day each week and at the same time of day.

Consider how habilitation might have worked for Linda and her mother, Diane. "My daughter won't let me do the laundry anymore," Diane moaned at a patient support group meeting. "She says it makes more work for her when I do it. She claims I put whites in with colors, but I know I don't do that. She says I forget the detergent. Imagine that. 'Don't go near the wash while I'm out, Mama,' she says to me, as if I'm a child. I might as well put the TV on and sit like a lump all day if no one thinks I can do anything."

As Diane's ability to sequence the chore eroded, she probably was making the laundry chore harder for her daughter. But rather than emphasizing Diane's mistakes, the focus should be on what strengths she still had. Linda could give her mother the clean laundry and ask her to fold it — a repetitive task that Diane could still accomplish. Yes, she would take an hour longer than her daughter to finish the chore, but time is not the issue. Dignity is. Linda would praise Diane at the end and thank her for helping out. As a result both Linda and Diane would feel good.

Even for people with Alzheimer's disease, life is about doing, not just being. "What can I do — to help, to serve, to feel like a contributing part of family and community" is the silent plea of people with progressive dementia. Just receiving basic comforts and palliative care is not enough; these people need to feel useful to whatever extent is possible for them.

Focusing on What Remains

Family members often report to the doctor or nurse that the person with Alzheimer's disease cannot perform certain seemingly routine tasks long before the disease's normal progression suggests the need for hands-on assistance. In the parlance of health care professionals, this problem is called "excess disability." In an effort to keep the patient from attempting a task that might prove difficult, a well-meaning care partner may simply do the work for him. Although this might seem the best solution in the short term, it is likely to mean that the patient will soon not be able to perform the task at all.

Consider how habilitative principles could have helped Peter. His disease had led him into a world in which some of the simplest activities of daily living had become sources of frustration. In response, he strove even harder to maintain his independence, resisting the efforts of his family members who, he thought, were determined to infantilize him.

One morning Peter woke up early, as usual, and went into the bathroom before anyone else arose. This was his way of trying to take care of himself on his own. Once in the bathroom, he stood in front of the sink, wondering what to do next. He vaguely recognized where he was, yet he wasn't sure why he was there. After a while his pajama pants felt wet and warm.

Next he examined the many objects in front of him. He was

unsure which ones were used for what purposes. Aha. "Tooth stuff," he muttered as he picked up and squeezed a red and white tube. He cautiously smeared on his teeth the green paste coming out of the tube.

A few minutes later, Peter became thoroughly annoyed at the wetness and the cold feeling of his pajama pants. He tried to slide the pants off, but a drawstring fastened them tightly at the waist. He sat down on the edge of the tub and began to tug harder and harder until the cloth tore apart. He smiled with satisfaction as the cotton began to shred into long strips suspended from his waist.

Suddenly his wife, Abby, burst through the bathroom door. Horrified, she shouted, "Look what you've done. You've ruined a perfectly good pair of pajamas. And you have toothpaste all over your face. What am I going to do with you?"

She started to wash and dress him, calling for her daughter to come in and help, doing just what Peter most feared — treating him like a baby. If Peter could have articulated his feelings, I think he would have said, "I am still here. I am not gone. I'd rather try and fail than have you do these things for me. Please give me the chance to do one little thing for myself, and if I end up with my BVDs on my head, so what? Imagine how good I feel doing things myself. Please focus on how I feel and not on how I look."

Using the principles of habilitation, Abby could have helped Peter retain more independence in his personal habits. If he had had elastic-waist pajama bottoms, he could easily have removed them himself when the wetness made him uncomfortable. Abby could have placed toothpaste on his toothbrush, laid the brush on the sink top, and put the paste out of sight. She could have removed the other bathroom items, putting his brush, comb, shaving cream, and safety razor (which isn't dangerous if he has always used one) on the vanity.

While Peter was grooming, his daughter could have laid out

his day's clothes, sequencing the items by placing the first article of clothing he would put on — his briefs — on top, followed by his undershirt, trousers, and socks — in the order Peter had always put them on. When he had completed his basic dressing routine, his daughter could have held up two appropriate shirts and asked, "Which would you like to wear today, Dad?" assuring that her father still felt in control and able to make personal choices.

In this scenario, everyone would have won: completing the task would have preserved Peter's vital self-esteem, and he could have conducted his toileting and dressing without Abby's using negative words or losing her temper. The objective of habilitation is to find each patient's optimal ability to function independently. Clinicians gauge how well a person can get along in a home setting according to how well she can perform specific activities of daily living. (For detailed suggestions and help with activities of daily living, see Chapter 8.)

Sometimes it is difficult to figure out how much independence the Alzheimer's person can use, as Michaela described at a care-partner support group. Her husband, Laurence, had repeatedly said he wanted to use their snow blower to clear the driveway of the heavy snow that had fallen. She finally decided to let him do this, so she started the machine for him and gave him initial instructions.

Back indoors, she realized that the blower's hum seemed rather distant. Looking out the window, she noticed six feet of snow piled in front of their neighbor's garage doors, where Laurence was blowing the snow from the driveway. Michaela still wanted her husband to succeed at the task, so when he begged for a second chance, she gave him simple, clear instructions on how to blow the snow from their own driveway onto the lawn. But some minutes later she again found him at their neighbor's, this time blowing all the snow from the lawn onto the driveway, which had been professionally plowed earlier that morning.

Once again Michaela walked over to the neighbor's yard; gently taking hold of the snow blower handle, she shut off the engine. "Laurence," she said, "the engine seems to be overheating. Let's give the machine a rest." As she took his hand, she said, "I need a cup of coffee. How about you? Want some chocolate cake?" Together they began trudging home through the snow, leaving the blower and the comical scene for her teenage son to remedy.

Every care partner must find a balance between allowing the person with Alzheimer's enough independence to have opportunities to succeed, but not so much as to cause new failures. Formulating and consistently revising a workable plan of care will help the habilitator assess the person's abilities.

The care partner should also look for repetitive tasks that the patient can do successfully. Tasks that do not require a great deal of supervision allow the person with Alzheimer's to still feel independent and useful, with minimum assistance from others. Repetitive tasks, such as rolling dough for pie crust or raking autumn leaves, are often the best choice to compensate for cognitive losses such as attention span and sequencing. Any activity that offers the patient a chance to feel useful and successful — dusting, sandpapering, vacuuming, weeding, shoe polishing, or sorting objects — can be rewarding activities if the care partner makes them so.

One evening I entered my kitchen after dinner to find my husband standing at the sink with my brand-new Teflon-coated frying pan in one hand and a wire scrubber in the other. Teflon cookware was fairly novel in the early 1970s, and I had saved to purchase this one. My heart sank when I saw him. But he was smiling as he began the task of getting the Teflon off the pan — scrubbing and scrubbing, smiling and smiling. The task took him about two hours to complete. By the time he left the kitchen, proudly holding the frying pan in the air and proclaiming victory over Teflon, I had bathed a toddler, looked over homework assignments, ironed shirts for the next school day, and finished a host of other chores. I hugged him and told him it was the best darn job I had ever seen. The kids joined me in applause.

The next morning he was still smiling, though I don't think he remembered what had made him so happy. But that wasn't important. Praise and thanks go a long way in combating injured self-esteem and feelings of helplessness.

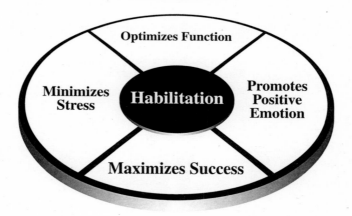

The habilitative model produces critically important results.

Domains

As the care partner fosters independence and self-respect, another aspect of habilitation to consider is what my friend and colleague Dr. Paul Raia calls "domains." While the five tenets are the *tools* that care partners will use to make the Alzheimer's patient function in the best way possible, the six domains discussed on the following pages are the *locations* — either physical or mental — in which the tenets can be implemented.

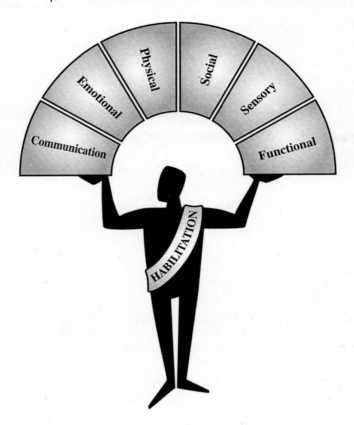

The Six Domains

Physical issues, such as grooming and dressing, and the patient's emotional styles are the foundation blocks of a meaningful habilitation program, along with functional support, which includes elements of the environment such as paint, lighting, and colors. With those three "bricks" in place, the care partner can concentrate on the patient's sense of the world and his interactions with others. When the bricks are balanced, the patient can communicate meaningfully with others even without using words. But if one brick is removed, the others will fall down as well.

1. The Physical Domain

As the disease progresses, surroundings that were once a familiar aspect of the patient's daily existence become less familiar, leaving him with feelings of apprehension and confusion. At this point, he is likely to act out frequently, expressing fear or dismay through an outburst of agitation or aggression.

Since these acts are the patient's way of seeking self-protection, the care partner can try to reduce his anxiety by recognizing that he is probably having growing problems with visual perception (the ability to see contrasts, colors, depth, and motion), cognition (intellectual functioning), and orientation (familiarization to people, places, or time).

Painting a bathroom wall a deep or bright color can draw the patient's attention to the contrasting white toilet, for instance. Enhancing personal areas with memorabilia, eliminating clutter, illuminating task areas, and doing away with sources of shadows can also help. Such changes give patients the greatest chance of being able to function at their highest level for a longer time. Chapter 6 discusses these ideas in more detail.

2. The Functional Domain

The routines that the person followed before she was afflicted by Alzheimer's should be the foundation for keeping her active in her own care and thus relatively independent for as long as possible.

The care partner can offer simple prompts to foster the patient's remaining skills in activities of daily living, which include bathing, dressing, eating, toileting, and sleeping. Place the toothpaste on her toothbrush before she goes into the bathroom for morning grooming. Lay out her clothes in the order that she will put them on. Schedule her shower at the time when she is most relaxed, alert, and cooperative (usually when she wakes up in the morning, before the day's challenges begin). At the dining table, the habilitator should eliminate meaningless utensils and many condiments, because several choices may prove to be overstimulating. And if the patient fails at complicated tasks, assist her with a simpler version of the chore. For instance, if planting the vegetable garden becomes overwhelming, perhaps she can help decide what vegetables to plant.

3. The Social Domain

Almost all of us have an innate desire to be social. We perform better, laugh more, and feel more emotionally secure when we feel the closeness of other people and, perhaps, pets. This desire for closeness does not disappear when someone develops Alzheimer's disease. Many health care professionals in this field report that even patients who are said by their families to be quite unsocial or who have lived for decades without close friends, as well as those who live reclusively because of their illness, have enjoyed relationships with new friends and old family members as the disease progresses. With the loss of inhibition and control, perhaps these patients can now enjoy the company of others, feeling more grounded and safe when people are around.

People with progressive dementias who spend much of their time doing nothing show many more signs of anxiety, depression, and paranoia than their counterparts who are occupied in daily chores and activities. Too much leisure time adds to the patient's feeling of being devalued as a noncontributing family or community member. Everyone, including people with Alzheimer's, needs opportunities to feel successful.

To prevent social problems from building, care partners should constantly include patients in conversation and have friends in to visit one on one. Reminiscing, enjoying music, engaging with children or pets, pursuing hobbies, or participating in religious events can provide feelings of enrichment and accomplishment. Such responses help the patient remain oriented and engaged, maximizing his or her strengths while minimizing isolation.

4. The Communication Domain

Our ability to communicate with language sets us apart from other animals. The loss of language, therefore, can feel dehumanizing. But the habilitation model of care provides a profound opportunity for communication as a way to elicit positive emotions.

The habilitator's tone of voice, gestures, and facial expressions can help counteract the patient's failing language patterns. The care partner can also communicate with pictures rather than words. The method chosen should be appropriate to the individual, and it must change as his communication abilities alter. For instance, a patient who has just begun to need some assistance with word finding may find it demeaning to have words replaced with pictures. In a more advanced stage, however, looking at pictures of infants, for example, may elicit far more delight than trying to have a conversation about babies.

The overall goal is maintaining the emotion of personal value, and the less frustration the patient experiences from verbal errors, the longer he will continue to interact with others. A care partner will not be able to change the imperfect language of a person with Alzheimer's, but the helper can do much to modify his or her reaction to this ongoing loss.

5. The Sensory Domain

Researchers have long identified the senses as an area of particular interest. This domain involves both receiving the sensory signals — sights, sounds, odors, tastes, and textures — and processing these signals in the brain. Alzheimer's disease may scramble the processing of these signals to the point that the patient is unable to share information about what she is seeing, smelling, hearing, tasting, or touching. Yet sensory signals still enter the brain, and they may affect the person on a deep, emotional level, for good or ill.

For example, smell is the oldest and most powerful of our senses, and smells can be used to calm a patient. Once, after I visited one of my grandsons, my daughter dropped me off at the airport. As she drove back to their house, my daughter suggested to her teary six-year-old that they stop and buy a pizza. "No way," he replied. "I don't want anything in this car to take away the smell of Mummum." The fragrance of my bath powder in the car had evoked and sustained a pleasant memory for him. In the same way, many good Alzheimer's programs now use aromatherapy to help evoke pleasant memories.

As for hearing, at some point in the progress of the disease, the person will have difficulty separating one sound from another. Then the care partner needs to minimize distracting or overstimulating noises that may unnerve him. The same effort to minimize and simplify will help those in whom the disease has altered the ability to interpret color, shape, contrast, and motion. For instance, the person may perceive shadows and lights as threatening. If his tactile senses are affected, he may not be able to identify items in his pockets. Someone whose taste buds have changed may enjoy his food more if it is enhanced with herbs and spices.

As the disease progresses, perceptions become ever more problematic until, finally, messages from all of the senses become tangled.

6. The Emotional Domain

As I've suggested, problems in the other domains can lead to emotional problems if a care partner does not use the habilitative approach. In my experience, it is habilitators' unrealistic expectations that most often trigger frustration, verbal agitation, and physical aggression. Most behavioral changes in a person with progressive dementia are rooted in the frustration of being unable to master an emotional and physical environment that feels like foreign territory.

An afflicted person may ask her lifelong spouse, "Who are you?" Or say, "I don't belong here," gesturing to the kitchen of the house where she's lived for forty-seven years. The statement may be cognitively absurd, but the underlying emotion — in these cases, fear — is real. Such statements are both clues to the person's emotional state and warnings that a behavioral change, driven by apprehension, is about to occur.

The habilitation approach accepts that a care partner can influence behavior only indirectly, by changing the patient's environment and by adjusting his or her own attitudes. Trying to use rewards to reinforce positive behavior makes no sense after the point when patients can no longer understand the link between a behavior and a positive reinforcement.

For example, if Travis continually tries to open the door and get out of a moving vehicle, the answer is not to offer his favorite strawberry milkshake if he sits still for the duration of the ride. He no longer sees the connection between his behavior and the reward or lack of reward. The appropriate way to control this problem is to stop taking Travis for rides in the car for a while, until this particular behavior subsides. As for the milkshake — give it to him anyway.

Families and professionals must be aware of the ongoing need to reassess the patient's domains and to modify the care partner's actions and reactions. With education, practice, patience, and support, care partners can learn how to reach patients through their remaining capacity to feel and exhibit emotions.

Seeing the World from the Patient's Perspective

I've danced,
I've sung,
I've given birth,
I've laughed,
I've succeeded.
Why is everyone
so sad?

AT AN EARLY-STAGE Alzheimer's group meeting, Jim described how people began to speak more loudly to him after they learned of his diagnosis. "One jerk even said to my wife, 'Ask him if he wants coffee.' I screamed back at him, 'Yes, I do — with sugar!' You should have seen the look on the guy's face." Jim chuckled. The rest of the group nodded with recognition. They had all experienced similar reactions.

To the patient, a diagnosis of progressive dementia means the recognition of a disease that is already active and that will, presumably, continue for a relatively long time. But too often, outsiders think they should start treating the person differently, without recognizing his existing abilities. Or they may worry that if they speak to him about the disease, they are being too personal. But speaking with and listening to the patient — allowing him to talk openly about feelings and abilities — helps significantly. In 1996, researcher Mary Mittelman, a professor of psychology at New York University Medical Center, published an article in the *Journal of the American Medical Association,* about the crucial importance of families and patients speaking and listening to one another about the diagnosis and the disease.

Listening is the best way for the care partner to seal a positive pact with the afflicted person. The language that the patient uses is of little importance. What matters is that someone is listening with heart and soul, unconditionally and without interruption. Listening tells the patient "I value you" louder and clearer than almost anything else. Listening also helps the care partner understand how the patient is reacting to this disease and to the way people treat her. This has an even greater impact since most people, including health care professionals, generally do not include patients in conversation. But people with Alzheimer's resent being seen as deaf and dumb. Many of them will talk much less than they did before the diagnosis, and some will stop talking completely, fearful that they will make mistakes.

In talking to a person with Alzheimer's, the goal is to stimulate conversation and win trust on a personal level before expecting her to open up. The particular subject isn't important; I often talk about movies I've seen or parties I've been to. Weddings are a favorite topic with women; ball games rate high with many men. Maintain eye contact to assure the patient that you truly are listening. Be aware of the expression your face is conveying. Every chance you have to nod or pat the patient's arm in affirmation will encourage confidence, and that will help the Alzheimer's person to speak out, even if language is a challenge.

Whenever other people are present, show them how to include the patient, even the most profoundly speech-deprived, by addressing him directly, referring to him, and incorporating him into the general laughter and body language. A wink is a great way to convey a sense of inclusion. The person with Alzheimer's disease — like anyone with memory loss — may soon forget what you say, but he will never forget how you made him feel.

Can we do This?

Talking about the Disease

People with Alzheimer's will let their friends and loved ones know they want or need to talk about the disease. The dilemma is that the friend or family member may not be ready, or prepared, to talk about what is happening and may either deny that the person has the disease or just brush off the attempt to talk about it.

In an early-stage patient support group meeting, Rachel commented, "I long to have someone take my hand and say, 'This must be awful for you.' Instead, my daughter looks at me with tears in her eyes and goes into another room. When I ask my husband if I'm losing my mind, he says, 'We're all getting old' and that's the end of that. I know what's happening. Why won't my family talk about it?" Rachel went on to describe how, after her younger sister was diagnosed with cancer, the whole family rallied and helped her make plans. The contrast makes it all the more difficult for Rachel to comprehend the silence surrounding Alzheimer's.

If patients want to discuss the disease, most often they ask such questions as "Am I losing my mind?" "Am I going crazy?" "What's wrong with me?" Or their desire to talk may take the form of statements such as "I feel like I'm becoming senile," "I'm no good anymore," "I can't seem to think straight," or "I'm so forgetful these days."

No matter what form the comment takes, these personal assertions often have a single meaning: *Tell me why this is happening. Help me understand.* As soon as the person with Alzheimer's broaches the subject, say something like "The brain disease makes you feel that way. Let's talk about it." Talking about the disease helps relieve the patient's anxiety and can often deepen the relationship with the care partner.

A patient may try to broach the subject with her physician — and if the physician is skilled in communicating, that may be a good idea. The physician certainly can discuss the physical, mental, and emotional ramifications of Alzheimer's and may be able to offer intelligent, thoughtful comments and advice when others who are close to the patient feel tongue-tied and ill equipped to discuss these issues.

Since memory loss produces great anxiety, a normal coping mechanism is to try to hide the problem or deny that it is occurring frequently. One time Richard poignantly described how fearful he felt almost every moment as he declined. "Suddenly I'm having trouble remembering my neighbors, although I've lived beside them for thirty-six years. I glance over the evening paper at my wife and fight to recall her name. Still, there are times when I feel like my old self, ready to teach another chemistry class, ready to watch a Packers game, ready to win a hand of bridge. At those moments I think nothing is wrong, maybe I was just overtired. Sometimes things are losing meaning as I breathe. I wish I could tell the people around me how I'm feeling when these 'brain attacks' happen. I'm afraid I'll lose my job or won't be invited to play bridge anymore or will just be treated differently."

When attacks of memory loss increase to the point that they must be acknowledged, a patient's fear grows. At this point, a thoughtful care partner can make all the difference. I was impressed with the way Ernie's daughter, Stephanie, dealt with her father's memory problems without perturbing him.

Ernie was heading to the dining table for lunch when he saw a cardinal perched on the bird feeder outside the family-room window. "Wow, will you look at that!" he said. He followed the bird's flight from the feeder to the cherry tree and then to the neighbor's roof. When the cardinal was out of sight, he returned to his chair in the den, picked up the morning paper, and perused the front page. His soup grew cold on the dining room table.

Stephanie recognized Ernie's ability to focus on only one thing at a time. She reheated the soup, then appeared at his side and used verbal prompting to get him to eat the soup. "Come on, Dad, let's have lunch together." She prompted him without using any chiding or negativity. And calmly saying the word "lunch" was enough to trigger the memory of what he had been about to do before the cardinal captured his attention.

"Oh," he said sheepishly, "I was supposed to do that a while ago, wasn't I?"

Don't Worry about Rejection

Family members, friends, coworkers, and acquaintances are often put off by what appears to be the impaired person's lack of interest in them or downright rejection. Why wouldn't they be offended? After all, someone they have known for years seems now to be snubbing them, averting his eyes when they meet by chance, acting downright bizarre. At other moments, this strange person becomes once again the husband or friend or neighbor he has always been.

The more we understand that his behavior is a result of a disease process and not an intentional desire to be aloof, the more we can help the person who is losing his memory or his ability to focus. At the same time we can be relieved of wondering what we might have done to cause the rejection.

If the person with Alzheimer's has had an outburst when friends are visiting or in the company of others, don't remind her of the incident. Consider only what can be done to keep it from happening again. An outburst may be a direct response to her realization that she no longer fits in. Although she may not know exactly what to do, she may be very much aware of her loss of control. Becoming remote or seeming indifferent is a way of dealing with uncertainty about how to act.

When visiting someone else's home, even a familiar one, the Alzheimer's patient may have hallucinations (seeing or hearing something imaginary), delusions (believing something that is invalid — for example, "I hear people talking about me"), or even paranoid reactions (blaming others for something he himself has done or something he cannot make sense of — for example, "You're stealing all my money!" or "Where did you hide my keys?"). Explaining or trying to clarify what is happening will not help and may make the situation worse by increasing the person's anxiety.

A thoughtful habilitator can calm the anxiety, however, by addressing feelings of fear or sadness directly and by altering the environment in some way; emotion or the environment may be the cause of the hallucination, delusion, or paranoia. Remember that the altered state of perception is real to the patient — don't try to suggest otherwise.

One day Ginny told our care partner support group that her mother Rosalie had called her six times one morning. "Where are you?" Rosalie demanded. "Don't you understand? Someone is robbing me! I want you to do something about it *now*."

"Mom, this is the sixth time you've called. If you'd stop calling long enough for me to get dressed and come over, I'll be right there."

"More things will probably be missing by then!" Rosalie shouted as she hung up.

Take a deep breath, Ginny told herself. *Poor Mom really believes that someone is stealing from her. I must not let my feelings get in the way of helping her through this. Denying that it is happening or reasoning with her sure hasn't helped in the past . . . in fact, it seems to make it worse. I wish I hadn't been so short with her on the telephone.*

Rosalie's front door was unlocked, so Ginny walked in.

"Oh, you scared me!" Rosalie said, starting in surprise. "How did you get in?"

"I walked in. The door was unlocked."

"It certainly was not! It was the burglars — they left it open. They've taken some silver and crystal and money and Lord only knows what else. This is the third time I've been robbed, and the police won't do a thing. What are you going to do, Ginny?"

Ginny knew Rosalie had forgotten that in previous incidents the police had conducted a brief search and found the "missing" objects, which had simply been misplaced. This time Ginny dutifully sat with her mother over a cup of tea and made a list of all the missing objects. Some of them she could see in the china closet, but she wrote them down anyway. Slowly the conversation turned to life in the city today and how it had changed over the years. Rosalie expressed some of her fears of living alone and Ginny again suggested door alarms so she would know if someone was trying to come in. This time Rosalie agreed, and Ginny returned later with the alarms.

Moving to a safer place with people her own age was beginning to sound like a better idea to Rosalie than it had the month before. Meanwhile her feelings had been validated, and Ginny felt one step closer to establishing a more appropriate environment for her mother. Rosalie's issues are typical among patients moving down the road of Alzheimer's disease.

Lights along the Way

Some people with Alzheimer's, fortunately, have jumped at the opportunity to give helpful suggestions for others on the same journey. Sometimes, they counsel, you may stumble, sometimes you will succeed, sometimes you will dance, and you will always need validation.

Over the past fifteen years, along with my colleagues Paul Raia, Elaine Silverio, and Lois Pecora, I have asked early-stage support groups about living with Alzheimer's. The insights the groups have offered have taught us a great deal. Following are some comments by people in these groups.

- I don't know how to act — I've never been here before.
- I cannot function when there is noise — even the sound of my own breathing scares me at times.
- I am waiting for the next shoe to fall.
- Not only is my brain getting smaller, but so is my world.
- Don't "test" me with questions — that does not make me better, it makes me sadder.
- I think my neighbors fear that I'm a madwoman.
- I am still here — parts of me are missing, but parts of me are still damn good.
- I never taught my children how to hear my pain. I was too busy telling them to listen.

These group members were asked what helps the person with Alzheimer's disease to function at the most optimal level, and what suggestions they would have to help others in their situation live more positively. They had the following tips:

- Share your diagnosis with friends and family. As Jake told us, "It is far better to have them walk with you through the disease than to have them run away from you because they think you are losing your mind or have had too many martinis at lunch."
- Cherish each moment. Don't waste a lot of time looking ahead or back. This minute is good only if you make it so, and a lot of little minutes add up to a full day.
- Know that some days or hours will be better than others. Even if today was not such a good day, tomorrow still can be.
- Find humor whenever possible, especially if it means laughing at yourself.
- A peaceful environment is much easier to function in, so keep sounds, like TV, to a low level.

- Tell those you love that you can do almost anything if the steps are easy.
- Have patience with your loved ones; they are learning, too.
- A pocket-size notebook may help you remember appointments or events. Keep this notebook with you at all times and write down everything that occurs during the day. Review your notes at night, highlighting facts that seem significant.
- Buy large-face clocks with black numbers on a white background or vice versa, to aid failing perception.
- Tell storekeepers about your memory problems. Chad carries a card that simply states "I have memory difficulties. Please be patient." He hands the card to wait staff and salespeople. "Most of the time," he says, "I try to revisit familiar places where they already know my condition."
- Increase your support circle by reconnecting with old acquaintances and family members. Long-term memory remains intact for a long time; old buddies can reinforce these memories and share tales of days gone by.
- A "one-day-at-a-time" calendar can help you focus on today and not let the bigger picture overwhelm you.
- Take advantage of every opportunity to feel uplifted. You know the adage about "taking time to smell the flowers." Well, don't forget to feed the neighborhood strays and examine snowflakes and consider the vast difference between an oak leaf and a mountain ash leaf. Steve says he never realized how many kittens came to visit his yard until he had Alzheimer's. "Now I feed every one of them, and I've named them all. I never quite recall their names from one day to the next, but they don't seem to care."
- Register with the Alzheimer's Association Safe Return Program (see Further Resources, page 217), even if you feel certain you will never get lost. This program helps find people

with memory impairment and provides a central structure for monitoring the search for a missing person. Communication with the family awaiting the return of loved one is an integral part of this program.

- A support group for patients is the perfect place for sharing your feelings and concerns. "I feel that I am not alone," says group member Ruth. "No one else ever asks me how I feel. In fact, no one ever seems to think that I do feel, and I feel deeply. My family is crying all the time about losing me — well, so am I."

We need to hear the patient when she asks us to listen. We must support her failing words. Instead of abandoning previous relationships, we need to expand them. We must be innovative, courageous, and flexible and realize that the patient is courageous, too.

We must know, deep in our gut, that the time when the afflicted person is the least lovable is probably the time when he needs love the most. This journey has no guideposts to help us along the way. But we can use our new perception to take slow steps together into this land of altered communication forms. We always need to be mindful that outside appearances give no real clue to what remains within.

The Five Tenets
of Habilitation

· 6 ·

Tenet #1: Make the Physical Environment Work

Sometimes, something is familiar to me.
Most times there is no recognition
of the fabric of my life.
Only frayed remnants of who I once was.

T<small>HE NEXT FIVE CHAPTERS</small> discuss the five tenets of habilitation in detail and in the order that will allow a habilitator to make use of them most easily. To work properly, however, the tenets must be applied all together; the difficult part is often learning how to apply them in a particular situation.

This chapter focuses on the physical world around the person with Alzheimer's and gives specific suggestions for altering the environment to improve the quality of life for both patient and care partner. To begin with, pay close attention to what the memory-impaired person sees, hears, smells, and touches in a world that is becoming increasingly less familiar. These clues will help you adapt the environment to maintain a certain level of self-care, create chances for feeling successful, and minimize distress.

Although none of us lives in the world that the Alzheimer's

patient now inhabits, we can try to understand how the disease may be affecting him. Imagine these difficult experiences:

- Looking at a staircase and seeing a wall.
- Gazing into a mirror to find what seems to be someone else staring back at you.
- Having someone tell you to sit down when you cannot find a chair.
- Hearing many sounds — television, voices, traffic — that others don't hear.
- Feeling keys in your pocket but not knowing what they are.
- Smelling the odor of mothballs in your grandmother's attic — but where is the attic and where is Granny?

Next, consider the feeling of having many senses bombarded at once and having ever greater difficulty separating today from yesterday. Doesn't it feel frustrating and scary? Remember these emotions whenever you interact with the patient. Even in the earliest stage of the disease, she may have some of these feelings. Try to see, feel, hear, taste, and touch as she is — and always remember that no matter how well she is performing, the disease is affecting her perspective, so it is different from your perception.

Next consider how the person's surroundings may affect the changes in perception. You can and should alter the environment so that it helps prevent problems for the patient. The overarching idea is to make the surroundings as simple as possible.

Lighting

Start by thinking through how lighting can help control behavior, increase safety, and offer comfort and a feeling of security to the patient. The goal of lighting is to mimic daylight, which is the most comfortable kind of light for patients. Many distributors now offer bulbs under such names as "day glow," "vita lite," or "pink light." You can also make a fluorescent ceiling fixture feel more like natural light by replacing the cover with a parabolic grid, which resembles rows of two-inch plastic cubes. The grid diffuses light and eliminates shadows. Focused-task lamps should be used only on a desk or a table where the patient works. Having a number of lamps on creates too many shadows, which an Alzheimer's patient may misinterpret or find threatening.

It may seem impractical to leave lights on at night, but accidental toileting problems are not practical either. Nighttime incontinence may just be the result of not being able to find the bathroom quickly enough. At most hardware stores you can purchase a roll of sticky-backed reflector tape, which you can run from bedside to bathroom to mark this most important path, illuminating it with several nightlights. Even better, 3M produces a reflector tape that needs little or no light; it is pricey but worth the cost.

Install dimmer switches throughout the house and turn up the lights as the sun starts to go down to help the patient who may become influenced by "sundown syndrome." Often a patient's aberrant behavior begins to surface at that time of day and may continue for several hours. "Sundowning" generally occurs between three o'clock in the afternoon and eight in the evening, depending on the season.

As part of the effort to simplify the environment as much as possible, try to replace floor lamps with lighting that is attached to the wall. That will help make the house as clutter-free as possible.

Color Schemes

You can also help an Alzheimer's patient by choosing indoor and outdoor color schemes carefully. Researcher Dr. Alice Cronin-Golomb, in the psychology department at Boston University, has found that the disease affects patients' reactions to colors. Sandra Harris, who specializes in interior design for Alzheimer's patients, has found that using unique colors for different areas and spaces can help keep the patient oriented in her home and can enable her to travel from one room to another without getting lost. Flat rather than high-gloss paint on walls helps eliminate both glare and shadows.

Try to find wall colors that contrast with the functional objects in a room. For instance, if the furniture in a room is light-colored wood, you may want to paint the walls deep aqua or a warm peach; if the room has dark, varnished wood furniture, then light-colored walls will provide a good contrast. Bright colors can help balance failing perception of depth and contrast. You may be able to help a patient's orientation by putting colorful cushions on dining chairs, choosing frames in primary colors for her favorite photos, and placing lively place mats under table lamps. The use of colors for definition and contrast will allow the patient to continue using household objects, such as cooking utensils, hobby materials, and small pieces of furniture, for much longer.

Paint the wall behind the toilet a darker, contrasting color so it's easy to spot from the bathroom doorway. If sofas and chairs blend with the background, use colorful throws or afghans to draw attention to where the patient should sit — his altered perception may make it difficult to decide.

Color can be used not only to highlight utilitarian items but also to camouflage objects to avoid. To keep a patient out of harm's way, you can place a black mat inside the front door to suggest a dark chasm that can't be crossed. Many fine long-term-care facilities specializing in the care of Alzheimer's patients have found this to be a great way to keep their residents from wandering off. Staff members report that the most positive aspect of using black mats is not having to issue negative commands. When the Alzheimer's resident sees the "hole," he simply turns back in the other direction.

Along the same lines, painting or wallpapering entry doors to match the surrounding walls makes them harder to see. Place functioning locks, and even doorknobs, up high or down low on doors, leaving the useless locks and knobs in place; the person will often believe that the nonfunctioning lock or knob is broken or stuck and will not see (or look for) the newly installed hardware.

If the patient's bedroom is kept simple, with only a splash of color on the bed to draw her attention, she will tend to use the room only for sleeping at night and dressing rather than for napping during the day.

Consider the following scenario:

Where's my underwear, Wanda?" Burt hollered.

"On the bed, where I always put it. Look on the bed."

Burt tore the bed apart. "It's not here! Where is it? I'm stark naked."

Wanda came into the room. "Look, it's right where I put it. Here on the pillow."

Wanda had made the mistake of placing the white briefs on a white pillow, making it very difficult for Burt to see them. Had she laid Burt's white briefs on top of the navy bedspread, he would easily have spotted his underwear on the contrasting visual field.

By and large, stick to a palette of solid, strong, simple colors. If you are able to visit a paint store and look at paint sample cards, the middle section, working toward the darker end, will include the shades that enable patients to function best. For Alzheimer's patients, the lighter shades seem to blend together, making it difficult to differentiate a chair from the wall behind it, or the sofa from the floor. Checks, stripes of contrasting colors such as black and white, and polka dots create visual confusion and should be avoided. Simple geometric or repeat designs, plaids, and florals are more welcoming.

Flooring

Next consider flooring. At some point, a patient's gait will become shuffling and perhaps scissorslike. Many patients have a history of falls, and frequently the floor covering is to blame for such mishaps. Care partners should adapt the floor surfaces to accommodate the afflicted person's needs. Before altering the flooring, however, start by checking his footwear — especially if he walks with a "shuffling" gait.

You will probably want to continue to use whatever flooring you already have. But if a room has tile floors, for instance, do not spend time trying to get the perfect shine; cleanliness with a dull finish is fine. Shininess or glare tends to create an illusion of water, ice, or other fear-provoking mirages. Wall-to-wall carpeting, without scatter or area rugs, offers a uniform, secure walking surface, but spills and maintenance may present a problem.

Light-colored carpeting is best, since it tends to make a space seem larger and less confining. Since scatter or area rugs often cause accidents, eliminating them is a good idea for safety. Always be mindful, too, of shadows that may be created on flooring, and adjust window coverings or lights to eliminate the sometimes terrifying visual illusions that can form in the perception of a person with Alzheimer's. For safety's sake, repair or level uneven flooring.

If you have the opportunity to choose new flooring, the ideal surface is a simulated hardwood floor (it can be found in most large home improvement centers), because it is reminiscent of older homes and is easy to care for. It is the first choice of interior designers and architects who build facilities for memory-impaired people.

Interior Pathways

Establishing clear interior pathways will help the person with Alzheimer's negotiate spaces safely. He will also feel a sense of accomplishment at being able to find important places — the bathroom, kitchen, or even a favorite chair — more easily.

Consider placing a colorful wallpaper border at waist height along the walls in the rooms where the patient will be spending time. Unsafe entries and exits can be camouflaged by continuing the border across doors and on the surrounding walls. To someone with failing perception, the doors then seem to be just part of the walls.

In a care facility, scenes or designs can be painted on doors to help deceive the residents while ensuring their safety. Bright thematic borders, such as cactus and tumbleweed for Texas, cornfields for Oklahoma, and so forth, can direct residents to activity rooms, while colorful arrows can show the way to the bathroom. An awning hangs over the entrance to the dining room in one of my favorite facilities.

Furniture and Hangings

Remove furniture that is difficult to get into and out of. As the person's motor skills diminish, balance becomes more tenuous. She will require sturdy chairs with arms to push up from and seats with short depth from front to back. Large, overstuffed furniture can prove difficult for the person with Alzheimer's. A glider is a wonderful addition at this time, both for comfort and for recalling memories of rocking chairs. Unlike rocking chairs, which can be quite hazardous, gliders do not actually lift off the floor — just the seat slides to and fro, providing safe hours of enjoyable rocking. Also, recognize that to someone with changed senses, large pieces of furniture that wobble or move when touched, even if safe, may appear ready to topple. Built-in shelves are always safer and less threatening than freestanding units, and they help to keep areas clutter-free and simplified, thus increasing safety and reducing the sense of being threatened.

Simplicity is the watchword for any item that hangs on a wall. For instance, at some point in the middle stage of the disease, mirrors do more harm than good. A glance in the mirror may make the Alzheimer's person believe that another person is in the room — someone who has not been invited, an intruder, some-

Faye is re-arranging all the time

one who is there to do harm. Because the image seems vaguely familiar, the person may perceive it to be an older, possibly deceased relative — a mother, perhaps, or a father who passed away long ago. This can cause great distress and frustration to someone who can't separate facts of existence from unreality. When you first become aware that the patient is no longer using a mirror to inspect his image, replace it with a different wall decoration. (The same principle holds true for hand-held mirrors or those that rest on surfaces, of course.)

You should think carefully about other wall hangings, too. The cognitively impaired adult can easily misinterpret photographs and pictures on the wall, especially if they are protected by glass. Replace reflective glass with no-glare glass to help the patient focus on the painting or photo and not on what might be generated in her mind from shadows and reflections. Remove images that are abstract or show complicated scenes. Instead, simple pictures of flowers, children, and animals evoke harmonious memories. Textured wall hangings and ones that can be touched, including quilted shams, are a source of great enjoyment. Children's artwork and unframed needlepoint images hung on walls can serve as tactile or conversational pieces.

Faux windows with views of, say, a Maine lighthouse or California coastline can break up stretches of blank wall. Patients react to these "windows" so positively that many such scenes are being created solely for use in Alzheimer's facilities.

Eliminate reminders of hobbies that the patient can no longer take part in — any activity that requires fine coordination, for example. At the same time, to encourage hobbies that he can still perform, keep the crafts or tools in clear view, perhaps near a favorite chair.

Finally, a piece of "furniture" that you may want to add is a sturdy fish tank, which can provide hours of viewing pleasure and a chance for the patient to be nurturing by feeding the fish. You'll have to establish a feeding schedule so the fish aren't fed too often. And set a comfortable chair in front of the tank — not beside it — so the patient can watch the fish. Do not depend on the person with Alzheimer's to set up the viewing arrangement.

Use Images to Replace Words

As directions become more difficult and memory less reliable, use images of items to supplant words. Put a picture of dishes on the door of the cabinet where the dishes are stored, a picture of panties on the front of the underwear drawer, a picture of a toilet on the bathroom door or next to the door if you want to leave the door open, especially at night. Frequently assess the environment to adjust or compensate for changes in the patient.

Safety Devices

Many devices can make a patient's surroundings safer. For instance, at the top and bottom of the stairs, you can install child safety gates. Keeping a person with Alzheimer's from climbing stairs is as important as protecting her from falling down them.

Closets also present problems. If the closet doors have knobs, you can install childproof locks on them. These locks, which do not have keys, require some finger dexterity to open but they are quite manageable for most care partners and too complicated for someone who is cognitively impaired. Use these locks to prevent the patient from entering any area where harmful substances are stored, where last season's clothes have been placed out of sight, or where you don't want her to explore. You can also employ these locks to secure items such as medical, cleaning, and other supplies in drawers; one unsuccessful attempt to open a drawer is usually enough to keep the patient from trying again.

If your home has a fireplace, you may want to camouflage the opening by placing something colorful inside it, such as a large basket of yarn or a silk flower arrangement. Remove any firelace screen or door and put it out of sight. Of course, keep matches and other lighting implements well hidden at all times.

If your stove or oven is electric, have someone install a "kill switch" in a place known only to you. Such switches allow the habilitator to use the stove or oven at will but make it impossible for the patient to turn on. If you have a gas stove or oven, consult your local gas company on how to make it tamperproof. The patient should think of the appliance as broken instead of believing that he is unable to make it work. Keep in mind that the afflicted person's physical safety is not the only concern; his feelings of success also count.

Home Areas

Encouraging socialization is an important part of the habilitation approach, and care partners can generate social interaction by placing chairs at angles to one another to signify a place for conversation. A person with Alzheimer's may not be likely to initiate conversation without such clues. And the creation of cozy spaces often makes a patient feel more emotionally comfortable. In a home in which an afflicted person has lived for many years, rearrange furniture to encourage conversation while keeping the arrangement as close to the original pattern as possible. Coziness can be enhanced, for example, by eating meals in the kitchen rather than in a large dining room, or by eating only at one end of the dining table, after making it distinct from the rest of the table. Keep in mind, when entertaining, that large spaces make people with Alzheimer's particularly uncomfortable, especially in social situations.

Of course, at times we all need solitude. Sometimes, in long-term-care settings, staff members believe that patients need to be constantly engaged; but this is no more true for Alzheimer's people than it is for anyone else. No one wants to have every moment filled with activities that may have little meaning to one's past lifestyle; we all need opportunities to be alone, gathering our thoughts, assessing our feelings, and reviewing the past. The patient may have a much stronger perception of the past than of the present, so offer her many chances to review it happily and comfortably.

Toward this end, you can put a favorite chair in a corner of a room to encourage her to be alone at times when she seems to need quiet and introspection.

Outdoors

Repair cracked, uneven, or potholed pavement, trying to make the surface as level and smooth as possible (but not slick, of course).

Being outdoors and having contact with nature can contribute to the patient's well-being and sense of security. Bird feeders and houses, birdbaths, wind chimes, and colorful windsocks may all be points of interest. If the afflicted person likes gardening, whether the enjoyment is in planting or simply experiencing warm earth running through the fingers, worms and all, create a raised flower bed, about three feet high, so it can be comfortably reached. Plant a few flowers or herbs to make the purpose of the bed visually obvious at eye level. The height also saves patients from strained backs. Parsley, sage, rosemary, and thyme are wonderful choices for an outdoor (or indoor) herb garden because of their wonderful perfume, splendid foliage, and great taste when eaten. Chives have fine stalks and offer a pale purple bloom, and yellow nasturtiums — like the other plants I've mentioned — are harmless if ingested. All are easy to care for and have a sweet aroma and interesting colors. (Patients cannot always distinguish edible from inedible plants, so check with the local poison-control center to ensure that all outdoor plantings and houseplants are safe.)

If you have a good-sized yard, creating paths for the patient to wander along can help his serenity. Plant bright annuals, such as geraniums, impatiens, and marigolds, along the paths. The flowers act as guideposts and keep patients away from areas that are uneven or otherwise problematic. Make sure that the plants and flowers within reach are not poisonous, since people with Alzheimer's often mistake plants for food.

A bench or outdoor chairs placed at the end of a walkway can serve as a social area, and possibly as a deterrent to going beyond the walkway. A sturdy six-foot fence around the yard might also be necessary to keep the Alzheimer's person out of harm's way. A fenced area also provides a respite for the habilitator, who knows that the patient can enjoy the outdoors without danger of wandering away. Choose a fence material that cannot be seen through — solid wood, perhaps, or brick, rather than chainlink; that will lower the chances of the Alzheimer's patient becoming overstimulated by objects beyond the fence, and will also reduce her desire to get to the other side. Planting bushes and seasonal flowers in front of the fencing will reduce or eliminate feelings of imprisonment.

Noise and Sound

Noise is also part of the environment. The patient's ability to hear does not change, but he interprets sounds differently as time goes on. Research has shown that many of the sounds we take for granted actually disturb patients with progressive dementias. The sounds of television, telephones, flushing toilets, running water, radios, doorbells, alarm clocks, and traffic, for example, can be overstimulating and agitating to a person with Alzheimer's.

Monitor the patient for signs that she is not able to understand words or separate sounds or that she is scared of noises. Does the soft whirr of an air conditioner seem to be an ever-present annoyance, no matter how loudly she tries to talk over it? Does she fear that every passing car is going to crash into the house?

Unfortunately, as of this writing, there is no test available to evaluate exactly what sounds the patient is hearing or differentiating. But many early-stage patients have said that they function best in a quiet space, and that they become lost in a conversation if more than one person speaks. Furthermore, two or more sounds occurring at once — a bird singing while a baby laughs, for example — can easily overwhelm a person who is struggling to sort out simple information. And an additional background sound, such as that of a furnace, can truly be confounding, as if the noise is coming from within the patient's own head.

If an unexpected sound frightens the person with Alzheimer's, quickly show him what made the sound and repeat the incident. If a pan drops on a floor, for example, drop it again, and point out that you, too, were shaken by the sound. Of course, it's good to avoid having things fall noisily on a tiled floor, for example, and cause clattering; place a nonslip mat on the floor when doing kitchen chores to cushion the sounds and limit breakage.

Sometimes sounds may be frustrating to a patient by reminding her of her shortcomings. Sounds of a meal being prepared can bring back memories of what she can no longer do. Being aware of and sensitive to this problem will help you discover some ways to solve it. You may be able to arrive at an answer without too much trouble.

For instance, at certain times of the day Elliott noted that Janelle's conversation would get louder and louder. All too often, he said, his wife would shout so strongly that neighbors would come over to see if everything was all right. Elliott was stumped. The commotions did not happen all the time and never after the couple went to bed, even though they often had long conversations about the day's happenings then. Elliott also realized that the shouting occurred only in their home. Clearly, Janelle was trying to speak louder than some bothersome sound she could not identify. Using a behavior log to keep track of this troubling behavior when it happened (see Chapter 9), Elliot uncovered the source of her agitation: the noise of warm air humming through the heating ducts. Elliot was so accustomed to the noise he never noticed it, but Janelle registered the sound as something new, an annoyance that could be overcome only by speaking at the top of her lungs. Elliot called in a heating company to wrap the pipes to deaden the sound. He also installed carpet on the cellar ceiling to further muffle the sounds of the furnace.

If you have an area where noise is particularly bothersome, try installing some temporary acoustical ceiling tiles on the walls. You can place sound-diffusing transparent contact paper on windows if street sounds are an annoyance. And don't hesitate to draw the draperies and turn on lights in broad daylight if that will produce a quieter situation. Textured wall coverings (either paint or wallpaper) can help to diffuse sound.

You can also use noise to enhance the patient's safety. Jingle bells or sleigh bells hung on a door or gate can alert a care partner to an attempt to get out, averting a potentially harmful situation. Some hardware and department stores have "traveler's locks" that hang on a doorknob and emit a shrill sound when the knob is turned.

Research has shown that patients' difficulty processing sounds is upsetting for only a short period during the progression of the disease. Perhaps as the person with Alzheimer's retreats more into her own world, she is bothered less by the noises and acoustical interruptions from the outside world. It is very important, however, to pay attention to what is happening during the period when she feels assaulted by noises and is unable to separate or identify the various sounds.

The $100 Hardware Store Revolution*

- Purchase an emergency power-failure light (less than $15).
- Pick up a hand-held shower (about $25).
- Buy a door alarm (about $40).
- Spend the rest of the $100 on halogen light bulbs and double-sided tape or other skid-proofing for throw rugs.
- Throw in another few dollars and buy a timer for the outdoor lights.

---

*Courtesy of Jeanette Rosa-Brady of the Massachusetts Alzheimer's Association.

Habilitation requires care partners to think creatively, applying the five tenets to each situation to arrive at resourceful adjustments. Consider the following examples.

Early one morning, Steve looked out his window on the second-floor landing. The day was going to be beautiful. He smiled as he felt the warm sunshine on his face, then he took two steps forward and toppled headfirst down a flight of stairs. An early-stage Alzheimer's patient, Steve was having trouble distinguishing depth and contrast, and he did not see the stairwell's empty space. That afternoon Steve's son, Tom, laid strings of white Christmas lights against the wall along one side of the stairs, outlining each step, and installed an overhead light to illuminate the stairwell. A timer automatically turned on all the lights at three P.M. and shut them off at nine A.M. Tom also painted the stairwell yellow to contrast with the white walls of the upstairs hall. Tom smoothly altered the environment to solve a potentially hazardous situation without resorting to safety gates or moving Steve to a downstairs room.

Lois's problem was more difficult for her care partner to pin down. One day she stood in the middle of her living room, staring at the floor, for over an hour. Her husband, Ron, begged her to sit down or come to the den. Each time he spoke, Lois looked up and seemed to see him for the first time. Then she quickly looked down again. Ron finally realized that Lois was dealing with an overload of visual information. Standing amid piles of familiar, memory-laden objects, knitting magazines, and photographs, she could not decide where to sit or what to do. Ron discarded unneeded items and cleared off table surfaces. He replaced standard lamp bulbs with bulbs that mimicked sunlight and hung new, sheer curtains to replace the worn blinds. (The late afternoon sun had cast frightening shadows across the walls.) Leaving a space beside Lois's favorite chair where several mementos and her knitting bag could have the place of honor, he threw a bright afghan over the back of the chair to draw Lois's attention to it. Finally, anticipating problems to come, Ron painted the front door and trim the same color as the walls to help camouflage the exit. Utilizing just a handful of habilitation techniques, Ron made it possible for Lois to enjoy her knitting and other daily tasks for the first time in a long time.

One day Sean, who was having memory problems, tried to call his sister, just as he did every day. But the woman who answered was not Annie; he had dialed the wrong number. He dialed again and got a telephone company recording. Realizing that he had been unable to recall her telephone number four times in as many weeks, he sat in his chair, looking at the telephone. Finally it rang, startling him. His sister, who had recognized that something must be wrong with Sean, was on the line. The next day Annie bought him a new telephone with oversized buttons. She programmed each button with Sean's most important telephone numbers and replaced the numerals with a photograph or symbol: Annie's picture on 1, Sean's best friend on 2, an ambulance on 3, and the image of a hypodermic needle (for Sean's physician) on 4, and so on.

Like the care partners in the above scenarios, you will not need to incorporate every one of the recommendations in this chapter. But a few simple adaptations will make the home safer and more habilitative, a setting where the patient and family can thrive. Don't hesitate to be creative — the issues will vary from patient to patient and from day to day, and they will have to be revisited often as the disease progresses. Making the most of the surroundings will maximize the Alzheimer's person's abilities.

7

Tenet #2: Know That Communication Remains Possible

You are smiling at me.
I see my reflection in your eyes.
I've finally found someone
who speaks my language.

REMEMBER THAT the emotions behind failing words are far more important than the words themselves — and it is the emotions that need to be validated. Although many losses occur with this disease, assume that the patient can still register feelings that matter.

Difficulties with Language

"Shut," Stacey screamed at her husband with her hands held tightly over her ears. "Shut, shut, shut!"

Russell had no idea what he had done to elicit this angry response from his usually soft-spoken wife. He crossed the room to where she was standing and gently enfolded her in his arms, letting her sob gently against his chest. It seemed like such a short time ago that Stacey had gone from having difficulty finding words to making up words to struggling to say anything.

"I've been talking too much, haven't I, Stacey? You want me to just shut up, and I don't blame you." Her husband understood that she was struggling, and as her comprehension declined, that the inability to communicate was becoming unbearable. Angrily placing her hands over her ears and yelling "Shut" was her way of letting Russell know she was overwhelmed by his talking. Even though words failed her, her emotion came through loud and clear.

Difficulties with language often cause emotional outbursts such as Stacey's. We must always look for human emotions and qualities that are being repressed but are ready to burst free when the afflicted person wants to make a statement.

Imagine the anguish of having your ability to talk with loved ones, chat with friends, and exchange greetings with strangers slowly taken away from you. Imagine the frustration of thinking you are saying something clearly, then realizing that the person you're addressing does not understand a single word coming out of your mouth. Imagine, too, listening to someone speaking to you and not being sure what language she is using. This is the reality of life for people with Alzheimer's.

In the early stage of the disease, speech problems range from occasional word-finding difficulties to a profound loss of language. Then the ability to process and store information declines. Clinicians agree that in the middle stage a "verbal casserole" becomes common, with disconnected thoughts spoken aloud and invented words and sounds replacing real ones. In the final stage of the disease, speech all but disappears. Throughout the process, the emotional toll on both patient and care partner is enormous.

Reading and writing abilities also change, and for some patients, following a story line becomes impossible. With diminishing attention, memory, and comprehension and declining ability to think logically, understand metaphors and idioms, and make one's needs known, many people with progressive dementias become silent. They do not wish to make verbal errors, and they're frustrated knowing what they want to say and being unable to say it. They become agitated when we do not take the time to figure out the message or when they see negativity or hopelessness in our eyes.

Often the patient will misuse, bastardize, or alter familiar words altogether. Get to know the patterns and be sure to explain any important "words" to other care partners watching over the person with Alzheimer's, even if only temporarily. My husband, for example, used the word "smish" for sandwich. After a while, "smish" meant "food," and he would say "smish" whenever he was hungry.

Remember that in the person with Alzheimer's, the way the brain processes outside stimuli physically changes. Although you are clearly saying, for example, "I bought some lamb chops. Would you like one for dinner?" he may be hearing, "Wooden lamps are dimmer" — and wonder why you are repeating yourself and seem to be waiting for a reply.

If the person doesn't seem to understand you, break down your sentences into less complex patterns, establish eye contact when possible, and use simple, short statements to alleviate the stress related to failing communication. Remember that processing language will take longer than before — give the person time to think. At some point, the processing mechanism may fail completely. The patient just won't understand what's said.

To further complicate matters, when a person with Alzheimer's is word-searching or using clearly incorrect words, he or she may still be able to understand spoken language. Similarly, a patient who is speaking fairly well may have great difficulty comprehending what is being said.

The upshot is that you should always assume that the person understands language and is included in any dialogue. Even if she appears uninterested or bored, speaks out at inappropriate times, or is not speaking logically, continue to show her that she is valued and is still a part of social or family life. A chief complaint of early-stage patients is not being included in conversations.

People with Alzheimer's often complain that others ignore them in conversations — intentionally or unintentionally. Outsiders who do not include the person in conversation often assume that it is no longer worth talking to the patient. This problem may begin when the doctor gives the initial diagnosis. A couple I know were with their doctor, going over the husband's test results. The doctor looked up and said, "Well, Cristina, I think you need to take Jason on that vacation you've both been waiting for. There's a possibility you won't be able to travel too much longer. I'm sorry to say it, but it looks like Jason has dementia of the Alzheimer's type."

At this juncture, Jason stood up and, banging his fist on the doctor's desk, said, "Damn it all. Am I invisible? This is *my* disease you're talking about — I'm still here. Talk to me. Me!"

The doctor apologized, looked directly into Jason's face, and told him, "Your diagnosis is most probably Alzheimer's disease. Most of the tests point in that direction. Let's do another MRI scan in six months and compare it with the one you took last week. Does that sound logical?"

"Yes," Jason said. "Thank you for telling me."

Communication difficulties may begin at the same time as other problems, making the situation even more difficult. For the person experiencing cognitive decline, the slow loss of coherent speech will be compounded by a declining ability to draw conclusions.

"It is so cold," Nancy said, gazing out the window. "And it's raining so hard outside." At that point, her husband, Douglas, nodded at her, roused himself from the chair where he been sitting for the past few hours, and proceeded out the front door without putting on any kind of raingear. For Douglas, the cause-and-effect thinking that the rest of us practice subconsciously every day no longer existed. The last word he heard Nancy utter was "outside," so he followed that verbal cue, with no thought of protecting himself from the elements.

Many care partners tell me they use this "last-word connection" to their advantage. They relate that this technique actually can help a person with Alzheimer's feel in control of decision-making. Here's how the technique works. The care partner asks, "Would you like to wear this green shirt today, or the one that's blue?" Nine times out of ten, the patient says, "Blue" — simply because it was the last word he remembered hearing. If you ask, "For lunch today, do you want a tuna fish sandwich or cheese?" the response will be "cheese." The wonderfully habilitative part of this technique is that the afflicted person, who is prone to feelings of failure or defeat, now feels able to make choices.

Yes re groceries!...

Emotional Communication: Beyond Words

Words are only one part of communication, of course. When visiting an Alzheimer's unit in a long-term-care facility, I frequently come across small groups or pairs of people relating to each other as dear old friends. They appear to be reliving more youthful times and laughing together as they share stories of their past. Upon closer inspection, I sometimes find that each person is speaking a different language, perhaps the foreign language he or she grew up with. Yet even with no words in common, the emotional communication takes place.

I can only assume that Alzheimer's patients focus on the speaker's eyes and determine meaning through tone and gestures, much the way we can watch television without the sound on and still understand the plot. In the same way, if your boss has ever instructed you to come into her office and then has proceeded to take a telephone call, you don't need any words to tell you how she really feels about you.

Everyone uses gestures and pictures, tone and voice pitch, facial expressions and body movements, to convey messages to friends, colleagues, family, and strangers. At times, body language

:) COVID ≠ no body language

seems more honest and reliable than words. People with Alzheimer's, in trying to compensate for their cognitive and sensory losses, pay more attention to this nonverbal communication and become quite adept at understanding it.

Consider a situation in which I found myself three decades ago. I was trying to direct my husband to sit in a chair. Several attempts had failed, and I felt close to the breaking point at the end of a long day. I had helped with fourth-grade homework, made brownies, diapered and rediapered a toddler, and now this.

"Just do it because I love you," I said in a flat tone.

He immediately stepped close to me and placed his forefinger gently on my eyes. "No," he said clearly and, touching my eyes again, repeated, "No." And he was right. At the moment that I was declaring love, my eyes denied the words. In his own way, he was saying loudly and clearly, "Your eyes don't love me."

Whenever you need the person with Alzheimer's to complete a task, you will be able to communicate your message in far less time by showing patience and confidence through body language as well as words. As we've seen in the context of dining and bathing, taking time to sit with the patient, to talk about simple things without expecting a response, is one of the best ways to win cooperation. Communication says that we value the patient. Also, never underestimate the power of physical communication with a person who has Alzheimer's. Touch is a marvelous expression of nurturing and security.

Here are some specific guidelines for communicating positively:

- Approach the person in a calm, gentle way, and always from the front, to foster trust.
- Set the stage for discourse with a tone that reflects respect.
- Speak slowly, in a low tone, using simple sentences rather than complicated language patterns. The patient's hearing is not the problem, so raising your voice is not the answer.

• Be patient; the person with progressive dementia takes extra time to process information.

When people other than family members are going to be with the patient, be sure to tell them about his personal vocabulary, so that they use familiar terms for any concepts they are trying to communicate. If the last meal of the day has always been referred to as "dinner," then calling the patient to "supper" will not achieve the expected response.

Use simple language, because idioms, metaphors, slang, and other speech variations are extremely difficult for a person with Alzheimer's to interpret. If you suggest to a patient that she is "pulling my leg," be prepared for her to literally do just that.

When you need to have a serious conversation, find a quiet place where the patient will not be overstimulated. The best place is one where you can sit at right angles to the patient, establish eye contact, and hopefully touch him to show your support, concern, and love during the conversation.

Assure the patient frequently that her communication is successful. She knows failure all too well and needs constant reassurance that she is still a functioning human being. When the patient's words are mixed up and seem nonsensical, smile, touch her, and simply say, "I am having a problem understanding." This underscores that she is not the problem.

Avoid asking open-ended questions. Statements are preferable because they do not call upon the person to make decisions. "Let's have a cup of coffee" will reap a response, while "Do you want a cup of coffee?" may garner a "no" when, in fact, he or she would love coffee but can no longer verbalize the choice. "No" often seems the safer reply to a question. A person with Alzheimer's is likely to perceive questions as a kind of testing, which makes him feel like a failure.

Humor remains the best way to communicate. Laughing at oneself is a true gift; laughing with someone else is the greatest joy. Watch comedy videotapes together, listen to humorous audio cassettes, and read aloud funny anecdotes. Often it is the laughter itself that brings pleasure; the patient doesn't necessarily have to understand the punch line. Recall amusing situations you have shared, and laugh together until your sides hurt.

Remember the power of music, a universal tool for communicating with those whose language is impaired. A Mozart flute concerto speaks to people from many countries and backgrounds; people of all ages and many ethnicities clap along to a Sousa march. Ethnic and religious music can be used to lull someone to sleep, to encourage recall, and to calm obstreperous behavior. Of particular therapeutic value is the music from a person's early cultural background. And many people with progressive dementias who are described as nonverbal can still sing every word of "Happy Birthday." (The best Alzheimer's programs employ a music therapist as a permanent staff member to reach nonverbal residents through song and dance, exercise, and reminiscing.)

Always listen to the emotion behind the patient's failing words. The emotion is still intact; at some elemental level, you can still reach it. The actual words are not important if you can understand the feeling behind the attempt to communicate.

8

Tenet #3:
Focus on Remaining Skills

I suffer most for my loss
of self-esteem,
not for the loss
of choosing my wardrobe.

Focus ONLY on the skills that the patient still has. Value whatever abilities remain. Help her compensate for any lost abilities without bringing them to her attention.

Those of us without dementia can go through our activities of daily living without thinking or rehearsal. While other thoughts occupy our minds, we shower, dress, eat breakfast, listen to the morning news, tie a Windsor knot, fasten jewelry, and take on the day. That's not true for Alzheimer's patients, of course.

Bathing

Of all the activities of daily living, the biggest single problem for most care partners appears to be keeping an Alzheimer's patient clean. Why, adult children wonder, does Father want to be dirty all of a sudden? Why does Mom refuse to take a shower? A wife can't understand why her husband behaves like a lion when faced with a washcloth; a husband is frustrated when his wife screams when she looks into the bubbles of a warm bath.

Unfortunately, the battle of the bath begins early in the disease process and, without the habilitation approach, continues till the end. Consider the scene Paulette and her health-care aide, Jayne, had during one bath time. Jayne had been trying to coax Paulette, who exhibited most of the typical signs of the middle stage of Alzheimer's, into the tub for almost twenty minutes. Paulette was standing beside the bathtub shivering; the towel wrapped around her midsection did little to warm her or to protect whatever vanity remained.

"Just get into the nice bath," pleaded Jayne. "You haven't had a good bath in days."

Paulette, who had limited language use, first replied, "Go, go, wo, wo, wo." Then she started talking louder and began shaking her fist at the mirror.

Tired of the battle, Jayne leaned over slightly to lift one of Paulette's feet into the warm water.

"No, no, no," Paulette screamed, suddenly pummeling and scratching at Jayne's face and arms. "No, no, no!"

Jayne gave up and took Paulette back to her bedroom.

Every day, thousands of patients and care partners in homes and facilities go through this kind of battle. In most cases, the habilitation approach can ameliorate the situation.

Although I have stated this before, it is well worth repeating: *Never attempt to reason with someone who has lost her reason.* Twenty minutes was far too long a time for Jayne to try to coax Paulette into a bath. A long discussion about the need for a shower or bath will lead only to confrontation and a fractured ego. And Paulette's fear, suspicion, and chills must have grown during the course of the standoff.

What's more, Jayne should have kept Paulette thoroughly wrapped until she stepped into the bath. A care partner should remove the warming garment at the last moment, even if that means getting the edges of it wet. Clothes and towels dry quickly — spirits take far longer to heal. Jayne should also have removed the mirror from the bathroom, since it's very likely that Paulette became even more distressed by the perception of an additional person in the room.

Next, Jayne needed to be more attentive to Paulette's emotions, taking the time to reassure her and to establish trust. For example, Jayne could have chatted about a topic of interest to Paulette while making the bath preparations, letting Paulette feel that she was involved in the process.

When Jayne leaned in front of Paulette, she would have been much safer if she had first given the patient a washcloth to hold and focus on. Paulette would then not have had time to be afraid or worried. Intimidation and fear are generally the triggers for malevolent behavior during bathing time. Resistance is not a conscious choice — the patient truly does not have the cognitive powers to make the decision to fight.

Several problems may crop up each time a person with Alzheimer's faces a bath or shower:

- The patient may perceive the bath or shower as a first-time ordeal every time. He simply may not remember the expectations of bath time.

- Removing clothing — or having it removed — can increase feelings of loss of control. The inability to articulate those feelings can raise the patient's anxiety.

- The sound of running water may induce fear in someone with failing auditory perception.

- Impaired perception of color, depth, and contrast may keep the patient from seeing clear water. Adding a blue or blue-green coloring agent to the tub helps make the water visible.

- The feeling of water suddenly splashed on the face can cause fear. If possible, wash the patient's face and hands separately,

Where is Mom on This? 4/21

not in the shower. Shampooing can also cause anxiety, so shampoo only when you must do so, and use dry shampoo whenever possible.

· The odor of an unfamiliar kind of soap may induce fear.

The person's shortened attention span may cause another problem. Don't ever suggest that the patient "wait a minute" while you get something ready. One woman in a care-partner support group told us how she had her husband all prepared for his shower when she realized she had forgotten fresh towels. "That's when the fateful 'wait a minute' escaped my lips," she said. "I went to get the towels and he went for a walk, stark naked, out the front door." Her husband simply did not have a long enough attention span to wait.

The habilitator trying to instill confidence should maximize the creature comforts. Light a lavender-scented candle, offer a soothing cup of tea or glass of wine (be sure the cup or glass is plastic, however). And why not play some soft background music? The bathroom should be warm, well lit, and have nonskid rugs and safety bars. Place a shower chair in the stall or use a bath bench (see Further Resources, page 227) in the tub, close the shades or curtains, and shut the door. If you are giving the patient a shower, use a hand-held nozzle and work from the feet up. This method gives the person a chance to feel the water's warmth and a sense of pleasure as the water slowly moves up his body.

If you know that the person you are helping will become anxious — as Paulette did — give her something other than the bath to focus on. Along with washcloths, sponges and loofas work well. One care partner I know placed a lava lamp nearby to capture her husband's attention while she gave him a scrub.

If a bath or shower causes panic, try giving just a sponge bath. Sequencing the steps will help keep the patient as involved as possible. First, with the patient wrapped in a terrycloth robe or towel, you might say, "Hmm, this is a nice warm cloth." Wait a moment, then hand it to her, saying, "Wash your face." Have a towel ready and, when she is done, let her dry her face herself. Then move on to the next body part, exposing only whatever is necessary. Offer simple instructions, demonstrate with gestures, and show that you are not in a hurry. Offer praise whenever possible, of course.

Giving a bath may require some real ingenuity on your part. My friend Susan gave new meaning to the term "sponge bath" when her husband, Tyler, made it quite clear that he was never going to bathe again. A six-foot-four-inch-tall career marine, Tyler one day underscored his determination by picking up his five-foot-two wife and plunking her down on top of the washing machine in their townhouse. Tyler's language had failed considerably, and he rarely spoke, but Susan understood what he meant. Determined to find a way to get her husband clean, this feisty woman, equipped with a pail of warm sudsy water, waited for Tyler to fall into his "snoring stage" of sleep each night, and then she got out her sponge and started to work.

If he began to wake up, she said, "I would throw a towel over him, pull up the covers, and run like hell. He never ever caught me, and he was relatively clean from then on. Boy, was I proud. It took four days to get his whole body clean and then I'd start again. But he never caught on." That was creative care partnering.

Dressing

Outsiders often perceive a patient's careless or sloppy dressing as showing a lack of interest, when it actually may just be the inability to cope with buttons, zippers, snaps, or jewelry, all of which require considerable finger dexterity. Having put together a fairly unconventional ensemble by herself, the patient may feel well dressed. But she may register the care partner's expression of embarrassment, anger, or frustration. And later in the disease, when the patient certainly requires assistance with dressing, how a care partner does this can affect the patient's emotions for several days.

Consider the patient's reactions in these two situations, which were discussed in one support group.

Scott was filling the dishwasher with the breakfast cutlery as Beverly came down the front stairs ready for her Saturday morning hairdresser appointment. Scott finished up, stepped around the corner, and looked at his wife.

"What the heck do you think you're doing?" he said.

His response took Beverly aback. "What do you mean?"

"Look at how you're dressed. Now go back upstairs and put on the right clothes. And hurry up or we'll be late."

Beverly went back up to her room, lowered herself onto the edge of the bed, and waited for some time. Scott's voice broke her reverie. "Beverly, are you ready? We have to go right this minute or we'll be too late. C'mon, let's go — now."

Beverly gathered her pocketbook and started down the front stairs, hoping that Scott would already be in the car and that they could avoid another confrontation. But when she stepped outside, Scott saw her and jumped out of the car. He raced toward her, grabbing her arm, and hurriedly ushered her back inside the house.

"Ow! Scott," Beverly whimpered. "What did I do? Why do you hate me?"

"I don't know why you are doing this to me! I can't take you anywhere dressed like this. For cripe's sake, those are your gardening pants, and that's the blouse you wore to the Valentine's Day dance at the club. All the people at the salon are going to think you're nuts — or that I am, for letting you go out like that."

Beverly ended up in bed in tears, with Scott phoning the salon to cancel her appointment.

Contrast that scene with another scenario. One Thursday, as was their custom, Jan took her mother, Melanie, to a local seafood restaurant for a four o'clock "early-bird special." It was raining, and Jan was late picking up her mother. Melanie was already bundled up and ready to go.

When they reached the restaurant, the maitre d' showed them

to their table, and Jan suggested that Melanie remove her coat. When she did, there she was in all her glory, clothed only in a thin, well-worn pink slip, with one strap held up with a tiny gold safety pin.

Jan's response was the best way to turn what could have been a humiliating catastrophe for both mother and daughter into a seemingly normal evening with no loss of self-esteem. She leaned across the table and said, "It's so chilly in here tonight that I'm keeping my coat on — how about you?" Her mother nodded in agreement, and let a blushing young waiter help her back into her wrap.

When I asked Jan if she had been horribly embarrassed, she replied that she felt the situation wasn't about her — it was about maintaining her mother's dignity. That night Jan and Melanie's dinner was lovely, as always. The experience underscored a habilitation lesson: it isn't Alzheimer's that takes away the person's dignity; it's other people's reactions that do.

Think about how the situation with Beverly and Scott could have been improved. "That blouse is so beautiful," he could have said, "I think you should save it for when we go out to dinner tonight. And how about if I find your sweater that's brown, the one that goes so nicely with those slacks, which are brown?" (Repeating the word "brown" and ending the sentence with "brown" would make Beverly more likely to remember it.)

And if Beverly had resisted the change of clothing, the worst-case scenario would have found her at the beauty salon decked out in an odd outfit — but that probably wouldn't have bothered the hairdresser, who must have already noticed the changes in Beverly's behavior. Every care partner needs to smile tolerantly at a few odd fashion statements if she is going to survive. Remember whose problem it is — and whose dignity you are trying to save.

After Scott brought up Beverly's dressing problem in his support group, he figured out how he could better handle such situations in the future. Scott asked his daughter to come over and begin weeding out Beverly's closet. Along with making sure that only seasonal outfits remained, the daughter hung matching pieces together, choosing as many solid colors as possible. When Beverly noticed that some of her clothes were missing, Scott mentioned that the garments were in storage — a "fiblet" that brought peace.

Several weeks later the daughter returned to remove a few more items, and she kept doing so until the closet contained only those clothes that would complement each other. Although Beverly's clothes choices would not make her look the way she used to before her diagnosis, they were reasonably appropriate. Most important, she could feel a sense of control in her world.

How to Help a Patient Dress Successfully

Choose clothing for:

- Ease. The garment can be put on and taken off easily.
- Comfort. The clothing does not restrict movement.
- Recognizability. Try to use clothing that the patient can easily recognize. Buy the same outfit again and again; if it wears out or is too stained, you know it is a favorite.
- Familiarity. Do not introduce new styles or faddish clothes.
- Color. Choose colors that you know the patient will enjoy or would have chosen for himself.
- Touch. Use textured clothing when you can. Velvet and silks are lovely to touch.

Here are some clothing choices that have proved to be useful:

- Simple, comfortable socks and shoes
- Slip-on, Velcro-tabbed shoes or sneakers
- Ankle-high socks (all the same color and type, to avoid mismatches and reduce anxiety)
- Knee-high stockings for women
- Open-collar shirts and dresses
- Clothes that are one size larger than usual
- Shirts and dresses that pull on over the head
- Elastic-waist, loose-fitting pants
- Avoid clothes that have zippers or buttons, are tight or otherwise restrictive, or confuse the patient.

Never act as if you're in a hurry if you need to assist a patient dressing. A person with Alzheimer's disease needs considerably more time to process information and can usually handle only one command at a time.

Try to schedule appointments in the afternoon whenever possible. When you have no alternative to an early schedule, be sure to set out the afflicted person's clothes the night before, so they are ready to be put on in the morning.

Other problems may also make an Alzheimer's patient unable to dress as she used to. Muriel, for example, was in the late-middle stage of Alzheimer's and, much to her sister Nina's chagrin, she wore the same yellow dress day after day. Sometimes Muriel even wore the dress to bed. And she often wanted to wear it when shopping with Nina; no amount of cajoling or reasoning changed Muriel's mind. Probably Muriel wasn't aware that the dress was soiled and wrinkled, since she was no longer sensitive to hygiene and tidiness.

Nina could have found a way to bypass this common situation. She could wait until Muriel was asleep, remove the yellow dress, and then buy several similar dresses that offered the same simplicity and comfort and color that made the dress so appealing to Muriel.

And don't worry about buying clothing that you would not have purchased for the patient in the past. Although you may never have imagined your mother in a sweatsuit, for example, the time may come when such a suit is the most comfortable way to dress, particularly in the late stage of the disease.

A problem that crops up with many people who have Alzheimer's is wanting to undress at inappropriate times. For the patient who loves to disrobe, the answer can be a one-piece jumpsuit with a zipper in the back. Or you can give the person a "busy apron" to distract him when he tries to remove his clothes. A busy apron is nothing more than a regular apron with many items sewn onto it — for example, buttons, zippers, ribbon, flowers, dangling objects, keys, and so on. It keeps the patient's hands en-

? Yikes! OK!

gaged and minimizes frustration. (The Products section of Further Resources, page 227 lists suppliers of comfortable clothing and useful gadgets.)

You may also find that when a woman requires assistance with grooming and dressing, you can help her by applying a little fragrance or makeup, even if she has never used such niceties before. When outsiders pass her in the supermarket or the corridor of the nursing home, they may smile or compliment her.

Similarly, don't forget the value of complimenting a patient on his looks. Complimenting someone with progressive dementia may not only add to feelings of self-worth, but, as inhibitions dissipate with the progress of the disease, may result in an effusive affirmative reaction. Stephanie shared with her support group what happened when she complimented her shy father, who was dressed in his "usual navy suit." Her comment, "You look really great today, Dad," resulted in his sweeping her up in a bear hug, and suddenly involving her in a two-step dance around the living room. Stephanie said she had never felt so close to her father; her compliment and his response were the beginning of a new phase in their relationship.

Eating

Care partners often become frustrated when soup cascades down a patient's shirt front, fingers end up gloved in bright orange squash, or coffee swims over mashed potatoes on a plate. This is what was upsetting Fran when she called me about her father. "From now on I am going to feed him myself," she said. "I can't take it anymore. He was always so well groomed. He'd die if he knew what he looked like now — covered with food. And he runs the other way when he sees me."

Fran needed to learn that the goal is not impeccable social dining skills but — at this point you know the answer — as much independence as possible. The biggest challenge for care partners is in adjusting their attitude, accepting the patient as he is now, not expecting him to be who he once was. Fran was projecting her disdain onto her father, with the result that he actually ran the other way when she approached him.

Patients can have trouble dining for several reasons, including the following:

- Inability to recognize how items are used
- Failing visual perception
- Diminishing attention span
- Language difficulties
- Declining motor skills
- Reduced social graces

Introduce finger foods when the patient is in the early stages of the disease, before the need becomes imperative. Finger foods are the best choice for maintaining dignity, providing opportunities for success, and encouraging proper nutrition. Such foods don't require utensils, condiments, or plates and can be served at any time of day as snacks or at regular mealtimes. Finger foods can be served throughout most of the disease process. (See the Appendix, page 207, for finger food suggestions.)

In the example below, see if you can identify habilitative methods that would improve the outcome. (Coming up with answers for at least six problems will earn you an A.)

At Jameson and Louise's small dining table, Jameson set the radio so he could listen to a football game. Louise laid a flowered place mat on the striped tablecloth and set the table with silverware and a plate. Next she brought in the teapot, sugar bowl, creamer, salt and pepper shakers, and a carefully folded napkin. She set a white porcelain bowl of fruit in the middle of the table. For years the couple had used this arrangement for their meals. Jameson would listen to sports games at the table, while Louise would carry her plate to the den and watch television as she ate.

Louise next brought out a large bowl of macaroni and cheese and set it in front of her husband, saying, "Try not to make too

for Visits with Faye

much of a mess." As she walked away, she heard a crash. She turned around and saw Jameson half standing, with the macaroni bowl and the food at his feet. What's more, he was eating a bright orange tangerine — peel and all.

What could have been changed to make the experience easier for both Jameson and Louise? First, Louise should have turned off the radio. Mealtime is the wrong time for extra sound, with Jameson needing every grain of his remaining attention capability to focus on eating. And the time of the meal could be changed so he could listen to the game later, since it was such a source of enjoyment for him.

Setting a place mat on the tablecloth provided too much visual stimulation for Jameson. The different patterns created a sense of visual bombardment. The best choice is a mat that contrasts with the table and with the plate, to aid both visual contrast and depth perception. For example, on a wooden table, use a solid-color mat and a white plate: the plate will contrast with the mat, which in turn contrasts with the table; the food will be the primary focus of attention.

Jameson never noticed the macaroni and cheese, which in his simplified color palette matched the white bowl. Louise could have put the mainly white food on a brightly contrasting plate. Or she could have shaken some red paprika on top of the food, or chopped chives, ketchup, or grated yellow cheese. (These tricks also work for white vegetables, such as cauliflower, and fish.)

Louise should have put out only the silverware Jameson would need for the food she was serving. All the silverware created an additional stimulant for him. Just a soup spoon or tablespoon would have been fine for the macaroni and cheese, given Jameson's declining motor skills. Serving a sandwich would have been even better, since then Jameson would not have needed any utensils. (According to the same habilitative principle, the best way to present soup is in a mug.)

Like many people with Alzheimer's, Jameson could not distinguish the edible part of the fruit from the inedible skin. One day I searched for a missing banana, only to learn, hours later, that the patient I was working with had devoured it, peel and all; another time he ate a tea bag. Fruit should be kept out of sight or peeled and left out as a handy "help-yourself" snack. Frequent small meals might have been better for Jameson if he had a short attention span. Leaving easily spotted, nutritious finger foods in various places can help a person with progressive dementia get the nutrition he needs.

Finally, Louise's derogatory remark about a mess did nothing to boost Jameson's feelings of self-esteem. Even when cleaning up after a mishap, a care partner using the habilitation approach tries to avoid making the person with Alzheimer's feel responsible for the problem. The day will come when you no longer have to deal with accidents and calamities. Believe it or not, you may miss them.

Eating, of course, is not just a matter of physical skills but also a question of nutritional intake. The care partner needs to monitor changes in the patient's weight and eating habits, evaluating whether the alteration may be the result of a physical or medical condition. Can the patient say that she is cold or thirsty? Does she recognize food as the answer to hunger?

Stay on the lookout for possible dehydration, which may occur because the patient no longer recognizes the signal of thirst, because she is taking certain medications, or because she is simply not drinking enough fluids. You should offer fluids throughout the day, but not after supper, to discourage urination at night. If you notice that the person with Alzheimer's seems to be losing weight, check for ill-fitting dentures or aching teeth. He may not be able to report such problems, which might make eating more difficult.

What if the person doesn't seem to be hungry at mealtime? To stir up an appetite and bring the mind around to thoughts of mealtime, offer a bit of wine or grape juice in a cocktail glass before dinner. The only snacks offered before meals should be a healthful selection of sliced vegetables and a dip to take the place of a vegetable served during the meal.

Recognize that large portions can easily overwhelm the patient, even if big servings pleased him in the past. Tastes also change, and at some point you may need to augment food with condiments, herbs, and spices for someone with progressive dementia. You may be able to encourage the patient to eat by adding a little sugar to the food, even if she previously didn't care for sweets. Many care partners sprinkle brown sugar on scrambled eggs and mix softened chocolate chips into whipped potatoes. These combinations may not be to our taste, but we're not the ones with the disease.

If the patient is reluctant to take medications, you can in many cases purchase the medicines in liquid form and blend them into an appealing shake (see the Appendix, page 210, for blender recipes). Shakes are a good way to provide additional nutrients when the person is not eating well.

Sometimes the person with Alzheimer's simply needs a visual cue to start eating. A quiet table for two is a good setting for engaging the patient in the social ritual of eating. Eat with her whenever you can, for the need for human interaction is constant. What's more, some social graces may surface when least expected. The afflicted person may be only a passive conversational partner, but you can chat about pleasant happenings in the world or your life. You can talk about books, movies, sports, or fashions, even though the discussion will not be what it was before the impairment. And, as a bonus, dining together is an opportunity for the patient to mimic your dining style — a built-in cueing system without words but with a positive use of body language.

Whether or not you eat with the patient, make sure that the lighting is good enough to focus clearly on the meal, yet not so bright as to cast shadows, which can be disruptive. As I've mentioned, shadows may elicit hallucinations or raise the level of the patient's stress.

It is a good idea to cover the patient's clothing to keep spills from becoming a problem, but don't use a childish bib. Cover yourself the same way you cover the patient and say, "This may be a messy meal for both of us," as you spread the lap towel. To avoid confusion, serve no more than one item at a time. You might put a mug of soup in front of the patient, then remove the mug when she has finished, before bringing in a sandwich.

If you are the care partner but not a family member, find out about the patient's favorite foods and accustomed dining schedule from someone who knows her more personally. Ask when she eats the day's biggest meal. Learn whether she likes to have coffee or tea at certain times of the day, and what she likes in the beverage. Inquire whether snacking between meals is the norm. Routine and familiarity are cornerstones of habilitative care.

Consider what can happen if you don't know such details. When Rob's nursing-aide agency assigned him to be a live-in companion for Connie while her family spent a month vacationing, he thought the undertaking would be rather easy. Connie's family had described her as easygoing, affable, and pleasant. She rose early, spent most of the day in the garden, and retired by nine P.M. Although she was in the early stage of Alzheimer's, she had a profound loss of language skills. Otherwise, Connie was quiet and kept to herself.

Waking before Connie on their first morning together, Rob prepared a breakfast of bacon and eggs, which he set before her. He poured her a cup of coffee.

"Milk?" he asked. "Sugar?"

"Not." She shook her head, frowning, pushing the untouched plate away.

Rob pushed them back. "C'mon, Connie, you have to eat. I made these special for you."

Connie rose from the chair and went back upstairs to her room. Later she went out into the garden, and, unknown to the aide, drank water from the hose. Rob prepared a fresh pot of coffee for them and offered Connie a cup on the patio.

"Not, not, not," she said, her voice rising.

"What do you want? You haven't eaten anything. It's almost lunchtime. What should I make you for lunch? Do you want a salad? I'm going to make one for me. I'll make you one, too."

Connie returned to gardening. Rob prepared the salads, but again Connie did not eat (although she drank some more water from the hose).

Their interaction continued in that way, with Rob preparing meals and Connie refusing to eat and becoming angrier with each meal. Where was the sweet patient her family had described? Finally, sometime during the second week, Rob, at his wits' end, suggested that Connie go shopping with him.

"You pick out what you want. I don't care what it is. I will make it for you."

She seemed at first not to understand. Then, as they slowly ambled the aisles, she began touching familiar items. The first was tea bags. *Of course,* thought Rob. *Tea, she drinks tea, not coffee. No wonder she pushed the coffee away. Wouldn't you think the family would have told me?* He grabbed the box of tea bags and tossed them into the basket. Connie smiled. A new partnership was beginning.

Nothing could have been more important than for the family to tell Rob about Connie's likes and dislikes — where she liked to have her meals, what snacks she enjoyed, and what time meals were served. This kind of information not only keeps the patient scheduled and on familiar grounds, but helps to seal a positive relationship between the person with Alzheimer's and any temporary companion.

As the disease continues, the care partner needs to be on the alert for more serious issues concerning food. In the late stage, a person with Alzheimer's may have difficulties with chewing and swallowing, for instance. When such problems start to occur, the patient's physician or other health care provider should refer the person to a speech therapist. That specialist can give tips on the best feeding methods and types of food, such as soft, thick foods. These recommendations will maximize comfort for both the patient and the feeder.

Toileting

Thank you
for hanging a picture of a toilet
on the bathroom door.
Thank you
for not mentioning it.

Problems with toileting may arise in early stages or may not be a threat until the late stage. Over the past few decades, most clinicians who have worked with Alzheimer's patients have concurred that early in the disease, incontinence is not related to medical or physical causes so much as to environmental or other treatable conditions. Some people with Alzheimer's seem to think that it is safer to urinate outdoors than to try to find the appropriate place indoors. In many cases, the person once lived on a farm, was allowed to use the outdoors during the summer, or even had an outhouse as a young person. Being aware of the patient's background and social history enables family members and health care professionals to prepare for disconcerting situations such as inappropriate outdoor toileting.

The basic assessment for habilitative toileting includes learning whether the patient can find the bathroom and toilet, can indicate that she needs to use the toilet, and can undress quickly enough.

Marc awakened just after midnight, realizing that he had a strong urge to urinate. He rose from the bed he shared with Danielle, slipped into the sandals near his bedside, and went to the bathroom. Marc returned to bed and immediately fell back to sleep. Later Danielle reported that for three nights in a row, he walked over to the closet next to the bathroom, opened the closed door, and "peed all over my clothes."

Solving that problem was straightforward. Danielle stuck reflecting tape on the floor between Marc's side of the bed and the bathroom door. At night the tape acted as a one-inch-wide bright green pathway, guiding Marc to the bathroom at night. During the day the reflector tape did not show.

Also, Danielle used several inexpensive "touch" lamps in the bathroom to help Marc. (She had previously attempted to leave the bathroom light on many times, but frugal Marc would always shut it off before going to bed.) Danielle touched the lamp's plastic domes before retiring, so that a soft light emanated — just enough to offer a warm beacon to Marc as he approached, drawing his attention away from the closet and to the bathroom.

Danielle happily reported to a group of care partners that Marc had learned to use the bathroom, and she had successfully cleaned her clothes. (By the way, if urine odor is permeating a room of your home, the products offered to rid areas of the smell of cat urine work on human mistakes too.)

Danielle used some of the techniques I have found most helpful. Along with adjusting the environment to deal with the toileting issue, she replaced Marc's cardigans with pullovers to eliminate the struggle with buttoning, and she placed each day's medication in a small bright red plate at mealtime to draw his attention and aid his feeling of independence. She also greatly decreased his frustration when he was searching for a word by quickly saying it to him. These methods center around the patient's ability to find his way; attention span; depth, color, and contrast perception; fine motor skills; short-term memory; verbal abilities; and problems with medications or other illnesses.

To reduce visual problems, pick out a bright paint color that you can live with for a few years; turquoise, plum, terra cotta, and emerald green are great choices. Paint the bathroom walls a contrasting color to the toilet and sink, remembering that it's not likely that an interior-decorating magazine will be calling to photograph your décor. The white porcelain sink and toilet (and, perhaps, bathtub or shower) will be much more visible.

In many cases it is essential for the care partner to suggest to the person with short-term memory problems that it's time to make a trip to the bathroom. You can do this with habilitative language that does not imply that the patient needs to be reminded. You can say, "I think I'll scoot into the bathroom, Dad, why don't you go before me?" or "I'm going to use the upstairs bathroom, Mom. You can use this one over here. The one with these great blue walls." Many habilitative long-term-care programs offer two-hour toileting schedules; care partners guide residents to the bathroom while chatting about other matters. When they reach the destination, they say something like "I'll wait out here for you."

Because of short-term memory or attention-span problems, the person you're caring for may not equate the sensation of a full bladder with the need to find a toilet. Often, by the time the feeling is processed, he or she needs to get there speedily. Placing a stable commode at the patient's bedside may make nighttime toileting easier for both of you. And, as I mentioned earlier, have the patient wear elastic-waist slacks and skirts rather than tight outfits with buckles and buttons.

Also, place a disposable bed pad under the bottom sheet on the patient's side of the bed before nighttime incontinence becomes an issue. And if incontinence becomes a way of life, place sturdy plastic sheeting under the sheets, even if the patient is wearing diapers overnight. Eliminate fluids after evening meals if the patient is urinating during the night, and try to keep the bathroom door open and the light on. If a patient visits a friend or family member, mention her special toileting needs to the host.

Check with your physician if the patient you are caring for suddenly has problems controlling his bowels or bladder. You may find that a medication or illness is causing the problem. And if constipation becomes an issue, try adding stewed prunes, apricots, or other fibrous foods to the daily diet, and seek the help of a nutritionist if you need to. (A padded or elevated toilet seat can help make a long sitting more comfortable, and sometimes some soft music will help.) If the patient doesn't seem able to sit on the toilet long enough, give him a familiar object to stimulate interest in sitting. One or two photo albums, a magazine, dolls, or a busy apron may occupy the person long enough to accomplish the task.

And to help with patients' failing verbal abilities, when phrases such as "the women's room," "bathroom," or "lavatory" no longer have meaning, some habilitative facilities place pictures of toilets on bathroom doors. Plumbing-supply stores have books of appropriate bathroom photographs from which you can request one to hang at home.

Whatever techniques you try with a patient, do not treat early-stage incontinence by moving directly to geriatric diapers. Giving in to the lowest expectation will cause the patient to feel embarrassed, hostile, a failure. However, when the need for some incontinence measure is clear, you may want to begin by using women's sanitary pads as panty or underwear liners, which are easier to put on and remove than full diapers. Using pads along with a strict toileting schedule (every two hours), you may be able to defer serious incontinence for a while longer.

Finally, ignore accidents, and praise results. Your objective is to lessen the patient's embarrassment, shame, and apprehension. Habilitation offers the opportunity for long-term feelings of success — as well as dry pants.

Sleeping

In many cases sleeping problems are the final straw for the care partner; when sleeping becomes a major issue, the habilitator quite often admits defeat and starts seriously pursuing out-of-home care options.

Many people with progressive dementias sleep for only about

six hours at night. Those who take several naps during the day sleep even less after the sun goes down. You do not need to be a mathematician to figure out that if the person with Alzheimer's retires to bed at eight P.M. and receives a "good" night's sleep, she may be ready to start the day at two in the morning. The care partner may be just drifting off at that hour and is hardly ready to go back on duty to oversee waking activities. Add into that the care partner's worries that the patient may find hazardous items or areas or may leave the house.

The result is stress, tension, and frustration between patient and care partner, which can lead to outbursts. Those, in turn, add guilt to the care partner's emotional overload. No wonder that sleep deprivation of the worn-out care partner is a primary reason for seeking to place Alzheimer's patients in nursing homes.

Do not panic, assuming that all your nights as a care partner will be sleepless. Many people maintain the same sleep pattern they had before Alzheimer's disease became a part of their lives, or they develop a new, reasonable sleep pattern.

For some patients, however, night and day become twined together, and no care partner can unravel these mysterious threads of time. If changes in sleep habits occur, you should assess whether the disturbances are linked to physical, medical, or emotional events rather than to the disease process. The patient may be getting a cold or the flu, may be dehydrated or hungry and unable to relate her discomfort, may need to use the toilet, or may desire to open a window. Perhaps the designated bedtime doesn't work because she worked the night shift earlier in life.

When Charlotte came to the support group, she slumped into a chair. She had dark circles around her eyes. "Mother is up at all hours of the night. I have to get up so early to get the kids ready for school and get her ready for day care that I am exhausted by the time I get to work." Given the group's advice to find out if an unrelated problem existed, Charlotte took her mother to the doctor, who noted changes in the joints in her arthritic hands and knees and prescribed a medication to help with inflammation.

Soon afterward both Charlotte and her mother were sleeping through the night.

In another scenario, Elizabeth, who had Alzheimer's, suffered horrible nightmares until her husband discovered the cause quite by chance. One of their traditions as a couple had been watching the eleven o'clock news. Even after her disease had taken away her ability to comprehend a news story, Elizabeth sat each night staring at the sights and sounds flashing across the television screen. Then she would go to bed, only to awake screaming in the night. Only after their cable service was disrupted did Elizabeth's husband discover that the images on the screen of warfare, automobile accidents, and assorted acts of mayhem were causing his wife's nightmares. As soon as they stopped watching the news, Elizabeth began to sleep peacefully until dawn.

Whatever the reason for the patient's sleep problems, the care partner should establish a truly habilitative environment to protect the person at risk. You will be able to rest easy if you have carefully put away all dangerous household items, placed childproof locks on cabinets, and installed bells or traveler's locks on doors.

Other suggestions for creating a habilitative setting for sleep include singing or using a tape recorder to softly play a lullaby in the bedroom. Familiar, comforting tunes can induce sleep for older people, just as they do for babies.

And if the patient's sleep-wake cycle seems confused, try keeping her awake all through the day until bedtime. You may need to start gradually by keeping a record of the times when she naps during the day. Once you find the pattern, arrange to take a walk with her ten or fifteen minutes before she usually falls asleep during the day. Eventually, she will sleep longer during the night. Naps during the day often reflect boredom, as well; the patient may need some new task, chore, or hobby to keep busy with.

An evening stroll helps to relax both care partner and patient in preparation for a good night's rest. And don't underestimate the soothing effects of warm milk and back rubs. My mom paid her grandchildren to rub her feet with glycerin and rosewater. At ninety she still had beautiful tootsies and always slept like a baby.

A sleeping medication for the patient might become necessary to enable the care partner to get a good night's sleep. At home the medicine may be needed much sooner than it would be in a nursing home. If you go this route, recognize that many choices of sleeping medications exist, along with many controversies about the drugs. Of course, consult with your doctor or pharmacist, and tell them about the patient's body size, age, diagnosis, and any other medications he is taking.

Whatever you do, recognize that if the person you work with develops a sleeping problem, you must find support and relief of some sort. You might have a "family sleepover," letting several family members take turns being the "guard" during the night. Or have a home-health aide stay over occasionally. Both care partners and patients need a good night's sleep.

9

Tenet #4: Live in the Patient's World: Behavioral Changes

I can no longer
make apple strudel,
but I can chop pecans or roll the dough or peel the fruit.
I am here.
I've not yet gone.

NEVER QUESTION, chastise, or try to reason with the patient. Join him in his current "place" or time, no matter when or where that may be, and find joy with him there.

At a recent patient support group, I turned to a friendly woman next to me and said, "How wonderful to see you."

Puzzled, she looked at me for several seconds before saying, "Have we met before? You don't look at all familiar."

Even though she had attended the previous three meetings, I replied, taking her hand in mine, "It is always so nice to meet new friends." She smiled, noticeably relaxing as she grasped my hand. The accuracy of our interchange was unimportant; her self-esteem was all that mattered. Meanwhile, I had enhanced her day, and I felt buoyed as the care partner of the moment. I had entered her world, and it seemed like a nice place to be for a while.

A host of techniques can help you work appropriately with Alzheimer's patients as they encounter typical behavioral changes, such as not recognizing people and having difficulty making choices. To start with, when a patient's behavior seems to be changing, check out his basic physical comfort. Is he thirsty? Hungry? Does he have to go to the bathroom? Too hot or too cold? Overmedicated? Do hearing aids or eyeglasses need to be checked? Does he need to talk to someone about what is happening to him?

Remember that the person may not be able to communicate in words what seems to us to be simple information. Check often on her medical and physical well-being to ward off negative behavior before it has a chance to appear. If she is out of sorts, cranky, agitated, or aggressive, first determine whether she has some illness or physical discomfort that she may be unable to articulate — constipation, arthritic pain, sore throat, earache, headache, or bellyache. An impending illness or other physical ailment may be the cause of the distress. Have the patient's primary care physician check her for any medical problems before assuming her behavior is just another trial of Alzheimer's.

If you have to take a temperature, try to do it before a meal to ensure the most accurate reading. If the patient refuses to let you take her temperature, buy a second thermometer and take your own temperature at the same time, explaining that the doctor is checking everyone for flu.

How to Deal with Typical Behavioral Changes

The behaviors listed here roughly follow the order of the list in Chapter 3 of behavioral changes as the disease progresses.

Forgetting Appointments or Events

If a person in the early stage of Alzheimer's forgets an appointment, don't make her feel that she made a mistake; it's far better to make up an excuse or blame the incident on an intervening event: "It's just as well; the doctor was running late anyway."

Losing Track of Time

In the early stage, an Alzheimer's patient may forget that he just ate and, ten minutes after polishing off a sandwich, announce that he's hungry. Rather than saying "You just ate," distract him — "Oh, look, your favorite show is coming on" — or somehow modify his behavior: "You know, I'm still full from lunch. Let's have tea now, instead of dinner."

Repetitiveness

When the person with Alzheimer's repeatedly asks the same question ("What time is it?!"), keep in mind that she doesn't want the *question* answered; rather, she wants to articulate some feeling behind the question. What is her face saying? Try to find the meaning, the emotion, behind the query. The two most common questions that occur daily are "What time is it?" and "Where is my mother [or father]?" The question about time means that the patient is asking for something to occupy her time. The second question means that she is seeking comfort and reassurance.

Not Retaining Information or Memory of Events

When the person shows that he has forgotten some information or event, don't try to help him remember it. Simply change the subject and move on to a subject he is comfortable with. Or discuss the event from your own frame of reference. If, for instance, he has forgotten attending a recent wedding, you could say, "Oh, we had such a lovely time at the wedding. We saw your cousin John and ate chocolate wedding cake." Include the patient in the memory: "You and I danced until eleven o'clock." It doesn't really matter whether the details are accurate — some memories can use a bit of dressing up.

A patient in the early stage who is independent enough to do some things alone may still need some help remembering certain information. Peggy, for example, had trouble at the checkout line of a market. When told the bill, Peggy handed Lynn, the checkout person, a quarter and a cherry Life Saver and whispered, "How's that?" Knowing about Peggy's situation, Lynn was able to help her find the correct amount of money. The patient should be guided to establishments where personnel are acquainted with her needs and won't embarrass her.

Many chapters of the National Alzheimer's Association offer a small, wallet-sized "memory" card that a patient can carry. The card states, "I have a memory problem. Please be patient." Or a care partner can easily craft a similar card.

Not Recognizing People

If the person with Alzheimer's fails to recognize you as a friend or acquaintance, simply reintroduce yourself. You've preserved his self-esteem, and the conversation can continue smoothly.

Word-finding Difficulties

When the person with Alzheimer's is struggling to remember a word — either written or oral — simply say it to her if you know it. The more time that is wasted searching for the word, the more likely that the person will lose the thought altogether. Your goal is to make communication as smooth and easy as possible.

Difficulty Making Choices

Remember that you cannot reason with someone who has lost the ability to do so. Instead, limit any choice to two items: "Shrimp or steak?" "Black dress or red?" (The person will probably choose the second possibility, making the "last-word connection," as I mentioned in Chapter 7.)

not on issue in Panderville

Diminished Concentration

Keep a task going for a manageable length of time, bringing it to a close before the patient becomes exasperated. A care partner is generally able to tell when the person is getting bored or frustrated, signs that he will soon flare up or express unhappiness.

Accusatory Behavior

Since the patient has lost the ability to reason, agree immediately with her version of events or offer a very reasonable explanation for her concerns. To the accusation "You stole my special coat," the answer is "I forgot to tell you that I put it in storage for the summer," even if the coat was sold twenty years ago. For "The aide is stealing," the answer is "I'll talk to him. It won't happen again." (Of course, tell the aide about the false accusation and your habilitative response, so that he understands the need for this white lie and stays on your side.) Paranoid behavior is usually directed at the closest family member, and that person should remain in the patient's world throughout the discussion, no matter how bizarre the accusation.

Difficulty Separating Fact from Fiction

Since a patient cannot always be in our world, it becomes essential to monitor where she is in her interior world — and to join her there if necessary.

Todd and his wife, Lucy, were watching the presidential election convention on television. Lucy, in the middle stages of Alzheimer's, became increasingly restless. Todd turned off the TV to assess her obvious distress. Immediately Lucy breathed a great sigh of relief and said, "Oh, thank God. I didn't know how we were going to feed all those people." She had perceived all the conventioneers as being in her living room.

"I took care of that," Todd replied, smiling. "Now there's just the two of us. Let's eat. I'm so hungry."

Todd, practicing habilitation, did not chastise Lucy for her impossible scenario, nor did he try to reason with her or explain why these people could not be in their living room. He simply went into her world for the necessary moment to reassure her, then changed the subject and turned it into a pleasant experience.

Impaired Ability to Translate Thoughts into Actions

At first, this behavior may be difficult to figure out, since the only thing that is apparent is the person's frustration. If you notice that the patient is acting frustrated, it may be that he cannot perform the task at hand or cannot communicate what he would like to do. Distract the patient with another task, food, or a different situation.

Changes in Judgment

People in the late early stage of Alzheimer's have an impaired ability to make and remember judgment calls. Someone at this stage can reach out and touch a hot stove, burn himself, and ten minutes later reach out again to touch the same hot stove. He may have difficulty understanding the weather — going outside in winter, for example, without boots, hat, gloves, or coat.

Constantly monitor a patient for the ability to make and recall sound decisions. Try to make the environment interesting enough, simple enough, and safe enough to avoid problems before they start.

Diminishing Ability to Sequence Tasks

If the patient has difficulty brushing her teeth, put toothpaste on the toothbrush, place it on the counter, and leave the water running *before* she goes into the bathroom. If she wants to bake a cake, measure the ingredients ahead of time and put them on the counter. And don't call attention to what you have done.

Difficulty Writing and Understanding Written Language

Before writing difficulties become pronounced, try to take over any writing chores. Monitor the situation for frustration, and distract the patient if necessary.

When a patient no longer understands written words, don't speak about it or ask questions about what she is reading. You don't need to take away books and magazines — keep them around if she is used to them.

Getting Lost in Memories

If the person with Alzheimer's mistakes someone for a person from the past or thinks he is in a different place entirely, allow him the leisure and liberty to take you where he wants you to go.

Not all memories are pleasant ones, of course. If, for example, the patient starts crying because she sees a parent in the mirror, acknowledge the issue ("It's making you unhappy to see your mother right now, I understand"), distract the patient ("Here, have a cookie"), and remove the trigger of the unhappiness (get rid of the mirror). Happy or not, though, getting lost in memories may indicate that the patient needs to discuss the past — perhaps not at that moment, however.

Impaired Computation Abilities

When you notice that the patient is having trouble with simple math, you will have to be ready to take over or oversee any transactions that require an understanding of numbers. This includes balancing the checkbook, paying bills, making change, paying a cashier, leaving a tip, measuring for recipes, reading a thermometer, setting the oven timer, and many other such tasks that we do daily. Guide the patient or take over as inconspicuously as possible to allow him to maintain a sense of control for as long as possible.

Changes in Reaction Time

When the patient begins to take a long time to react to a situation, do not put him in a situation that will require quick reflexes, such as baby-sitting or driving. If he was once a great ball player, but now his slower reactions make playing outfield impossible, toss him a large rubber ball in a game of catch. Don't stop playing! Even though reaction time is slower, that does not mean the person with Alzheimer's must now be excluded. The caveat, of course, is safety.

Not Recognizing Objects

This occurs especially with dining implements (forks, spoons, knives), keys, and other small objects. Eliminate all items that the patient no longer recognizes, even eyeglasses, hearing aids, and dentures. Don't try explaining what the object is for; that results in a sense of failure as well as confusion and frustration.

Lack of Social Appropriateness

Social graces may disappear when self-control no longer exists. "You have big boobs," a patient once told me, her loss of inhibition and control allowing her to say whatever she saw as the truth — much as a youngster will often do. You will have to judge each social situation as it arises to decide whether the patient's lack of social appropriateness will be problematic. Dinner at a dear friend's home is quite different from cocktails with your boss. Remember above all else that it is the disease causing the behavior and not the patient's desire to be naughty or to embarrass you. There are no medications to curb the lack of social appropriateness, but this stage will pass as the disease progresses. And if you *really* want to know how your new hairdo looks — just ask him!

Frequent Emotional Changes

Sometimes the patient will experience a whirlwind of emotions — laughing one minute, weeping the next, then laughing again. Follow the patient's lead and go with her emotion; remember that it is real to her. And remember that these outbursts are generally short-lived.

Problems with Holidays

Holiday celebrations can be difficult for people with Alzheimer's because they can't perform as they used to, and they're aware of it.

So much is going on, and they don't feel as if they're part of the action. Try to convince a patient to help in whatever way he can. Making the family's traditional Thanksgiving apple strudel may no longer be possible, but perhaps he could help roll out the dough.

Formulate a specific plan of care for the holiday. Plan on having the person with Alzheimer's be with only one person at a time, to cut down on confusion and overstimulation. Ahead of time, assign different people to be with her at particular times. Someone should always be with the patient, without her knowing that this has been planned. Be sure to have a secondary plan as well. You may have to leave the event if the patient has an outburst, for example. In that case, who will accompany the person home? Is everybody ready to leave, if that's the best solution?

Not all situations, of course, can be anticipated and outlined here. When confronted with a new behavioral change, keep the following solutions in mind:

- Don't reason with someone who has lost the ability to do so.
- Distract the person with another task, situation, or thought, instead of dwelling on the problem.
- Follow the patient's logic or thought pattern, entering her sense of reality. Then gently lead her back to your world.
- Don't hesitate to use white lies to keep the situation manageable.
- Physically remove items that may cause problems.

Because habilitative techniques have not been widely used in the past, common behavioral changes have truly been challenging to well-intentioned care partners, both professional and family. The use of habilitation techniques will do much to help everyone feel more comfortable in dealing with these challenges.

Aggressive Behavior

I did not mean to strike you.
I was protecting myself
against insensitivity:
My-self defense.

Jeanne sat in her favorite spot facing the large bay window and the bird feeders she had hung so carefully so many years ago. She smiled as the chickadees landed and pecked away at their lunchtime snack. Carolyn, Jeanne's home-health aide, entered the room and, not wanting to break Jeanne's limited concentration, walked softly behind the chair. She leaned over and placed the lunchtime bowl of chicken noodle soup on the table. Jeanne picked up the bowl, stood, slowly turned toward Carolyn, and threw the warm liquid in her face.

"Get out of my house," she screamed. "Get out now! Right now, or I'll call the police!" Jeanne picked up a magazine lying nearby and threw it as well, then ran after her aide, yelling, "Go, go now, I'm calling the police!"

This kind of behavior is known as a "catastrophic reaction," an overreaction to a situation created, usually, by a care partner or by the environment. In the above scenario, the sudden appearance of the aide and the soup startled Jeanne, so she reacted to protect herself. The situation had confounded and therefore frightened her.

Carolyn did leave. She sat in her car for a few moments, wiped off her soup-spattered face, removed her sweater, and returned, this time to the back door. She knocked gently and, when Jeanne answered, Carolyn took a deep breath, smiled, and said, "Hello, I'm Carolyn. I've come to do some chores for you. Where do I begin?"

"Come on in," Jeanne said. "Would you like to have a cup of tea with me?"

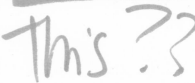

Aggressive behavior such as Jeanne's is the greatest concern for many care partners and provides the most fodder for discussion at family support group meetings. Such behavior is upsetting and possibly terrifying, particularly for a frail, elderly care partner who has never before been confronted this way. Fortunately, because the behavior is usually the result of a care partner's action or of the environmental setup, it can be avoided. If Carolyn had approached Jeanne from the front and told her what she was doing, Jeanne would not have been frightened and felt it necessary to defend herself against something that she simply did not comprehend. Had the aide announced as she approached that she was bringing in the soup, then stated that the soup was "chicken noodle today," Jeanne would have been aware of Carolyn's presence and of the arriving soup. With that preparation, she would not have reacted catastrophically.

Aggressive or challenging behaviors can stem from many problems related to Alzheimer's disease. Paranoia, hallucinations, repetitive behaviors, continual anxiety, changing sexual desires, or illness may cause the patient to act out or overreact. Using the habilitation approach, care partners and others who deal with patients with progressive dementia can come up with different, successful game plans to deal with challenging behaviors. Each care partner's approach will depend on many factors, of course, including his past and current relationship with the patient, his personal coping skills, and the available support systems.

Whenever you have to deal with challenging behavior, remember to make eye contact, speak calmly and slowly, and break down your speech into simple, short statements. It takes an emotionally charged patient even more time than usual to process language.

Unresolved issues that existed between the care partner and the patient before the onset of Alzheimer's disease may add to the challenge of dealing with behavioral matters. The care partner may think the patient is purposefully being obstinate or unreasonable, but that is not usually the case. If you think that a trying situation relates to your past relationship with the patient, talk to your doctor or a psychotherapist, presenting a realistic picture of how you and she interacted before progressive dementia complicated the picture.

No matter how dismaying a patient's "acting out" in public is for you or your family, it is usually not so stressful for the patient. When you have to deal with a challenging behavior in public, first recognize that, by and large, the behavior results from the disease. "It is not the person, it is the disease" is a favorite verbal reminder among my support-group participants. Care partners sometimes repeat this slogan aloud three or four times while their loved one is doing something embarrassing in front of neighbors or at the grocery store.

Ways to Reduce Challenging Behavior

Perhaps the most useful habilitation tool for figuring out the cause of aggressive and challenging behaviors is the Alzheimer's disease behavior log, which can isolate an underlying problem before it becomes serious. If the thought of keeping track of difficult behaviors sounds overwhelming — you probably feel that you have hardly enough minutes to do what is called for now — remember that if discovering the cause of the aberrant behavior leads to tempering or eliminating it altogether, the investment in time may make the difference between a frustrating and a satisfying day. Recognizing that certain confrontations are inevitable will also help you endure the disease. Time spent in anger, frustration, tears, and remorse is time wasted.

Keeping a behavior log involves collecting information of several kinds: the time of day, the exact location of the behavior, and a thorough description of environmental elements such as odors, sights, and sounds. Keep a record of these factors for each specific behavior and, generally, within ten entries you will see a pattern emerge that makes the trigger obvious. In the log it is also useful to record others' reports of the same behavior. Occasionally, you will understand the pattern after only three or four entries. The behavior may be triggered by the time of day, rainy weather, a visit by a certain relative, or a specific television show. When you know what to look for, you can then plan to keep the patient occupied during the difficult time slot; pull the shades on a rainy day and watch a video, perhaps, or explain the dilemma to the relative and ask that person to stay away until the behavior passes, or shut off the TV.

Here is the way a behavior log might look for Chad, whose challenging behavior is to bang loudly on the door with his fist.

Time, day, and date	Where	Full environmental description
10:15 A.M., Thurs., Oct. 5	back door	Cold outside and in — fire in fireplace — lights on everywhere in house — shades open — wind blowing — coffee brewing
2:04 P.M., Sat., Oct. 14	cellar door	Neighbors in for tea — light snow beginning to fall — wind blowing — candles lit — shades closed — house warm
6 P.M., Wed., Oct. 25	front door	Dinner placed on dining room table — house warm and cheery despite windstorm and blowing snow — church bells ringing in the distance

After only three entries, you can see that the wind was blowing each time Chad banged on the door. Evidently the sound of the wind evoked an emotion in him. What that emotion was doesn't matter; this information allowed the care partner to try to thwart the behavior before it caused more distress. Turning on soft music to mask the sound of the wind could work nicely. Keeping Chad occupied in a part of the house where he is least likely to hear the wind howl would be another option.

Here's another behavior log, this time for Laurie's unexpected frantic pacing:

Time, day, and date	Where	Full environment description
3:03 P.M., Sun., April 13	throughout the downstairs	Laurie's favorite TV show playing — curtains open — dinner is in oven — we are waiting for company and for the kids to come from the movies — I'm setting the table
4:11 P.M., Tues., April 22	downstairs hallway	Music is on — gray day. I am peeling potatoes. Kitchen lights are on. Draperies are drawn. Kids are at baseball game.
3:45 P.M., Fri., May 1	living room to front door and back	Preparing meal early to be ready for going out this evening. Kids are helping. Beautiful spring day — many neighbors out raking and gardening. Windows open and draperies too.

No need to make more entries in this log. Laurie begins her frantic pacing each day in midafternoon. Checking to see what is happening elsewhere, we notice that family members are active at that time. Laurie is sundowning, exhibiting her challenging behavior as the day comes to an end. This once busy homemaker appears to be confounded by her uselessness. Her mind may be racing: "What should I be doing?" "Are the children home yet?" "Have I made dinner yet?" "I have so much to do but I don't know what it is." Whatever she's thinking, the antidote for her sundowning is to fill this time period with some pleasurable contribution to the family life or, at the least, with work that distracts her.

Afternoon would be the ideal time to have someone take Laurie for a walk or to interact with her on an individual basis, particularly if exercise can be involved to dissipate some of the energy that Laurie is expending through pacing. If the children are home, they could be called upon to engage their grandmother in "helping" them with homework or outside chores. Assisting in the kitchen with readying the meal or arranging the dining table also could occupy the time now spent pacing.

Some experts speak of Alzheimer's as a disease of behavior. I think of it as a disease of the emotions, however. By understanding, working with, and to some extent controlling the patient's emotions, it is possible to encourage behavior that is acceptable. This approach works much better than running away from the challenging behavior or medicating the patient heavily. Of course, at times every habilitator will want to separate herself from the person with Alzheimer's and go into a quiet room where she can throw pillows, swear uncontrollably, or cry. That is a human response when someone we have known as friend, mother, brother, or husband has taken on a different persona, has become someone we don't know.

The behavior log can be remarkably helpful. In just a few seconds, you can record what happens just before the emotional change. After studying several records in the log, you can often determine the trigger and eliminate it. The patient will feel more in control of his world and will not build up his levels of frustration, agitation, and aggression.

Triggers for Challenging Behavior

Now consider some common triggers that can result in challenging behaviors, and how care partners can deal with these situations.

Paranoia and Hallucinations

One night Irene heard her husband scream, followed by a loud crash. She rushed into his bedroom to find him waving his cane and beating the white shade, which now hung in shambles from his window. A shattered lamp lay on the floor.

"Get out of here, you lousy bum. Get out of here!" Keith roared as he swung the cane.

"He's gone," Irene said softly as she stepped closer. "I saw him running across the lawn." She waited for Keith to calm down. Then, after he had lowered the cane, she said, "Come sit here on the bed. You're all out of breath."

Keith sat beside her, still panting, but reassured. Five minutes later, he put his head on the pillow and let Irene swing his legs onto the bed and cover him with a quilt.

By reacting calmly and immediately becoming part of Keith's world, Irene turned his fury into reasonable peace. She quickly realized that the stimulus behind Keith's hallucinating and paranoia was the shadow from the neighbor's flag moving across the window shade. The next day Irene replaced the shade with a darker color and put up some new, heavy drapes that she could close at sundown and so eliminate Keith's hallucinations.

Irene was also smart not to remind Keith later of the incident, which could have made him feel chagrined about losing his abilities. Many people with Alzheimer's have paranoia and hallucinations at some time during the disease. A patient might say, for example, "I hear people talking about me." Or she may blame others for things she has done or something she cannot make sense out of, resulting in comments such as "You're stealing all my money" or "Where did you hide my keys?" The way to calm such a person is to address the underlying feelings of fear, anxiety, or sadness, and to find ways to change the environment to lessen these problems.

Continual Anxiety

A patient who appears anxious can also create challenging situations. The person may repeatedly think about his past duties: having to get ready for the office, prepare lunch for a spouse, or be home in time for a child's school bus. Thoughts such as these may add to the anxiety he already has about the disease. If he isn't occupied for a time, he may suddenly say, "I need to be going home now," and try to act on that idea.

As you do with repetitive statements, think about what the veiled words really mean, such as "I need to feel useful right now." Again, giving the patient a task she can do may help her feel useful and still able to function as she did in the past. Even if she can no longer set the table properly for Sunday dinner, she may be able to put the silverware or plates on the table. If the plates wind up in the wrong places, so what? Rearrange them when the patient isn't looking and praise her for her help. Challenging behavior becomes far less likely when the person with Alzheimer's feels that she is still a functioning part of the family.

If continual anxiety is not easily modified, however, a deeper problem may be involved. Contact your physician for appropriate tests and, perhaps, medication that can ease the patient's suffering.

Sexual Behavior
Other challenging behaviors may deal with sexuality. The person with Alzheimer's disease has the same drives and desires as the rest of us but may have problems describing or acting on his sexual urges and in determining where and with whom the actions are appropriate. The patient may, in fact, develop a much stronger sense of sexuality, or hypersexuality. Changes in the brain may cause him to lose control and inhibition, resulting in sexual behavior that is disturbingly different from anything he has done in the past.

In the early stages of Alzheimer's, when the person's outward appearance has not yet changed, frustration often results from the loss of ability to communicate feelings about intimacy and sex. The person may be further upset if a care partner with whom she has been intimate is now uncomfortable speaking about sexual matters. When the disease has disrupted sexual expression and communication, a couple may need outside help to assure both partners that intimacy and affection can continue at this time when they are needed most. Just as a doctor routinely checks a patient's blood pressure and cholesterol level, she should ask about his physical needs and behaviors. If the doctor does not make these inquiries of the Alzheimer's patient, don't feel shy about bringing up the matters. A medical specialist, such as a nurse practitioner, may be able to offer advice.

An early-stage patient, after listening to a racy story or comment, may be unable to process the humor and join in with others' laughter. He may feign understanding, but underneath the facade feel lost, and even withdraw from the social setting. A care partner needs to vigilantly protect the impaired individual in such a situation, perhaps by reassuring him that the joke was obscure.

Later in the disease, the patient may not recognize her partner at times, or she may express sexual interest in someone else. In such situations, the care partner needs to be extermely sensitive and patient to keep both the patient's dignity and his own intact while struggling to deal with the situation. (Many care partners have told colorful tales of donning a wig or flirting outrageously with the unsuspecting spouse before inviting the patient into bed. Sometimes habilitation requires a great sense of humor.)

And if the patient expresses sexual desire much more often than in the past, remember that sexuality is not limited to intercourse. Intimacy includes touch, loving words, and so much more. An act as simple as a back rub may dissipate some of the sexual feelings that so often build up in a life in which normal sexual expression is blocked. Sometimes nothing is as wonderful as a hand rub or a warm hug. If the person with Alzheimer's is obviously intent on intercourse, treat the gesture as you would have in the past. If the early-stage patient becomes overbearing in the frequency of demands for sex or in making unsuitable propositions, to the point that you feel uncomfortable with the advances, then talk honestly about the issues. If hypersexuality becomes a problem in the more advanced stages, then speak to your physician about medications that will help subdue sexual urges.

If you are not the patient's partner or spouse and find yourself fending off unwanted advances, firmly but gently explain that this behavior is not appropriate for you. If possible, distract the patient with some other activity.

In some cases, behavior that seems to result from hypersexuality may come from a completely different need. A man who appears to be masturbating may actually have to urinate but cannot express the need. Someone with progressive dementia who is stripping off her clothes may just be too warm or may need to go to the bathroom.

Sometimes the healthy partner no longer feels a sexual attraction to the patient. If this reaction causes a care partner to feel guilt, failure, anger, embarrassment, or sadness, he or she should try to talk with other people who are experiencing the same feelings. A support group, private counseling, or discussions with a trusted friend can help.

Depression

Some other causes of challenging behavior may require medical intervention. Be on the lookout for signs that the patient is depressed and is no longer able to express his feelings. Signs of depression include napping frequently throughout the day, sleeping poorly at night, and having a poor appetite. Depressed patients are in great need of counseling so they can articulate fears and concerns. They also need to see a doctor to determine if short-term medication can alleviate the anxiety or depression.

We cannot feel what the person with Alzheimer's is feeling. But we can all recall the frustration of trying to remember a word or a name ("It's on the tip of my tongue") or the frustration that arises when we misplace our car keys. Multiply those feelings by one hundred, and you'll have a glimpse into the emotional state of the Alzheimer's person when he or she is acting out. Then slowly count to three, and respond to the patient as you would want someone to respond to you.

10

Tenet #5:
Enrich the Patient's Life

I am seeking,
I am not lost.
I am forgetful,
I am not gone.

CREATE MOMENTS for success, eliminate possible moments of failure, and praise frequently and with sincerity. Attempt to find joy wherever possible.

While driving into Boston one day, I received a call saying that my meeting had been canceled. Delighted, I took the next exit off the Massachusetts Turnpike and began to calculate whether I could stop by to see a family in distress and still surprise my grandson at his softball game. Then I wondered whether, if I planned my time right, I could return six overdue telephone calls while I watched the energetic nine-year-olds run the bases. I'm pleased to say that I was able to accomplish everything on that list. But, more important, I was able to plan, improvise, figure out shortcuts, and make choices about the order of these items.

How different my reaction to the canceled meeting was from

that of a person with early-stage Alzheimer's. The interruption in schedule might well have overwhelmed him. He might not have been able to figure out how to spend the free time, having few skills with which to think through and design a new course of action. Early on in the disease, carrying out chores, tasks, sports, hobbies, and pastimes becomes much more difficult, and friends and family members who once shared activities become unavailable.

The patient's loneliness is often compounded by the withdrawal of friends. Years after my husband's death, some of my friends explained that they simply did not know how to behave with him or what to say, and the fear of doing or saying something hurtful kept them away. Although they realized that their response to his illness was selfish, they were unable to overcome their feelings of discomfort. But the patient needs familiar visitors, and the care partner certainly needs the change offered by conversation with others.

As a result of this isolation, patients spend much of their time in apparent idleness. Care partners often complain that the person with Alzheimer's "just sits around all day." But in fact, while he may appear to be doing nothing, he is trying to think through his situation; because he is not being productive, he feels unworthy, valueless, undeserving — a failure.

As I've mentioned repeatedly, the person with Alzheimer's needs to have a sense of being a part of the society she lives in. She not only requires enrichment in daily life, but she also needs to feel that she is doing something that enhances someone else's life, just as we all do. Despite having a terminal illness, the patient wants to be considered a productive, contributing human being.

To help the patient fulfill these needs, the care partner needs to initiate activities, to plan and organize with creativity, resourcefulness, and a great degree of patience. Above all, care partners need to think of ways to compensate for lost skills, recognizing that even the simplest activity involves a sequence of steps that depend on cognition, recent memory, a sense of cause and effect, and a long-enough attention span. More complex activities involve motor skills, verbal communication, problem-solving, and patience.

Here's how Wendy, a care partner in a support group, altered the way she tried to engage her mother in a social activity. She first moaned to the group about the disaster she felt she had come up against when she invited some "friends from my mom's bridge club in to play cards. What a fiasco. Her friend Kate kept having to play the cards for her. I couldn't wait for them all to go, and I'll never ever invite them in again!" Wendy's mother hadn't been upset. But, Wendy said sheepishly, "I was having a nervous breakdown. The TV was on — they all love Jerry Springer — somebody was mowing the lawn, and there must have been half a dozen neighborhood kids running around our yard. I was so afraid she was going to do something wrong."

Recognizing that it's important to help Alzheimer's patients engage in sociable activities, the support group encouraged Wendy to try again. This time she arranged for the function to take place in the familiar setting of her home. She made sure that the get-together consisted only of women whom her mother knew well and that there were no additional stimuli, such as small children nearby or a television or radio playing in the background. Since her mother could no longer play bridge, Wendy came up with a simpler event — an afternoon tea — to fill time and maintain companionship. To help anyone who felt timid about conversing with Wendy's mother, who was struggling with language, Wendy decided upon a topic — a vacation the women took together — to start the conversation.

Wendy did invite her mother's friends over again. She listened to her mother giggle in the other room with her girlfriends as they reminded one another of their glorious week by the sea in "the good old days." "Weren't we devils?" she heard her mother say. Later, several of the women told Wendy that her mother seemed to have far fewer speech problems than she had had when they came over for bridge and seemed much more like her "old self." The memories of the long-ago vacation were more vivid for her mother than the recent card game.

Wendy had learned that trying to get a patient to perform the way others can causes more harm than good. Care partners should be honest and let visitors know that revisiting happy times long past makes for the most fruitful exchange. Giving friends and relatives an opportunity to rise to the occasion will not only make them feel good about their visits but will enable the patient to feel valued and appreciated.

Enrichment also means involving the person in tasks or chores. An Alzheimer's patient will be interested in a task for only a short period, because of her reduced attention span and limited patience. Still, she may find repetitive activities quite gratifying — folding, raking, polishing, sorting, whipping batter, planting. During tasks the care partner should remember to keep the patient included in simple conversation, even if her verbal skills are diminishing. And the care partner can use this as a time to hone his "emotional listening" skills. Working on chores also affords wonderful opportunities for the care partner to offer praise and gratitude for help.

Enriching Exercises

Another way to enhance a patient's life is to work on the mental-enrichment activities developed by neuropsychologist Dr. Paul Raia. The goal of the activities is to help the patient hold on to existing memory skills by stimulating parts of the brain that have not yet been used.

Dr. Raia's theory stems from research findings that older people can develop neurotrophins, hormones found most frequently in infants and small children, which are involved in making new connections among brain cells. Preliminary research has demonstrated that performing the kinds of activities Dr. Raia has worked out can result in the formation of neurotrophins, which allow the brain cells of Alzheimer's patients to make new connections and pathways around the area affected by the disease.

The fifteen activities below — which Dr. Raia calls "mental floss" — focus on stimulating areas of the brain that will eventually be affected by Alzheimer's disease. When you try these exercises with a patient, introduce them by saying, "Here are some activities that may help you with your memory." If the patient refuses to do them, don't force the issue; perhaps you can introduce them at another time. Be sure to start slowly and try only a few activities in one day. And if at any time the patient seems to be getting frustrated, agitated, or upset, slow down or stop the activity. Focus only on the activities she enjoys, since you want her to succeed.

What's the Main Idea?

Materials needed: tape recorder/player or CD (compact disk) player; book or short story on tape or CD.

Activity: listen to a paragraph from a book on tape or CD, then stop the recording. Ask the patient to tell you the main thoughts in that paragraph. Repeat this process five times using five different paragraphs. This activity helps memory and listening.

Touch and Tell

Materials needed: an opaque bag; miscellaneous household objects, such as a sponge, screw, button, plate, and candle.

Activity: place objects in the bag without letting the person see what they are. Instruct him to reach inside the bag and, by touch, identify each object. Repeat the exercise four or five times. This activity helps memory, sensory perception, and communication skills.

Mealtime

Activity: have the patient eat a meal with her nondominant hand. The purpose of this exercise is to transfer information from one side of the brain to the other, to build up the nondominant side. For this and other potentially messy activities, be sure to cover the person with a garment protector (see the Products section of Further Resources, page 223).

What Time Is It?

Materials needed: a piece of paper with ten clock faces drawn on it. The faces should have numbers but no hour and minute hands.

Activity: say aloud a particular time, such as quarter past ten, and ask the person to draw the hands on the clock in the correct positions. This activity helps physical and computing skills and memory.

Stimulating the Senses

Materials needed: blindfold.

Activity: blindfold the person and have her walk slowly through the house. Monitor her to ensure that she cannot bump into or trip on anything. This activity allows the person to pay attention to senses other than sight.

Banging along with Bach

Materials needed: a recording of music by Johann Sebastian Bach

Activity: play a recording of Bach (or any musical piece with an easy, steady, beat — preferably a 4/4 rhythm — that the person enjoys), and ask the patient to clap the rhythm. This exercise helps the patient focus.

Which One Is Different?

Materials needed: three index cards with magazine or newspaper pictures pasted on them. Two cards should have images that are similar in some obvious way; the third card should have a different picture. (For example, you might use two images of a one-story house and one picture of a two-story house.)

Activity: present the three index cards. Ask which card is different and why. This makes the person pay attention to visual details, hold things in memory, and make decisions.

Making Items with Clay

Materials needed: modeling clay.

Activity: ask the patient to form shapes of familiar objects — a car, a house, or even a circle or square. Forming things with his hands helps fine-motor control, while also allowing him to enjoy the feeling of touch.

Reading by Tens

Materials needed: a magazine or book, paper, pencil.

Activity: ask the patient to read, either aloud or to herself, a long paragraph from an article or book and copy down every tenth word. This activity involves counting, reading, focusing, and holding attention.

Stimulating the Sense of Smell

Materials needed: three or four small bottles or vials with caps; cotton balls; aromatic scents such as vanilla flavoring, orange peel, cinnamon, wintergreen mints and peppermints, vinegar, lemon juice, and ginger.

Activity: insert a cotton ball into each bottle, adding a drop or two of aromatic scent or a sprinkle of orange peel, cinnamon, or ginger.

If using four bottles, have one aroma that matches one of the other three. If using three bottles, have one aroma that matches one of the other two. For example, put a drop of vanilla into two bottles and orange peel into a third; a wintergreen candy in two bottles, and a peppermint candy in a third; ginger in two bottles and cinnamon in the third.

Take the cap off one bottle and present it to the patient, asking her to smell the bottle. Present each bottle in turn until the patient can identify the two bottles with the same smell and the one different bottle. This activity stimulates memory as well as the sense of smell.

Counting Backward

Activity: ask the person to count backward from one hundred by threes. Then ask him to count back by sevens, eights, and so forth. This activity stimulates memory and sequencing.

The Carrots on the Hat Rack

Activity: go to a particular area of the home and decide on a stopping place. For example, go to the front door and choose the hat rack in the entranceway as the stopping place. Then find another stopping place — the couch in the living room, for example. The dining room table can be the third stop. Make sure the person with Alzheimer's can name the three stopping places.

Then give the patient a list of three items — the more absurd the better — and ask him to visually associate one of these items with the first stopping place, a second item with the next place, and so on. For example, on the hat rack, he could visualize a hanging bunch of carrots. (The visualization's absurdity gives him the best chance of remembering the stopping place.) Next, take him to the first stopping place and ask him to visualize what goes there — the bunch of carrots in this case. Do the same at the second and third stopping places. This activity forces the person to use mental imagery, which is processed in a different part of the brain from memory. The exercise can help compensate for lost memory.

Floor Plans

Materials needed: paper, pencil.

Activity: ask the patient to draw a floor plan of her home and label the various rooms. Then ask the patient hypothetical questions — for example, "Say you were in the living room. How would you get from there to the bathroom?" Ask her to draw the route with the pencil.

This exercise helps the patient with mental images and spatial relationships. This visual problem involves thinking abstractly and seeing how things are connected.

Fun with a Puzzle
Materials needed: jigsaw puzzle with about fifty pieces.

Activity: ask the person to put the puzzle together. This task involves visual images and abstractions, as well as memory and fine motor skills.

Proverbs
Materials needed: a book of proverbs or a list you have made of proverbs.

Activity: read aloud a proverb, such as "A bird in the hand is worth two in the bush" and ask the patient to explain what it means. This activity helps abstract thinking, as well as verbalization.

More Activities for Early-Stage Patients

My colleague Lois Pecora, the director of Alzheimer's services for the Salmon Family of Health Care Services in Massachusetts, and I have shared facilitating both an early-stage support group and a care partner support group for the past five years. Here are a few activities that we use in our groups and pass on to at-home habilitators.

- Read a newspaper advice column and ask the patient to suggest responses.
- Challenge the patient to list as many words as possible that can be made from a longer word, such as "megaphone."
- Pose questions that have no wrong answer, such as "What three books would you take for a week's vacation alone?" or "What is your favorite dessert?" These kinds of questions will most likely foster further discussion on the chosen topic.

- Describe news, sports, or fashion stories of interest and ask for comments about them.

- Ask questions that involve making choices. For example, "Would you rather go on a picnic or to a five-star restaurant?" The answers can be a gauge of the person's ability to make decisions. At some point in the disease, the patient will reply, "Wherever you want to go" — or, using the "last-word connection" (see page 81), come up with an answer that involves no choice on his part.

- Describe a situation in the news and ask how the patient might solve the problem — for example, a budget deficit or a crisis in another country. Make sure the person understands that his response is of interest to you.

These are the kinds of conversational and thinking activities that well-organized adult day care and assisted-living situations offer in a social setting. A patient's failed attempts at conversation are usually met with chuckles, a pat on the hand, and a sly comment from another patient, such as "I know how you feel."

As you carry out any activity — whether in a social setting or at home — notice the patient's emotional state during and after the experience. As Dr. Raia has said, if you see signs of frustration, agitation, or anger during the activity, slow down or stop what you're doing. Also recognize that anger or befuddlement afterward may be triggered by something other than the activity itself. Try to identify the trigger and eliminate the problem causing the unwanted conduct or attitude.

A Daily Routine

Enrichment activities should be carried out within a structured daily routine. The need for routine doesn't mean you should curtail activities, however. A day filled with scheduled activities is often the catalyst for a night of pleasant sleep. An ideal, busy, practical, but quite attainable day in the life of a care partner and patient might include activities along these lines.

Early Morning

- Set the breakfast table together, according to the patient's ability.
- Have a leisurely breakfast, perhaps with a discussion of news headlines or sports news.
- Do breakfast cleanup chores together, including putting food away and clearing, washing, and drying dishes.
- Complete the bathing and grooming routines. The care partner should guide the person to the bathroom, allow him to do as much as possible, and find ways to handle his possible boredom or frustration.

Midmorning

- Put on clothes. To cue for dressing appropriately, the care partner can remind an independent patient of the day's events. For instance, she might say, "It looks like good golf weather today." For the patient who needs more guidance, the care partner can put out clothes in the correct sequence, without the patient's being aware of it. If the patient needs assistance, the care partner can place the clothes in position at night, to head off a potential confrontation the next morning.
- Go for a walk or engage in some other outdoor exercise. If a companion or family member can accompany the patient, the care partner can do necessary chores during this time apart.
- Exercise indoors if outdoor physical activity is not possible. Many videos feature aerobics and stretching exercises for older people, and most senior centers have solid exercise programs. Many clinicians believe strongly that physical exercise

promotes the Alzheimer's patient's well-being while slowing the downhill course of the disease.

- Take a coffee or tea break. If the patient is losing too much weight, the care partner can introduce a nutritious snack at this time. If weight gain is the problem, the habilitator can offer a light snack that will fill the void a bit before lunch. (See the finger food suggestions in the Appendix, page 207.) A snack at this time can be a reward for tasks already completed, which also means another chance to offer praise.

Late Morning

- Relax together, perhaps by watching a video, looking at a photo album, or reminiscing about past experiences (particularly those that elicit humor). If the patient is interested, she can pursue a hobby or avocation by herself. (This also lets the care partner finish chores.) A leisurely manicure followed by a hand massage will calm both patient and care partner.
- Weather permitting, take a short drive to nowhere or walk to a favorite local store. Sometimes an outing relieves the person's feelings of confinement and breaks up the monotony of being at home for long periods of time. The patient also gets a little exercise before mealtime. The care partner should be acutely tuned in to the patient's behavior after returning home. If problems arise, it may be better to stay at home, where the patient feels safe.

Noon

- Work together on lunch preparation. The care partner should guard against the patient feeling a sense of frustration or failure if he cannot complete the assigned task. The care partner should keep the table setting as simple and uncluttered as possible, and offer praise for any help.
- Eat lunch. The care partner may find it convenient to offer

the largest meal at lunchtime, and that is better nutritionally for the patient than a large evening meal.

- Do lunch cleanup chores together. The patient may function best at this time of day. Chores offer opportunities to feel useful and successful.

Early Afternoon

- If the patient doesn't have a problem sleeping at night, she can nap for an hour or less.
- If she has difficulty sleeping at night, have her engage in some sedentary activities. If she is able, she may be pleased to play card games, word games, or puzzles, to read, watch an old movie, or work on hobbies or projects. (As the patient's skills decline, the chosen activity should become less difficult.)
- Exercise enjoyably by taking a long walk, engaging in a sport such as golfing, dancing, or gardening, or doing household tasks.

Late Afternoon

- Take a coffee or tea break. Try to include other people at this time. A close friend or relative may be able to spend some time with the patient, giving the care partner some respite. Many people may be pleased to be asked to spend time with the patient and to help the care partner.
- If practical, work together on dinner preparation and table setting. A person with progressive dementia tends to have more cognitive difficulties late in the day (sundowning). He may require a lot of attention, so meal preparation may have to take second place.

Evening

- If the patient needs to retire early, perform bedtime preparations — brushing teeth, washing up, taking a sponge bath, putting out tomorrow's clothes. (Often people with Alzheimer's feel more secure when they have finished these chores.) As in the morning, the care partner should guide the person to the bathroom and allow her to do as much as possible for herself.

- Prepare for sleep, including putting on nightclothes and slippers.
- Relax in various ways, perhaps by listening to music, watching television, playing cards, taking a walk (preferably before changing into pajamas), singing, even dancing around the living room. (Doing the same activity at about the same time each day establishes a routine of sorts and may lessen stress and anxiety. This may be particularly valuable for patients who experience occasional sundowning.)
- Go to bed. The care partner may soothe the patient by giving a back, hand, or temple massage. Reading a poem aloud, even if a care partner has never done this before, often helps a patient fall asleep. The cadence of a metered poem read in a soft voice is very soothing. (Shel Silverstein's humorous poetry provides a great beat and can bring out a smile.)
- Ensure that alarms are set, doors locked, lights on in the bathroom, and preparations finished for tomorrow to make the day less stressful.

You can alter this schedule as necessary, of course. For instance, in the early stage of Alzheimer's disease, television can play a significant role in filling leisure time. This is fine, provided that the care partner exercises a little judgment in finding shows that engage the patient's mind — such as sports, nature shows, documentaries, or comedies. As the disease progresses, however, television may be overstimulating. As in the case of the woman who had nightmares after watching the news, the impaired adult may not be able to separate what is happening on the screen from real events. Select appropriate material that is simple to follow, and perhaps has just one voice speaking at a time (PBS or Discovery Channel documentaries, for example). Videos are also a good choice. Look for travelogues, videos from family gatherings, musicals, old television shows like *I Love Lucy*, and any favorites of the patient.

Physical Activity

Physical activities provide benefits beyond increasing strength, flexibility, and cardiovascular health. Exercising together affords both companionship and opportunities to participate in sensory activity. While walking, for instance, the care partner can talk about various odors in the air, can compare the bark on different trees, touch leaves on bushes along the way, or listen to bird songs.

Household tasks, both indoors and out, can be energizing and strengthening and can provide the best opportunities for praise and positive feedback. Remember that in later stages of the disease, the person may need a demonstration to initiate a task. But once the patient begins the task, he is likely to continue doing it for a while. After the early stage of Alzheimer's, you should plan any activity for no more than a half-hour, but you may find that the person wants to engage in some activities for a long time. Always, the object is not to complete the task but to be enjoyably occupied doing it.

Offer repetitive physical tasks, such as raking, planting, weeding, or vacuuming in the morning, when a patient's energy tends to be at its peak. Later in the day, physically repetitive activities may help tire the patient in preparation for a nap or bedtime. Don't complain if the person does the job repeatedly; just thank her profusely for helping with chores.

For every activity, prepare the supplies in advance; you run the risk of problems if you keep the patient waiting while you gather the necessary implements. Also, do not ask if he or she "wants to do" something; either begin doing the task or simply state the time when you will begin.

Most important, whatever you and the patient do during the

day, be sure to time activities with his previous routine in mind. Routine underscores a patient's feelings of security, well-being, and orientation. While you will have to make some compromises, your objective is to structure the patient's day while providing necessary time for other people to carry out their routines. A hired care partner or companion should also stick with the established routine throughout the course of the disease. Following the same course of events each day may be as important as any activity.

Keep in mind that activities are whatever we engage in to keep busy; they are the opposite of sitting with nothing to do or not knowing how to do anything. Keep the patient busy to fill leisure time and feel connected to the world through activity. Although much is lost, much remains. Focus on what is left, not on what is gone. Plan for contingencies, prepare for the terrible times — but use the techniques of habilitation to celebrate what can still be celebrated.

Enriching Activities

Try to fill empty times with activities that are creative or helpful, emotionally or spiritually enriching, or that offer the patient physical or cognitive benefits. Many of the activities in this list provide multiple benefits, and many can be used in nursing homes and assisted-living facilities.

Music
- Listening to music
- Engaging in sing-alongs, particularly of well-known, older songs
- Playing rhythm instruments
- Dancing
- Watching videos of musicals (especially older ones)

Food Appreciation
- Smelling and tasting foods with strong odors that evoke memories
- Feeling dough, Jell-O, pasta, and other foodstuffs
- Decorating cakes or cupcakes

- Making a salad or fruit compote from a set of ingredients placed on the counter
- Mixing ingredients for making latkes
- Preparing and baking cookies, cakes, or homemade bread
- Making applesauce
- Canning fruits and vegetables

Crafts and Hobbies
- Making and looking at mobiles
- Looking at or making scrapbooks and photo albums
- Making family collages, perhaps with seasonal themes
- Working on holiday projects, such as making valentines
- Arranging flowers, either fresh, dried, or silk
- Stringing popcorn or cereal loops to hang out for the birds
- Stuffing pinecones with peanut butter and seeds and hanging them for birds
- Dyeing Easter eggs

Spiritual, Inspirational, and Touch-based Activities
- Stringing beads for others
- Sewing, quilting, or making artwork for others
- Attending religious services
- Bird watching
- Spending time with pets in the home, visiting pets in other homes, or inviting someone with a calm pet to visit
- Cutting theme pictures out of magazines
- Sitting in the sun
- Walking on the beach
- Holding hands
- Receiving a massage
- Brushing hair
- Watching fish in a fish tank. The glass of the tank isn't dangerous, and the benefits of watching the fish far outweigh the grief of losing some. Even if the grieving period seems overly extended, it's all right for an Alzheimer's patient to feel grief.

Games
- Participating in trivia games, focusing on the eras the patient know best
- Playing "Finish the Pair," in which the patient tries to figure out the second item in a pair such as "Lucy and ____."
- Playing "Complete the Song Title," in which the patient tries to figure out the missing item in a song such as "You Are My ____."
- Piecing together jigsaw puzzles

- Answering "if" questions, such as "If ____ happened, what would you do?"
- Playing Pictionary — drawing a picture to explain the title of a television show, book, or movie
- Playing checkers, Chinese checkers, dominoes, or a children's form of an adult game such as Scrabble
- Playing simple card games, such as Old Maid or War

Outings*
- Spending time away with family or friends
- Collecting colored leaves
- Collecting beach glass or shells
- Building a snowman
- Attending social gatherings, as long as they are not overstimulating
- Going to cultural functions, such as dance performances or art exhibits
- Going to a library
- Shopping
- Taking historical bus tours through a city
- Traveling to a pick-your-own fruit farm
- Going to a nearby zoo
- Flying a kite

Activities to Stimulate Skills Affected by Alzheimer's

Verbal and Visual Skills
- Watching and discussing videos of old movies and television shows
- Discussing former occupations, service in the armed forces or other organizations, and past events, such as a first job, apartment, paycheck, or date
- Watching a children's performance or reading to children
- Being asked for advice about something the care partner is working on
- Listening to newspaper or magazine articles being read aloud
- Talking about great inventions and significant historical events
- Visiting or inviting in someone who has an infant
- Matching laundered socks

*After taking a patient in a nursing home or other facility on an outing, check with a staff member an hour or so after you return. If you find out that the patient became agitated after you left, suggest that in the future the staff have something ready for him to do upon his return. You may want to plan your outing to end just before a scheduled activity and have a staff member lead the patient into the activity as you depart.

- Looking at art books
- Writing a letter together

Motor Skills
- Sorting playing cards
- Tossing a ball
- Planting seeds outdoors or in pots indoors
- Clipping coupons
- Shelling nuts or peas
- Sorting buttons or screws
- Tossing bean bags, balloons, or a Frisbee
- Sorting playing cards by color, suit, or number
- Winding yarn
- Cutting seasonal or other thematic pictures out of magazines
- Polishing metal objects, such as brass doorknobs or candlesticks
- Helping to make a jack-o'-lantern
- Playing with children's clay (for patients with late-stage Alzheimer's)

Beyond
Habilitation

11

Caring for the Care Partner

Applause does not always come easily.
You must be a winner
of both Scrabble and life games.
It is not always enough just to know
that lessons learned in apple orchards
may be lost on concrete streets.

Don't let care partnering take all the energy out of you. Consider Garrett, who rose from his bed at midnight, went down the front stairs, stopped at the front door, and jiggled the knob. He went to the back door and repeated the action, then he went back into bed. At one forty-five, he went back downstairs, rattled the front door and the back door, then walked around the house. Garrett headed back upstairs once more, put on yesterday's trousers over his pajamas, then padded, barefoot, back down to the kitchen door and out into the yard. He picked up the ax that lay beside the woodpile and, in the moonlight, began to chop.

Around four A.M., Garrett came back inside, barely noticing his wife, MJ, who was sitting on the stairs. They both sat down in the large recliner, as they had so many times before, and fell asleep.

Garrett did not have Alzheimer's disease; MJ did. Garrett was simply burning out from the stress of giving care around the clock. Many times he had gone without sleep, trying to be alert to any need MJ might have. Without adequate sleep, care partners cannot maintain their emotional stamina. As discussed in Chapter 8, sleep alterations are common in a person with progressive dementia; she may sleep less or nap at various times through the day and wake in the night just when the care partner is finally drifting off, hardly ready to oversee her nocturnal activities. Add into that the care partner's worries that the patient may find something hazardous around the house or even leave the house.

The result, for both the patient and the care partner, is stress, tension, and frustration, which can lead to outbursts. Those stresses, in turn, add guilt to the rest of the emotional overload. No wonder that sleep deprivation is a primary reason that worn-out care partners seek to place Alzheimer's patients in nursing homes.

Care for the care partner is mandatory. While every habilitator has heard this time and time again, it bears repeating. The patient's care will be nonexistent, or very problematic, if the care partner's physical or emotional health is challenged beyond repair.

Keep in mind a sobering statistic: 30 percent of all care partners die before the people they're caring for do. If the care partner is no longer there, all of the promises spoken ("Of course I won't let you go into a nursing home"), all of the sacrifices made ("It's okay, I'll eat/sleep/relax later") are for nothing.

You must learn to recognize your limitations and acknowledge your needs. Even the most effective care partner has, at times, been exhausted, resentful, and discouraged. You can't provide for the patient if your physical or emotional health is shaky. You should see your primary-care physician or a psychological therapist right away if you suddenly find yourself having some of the following symptoms:

- Mood swings
- Unusual irritability
- Inability to fall asleep
- Inability to stay asleep
- Difficulty concentrating
- Digestive problems
- Unfamiliar aches and pains
- Increased desire for or use of drugs or alcohol
- Sense of failure or hopelessness
- Frequent bouts of crying, fearfulness, sadness
- Lack of interest in normal activities or family

As we often hear, getting enough exercise, nutrition, sleep, and time off can help guard against undue stress. The trick, of course, is not to wait until you feel frazzled to begin the regime but to exercise, eat healthily, and sleep properly all the time, so that when the difficult times arise you can handle them as well as possible.

The demands on the habilitator often push exercise, for example, to the bottom of the priority list. Keep in mind that Alzheimer's patients who exercise appear to have less need for medications (for heart problems, blood pressure, arthritis, and so on), which is a compelling argument to find ways for both the patient and care partner to include an exercise program in the daily regime. Exercising together can mean sharing a walk, a bike ride, a swim, or a game of tennis. These times can also afford a chance to hold hands, reminisce, and find pleasure, and perhaps even joy, together. And while finding the time and energy to prepare nutritious meals may seem as arduous a task as painting the house, placing nourishing snacks in strategic locations, not buying high-sugar snacks, and eating an abundance of fruits and vegetables can help a great deal. Finally, if nighttime sleep is elusive, make time for an afternoon nap (or at least a moment to sit back with your feet raised) when the person with Alzheimer's is napping.

One more necessity is to find some time to relax. You need free time, however you find help. You must commit beforehand to taking time for yourself on a regular schedule, or you won't follow through on your plan. And that won't be good for either you or your partner. Within reason, don't let anything stop you from having your chosen time off. Maintaining a social life and participating in activities outside of caring for a patient with dementia helps to release some of the negative emotion that may be building — with or without your awareness.

You also need to create a calm atmosphere in some part of your home. Surround yourself with items that induce repose, perhaps by evoking memories of restful times and idyllic places. For instance, an herb garden with odors such as rosemary or basil may help. Potted plants, a goldfish bowl, a bird cage, landscape paintings or photographs of favorite scenes placed on walls, or colored stones or glass marbles in a bowl of water or a basket may take you to nostalgic places. Try a water garden, a basket of pinecones or sage, an arrangement of branches, or a bouquet of fresh flowers.

I have come up with an acronym to help remind you of your own daily needs: COPE.

C — Communicate, not only with the patient but also with the doctor, other helpers, and supporters. Let them know how *you* are feeling, not just how the patient is doing. Speak up. Mention your level of fatigue or feelings of burnout.

O — Organize and simplify the details of your own life and the patient's life. Organize drawers, closets, attic, and cellar, throwing away anything that's no longer needed. Go through old documents and organize those that have to be kept — discard the others. Get others to help you do this work. Simplify the house slowly — one room a week or a month until it is done. Place bills to be paid in an expandable file or set up another system that works for you. Being organized means you will have more time to spend being a habilitator.

P — Prioritize your time. What needs to happen next? Can some matters be done at another time? Make a timeline of how you need to proceed and include legal and financial matters, visits to long-term-care facilities, and appointments to find appropriate doctors. A regularly reviewed plan of care will prove helpful here.

E — Energize your body and your brain. Along with physical exercise, do crossword or jigsaw puzzles and listen to music and read alone or with the patient. Find time to use a computer or practice the piano.

If you don't see how you can possibly create time for yourself, give yourself permission to ask one or more people to help you. Friends and family members may be able to help, but so may the teenager next door (see Chapter 12 for an in-depth discussion of other people in the home). Use delivery services for groceries, meals, and other necessities to the extent that your geographic location and budget allow. You may want to invest in hiring a housekeeper, home-health aide, or visiting nurse.

You must wholeheartedly commit to taking time for yourself on a regular schedule; the benefits for both you and the person with Alzheimer's won't happen unless you do so. Decide in advance how much time you truly need each day, week, or month and incorporate that time into your plan of care. Will the patient be napping? Will he definitely be in bed for the night? Will you need someone to look in on him while you are away from the house?

Here are some suggestions for scheduling time for yourself:

- Twenty minutes every day for six months (then revise if necessary). Soak your feet, sit outside alone and listen to the birds, walk the dog, read a magazine in the park, talk on the telephone with a friend — this is twenty minutes at the same time every day just for you.
- Two hours every other week for three months (then revise if necessary). See a movie with a friend, have lunch with a

Pandemic !?

buddy, take a trip to the library, the hairdresser, or the barbershop, treat yourself to a bubble bath with scented candles, work out at the gym, have a massage, go on a bird walk, or work on a hobby.

- Four hours once a month. Play golf, go the museum, go to a spa and have "the works," have dinner with friends, go to the symphony, play bridge, mahjong, or poker.

Whole shelves of bookstores are devoted to various ways to reduce stress and find relaxation, so I will not treat this subject in depth. The suggestions that follow are merely a few that I've seen work wonders in my own practice.

Specific relaxation techniques can ameliorate stressful situations. Many medical centers have stress-reduction clinics that can help you learn methods that enable you to calm down and cope; for these, check out the clinics in your area.

One technique that I use with both patients and care partners, which works almost anywhere (in the car, the shower, around the home, on a walk) is a simple breathing exercise: Close your eyes. Take a deep breath through your nose, and exhale through your mouth. Repeat ten to twelve times.

Another technique is to sit down, relax your muscles, and visualize the place where you feel the most relaxed. Try to push every other thought away, focusing only on that picture, letting it swallow up all of the tedium and difficulties in your daily life. A third technique is to focus on your toes, trying to relax them as much as possible; then focus on your feet, then ankles, calves, and so forth, until you work your way up to your head, making sure to relax your jaw muscles and the muscles around your eyes.

A Caution about Friends and Family

Some friends and family members may do more harm than good for you. One trait I see frequently is what I call the "Gee, He Looks Good to Me Syndrome." Friends and relatives often see what they want to see and don't understand how hard your situation is. A care partner once told me about a woman named Margaret, who said, as she left after a half-hour visit with her cousin, who had Alzheimer's, "He seems fine." But Margaret had not given her cousin a chance to talk, and he looked "fine" because the care partner had dressed him for the third time twenty minutes before the visit. At the end of such a visit, the visitor may turn to the care partner and essentially ask, "What's *your* problem [with the patient]?"

This situation often develops when a parent gets Alzheimer's and one adult child becomes the primary care partner. The other siblings are too busy or too far away; when they're finally forced to see the situation for what it is, they commonly say, "I don't know how you did it this long." Then they may become useful helpers. There's little that you can do about such misperceptions until the other person has the opportunity to walk in your shoes. Perhaps the person with Alzheimer's can stay with the relative for a few days, or the relative can stay with the patient while you're away "on business," if an excuse is needed.

In many cases, however, denial is the only way that people deal with Alzheimer's. In such situations, it's best to have the visitor visit as infrequently as possible.

You may have to be especially careful with family members with whom you or the patient has had difficult experiences in the past. Families for many reasons — particularly out of guilt — do not always acknowledge the good job the primary care partner is doing. It is a waste of time to hope that a relative's personality will change during this period. At some point you just may have to say, "You don't seem to understand, and your calling me [or visiting us] disrupts me and [the patient]. Please leave us alone."

Or the primary care partner may find himself barraged with supposedly helpful advice from someone who just wants to provide the advice, not the help. Listen if you choose; use the advice if you wish; but remember that you can say, "If you're not going to be here to help me, please don't make suggestions that I can't possibly do or handle." Use your energy to find solid support elsewhere rather than expending it on friends and relatives who aren't helpful.

Family meetings should always be encouraged, however, whether or not the family members get along. In therapy sessions with me, families often discuss issues they've had with the patient that have been under the surface all their lives. The only thing that has changed is that one member of the family has Alzheimer's, but the family dynamics remain the same. In such a situation, the crisis of dealing with the disease can actually be an opportunity to remedy long-standing negative family dynamics. But don't expect personalities to change just because a parent or other family member has Alzheimer's disease. Again: use the energy elsewhere. Accept pats on the back from anyone who gives them, and know that they are well deserved.

Support Groups

Once you recognize the importance of caring for yourself, you should seek a support group of other care partners. You need reassurance and validation; feeling the support of people in the same situation is a great beginning. A telephone call to the office of the local chapter of the National Alzheimer's Association should provide help in finding a nearby support group where you can share emotions, problems, and remedies with fellow care partners. Hospitals, nursing homes, assisted-living facilities, places of worship, libraries, councils on aging, and similar agencies host support groups that are generally open to anyone in the community. If at all possible, shop around and sit in on a few groups. Of course, not everybody can do this; some care partners may have to travel fifty miles to the nearest group.

Alzheimer's support groups offer families and friends an opportunity to focus on ways to care for the patient, skills to hone, humor to help you through the hard times, and education about the disease. Members find that they are not alone and have a forum to discuss ideas and concerns, to share hopes and even positive aspects of the disease. Giving others helpful feedback and offering compassion are steppingstones to your own self-care. This support system will replenish your energy as you gain the desire to smile through tomorrow.

A support group may also be able to provide clinical information about new medications and practical suggestions on how to influence a patient to stop driving, for example. Members may be energized to learn about organized advocacy or new strategies to help children deal with an afflicted parent. Remember that members steer the group meetings, so you can give to or take from your group as much as you need.

Generally, support groups are either closed or open-ended. Closed support groups run for a certain length of time (often eight to twelve weeks), with a group of people who have signed up. At the end of the specified time, the group disbands. These sessions are usually educational in nature, set up strictly for informational purposes. Open-ended support groups, on the other hand, meet year-round, through holidays and vacations, with no end date. New members may come into the group at any time. The facilitator of the group may be a care partner or a professional from a local assisted-living center or a nursing home.

Whether closed or open-ended, support groups can come in a variety of flavors. The most common are these:

- Early-stage support groups for caregivers (this may be the most common type)
- Groups for caregivers of mentally retarded adults with Alzheimer's (all people with Down's syndrome, for example, will develop Alzheimer's)
- Early-onset groups, for patients under sixty-five at the time of diagnosis
- Foreign/cultural support groups
- Men-only groups

• Groups for children of parents or grandparents with Alzheimer's

You may also want to look into early-stage patient support groups, which are for patients only. Such groups can be beneficial to the patient, who often feels able to communicate in this setting: instead of relying on wordless pleas for understanding, she finds others who can help her find lost words. Many family members who thought that a patient was unable to talk about her feelings have been surprised to discover that in a safe forum, with others bearing the same diagnosis, she could be remarkably insightful and articulate about these emotions.

The ideal is to find an early-stage patient support group and an early-stage caregiver support group that meet at the same time in one building but in different rooms. An option I find less effective is a single support group for both care partners and patients — often called an early-stage patient/caregiver support group. This option often doesn't allow either person to articulate her feelings freely.

Remember that support groups can go a long way toward reducing both emotional and practical stress. One of the best aspects is the opportunity for share-care (see Chapter 12), in which care partners in the support group take turns watching over several people with Alzheimer's — allowing the other care partners to have some personal time, with the knowledge that a trusted person is supervising the patient.

Caring at a Distance

You will also encounter stress if you are caring for a family member or close friend who lives elsewhere. Even if you are a long-distance care partner, you will still feel a loss of freedom, and you may well face anger, fear, and fatigue repeatedly. You might receive repeated telephone calls from another time zone — perhaps thirteen times a day or more. Or the manager of the apartment building where the patient has lived for the past six years might call you to report bizarre nightly behavior, wanting to know what you are going to do about the problem — and when.

To reduce your stress over the long run, begin as early as possible to keep a notebook about the faraway afflicted person's changes in mood, skills, behavior, cognition, and activities of daily living each time you visit. If the patient has some help, speak with the helpers before, during, and after each of your visits. Discuss the situation with the council on aging in the town where the afflicted person lives — perhaps you can arrange to have a case manager stop by and assess the situation. To get another opinion about the patient, contact as many people who know him as possible — neighbors, other family members, clergy. Determine whether the symptoms they mention are just signs of old age or indications of something more serious.

If you suspect that the person has Alzheimer's or some form of dementia, you may have to visit her and become an unpopular person for a while — especially if she is opposed to going to a doctor or getting a workup. You'll have to decide to take action, even if she will dislike you for it or do nothing, taking the chance that something terrible will happen that you'll have to live with for the rest of your life.

If you decide that an unwilling patient must see a doctor, you can take some steps to make the appointment more pleasant. Set up the appointment allegedly for yourself, and get the person to accompany you. Have an assessment done on him during that time. Or find a geriatrician who will come to the house — this is becoming a popular service. Your local chapter of the Alzheimer's Association will be able to recommend someone.

In most cases the person with Alzheimer's will have no helpers initially, so safety will become your primary concern. Touch bases with the Alzheimer's Association in the area and explain that you are a long-distance care partner, and you need to ensure the person's safety. Also, tap into the formal support network, which includes adult day care, home health care, the local Visiting Nurses

Association (VNA), Meals on Wheels, and any other supports that the Alzheimer's Association recommends. Frequently, the network includes sources of community help; ask for whatever help you think will be needed in the future. If your decision to bring helpers into the home meets with consternation on the part of the patient, point out that the aide's presence will ease your mind.

When you visit the patient, be sure to spend at least three or four days. Visit her friends, neighbors, primary-care physician, house of worship, closest hospital, and the council on aging. That will help you find out who and what services are available. Then, if a problem arises when you cannot make a quick trip to see the person, these contacts may be able to help out and perhaps even network with one another.

Set up interviews with medical doctors, home health care agencies, case management programs, and assisted-living centers and nursing homes. Take the time to visit them in person, using the assessment tools provided in Chapters 12 and 13. I have received many calls throughout the years from long-distance care partners in great distress after a hired helper has been brought into the home without an interview. Don't let this happen to you; visiting the various organizations and institutions will let you be prepared. (If you need to choose, say, a neurologist or a nursing home, narrow your choices to two in case one is booked when you need it the most.)

If you visit your loved one only at infrequent intervals, be prepared for changes wrought by the disease. Education about the disease process is a must. If you cannot attend a support group in your region, then get information from the library or the Alzheimer's Association on the manifestations of the disease and what to expect as it progresses (and see Chapter 3).

If you feel that the patient might be better off living near you, weigh all the possible alternatives before making the move. Consider whether the patient will have as many visitors and whether the care will be better. Do you want to visit her more often, and in a closer location? Would you like to take a greater part in her care? Are you considering the move to assuage your feelings of guilt? Will the move unsettle her and perhaps create new way-finding problems? Do the emotional positives outweigh the material negatives?

Maybe a move will help both you and the patient. Then again, the patient may see a potential move as an attempt to interfere with her life. Past history plays a major role in a patient whose long-term memories have become the bulk of today's thoughts. Trying to make up for negative past interactions by bringing your mother, say, to live with or near you at the end of her life may not buy you the solace you require. Your current relationships may have to take precedence over a relative living far away. Accept this situation with as little guilt as possible. Professional care partners who have learned the appropriate ways to interact with cognitively impaired adults can make the patient's life as good as possible. Often this arrangement frees the afflicted person from the stress of family history and the burden of having to perform well enough to hide the illness. An appropriate care partner will generally accept the person the way she is now. As she progresses through the disease, she will grow to love the care partner.

Be sure to show your appreciation to any far-away care partners. Call them often and offer praise and support. Send tokens of your appreciation and remember their birthdays. Whether friend, neighbor, or professional, they are helping you. And remember that every human being is unique and brings individual skills to the care-partnering experience. Don't compare your abilities with those of another care partner; we all have different resources — in terms of finances, family, personality, previous history, and more — to draw from. Don't be afraid to say aloud several times a day, "Not every marriage was made in heaven" or "Not every family relationship is okay."

Many years ago, I was at my grandmother's house after she died, going through her belongings. I came across an ancient faded box stuck in a corner. Opening it gingerly, I found a magnificent velvet hat adorned with tiny peach-colored rosebuds so perfect that I leaned down to sniff them, sure they must be real. A yellowed price tag still dangled from the brim.

"Why didn't Grandmother wear this beautiful hat?" I asked my grandfather.

He held the hat gently, the soft velvet a contrast to his rough flesh. "She was saving it, honey," he told me. "She was saving it for a special occasion."

Any moment can be a special occasion. A care partner needs to reduce the stresses in his life so that he — and the person he is caring for — can feel the special quality of their time together. As a care partner, try to *savor* more moments and *endure* fewer.

12

Receiving Home Care

*I am not running fast enough
to keep away
that furtive shadow chasing me.
Next I'll breathless stop
to find that same shadow
is all that's left of me.*

SHAY MCGRANEY, seventy-nine years old, was in the final stage of Alzheimer's. She spent her time in bed or looking out the window at her younger brother Edward's house in coastal Oregon. Edward had pasted a poster of the Irish countryside on the ceiling above her bed. A cassette player issued soft Irish music as a part-time home-health aide tucked in the rumpled blankets. Shay smiled.

She no longer used words to express thoughts. But Edward and the aide recognized the subtle facial movements that indicated when she was cold or thirsty, and they responded to those needs. Edward understood that Shay no longer knew how he was related to her. But he knew that she felt loved.

Home care is rarely as idyllic as that. But it can be the ideal situation for both patient and care partner — if, and only if, both are comfortable with the arrangement, if the past history between the two has been positive, and if the care partner wants to perform the care out of love, not guilt. If all those pieces are in place, home care can be the best choice because it enables the patient to remain oriented to the world as much as possible and is the easiest setting for implementing habilitative methods.

All care partners need to learn about what formal and informal support systems are available. Keep in mind that as the disease progresses, the person with Alzheimer's will require additional or different types of assistance; what is appropriate today, when the person is living alone in her own home, will be inappropriate tomorrow, when she is no longer able to take care of personal needs.

Here are the resources most commonly available, which are discussed in this chapter:

- Home care by one or more habilitators: Even if you are the primary care partner in your own home or the patient's home, you may also enlist other people to help with the care.
- Home health care agencies: These agencies provide personnel, including aides and housekeepers, for a variety of tasks in the home.
- Case management programs: A social worker from this program will set up and manage a plan of care.
- Adult day health centers: These centers offer enrichment activities to early- and middle-stage Alzheimer's patients. They have trained staff and may also have a trained nurse on the premises.
- Adult day care centers: Day care centers offer enrichment activities for all adults with medical problems; they may not have trained staff or an available nurse.

Home Care by a Habilitator

Home care is often the first and best choice for both patient and care partner. The surroundings are familiar and can be modified as the patient's condition changes.

At home you can monitor visitors — people both known and unknown to the person with Alzheimer's — more easily, so social situations are often more pleasant and more predictable. Routine activities of daily life will be less challenging for the patient because household objects are where they're "supposed" to be; odors are familiar; and the caregiver remains constant, without any surprising changes of staff or personnel. The person's hobbies, tools, and interests continue to surround him; leisure activities can continue relatively unchanged, so it is easier to fill up the day. Personal memorabilia provide opportunities for reflection and conversation. Being surrounded with much-loved objects in a long-known setting is one of the basic ways to keep an Alzheimer's patient in touch with the world: if the world is familiar, the patient feels more secure.

Home care is the most common solution to Alzheimer's. According to the 2001 National Public Policy Program of the National Alzheimer's Association, 70 percent of people with Alzheimer's disease live at home, with approximately three-fourths of home care provided by family and friends.

Before making the decision to become the primary care partner for a patient, assess the level of involvement that other people can assume. If the person with Alzheimer's lives alone, you may want to have a delivery service bring in groceries or other hard-to-carry items. If the person with Alzheimer's is living with the care partner, you may want to investigate local Meals on Wheels programs. The local council on aging or local chapter of the Alzheimer's Association should have information about what organization in your area may offer this service.

Find out about the availability of neighborhood teenagers,

adult neighbors, friends, family members, volunteers from religious or social organizations, housekeepers, and companions. For anyone you are considering having come in to help, observe whether she seems able to communicate with the person with Alzheimer's. The helper must seem to enjoy being around the patient, not frustrated or bored.

Introduce the helper in a way that doesn't leave the patient feeling as if he is the problem. "Joyce is here to help me get some things done," you might say. Don't leave the helper immediately with the patient — give him time to adjust to this new situation. If the patient seems to be acting up, stay in the room with the patient and helper several times, making the experience positive for everyone. Recognize that you may have to postpone your own plans at times to make sure that the patient is comfortable with the helper.

Asking family members and friends to help out can present certain complications. First, be honest, letting the person know exactly what is happening with the Alzheimer's patient, and explain that you need help on a regular basis — every Tuesday afternoon between two and five o'clock, for example — not "when you're able to come." The commitment has to be pleasurable for all concerned in some way. If the family member thinks this responsibility is a chore, the patient will know that. In such a case, it is far better to pay the teenager next door, who is willing to be polite and helpful for a few hours, to help out.

If a helper doesn't arrive on schedule, talk openly and honestly about the situation. "How can I meet your needs, since this doesn't seem to be working?" If the problems can't be resolved, you will have to replace the no-show with a helper who is more reliable.

What about seeking volunteer helpers from religious or social organizations? Good helpers of this sort are generally hard to find. Either the volunteers have no experience or they have little interest in dealing with someone with Alzheimer's. And if the patient, while attending a service or event, has been disruptive, the volunteer may feel alienated from him.

You may want to look for other organizations that can help out. Home health care agencies should be able to provide aides, nursing assistants, visiting nurses, companions, and housekeepers to help in matters such as:

- Personal care of the patient (bathing and dressing)
- Laundry services
- Escorting to medical appointments
- Light housekeeping
- Preparing meals
- Companionship (both in the home and in social settings)
- Case management (see page 172)

After determining the type of services the patient will need, try to find someone who is trained in taking care of Alzheimer's patients. Most home health care workers do not have this training, but you may be able to learn about agencies with trained personnel by calling your local chapter of the Alzheimer's Association, speaking with other care partners, or looking through the list of organizations in Further Resources, page 212. Here are the most common kinds of home helpers:

- Visiting nurse: comes to the house at a physician's request. The visiting nurse can perform most medical procedures that a doctor specifies — changing dressings, giving injections, performing physical therapy, and so forth. Note that this may be the only helper who is covered by Medicare/Medicaid; be sure to ask if outside insurance will cover the requested helper's services.
- Certified nursing assistant or aide: can do minor medical tasks such as changing bandages on scratches and scrapes, putting on leg braces, and assisting with bedpans or urinals

(be sure to find out the differences between "certified" and "uncertified" assistants, which will vary by state). Aides "cannot" (that is, they are not supposed to) give medications, although, as a practical matter, most do so.

- Nursing assistant or nurse's aide: can do personal care tasks, such as washing a patient.
- Companion: sits with the patient and provides companionship, takes him for walks, to restaurants, or movies; does not do cooking or cleaning.
- Housekeeper: does light housekeeping (does not clean refrigerators, gutters, or windows, for example); does not provide patient care.

Here's a checklist to think about when interviewing a home health care agency:

- Will the same helper come every time? (It's best for an Alzheimer's patient to see a familiar person. Any agreement should specify that the agency will send the same person each time.)
- Are the agency's personnel bonded? This helps guarantee higher quality of service and reduces the risk of theft and other concerns. Of course, you cannot be completely assured of a helper's honesty. Get references, if possible, and don't leave money, jewelry, or other valuables around.
- How long has the agency been serving the community? Length of time is often a good indication of the organization's reputation. (But keep in mind that new agencies open because of the lack of competent agencies.)
- How does the agency handle emergencies? Are some staff members on duty, or at least available, at all times?
- What services will they charge for?
- What supplies will they charge for?
- Has Medicare approved the agency?

- Will any governmental assistance (such as Medicare or Medicaid) pay for needed items?
- Will the agency be in regular contact with the patient's physician?
- Can the patient and habilitator help decide the patient's plan of care?
- Does the agency teach family members how to carry out the types of care it gives? If the agency person transfers the patient from bath to bed, for example, she needs to teach the family how to do this as well.
- Does the supervisor make regular visits to the home? Who at the agency checks to be sure that the services/supplies are being provided as promised?
- Who is the contact person for questions or concerns?

If the helper you hire through an agency is not trained in working with Alzheimer's patients, explain the five tenets of habilitation to him and emphasize how this approach makes the experience work better for everyone.

You'll know within a few weeks whether the helper you've hired is not working (if the house or the patient is repeatedly not clean, for example). Watch the patient's body language — notice if she is frowning a lot or acting more assertive or aggressive. If the helper is not doing his or her job, the person with Alzheimer's may be trying to communicate her displeasure. Sometimes even the nicest helper isn't the right person if he reminds the patient of someone else. If matters do not appear to be going well, check whether a symptom of the disease is causing the problem; the patient might make false accusations out of paranoia, for example.

If all goes well, the services of a home health care agency can be a godsend, providing the care partner a badly needed respite. The agency personnel can show you useful techniques for dealing with an Alzheimer's patient and can serve as a sounding board as you develop a plan of care. And if one aide doesn't work out, the agency should be able to provide you with another — which can be easier than advertising in the classifieds or trying to find someone through a network of friends and colleagues.

Care Partnering in Your Home, Not the Patient's

If you do not live with the patient, you may think about caring for him in your home. Bringing a person with Alzheimer's into a home with other family members presents a unique set of challenges that you need to consider ahead of time. First, have an open, honest conversation with everyone who lives with you about the situation. Do your family members genuinely like the person? If you have children, explain that the patient may act differently from other people. Several great books and videos about people with Alzheimer's are available (see Further Resources, page 217). Engage children in the discussion so that they can feel vested in the decision.

Another matter to consider before asking a patient to live with you is the need to modify your house, which may be time-consuming and financially draining. Keep in mind that an Alzheimer's patient requires plenty of space for perceptual reasons, as well as a room to himself: a small residence simply will not make sense. And if the house is shared by a number of people, the distractions may be overwhelming to the patient.

If you have a job, it may be difficult, if not impossible, to care properly for the person with Alzheimer's. Will your job allow you to leave unexpectedly if you need to? How often can you do that? And if you can't leave work to take care of an emergency, is someone else available to help? Overall, will your job be conducive to the home routine you'll have to develop?

Having an Alzheimer's patient in your home will definitely affect the neighborhood as well. She may act erratically or have a variety of behavioral problems that neighbors may find troubling or embarrassing. You should be prepared to communicate with your neighbors about the patient; reluctance to discuss the situation may cause discomfiture. You could write a letter alerting your neighbors to the likelihood of some irrational behavior. You might say, "My mother has come to live with us. She has Alzheimer's. If she walks into your house without knocking or does something that makes you uncomfortable, please welcome her in and call us immediately. Here's our phone number."

As soon as you have decided to bring the patient into your home, seek financial and elder-care legal counseling. If the person owns the residence where he has lived up until now, it may have to be sold to help pay for his care. According to the Alzheimer's Association, as of 2001, the cost of caring for a person with Alzheimer's was approximately $12,500 per year. Also make sure that the proper clauses concerning physical and medical matters are inserted into documents such as the power of attorney.

The decision to bring a patient into your home doesn't have to be a permanent one. If at some point the family no longer wants to keep the person at home, other arrangements can be made.

Share-Care

Share-care is one of the most helpful options available to primary care partners. Generally, two or three care partners in a support group will organize a schedule for having one person look after several Alzheimer's patients for a given period of time, in exchange for another person looking after them at another set time. This not only gives care partners time to relax, but it's a wonderful bonding experience with other care partners, since these people really understand your situation. And they can speak frankly if the situation is not working well. "Your wife's nice," I once heard someone say to another care partner, "but she's peeing in my petunias. I think we'll have to make other arrangements."

In most cases, share-care arrangements simply happen — someone mentions it in the support group, and the care partners work out the plan. Often support-group participants are from the same geographic area and have similar work and ethnic backgrounds, which makes it easier for the care partners to understand each other, and allows the patients to feel more comfortable in someone else's home. Share-care shouldn't begin on the first day of the support group, however — the care partners must learn to know and like each other and learn one another's fears and concerns.

To set up a share-care arrangement, first arrange a meeting for care partners and patients. Everyone must like and trust each other.

Case Management Program

When a patient cannot live with a local care partner, family members generally hire a case manager — a social worker — to organize and manage the afflicted person's plan of care. The local council on aging, which is state-run and thus has guidelines, is the best place to find a high-quality case management program. The Case Management Society of America produces a directory and Web site that lists case managers by state (see Further Resources, page 214).

Initially the case manager goes into the home of the person with Alzheimer's and does a complete assessment of the patient and the home, focusing on safety issues, environmental concerns, financial matters, and the like. The case manager can arrange for the services of a home health care agency, as well as for financial and legal services, personal emergency response systems, home-delivered meals from Meals on Wheels, and much more.

A case management program is ideal for a patient who wants to remain living at home for as long as possible, and perhaps through the entire course of the disease. Depending on the patient's income, Medicare and Medicaid may pay for the services. Long-term insurance may also cover them, if they keep the patient from having to enter a nursing home.

A downside to case management can be the cost, which may

range from several hundred dollars a week for individual services to fifty thousand dollars a year for full-time care. In addition, the patient may experience a sense of having lost control. A good case manager tries to keep the patient feeling that she is still part of the decision-making, however.

Generally, early-stage patients welcome case management programs. If the person with dementia can cognitively grasp that the program will allow her to stay at home, she is likely to cooperate well with the case manager.

Adult Day Health and Day Care Centers

Another workable alternative for patients in the later early stage and middle stage of Alzheimer's is an adult day health or day care program. Adult day health centers provide enrichment activities outside the home. These centers have trained staff and a trained nurse on the premises. Adult day care centers are similar, but are not required to have a trained staff or nurse available.

Be sure that the adult day health program staff is thoroughly trained in interacting with people with dementia. A well-run program can offer the habilitator a respite by providing meals as well as hours of structured programming — including bathing and naps, if necessary. Since filling leisure time is often a difficulty for the patient, a program that provides fun, socialization, and chances for success makes sense. It may not be the best choice for patients who are not functioning well, however, and could lead to greater depression if the afflicted person spends a lot of time with patients who exhibit signs of more advanced dementia. It is also not appropriate for very late-stage Alzheimer's patients — these programs should not be considered a "sitting" service.

Bruce's family had a meeting and decided that three days a week in an adult day health program would enrich his life with activities that were both physically and mentally rewarding. After entering the program, the seventy-eight-year-old became much more engaged and interested in everything. On his "home" days, he wanted to go on walks with his hired companion. He never seemed to remember exactly what he did at the day program, but when asked, he would respond, "Whatever it was, it was great."

Bruce's family was fortunate that he remained outgoing and open to new possibilities. Many care partners, however, find that convincing an Alzheimer's patient to go to an adult day health program is difficult at first, since change seems threatening and confusing. Here are some techniques that can make the move more comfortable for both patient and habilitator.

When introducing the topic, explain to the patient that the adult day health program needs him rather than saying he needs the program. If he is still functioning well, you may be able to convince him that the center needs a volunteer helper who will help the staff by setting up meals and programs, transporting people in wheelchairs, reading poetry, or directing sing-alongs. If this explanation fails, or when it is no longer sufficient, explain that you need time to accomplish chores around the house, go shopping, work, or garden, and his attendance in a program will make that possible.

Set a time limit on how long the person with Alzheimer's will attend the center; you might say, "Let's do it just for this week because I have something to do." The following week, you can repeat the same request. Be persistent and confident that the program is a positive choice for the patient — even if she doesn't believe it. Staff members are accustomed to dealing with resistant patients and are quite adept at changing the negative into the positive.

If the patient hesitates when he arrives at the center, be sure to have a trained staff member actually move him into the facility each day. Have the staff person meet you at the car if you're driving to the facility, or have the bus driver meet you at your door. Staff people are trained to deal with reluctant patients, and a patient will often more willingly go with one of them than with the care partner or another family member. If the patient refuses to get dressed, send him in pajamas. The centers are equipped for such situations.

Have the center take photographs or videos of the patient having a good time at the program. When she insists, at day's end, that she had a terrible time and won't go back, the photograph will remind her how much fun the program was and will ease your mind about sending her there.

13

Receiving Care Outside
of a Family Home

*Good decisions are born
out of fears overcome
and baggage left behind.*

MAL, EIGHTY-TWO years old and in the middle stage of Alzheimer's, lived with her daughter's family, which included two teenage grandchildren. Long before Mal was diagnosed, her daughter and son-in-law decided that they should always take care of her. Recently, when one of the grandchildren had some friends over, Mal walked into the family room clad only in a slip and boisterously exclaimed, "Prisoners, prisoners, peaches!" Clearly agitated, she shook the front doorknob, trying to get out of the house.

Later that night, Mal's daughter heard the two kids huddled together on the porch, talking about the "totally awful embarrassment" their grandmother had caused. "What are we going to do?" one said. "I don't want her to be here anymore — she's ruining everything." The other seemed equally upset. "I stay away from this wacko house as much as possible. Mom and Dad just keep saying they promised they'd always take care of Nana. But what about us?"

Mal's social ineptness, lack of inhibition and judgment, and difficulty with language are typical manifestations of middle-stage Alzheimer's. The negative body language of her grandchildren most likely confused her even more. At that point, for the sake of the family, Mal should have been moved to a setting designed to care for people with Alzheimer's disease. The family could visit for brief periods, contributing to Mal's care but focusing primarily on positive family interactions. In this more appropriate setting, everyone in the family would have been happier, better off, and, ideally, free of guilt and denial.

Consider the story of Michael and Jennifer, too. After their mother died, they sincerely promised their father, Renato, that they would take care of him in his own home "forever." Renato had cared for his wife at home and now he expected his children to do the same for him. No one expected, or planned for, Alzheimer's. But as the disease progressed, Renato's inability to live alone forced caregiving issues. Who would cook for him? Who would make sure he took his medication? Michael had troubles of his own that made it impossible for him to care for his father, and he began phoning Jennifer daily, begging her to take Renato into her home. "But he won't leave his home — and I promised him he could stay," Jennifer would cry, feeling powerless to go against her father's wishes even in the face of dementia. She tried to reassure herself, saying "He'll be okay. I stop by every day. I keep the doors locked. I bring him pizza. What more can I do? He doesn't want to leave. He sits and watches TV all day. But it's his life."

Then one night Renato, locked in his home alone, awoke in the chair in front of the TV, where he now slept every night, and shuffled into the kitchen. He turned on the burner under the teakettle sitting on the stove, returned to his chair, and fell back to sleep. The teakettle burned dry, then the papers on the kitchen counter caught fire and spread to curtains, cabinets, walls. Renato woke up to the wail of the smoke alarms, although he did not understand what the sound was. Seeing the fire, he cowered near the locked front door, where the fire department found him, suffering from smoke inhalation. Had they arrived a few minutes later, Renato would not have survived.

As the progression of their father's disease caused changes in his need for care, Michael and Jennifer's plans for him also had to change, even if they felt guilt-ridden for making that decision. If having Renato live with one of his children was out of the question, engaging the services of a visiting nurse, sending him to an adult day center, or placing him in a nursing home would have been appropriate options. And the decision would have been made out of love for the parent — not out of guilt.

Families rally more easily when a parent requires a short-term hospital stay for an acute problem. Long-term — or, perhaps more aptly, "lifespan" — care, however, presents more difficult choices. Plans need to be continually revisited and revised. Promises — to both the patient and other family members — can be fulfilled only if circumstances warrant it, and promises should not be made and kept out of guilt.

Many children have assured parents that they would never be sent to a nursing home. Such a promise — made at a time when the parents were cognitively intact and able to care for themselves — leaves the children riddled with guilt when, after trying everything else, placement in a nursing home seems the only option. It's extraordinarily distressing to feel you've failed to care for your parent or to feel you've broken your promise to the parent or other family members. Consequently — and perhaps too often unavoidably — the parent remains in a less appropriate setting or receives less than optimal care for far too long, all because of a promise made before the disease had progressed or had been properly diagnosed.

Promises made to others when the situation was simpler may be impossible to keep after Alzheimer's intrudes and causes tremendous changes. Disease complicates the decisions and necessitates new plans. Use love as your guide: *Do I love her enough, am I worried enough about her well-being, to have her be angry with me for a while if someone else can care for her better than I can?* For many patients and their families, home care is not the ideal option — everyone may be better able to thrive if the patient lives outside the family home.

If you are caring for a patient in your home, you'll know that the time has come to relinquish care when you go out to do an errand and no longer want to go back into the house when you return — that is, when the negative feelings of being with the patient fully outweigh the positives. Practicing the tenets of habilitation is impossible without love, trust, and comfort. You cannot successfully reassure and comfort the patient if you don't have the sensitivity born of these feelings. When that time comes, you need to have already chosen the next steps to take.

The following options can, if properly selected, allow a person with Alzheimer's to live with dignity and self-respect:

- Group home/foster-care setting: Several people with Alzheimer's living together in a primary caregiver's home.
- Assisted-living center: An establishment for patients (and their spouses) who require minimal assistance but need some help with directions and activities of daily living.
- Alzheimer's assisted-living center: An establishment designed to meet the needs of Alzheimer's patients (and their spouses).
- Nursing home: An establishment for patients with advanced psychosocial and medical needs.
- Special-care unit: A designated area in an assisted-living center or nursing home, set apart for people with progressive dementia.

Each of these support systems offers differing possibilities to allow both patient and habilitator to thrive rather than merely mark time.

Group Home/Foster-Care Setting

In a group home, several people with Alzheimer's live together in a primary caregiver's home. This wonderful, but fairly rare, situation typically comes about when family members who have kept a loved one at home have extra space and invite others to live with them for a fee.

Group homes usually have five or six people living together; each patient has his own room, and they share a living room, dining room, and kitchen. The setting is like a regular home except that a family member (or sometimes a professional staff person) sleeps in the house overnight. The care partners are usually trained to work with Alzheimer's patients and help create Alzheimer's-friendly activities, chores, and outings. This is as close to home care as possible.

The habilitation techniques discussed in this book are perfectly suited to this care option: patients have a great opportunity to feel successful, and the entire house can be modified for maximum comfort. In one house I helped design, we painted each patient's bedroom a different vibrant color — making the room easily recognizable, comfortable, and personalized. Each resident can spend time alone in her own room, yet other people are nearby for socializing, which helps alleviate feelings of loneliness and isolation. The care for each resident can be personalized; each can have his own schedule and routine.

Unfortunately, group homes are not funded through any third-party source — they are paid for only on a private-pay basis, and the costs can be prohibitive. If a group home is available to you, find out the costs up front, and be sure that they can be checked and detailed in the future. Make sure the care provider isn't just trying to make money by taking in patients — he or she should be properly trained and should understand the particular needs of people with Alzheimer's. Talk to family members of other residents; ask for references, and check with the local Better Business Bureau.

Assisted-Living Center

Assisted-living centers are for elders (and their spouses) who require minimal assistance with directions, bathing, meal preparation, medications, and so forth. Alzheimer's assisted-living centers are designed to meet the needs of Alzheimer's patients who are not ready for nursing home placement.

To assess an assisted-living facility, consider the following factors:

- Convenient location: Will family and friends be able to visit on a regular schedule?
- Facility tour: Can you drop by for a tour anytime, or does the management insist on a guided tour? You should be able to see the facility from the resident's perspective at any time. A staff guide will point out areas or programs that you may miss if touring unescorted.
- Patient control: Will the Alzheimer's patient be safe from the dangers of wandering into other areas of the building or on the grounds? Have security and emergency systems, such as door alarms or security cameras, been installed?
- Training: Is the staff trained specifically to interact with Alzheimer's residents? Local chapters or the National Alzheimer's Association can provide brochures for education of staff — see Special-Care Unit, below, for more details.
- Staff: Do staff members appear to enjoy their work interacting with residents? Does the staffing ratio assure individual attention and care? There should be at least one staff person for eight to twelve residents. Is the staff friendly toward you?
- Odor: A pervasive unpleasant odor can be an indicator of unsanitary conditions. (However, an offensive odor outside a patient's room is generally indicative of an accident and may not indicate poor housekeeping.)

- Common areas: Are they well designed and inviting, allowing for socialization? Are chairs comfortable and facing each other, making the space conducive to conversation?
- Private areas: Are the patients encouraged to personalize their rooms with memorabilia and photographs?
- All areas: Is the environment specifically designed for Alzheimer's patients rather than outsiders?
- Activity programs: Are the activity programs of interest to the Alzheimer's patient?
- Outside activities: Are there opportunities and areas for outdoor activities?
- Family involvement: Does the center ask for the family's involvement in formulating its plan of care?
- Food: Is the food appetizing, nutritious, and suitable for the declining skills of Alzheimer's residents? (See Chapter 8.)
- References: Will the facility provide names and contact information for family members of other residents?
- Peer interaction: If the Alzheimer's patients are intermingled with other residents, do these people sometimes treat dementia patients with less friendliness and support than they treat other people? Talk about this with other families of Alzheimer's patients.

It is important to consult with a financial planner before moving a person to an assisted-living center. You may too quickly spend down funds that will be needed later, when the patient needs to move to a more professional setting, for example. Also, assisted living may be suitable for Alzheimer's patients for only a short term. And moving again as the disease progresses can be traumatizing for both patient and care partner.

But assisted-living facilities provide a safety net for thousands of Alzheimer's patients who would otherwise fall into a gaping hole of residential care. These centers promote continued independence and provide enrichment possibilities for early-stage patients. Because residents bring their own furniture, the transition from home is often easier, and as the disease progresses, familiar surroundings can be a great comfort. Also, the companionship of other residents can be a godsend for care partner and patient.

Nursing Home

When Kristen was making plans to place her father-in-law, Mel, in a nursing home, she told her support group of her feelings of failure. "I feel that I'm abandoning him in some way. They don't know him the way I do or my husband does."

Kristen needed to keep in mind the reasons that prompted her to seek an alternative living arrangement. Mel had begun to need more care than Kristen, the mother of three young children, could handle. Although her husband tried to be helpful, he was disturbed to see his dad in decline, and there was less and less interaction between the two. Mel was wandering away from home several times a week and had aggressively threatened Kristen when she tried to stop him. Moreover, none of her husband's siblings had offered assistance. In short, there had been no other choice than to find good professional care.

The support group gave Kristen the reassurance she needed. They viewed her decision to place Mel in a good nursing home as an act of love, giving him a safe setting where wandering wasn't an issue and where his frustration and anxiety could be reduced. Also, the staff worked eight-hour shifts, which meant that every worker could return refreshed. Kristen's future visits with Mel would be warm and meaningful, and she could enjoy a more fulfilling life with her family.

At some point in the care-partnering process, the best way to care for the patient may be to relinquish some of the responsibility to the professional staff of a nursing home. Too often, family members seek a nursing home bed at a moment of crisis rather than planning this move thoroughly ahead of time. Planning such a move with the patient can also be beneficial by conveying trust in his remaining control and willingness to have him participate in the process.

The variety of names describing these facilities can be confusing. The most common terms, depending on the geographical area you live in, are nursing care or health care centers, nursing homes, rest homes, foster-care homes, adult-care centers or homes, Alzheimer's centers, or special-care units. The latter two categories are set up to care only for folks diagnosed with Alzheimer's or other progressive dementias. I discuss them in the following section.

Nursing homes have come a long way in offering care to people with various kinds of dementia. Many, however, have not come far enough; it is necessary to visit, tour, and ask questions of people both inside and outside of the facility. If you have any doubts about a facility, check with the council on aging, your local department of public health, police department, Better Business Bureau, and people in the neighborhood. After all, you are choosing a home for someone you care about; if you plan ahead, you should be able to have more than a single choice.

Placing the person with Alzheimer's in a good nursing home can leave you with feelings of ease and satisfaction, knowing that she is being given care perhaps better than you could provide. You can still have positive visits and provide ongoing love. Although long-term-care facilities vary greatly from community to community, some basic features should be present in the one you choose. Ideally, try to find a special-care unit (see page 189). But even these units vary greatly, ranging from locked wards all the way to completely habilitative programs. Be sure to obtain and read, early on, the Alzheimer's Association pamphlet on choosing a long-term-care setting (see the Alzheimer's Association listing in Further Resources, page 216).

When assessing a nursing home, consider the points listed above for assisted-living centers as well as the following:

- Family council meetings: Ask if the facility offers meetings run by the families of residents who are not able to speak for themselves, and without staff members present. These meetings allow families to collectively voice concerns and ideas. A trusted staff member may act as liaison between the group and administration. For those residents who are able to speak for themselves, a residents' council should be in place. Ask if the facility holds such meetings regularly, and perhaps ask to attend one.

- Family support: Unlike family councils, which discuss concerns about the facility, family support groups discuss the emotional side of dealing with Alzheimer's, and the meetings are led by a facilitator. Studies have shown that family support groups are often extraordinarily beneficial to families and patients alike. If such a group meets regularly, attend a meeting or two to see if you want to participate.

- Medical director: Do you approve of the medical director? This person makes the final decisions about your loved one's medical care. Does she have a reputation in the community as an advocate for people with Alzheimer's? Ask other residents' families what interaction they have had with her.

- State survey: Ask to see the latest state survey report on the facility; this is public information and should be readily available. The department that handles this responsibility (whose name is usually a variation of public health department) makes yearly assessments of any facility that accepts Medicare or Medicaid patients. The report is available for public viewing. The facility should get the highest grade; if not, the administrator should be able to easily explain the few deficiencies, and there should be demonstrable proof that efforts are being made to correct the issues.

- Medicaid: Does the nursing home accept Medicaid payments? Many don't. When all of the patient's funds have been expended, Medicaid will pay for nursing home care.

Don't settle for the first nursing home you find nearby — tour several and take notes. Drop in unexpectedly. Listen to your gut instincts. Often when a family tours a facility, they come away with a certain feeling about the place. The feeling may be negative, but not necessarily. A good facility will feel warm and homelike because the interaction between staff and residents is friendly, and the philosophy of the nursing home is obviously positive in all aspects, from dietary programs to administration.

As soon as Alzheimer's has been diagnosed, you should formulate legal plans for eventual long-term care. Consult an attorney or accountant who specializes in these issues, and see Chapter 3 for further information on powers of attorney and living wills. Few insurance policies cover nursing home placement. Many people with Alzheimer's or other progressive dementias have been duped into believing that "long-term-care insurance" will cover their situation. It usually does not. *Read the fine print carefully to be sure that "cognitive" disease or "mental incapacity" or "dementia" is not excluded.* Some states have special programs to help cover *some* costs of *some* care in assisted-living facilities, foster homes, retirement centers, and nursing homes. Check with your state's department of elder services. Medicare will help pay for some services.

The actual moment of bringing the person to the nursing home can be painful, but it need not be terrible. First, before the patient arrives, take some of her personal effects to her new room, so that familiar items will be waiting. Make sure clothing is in the drawers, favorite mementos are on the shelves, and so forth. The patient shouldn't arrive with a suitcase, as if he were going on a trip. Most important is that the new room possess a familiar odor associated with home — his brand of shaving cream, for example, or soap.

Have the aide or another person who will be spending much of the day with the patient (ask ahead of time who it will be) greet him at the door. Let that person take over the social dynamics, showing the patient around and introducing the other residents. Staff members do this regularly and know how to do it properly.

If the patient doesn't want to get out of the car, let the staff take over. Often the person with Alzheimer's is exercising control over the care partner — expressing anger or frustration may be her way of communicating her displeasure to you. Although she doesn't know the staff members, she doesn't have a past history with them, either, so she may not need to assert that she is still "in charge." The act of entering a nursing home, of being taken over by competent, professional staff, may actually be a tremendous relief, but the patient may not want to admit it.

When you get to the patient's room, stay for half an hour or so, then come up with a reason for having to leave. Figure out a reason ahead of time. If it's around lunchtime, have lunch with him, kiss him goodbye in the lunchroom, and leave. Discuss your leaving plan ahead of time with the staff. If the patient is angry, that is not necessarily a bad sign — it's a normal reaction. Her negativity will dissipate as time goes on and as she grows accustomed to the facility.

When the patient who has been sharing a home with a care partner moves into a nursing home, the care partner is very likely to feel guilty about relinquishing an essential part of loving (nurturing), or she may worry that others will see it that way. Even if the need for placement is clear, the action can be a powerful blow to the habilitator's self-esteem. Also, nursing home placement can lead to feelings of competition with the staff. If you have any of these reactions, look upon this change as an opportunity to share care.

After you place the patient in a professional home, the best way to care for yourself may be to take some time to rejuvenate and realize how important your role has been and continues to be in the overall care package. Most facilities will suggest that you take some time away from the patient to adjust, and allow the new resident to do the same. Four or five days should be enough time for the patient to become somewhat adapted to new surroundings and faces, while you catch up on needed relaxation. Telephone calls may help keep contact with the patient, who may have been told that you are temporarily out of town — a fiblet to help the adjustment.

Now that someone else is sharing the care, make the most of your visits to the patient's new home (remember that the nursing home *is* his home now). Check the schedule of activities or enrichment programs and arrange to visit when the person will not be involved in these periods of socialization. Plan to visit for half an hour to an hour, a long enough time for positive interaction without interfering with the patient's new routine. Keep in mind that he may simply stop paying attention to you.

Offering information about your loved one will help nursing staff and other professional caregivers connect with the patient through her long-term memories. Her previous routine should become the basis for the new plan of care. Making sure that the staff knows the patient's likes, dislikes, and food preferences will make the adjustment more pleasant. Hobbies can be started right away as part of a personalized recreational program. Physical activity is still important; when you visit, take her for a walk outside or around the facility. She needs familiar faces as much as ever, so encourage family and friends to visit, but to do so one at a time to lower the level of stimulation.

You can take to the nursing home a number of items that the patient will enjoy. For instance, he may like listening to an audiotape of family members' voices (label the tape and be sure the staff keeps track of it). You can take some favorite foods. (Again, label these, then put them in a refrigerator at the nursing home.) Take photo albums that the two of you can browse through during your visit. (If you plan to leave the albums with staff members, label the pictures. Then the staff can mention the descriptions as they peruse them with the patient.)

If you want to take the patient out of the home for a few hours, a whole day, or a weekend, follow the advice of the staff on whether that is a good idea. Then check in with them a few hours after you return to gauge the advisability of future ventures. Going out may prove more complicated than you think, as Hunter found out.

Hunter insisted on taking his brother Jerry, who had been in his assisted-living facility for only two weeks, out for a Sunday drive and an ice cream cone. When they returned, the two brothers shared a bear hug, and Hunter was sure that everything had gone well.

But on the way back to his room, Jerry saw the large grandfather clock. "It's six o'clock. Where's my supper?" he demanded.

"I'll see what I can find for you," the young assistant said.

"Find for me! I want a supper like everyone else. And now, now, now!"

Jerry's overreaction, a first for him, occurred because the outing had confused and disoriented him. He was trying hard to exercise control over something in his life, and it might as well be a meal. The staff suggested that Hunter visit with his brother at the facility for the time being.

Learning to communicate and work with the staff will help make the experience better for everyone.

Special-Care Unit (SCU)

A special-care unit is an area within an assisted-living facility, nursing home, or other health care facility specifically intended for people with progressive dementia. These units vary from facility to facility. An SCU may be no different from the rest of the facility except for being behind locked doors. Or it may have a special philosophy, well-trained and plentiful staff, and an environment that meets the specific needs of patients with Alzheimer's. (The Alzheimer's Association chapter in your area may be able to point out the better SCUs.)

When assessing a special-care unit, use the guidelines listed above for nursing homes, but expect to find considerably more information relating to programming, training, philosophy, and design. When I look at a special-care unit for program integrity, I am hoping to find:

- A mission statement specific to the unit and understood by every staff member. For example: *Our mission is to live in the residents' world and to try to hear what they are* not *saying.*
- Only patients with an admission diagnosis of Alzheimer's disease or a related dementia.
- Use of preadmission assessment and social history as the backbone for developing a specialized plan of care for each resident.
- Availability of physical, occupational, and speech therapies.
- All staff trained to work with patients with Alzheimer's in a program either offered or approved by the local chapter of the National Alzheimer's Association.
- Consistent staff assigned to the SCU only, with coverage twenty-four hours a day, seven days a week, assuring the same resident-to-staff ratio every day.
- Assigned activity staff (as opposed to regular staff) working only on the SCU every day, seven days a week.
- An outdoor area designated specifically for SCU residents and not used by other residents of the facility, so the Alzheimer's patients don't mix with people who do not understand their behavior.
- A quality assurance committee to ensure that problems are recognized, evaluated, and dealt with.
- A community volunteer program of people who regularly visit patients one to one or put on special programs such as musical performances or pet visits.
- A program director who oversees the philosophy, training, and support of staff, residents, and families.
- A behavior team that meets regularly to ensure that habilita-

tion approaches are used and that residents are not routinely medicated for behavior control.

- Infrequent use of behavior medications, such as antidepressants, antianxiety drugs, mood elevators and stabilizers, and antipsychotics. In a good SCU, only 10 percent of patients will be taking such medications at any time. All pharmaceuticals should be used for short periods only and should be reevaluated frequently.)

- Counseling services for residents and families, and possibly for the community, to help develop coping skills.

- Ongoing assessments to monitor changes related to Alzheimer's disease and create individualized programs and daily care.

- Team meetings held whenever necessary to discuss patient changes.

- Family involvement in recreational programs and family council meetings that provide input to the staff on behalf of the residents, who can no longer articulate their concerns.

- Attention to environmental design, including the use of color to identify and define spatial area and aid in way-finding; flooring that helps walking and reduces confusion; easily interpreted wall hangings that can be touched and handled; and acoustics that help residents process information by decreasing noise stimulation.

- A finger food menu.

- Secured doors monitored by a nonintrusive system (no loud alarms).

- Most important, happy residents interacting positively with happy staff.

You may not find all these items in your evaluation, but they provide a baseline for comparing different SCUs. A pervasive feeling of comfort and well-being can mean as much as or more than other, more tangible factors.

I am not a Pollyanna. I consider myself a card-carrying realist, leavened with a bit of altruism. I do not believe that every care-partnering relationship will turn into an idyllic situation. Some families are much better in a crisis, rallying to support their loved one during an acute hospital stay, than they are when faced with the complex problems of long-term care.

But all families will do far better when the considerations of lifespan care are dealt with on the basis of realistic assessments rather than on guilt. Most important, if families follow the tenets of habilitation, the result will be a far more positive collaboration that will enrich the lives of all concerned.

· 14 ·

Inspiration

I played as a child.
I danced when I was young.
I laughed yesteryear.
Today, I recall
the games, the music, the joy
over and over and over again.

In 2001 I attended the annual Public Policy Forum sponsored by the National Alzheimer's Association, and as always it was a wonderful experience. Every year a great many people with Alzheimer's from all fifty states attend the meeting, as do thousands of other people, including care partners, professionals, and legislators. The patients who spoke at the 2001 conference were nervous and often fearful. They were poignant in their silence as they collected words for their next sentence. But they were also passionate about their concerns, willing to share their personal stories, and eager to participate in life.

The audience gave a standing ovation to these heroes. Even more accolades should go to the many thousands of patients who speak at other conferences, talk about their lives on television shows, walk in Alzheimer's marathons, or write newspaper articles and letters to legislators. Acclaim should also go to patients who make videos to influence public policy, appear on educational panels, give college lectures on the disease, speak to school-age children, and, in the early stages of the disease, volunteer to help Meals on Wheels programs, or work in hospitals or nursing home activity programs, reading poetry, working on craft programs, playing the piano, and so forth.

People living with Alzheimer's are amazing, and talking to them can be helpful for anyone who faces becoming a care partner of someone with the disease. Patients continually remind us that they need us to recognize their determination, bolster their sense of self-worth, and provide appropriate support throughout the course of the disease. As I've emphasized throughout this book, care partners should recognize patients' remaining skills and create a positive emotional environment in which these skills may be used. Such a setting enables patients to feel successful, have good interactions, and maintain a sense of dignity. Patients say they want these three outcomes as they live daily with Alzheimer's.

Consider the comments of three remarkable people I know who have repeatedly inspired me as they live with this disease.

My friend Bernard Reisman, a former chair of the department of Jewish studies at Brandeis University, told me of both the sadness that living with Alzheimer's has brought him and his resolve to maintain his sense of self-worth. An eloquent man, whose bright eyes and wonderful smile transcend his professorial tones, Bernie always considered himself a role model and authority for his children and grandchildren and a mentor to students. His realization that he was losing hold of these positions made him sad.

"I don't know what I'll do when my sons no longer come to me for answers," he told me. "I wonder now if they look at me differently. Do they ask someone else for information that they once would have asked me? Will my grandsons ever think of me as a great scholar or just as an old man who repeats himself? I am like the great pitcher who injures his arm. Except that my super body part has been my brain, and now it's injured. Two more strikes and I'm out.

"But I'm not out yet — I'm still at bat. I've always been a fighter, and I sure as hell am not giving up now. You bet I'm sad. And angry, and damn ornery too, but I've learned to listen, and learn, and live for today. I'm trying, I'm trying hard.

"I walk, I play tennis, I swim. I take medications to help Alzheimer's — not to cure it but to ease it a bit. My family and I still travel around the globe. I just finished writing a book with my son. I go to an early-stage support group, and I'm part of the Alzheimer's Association speaker's bureau. I have to continue to teach — it's not easy for me to lecture and it's certainly not the way I used to. I can talk about how to live better with this disease, and no one can shut me up."

In 2002 Bernard Reisman received an honorary degree from American Hebrew University. He also spoke with fervor at a legislative breakfast, pleaded for more research funding at a national Alzheimer's Association annual meeting, appeared on the front page of the *Boston Globe* in a feature article about Alzheimer's, and traveled to Iceland with his wife. Bernie still has much to say and to give.

In 1995 tall, handsome Jim Anthony walked into our early-stage support group. Jim, in his fifties, had just been diagnosed with Alzheimer's and had lost his job because of problems caused by the disease. He had been misdiagnosed several times before that and now felt relieved to know conclusively, through a brain biopsy, that Alzheimer's was the cause of his cognitive problems. Numbers were particularly difficult for Jim; dialing the telephone, balancing his checkbook, and trying to manage appointments left him reeling. His vast lexicon remained intact, however, and he spoke about his daily life fluently and with great humor.

Jim was hungry to learn about habilitative ways that could help him manage his life. Having observed his mother going through Alzheimer's, he was distressed by what was happening to him and by knowing what was to come. But Jim always presented himself to us — and, as I write, still does — as a vital person who is supportive of others. When he spoke to visiting Japanese students at Harvard Medical School in 1997, he made a powerful impression on the audience.

Alzheimer's, he told the group, "used to be a disease that was not discussed. It was considered hopeless. But from a universal perspective, all life is hopeless — in that we all die.

"What is significant about Alzheimer's is that it has the potential to rob us of our understanding. The severity of the disease can be quite daunting. But people with Alzheimer's also work, raise children, go to movies, take vacations, give talks, and refuse to let the disease dictate their lives. People with Alzheimer's disease experience varying degrees of disability. This is not a one-size-fits-all disease.

"One notable dynamic I have observed is that people can become angry with people with Alzheimer's, especially partners and family members. I have seen it in friends, in my family, and in my own experience. The reason for this anger, I suspect, is that Alzheimer's is a frightening disease. One prefers to think that his or her companion is simply not trying hard enough, is being careless, obstinate, difficult, even deliberately trying to provoke his or her partner. And the partner is as puzzled as everyone.

"The anger is something that family members and friends have to own and work through for the sake of the couple, the family, for everyone concerned, even though it is appropriate. A loss of this magnitude cannot be dealt with lightly.

"This does not mean that you cannot laugh. I attend an Alzheimer's support group twice a month, and laughter is an important therapeutic component. Crying is too. We tend to deal with our grief privately. But in a support group, we understand the grief we all share. Our group is remarkable for its spirit of empathy, compassion, and truth-telling. Sometimes we sense that one member of our group is practicing denial. We do not rush in to help him or her get over it, though one or more of us may prod gently. A degree of denial is essential in Alzheimer's. Like someone drinking hot coffee, we sip the truth of our condition carefully and gently.

"One could, of course, rail at the universe, at God, at the physician who diagnosed [him or her]. It is a temptation, and all of us with Alzheimer's have done a bit of that. And adjusting to Alzheimer's is not a stately process like that of a king ascending his throne. It's a bit grubbier than that.

"My mother was diagnosed with Alzheimer's . . . She . . . developed an acceptance of life and its challenges and a wisdom that transcended her limitation. People with Alzheimer's have gifts to give. Do not underestimate their strengths and wisdom. They do not survive Alzheimer's without learning a thing or two.

"I do believe that the afflictions that come to us are nature's way of keeping the planet going. And I do believe that our efforts to sustain life with compassion and common sense are a reflection of our humanity. But we know that our lease on the planet is uncertain. We do celebrate longevity, but we celebrate to a far greater degree those who live well. I am far more interested in living well than in living long, though I am quite willing to hang around for a while. Since I have little control over it, I think I will take it one day at a time."

Jim and his care partner, Bruce, who now live in the Berkshire Hills of western Massachusetts, attend as many Alzheimer's forums and conferences as possible and keep abreast, via computer, of new findings about the disease.

Another outstanding person with Alzheimer's is Shirley Geller, who in 2002 stood before an audience of more than five hundred professionals at a conference in New England on Alzheimer's and spoke about what the disease was like for her. First she described the fears and problems she has encountered, such as recognizing that she will become worse and will have to move to a nursing home someday, that she will repeat questions, lose her ideas in midthought, and have other difficulties. But she also described another side of having Alzheimer's. Her friends have been "extremely supportive and caring," she said, and she felt blessed to have her "wonderful" family, a doctor who had listened to all of her questions, and a "very helpful" support group. "It's important to be able to share problems and concerns with others in the same situation and to have leaders who are able to help with good suggestions," she commented.

"Truthfully, I still enjoy life and get pleasure from it. People are amazed that with this problem, I still have a positive attitude." She concluded, "I am determined to get the most out of each and every day."

Although Bernie, Jim, and Shirley are quite different from one another in personality, social and work history, and disease process, they share many reactions to having Alzheimer's. They feel empowered, their emotions are validated, they live in the here and now, and they feel connected to others.

Having worked with thousands of patients and their families, and having spent many years remembering the meaning, and the emotion, behind the failing words, I want to speak on behalf of the remarkable people who live with progressive dementia. They can show us how to help them, if we listen:

- "Reminding and scolding me does not make me better, only sadder. When someone asks me questions about where I've been and who I've seen and what I did, and I can't retrieve that information, I feel stupid and unworthy."
- "Trying to fill my brain with new ideas and new equipment and new data will not work. My brain is full. Not one speck of space is left for new information to find a seat. If the information can't go in, it can never come out again."
- "Don't wish me out of reverie or worry about my silent times. I still have imaginative explorations to make, and dreams to dream. I have kisses to relive. I have a garden of memories before me, and everything is blooming simultaneously. Don't assume I am sad when I sit alone; most of the

time it is the sadness on your face that brings sorrow to my heart."

- "You can make me a part of this world only if you actively involve me, if your connection with me remains until the end. You must constantly reach out and touch me — physically, spiritually, emotionally."

- "You are the conduit to my failing world, a world that has so many possibilities to be filled with laughter, a few shared tears, and memories."

Having spent three decades in the world of the memory-impaired, I am emphatic about the profound change a habilitative care partner can make in the life of an affected person. I am equally sure that the habilitative approach provides the best care for the care partner, because this philosophy helps eliminate confrontation and unnecessary stress. In the end, care partners realize how much stronger they feel as they watch their loved ones relax, with dignity intact.

Habilitation gives us the gift of the present moment. We can speak the language of Alzheimer's, a nonverbal language that transcends illness. With the habilitative approach we can know, in our spirit and our heart, that we have done the best we could — that we have offered the patient chances to be successful, and that both of us can feel worthy.

Glossary

Appendix:
Good Food for People with Alzheimer's

Further Resources

Index

Glossary

Alzheimer's disease behavior log: A record of data on a patient's problematic behavior, including time of day, location, and environmental factors, in order to determine the cause of the behavior. (See page 119.)

Activities of daily living (ADL): The basic daily activities, including bathing, dressing, eating, toileting, and sleeping, that health professionals use to judge an Alzheimer's person's need for assistance with physical care.

Busy apron: A plain carpenter's or chef's apron to which various small objects and notions have been attached to occupy the patient. (See page 93.)

Care partner: The person who works with the Alzheimer's patient, providing habilitative cueing, supervision, assistance, and emotional, physical, and cognitive support through the changing stages of the disease.

Contrasting visual field: A light background against which dark objects can be clearly seen or a dark background against which light-colored objects will be more distinct.

Excess disability: A patient's inability to perform certain activities of daily living as a result of having had too much assistance when he was still able to perform those activities. (See page 37.)

Fine motor skills: Physical abilities requiring the use of small muscle groups in the hands, such as buttoning.

Geriatrician: A physician who specializes in elder care.

Habilitation: An approach to caring for a person with a progressive dementia that focuses on validating the patient's underlying emotions, maintaining dignity, creating moments for success, and using all remaining skills. (See the list of tenets on page 7.)

Habilitator: A synonym for care partner.

Long-term-care facility: A nursing home or other community-based health care center that provides care for the remainder of a person's life.

Neuro-psych evaluation: A method of evaluating cognitive impairment, as part of the diagnostic workup for Alzheimer's disease.

Optimal independent functional level: The highest-level physical, social, and cognitive performance that can be expected, based on the patient's stage of disease and environmental factors.

Orientation: The patient's recognition of time (day, year, time, holidays), place (country, state, town, facility, address, room), self, and relationships.

Palliative care: The routine care of a patient, not designed to cure.

Plan of care: A written plan that is regularly assessed to assure that the patient's physical, social, emotional, and spiritual needs are being met *over a specific period of time.* (See page 28.)

Safe Return: A program run by the National Alzheimer's Association that helps families find patients who have wandered away. (See page 221.)

Share-care: An arrangement among care partners to take turns looking after several Alzheimer's patients for a given period of time. (See page 171.)

Special-care unit (SCU): A unit within a nursing home or other facility that cares exclusively for people with progressive dementia. (See page 189.)

Sundown syndrome or sundowning: The occurrence of problematic behavior late in the afternoon or early evening. (See page 63.)

Verbal casserole: The fragmented language expression of some late-middle-stage Alzheimer's patients, often consisting of many words in no particular order or relationship. (See page 78.)

Good Food for People with Alzheimer's

Staples to Have on Hand

Keep your pantry stocked with a variety of easy-to-prepare foods. Here are some suggestions:

Canned cocktail franks

Canned fish such as tuna, salmon, and crab

Canned kidney beans, lentils, and chickpeas, to add to soups and salads for variety and nutrition

Canned soups, including broth and creamed soups. (Add cooked vegetables or pasta to soups for variety.) Soups provide a hearty snack or meal any time of day.

Herbal teas

Ice cream cones (place a small marshmallow in the tip to prevent dripping)

Juice drink boxes

Packaged bread or muffin mixes — for example, corn, banana, date nut, and lemon poppy seed. (For easier handling of the batter, use less milk than called for in the directions; for a buttery taste, use melted butter instead of oil.)

Pretzels, potato sticks, and other simple snacks

Quick flour mix, such as Bisquick, for making biscuits, pancakes, and desserts

Rice cakes
Small boxes of dry cereal

Finger Foods

Families and professionals who oversee the dining needs of people with Alzheimer's know that finger foods are the best choice for maintaining dignity, providing opportunities for success, and encouraging proper nutrition. Such foods require no utensils, condiments, or plates, and can be served at any time of day.

Removing extra silverware, condiments, and dinnerware from the table makes dining a nonthreatening experience for the patient. The care partner's presentation of a simple food to be eaten from the hand is a positive experience for both care partner and patient.

Preparing Finger Foods

Pita bread, tortillas, and hot dog rolls are excellent "wraps" for finger foods. They are easy to see and hold, and you can easily find whole-wheat and other nutritious varieties. Ingredients for wraps can be old standbys such as tuna, egg salad, or peanut butter and jelly, or they can be more exotic (see suggestions below). For patients in later stages of the disease, all kinds of foods can be blended and used as sandwich fillings. Don't let your own sense of what is palatable interfere with preparation or serving; watch the patient's demeanor for signs of a positive eating experience. The goal is to get the patient to eat — and do so independently. Weight gain is generally not a concern. And as the patient becomes less active in later stages of the disease, she may lose weight naturally.

Nutritious Sandwich Fillings

Cottage cheese and herbs (or fruit preserves)
Cranberry sauce (sliced) with cheddar cheese
Cream cheese and fruit preserves
Cream cheese and green olives

Cream cheese and pimiento

Cream cheese with flax seeds and drained crushed pineapple

Eggs, scrambled, fried, or boiled and cut up (because eggs are difficult to see, they may be best used as a sandwich filling)

Filling from frozen pot pies

Hummus — add soft chopped vegetables (scallions, red peppers, or fresh tomato) for added flavor and attractive appearance

Mashed black or kidney beans (canned) and tomato chunks

Mashed carrots with melted cheese

Mashed potatoes with melted cheese

Meat, deboned and cut into small pieces

Mild Mexican salsa

Peanut butter (with or without jelly)

Salmon salad with raisins

Soft or hard cheeses

Spaghetti, cut up, with thick sauce

Tuna, chicken, or egg salad (soak chopped celery and/or onion for ten minutes to make it easier to chew)

Vegetable spreads

Other Finger Foods

FRUITS

Apples, pears, or peaches, peeled and cut into wedges

Banana slices with peanut butter

Dried fruit

Grapes

Pears, sliced, with soft cheese spread

Pineapple chunks

Tomatoes (grape or cherry)

VEGETABLES

Asian vegetables, such as canned baby corn, water chestnuts, or bamboo shoots, or fresh, washed sugar snap peas, snow peas, or daikon (a Japanese sweet radish)

Broccoli, carrots, cauliflower, green beans, or zucchini, cut up and parboiled for three to five minutes to make them easier to chew; drain and serve warm.

Celery filled with peanut butter or flavored cream cheese

Cucumber, sliced and spread with hummus

Dry-roasted peas (sold in health food stores)

French fries (oven-roasted)

Potato wedges or puffs

Sweet potato cubes or wedges (oven-roasted)

Vegetable loaf (use vegetables in place of meat; cut into cubes and serve cool)

MEAT AND FISH

Chicken nuggets

Cocktail franks wrapped in triangle or crescent rolls

Fish sticks

Meatballs (small)

Shrimp (peeled)

Turkey meatloaf (cubed and cooled)

BREAKFAST FOODS

Bacon or sausage mixed into pancake batter, cooked, then rolled up

Boiled eggs (best served cut up in a sandwich)

Cinnamon toast strips

French toast strips made with thick bread

Nutritious dry breakfast cereals (mix with nuts or raisins, if desired, and serve without milk)

Waffles, especially whole-wheat

LUNCH

Cheese cubes

Grilled cheese on dark rye, cut in quarters

Grilled scrambled egg (and bacon if desired) on dark rye, cut in quarters

Pizza cut into small squares
Ravioli or tortellini without sauce
Spring rolls or egg rolls
String cheese
Ziti or other finger-sized pasta, plain or with Parmesan cheese

DESSERTS
Animal crackers
Ginger snaps spread with cream cheese
Jell-O made with fruit yogurt instead of cold water, served in an
    ice cream cone if desired
Pudding (instant) in an ice cream cone

SNACKS
Energy bars
Goldfish crackers
Granola bars (chewy)
Popcorn
Potato sticks
Pretzels
Sesame sticks or crackers
Shelled peanuts
Soybeans
Vegetable chips

Blender Beverages

If the patient dislikes taking medication, liquid forms can be dis-
guised in beverages mixed in a blender.

Banana Nana: blend 1 cup vanilla ice cream, 1 very ripe banana,
    and 1 teaspoon vanilla.
Berry Berry: blend 1½ cups cranberry juice, 1 cup frozen blueber-
    ries, and a dash of lemon juice.

Fruit Smoothie: blend 1 cup fruit yogurt, 1 cup sorbet, and 1 cup orange juice.

Ginger Snap: blend 1 cup peach ice cream, ½ cup crushed ginger snaps, and a dash of ground ginger.

Lemon Sparkler: blend 1 cup lemon sherbet and 2 cups lemonade. Remove from blender and add 1 cup sparkling or soda water.

Maple Delight: blend 1 cup milk, 1 large scoop vanilla ice cream, 1 teaspoon molasses, 1 teaspoon maple syrup, and 1 teaspoon vanilla.

Pistachio Green Goddess: blend 2 cups pistachio ice cream, 2 cups green tea, and 1 tablespoon sugar.

Strawberry Smoothie: blend 1½ cups strawberry yogurt, 1 cup apple juice, and 1 cup strawberries.

Tomato Energizer: blend 2 cups minestrone soup, 1 cup tomato juice, 2 teaspoons lemon juice, ½ teaspoon white pepper, and 8 ice cubes.

Vanilla Pick-Me-Up: blend 1½ cups vanilla yogurt, 1 teaspoon wheat germ, 1 egg, and 2 teaspoons vanilla.

Further Resources

UK Organizations

Alzheimers's Society
Gordon House
10 Greencoat Place
London SW1P 1PH
Telephone 0845 300 0336
Email info@alzheimers.org.uk
Website www.alzheimers.org.uk

Age Concern England
1268 London Road
London SW16 4ER
Telephone 020 8765 7200
Email ace@ace.org.uk
Website www.ageconcern.org.uk

Age Concern Cymru (Wales)
4th Floor
1 Cathedral Road
Cardiff
Wales CF11 9SD
Telephone 02920 371566
Email inquiries@accymru.org.uk
Website www.accymru.org.uk

Age Concern Northern Ireland
3 Lower Crescent
Belfast
Northern Ireland BT7 1NR
Telephone 02890 245729
Advice line 02890 325055
(weekdays 9.30am–1pm)
Email info@ageconcernni.org

Anchor Staying Put
(see www.stayingput.org.uk or
   telephone 0191 2706068 to find
   your nearest agency

Benefits Equiry Line (BEL)
0800 88 22 00 (8.30am–6.30pm
   weekdays, 9am–1pm Saturdays)

British Association for Counselling
1 Regent Place, Rugby
Warwickshire CV21 2PJ
Information line 0870 443 5252
(weekdays 8.45am–5pm)
Email bacp@bacp.co.uk
Website www.counselling.co.uk

British Heart Foundation
14 Fitzhardinge Street
London W1H 6DH
Telephone 020 7935 0185
Website www.bhf.org.uk

Carers UK (UK Office)
20/25 Glasshouse Yard
London EC1A 4JT
Telephone 020 7490 8818
Email info@ukcarers.org
Website www.carersonline.org.uk

Centre for Accessible Environments
Nutmeg House
60 Gainsford Street
London SE1 2NY
Telephone 020 7357 8182

Charity Search
25 Portview Road, Avonmouth
Bristol BS11 9LD
Telephone 0117 982 4060
(Monday–Thursday, 9am–4pm)

Citizens Advice Bureaux (CAB)
To find details of your nearest CAB
    look in the phone book, ask at your
    local library or consult the CAB
    website at www.citizensadvice.org.uk

Continence Foundation
307 Hatton Square
16 Baldwins Gardens
London EC1N 7RJ
National helpline 0845 345 0165
(weekdays 9.30am–1pm; calls
    charged at local rate)
Email
    continence-help@dial.pipex.com
Website www.continence-
    foundation.org.uk

Advice Work Department
Counsel and Care
Twyman House
16 Bonny Street
London NW1 9PG
Email
    advice@counselandcare.org.uk
Website
    www.counselandcare.org.uk

Crossroads – Caring for Carers
10 Regent Place
Rugby
Warwickshire CV21 2PN
Telephone 01788 573653
Website www.crossroads.org.uk

Cruse Bereavement Care
Cruse House
126 Sheen Road
Richmond
Surrey TW9 1UR
Telephone 020 8940 4818
Email
    info@crusebereavementcare.org.uk
Website
    www.crusebereavementcare.org.uk

Disabled Living Centres Council
Redbank House
4 St Chad's Street
Cheetham
Manchester M8 8QA
Telephone 0161 834 1044
Email dlcc@dlcc.org.uk
Website at www.dlcc.org.uk

Disabled Living Foundation (DLF)
380–384 Harrow Road
London W9 2HU
Telephone 020 7289 6111
Helpline 0845 130 9177 (weekdays
    10am–1pm; all calls charged at
    local rate)
Minicom line 0870 603 9176

DIAL UK (Disablement Information
    and Advice Line)
St Catherine's
Tickhill Road
Doncaster
DN4 8QN
Telephone 01302 310123
Fax 01302 310404
Email enquiries@dialuk.org.uk

Elderly Accommodation Counsel
3rd Floor
89 Embankment
London SE1 7TP
Telephone 020 7820 1343
Email enquiries@e-a-c.demon.co.uk
Website www.housingcare.org

Help the Aged
207–221 Pentonville Road
London N1 9UZ
Telephone 020 7278 1114
Email info@helptheaged.org.uk
Website www.helptheaged.org.uk

LawNet Ltd
First Floor, 93–95 Bedford Street
Leamington Spa, CV32 5BB
Telephone 01926 886990
Email admin@lawnet.co.uk
Website www.lawnet.co.uk

Listening Books
(National Listening Library for the
    Handicapped)
12 Lant Street
London SE1 1QH
Telephone 020 7407 9417

Mind
15–19 Broadway
London E15 4BQ
Telephone 020 8519 2122
Email contact@mind.org.uk
Website www.mind.org.uk

NHS Direct
Telephone 0845 4647
Website www.nhsdirect.nhs.uk

Patients Association
PO Box 935
Harrow
Middlesex HA1 3YJ
Telephone 020 8423 9111
Email mailbox@patients-association.
    com
Website www.patients-association.
    com

The Princess Royal Trust for Carers
142 Minories
London EC3N 1LB
Telephone 020 7480 7788
Email info@carers.org
Website www.carers.org

RADAR (The Royal Association for
  Disability and Rehabilitation)
12 City Forum
250 City Road
London EC1V 8AF
Telephone 020 7250 3222
Minicom 020 7250 4119
Email radar@radar.org.uk
Website www.radar.org.uk

Relatives and Residents Association
5 Tavistock Place
London WC1H 9SN
Telephone 020 7692 4302
Website www.relres.org.uk

Solicitors for Independent Financial
  Advice (SIFA)
10 East Street,
Epsom
Surrey KY17 1HH
Telephone 01372 721172
Website www.solicitor-sifa.co.uk

Stroke Association
Stroke House
Whitecross Street
London EC1Y 8JJ
Helpline 0845 3033 100
Email info@stroke.org.uk
Website www.stroke.org.uk

Further Resources

US Organizations

Administration on Aging. This agency of the federal government publishes a useful fact sheet titled "Respite: What Caregivers Need Most." Telephone: 202-619-0724. Available on the Internet: www.aoa.gov/factsheets/Respite.html.

AllExperts. A volunteer organization staffed with physicians, nurses, home care providers, and other experts who answer questions on-line about the disease process, nursing facilities, home care, and other issues. Only on-line services are offered: www.allexperts.com.

Alzheimer's Association. The most prominent Alzheimer's organization in the country, with chapters nationwide. It provides information, suggestions, referrals, and other support options to patients, care partners, and families. 919 North Michigan Ave., Suite 1100, Chicago, IL 60611-1676; telephone: 800-272-3900 or 312-335-8700; fax: 312-1110; www.alz.org.

Alzheimer's Disease Education and Referral Center (ADEAR). An affiliate of the National Institute on Aging (NIA) that offers current, comprehensive, and definitive information and resources on Alzheimer's. ADEAR Center, P.O. Box 8250, Silver Spring, MD 20907-8250; telephone: 800-438-4380; fax: 301-495-3334; www.alzheimers.org.

American Association of Homes and Services for the Aging (AAHSA). A national nonprofit organization offering information on more than 5,600 non-profit elder-care and Alzheimer's-care facilities. 2519 Connecticut Ave. NW, Washington, DC 20008-1520; Tekephone: 202-783-2242; fax: 202-783-2255; www.aagsa.org.

American Association of Retired Persons. Anyone over fifty can be a member of AARP. The organization deals with many age-related issues, including living with Alzheimer's disease. It offers brochures ranging from early diagnosis to dealing with loss. AARP has offices in cities throughout the country. 601 E St. NW, Washington, DC 20049; telephone: 800-424-3410; fax: 202-434-2588; www.aarp.org.

American Bar Association Commission on Legal Problems of the Elderly. The commission offers advice on advance planning matters, including quality-of-life issues. Its publication *Consumer's Tool Kit for Health Care Advance Planning* contains a variety of self-help worksheets, suggestions, and resources designed for ease of use. 740 15th St. NW, Washington, DC 20005-1022; telephone: 202-662-8690; www.abanet.org/elderly.

American Health Care Association (AHCA). A federation of affiliated state health organizations that provides information about nursing homes and other managed-care housing options. 1201 L St. NW, Washington, DC 20005; telephone: 202-842-4444; www.ahca.org.

American Society on Aging. One of the largest professional associations on issues dealing with aging, the ASA promotes the dignity and well-being of the elderly and provides excellent information on caregiving and housing options. 833 Market St., Suite 511, San Francisco, CA 94103; telephone: 415-974-9600; www.asaging.org.

A Place for Mom. A free national elder-care referral service that helps care partners locate, compare, and choose local assisted-living facilities, nursing homes, and/or Alzheimer's special-care facilities. The organization also provides help in finding long-term-care insurance and tips on visiting nursing facilities. There are representatives of the organization in every state. Telephone: 877-MOMDAD-9 (877-666-3239); www.aplaceformom.com.

Assisted Living Federation of America. ALFA provides information and referrals about assisted-living facilities. 9411 Lee Hwy., Plaza Suite J, Fairfax, VA 22031; telephone: 703-691-8100; fax: 703-691-8106; www.alfa.org.

Benjamin B. Green-Field National Alzheimer's Library and Resource Center. The largest Alzheimer's library in the world. 919 North Michigan Ave., Chicago, IL 60611; telephone: 800-272-3900 or 312-335-9602; fax: 312-335-0214; www.alz.org/ResourceCenter/Programs/LibraryServices.htm.

Calhoun County Medical Care Facility and Marian E. Burch adult day care center. The Web site lists the comparative costs of adult day care and long-term or permanent nursing home stays as a basis for comparison.

1150 E. Michigan Ave., Battle Creek, MI 49014; telephone: 269-962-5458; fax: 269-962-7011; www.ccmcf.com.

California Association for Adult Day Services. Provides a list of many types of adult day care services. 921 11th St., Suite 701, Sacramento, CA 95814; telephone: 916-552-7400; fax: 916-552-7404; www.cads.org/adultday .html.

Case Management Society of America. A professional organization dedicated to the continuing education of case managers, nurses, and other health professionals and to networking around issues such as case management, social work, disease management, and rehabilitation. The organization offers helpful resources and referrals. 8201 Cantrell Rd., Suite 230, Little Rock, AR 72227; telephone: 501-225-2229; fax: 501-221-9068; www.cmsa.org.

Children of Aging Parents. CAPS is a nonprofit association that provides help in finding care-partner support groups and in locating geriatric care managers. 1609 Woodbourne Rd., Suite 302A, Levittown, PA 19057; telephone: 800-227-7294; www.caps4caregivers.org.

Cognitive Neurology and Alzheimer's Disease Center. The center provides information and support to the Alzheimer's sufferer and care partner, including reports on the latest research. 320 East Superior St., Searle 11-450, Chicago, IL 60611-3008; telephone: 312-908-9339; www.brain.nwu .edu/.

Eldercare Locator. A service of the U.S. Administration on Aging. Nationwide toll-free service helps find local services for older people. Telephone: 800-677-1116; www.eldercare.gov.

ElderCare Online. An Internet-based resource committed to helping Alzheimer's and dementia care partners find support and understanding, as well as educational resources and information. 54 Amuxen Ct., Islip, NY 11751; www.alzwell.com.

Family Caregiver Alliance. A nonprofit organization that focuses on helping home care partners by supplying many publications and much useful information. The magazine *Today's Caregiver*, available in print or online, has special Alzheimer's sections. A subscription includes a free weekly e-mail newsletter; for subscription information, call 800-829-2734. 690 Market St., Suite 600, San Francisco, CA 94104; telephone: 415-434-3388; fax: 415-434-3508; www.caregiver.org.

Fisher Center for Alzheimer's Research Foundation. An on-line site provides information and links on elder care, care-partner and patient resources, and up-to-date information on Alzheimer's research. One Intrepid Square, West 46th St. and 12th Ave., New York, NY 10036; telephone: 800-ALZ-INFO (259-4636); www.alzinfo.org.

Hospice Foundation of America. With a national database of hospice providers, the foundation offers help in finding the right hospice. 2001 S St. NW, Suite 300, Washington, DC 20009; telephone: 800-854-3402; fax: 202-638-5312; www.hospicefoundation.org.

Information Source for Adult Day Centers. Provides an extensive list of state associations and other contacts as well as information for operators of adult day care centers. 5220 Beckwyck Dr., Fuquay-Varina, NC 27526; telephone: 919-552-0254; fax: 919-552-0155; www.theinfosource 4adc.com/Links.html.

Law and Aging Resource Guide. The American Bar Association publishes this state-by-state directory of legal resources and services available for seniors. 740 15th St. NW, Washington, DC 20005-1022; telephone: 202-662-8690; www.abanet.org.

Medicare Rights Center (MRC). An information resource on Medicare coverage. 1460 Broadway, 17th Fl., New York, NY 10036; telephone: 212-869-3850; fax: 212-869-3532; www.medicarerights.org.

Metropolitan Area Agency on Aging of Minneapolis/St. Paul. Provides a checklist for assessing day care centers. 1600 University Ave. West, Suite 300, St. Paul, MN 55104; telephone: 651-641-8612; fax: 651-641-8618; www.tcaging.org/com_adck.htm.

National Academy of Elder Law Attorneys. NAELA offers an on-line database of its member attorneys by location. 1604 N. Country Club Rd., Tucson, AZ 85716; telephone: 520-881-4005; www.naela.com/naela/resources.htm.

National Adult Day Services Association. NADSA offers information, standards, and referrals on many adult day care programs. 8201 Greensboro Drive, Suite 300, McLean, VA 22102; telephone: 866-890-7357 or 703-610-9035; fax: 703-610-9005; www.nadsa.org.

National Association for Continence (NAFC). An incontinence resource. P.O. Box 8310, Spartanburg, SC 29305; telephone: 800-BLADDER (252-3337) or 864-579-7900; fax: 864-579-7902; www.nafc.org.

National Association of Area Agencies on Aging (N4A). This umbrella organization for almost nine hundred area agencies on aging functions as a clearinghouse for information for elders and care partners seeking local support resources. Information is available in English and Spanish. 927 15th St. NW, 6th Fl., Washington, DC 20005; telephone: 202-296-8130; fax: 202-296-8134; www.n4a.org.

National Association for Home Care and Hospice (NAHC). Provides more than 22,000 resources for those seeking hospice or home care. The publication *How to Choose a Home Care Provider,* available on-line or in print, tells how to select the right provider and what to do if something goes wrong, and explains standard billing practices. 228 Seventh St. SE, Washington, DC 20003; telephone: 202-547-7424; fax: 202-547-3540; www.nahc.com.

National Caregiving Foundation. Produces the Caregivers Support Kit, which is designed to address every aspect of care partnering and simplify daily tasks. 891 N. Pitt St., Alexandria, VA 22314-1765; telephone: 800-930-1357; www.caregivingfoundation.org.

National Citizens Coalition for Nursing Home Reform (NCCHR). Provides useful information and referrals to nursing homes. 1424 16th St. NW, Suite 202, Washington, DC 20002; telephone: 202-332-2275; fax: 202-332-2949; www.ncchr.org.

National Consumer Law Center, Seniors Initiative (NCLC). Focuses on consumer issues, including bankruptcy, foreclosures, misrepresentation, fraud, and predatory sales practices. Publishes newsletters such as *Avoiding Living Will Scams*, *Medical Debt and Seniors: How Consumer Laws Can Help*, and *When You Can't Go Home Again: Using Consumer Law to Protect Nursing Facility Residents*. 1629 K St. NW, Suite 600, Washington, DC 20006; telephone: 202-986-6060; www.nclc.org/initiatives/seniors_initiative/index.shtml.

National Council on Aging (NCOA). The council is concerned with the "dignity, self-determination, well-being, and contributions" of elders. Brochures include *Alzheimer's Patient Guide* and *Alzheimer's Caregiver Guide*. 409 Third St. SW, Suite 200, Washington, DC 20024; telephone: 202-479-1200; TTD: 202-479-6674; fax: 202-479-0735; www.ncoa.org.

National Hospice and Palliative Care Organization (NHPCO). Offers several brochures about hospice and palliative care. 1700 Diagonal Rd., Suite 300, Alexandria, VA 22314; telephone: 800-646-6460 or 703-837-1500; fax: 703-525-5762; www.nhpco.org.

National Institute on Aging (NIA). This division of NIH offers a great resource directory, with information on the latest research and clinical studies, including state and federal agencies and resource centers. Bldg. 31, Rm. 5C27, 31 Center Dr., MSC 2292, Bethesda, MD 20892; telephone: 301-496-1752; www.nih.gov/nia.

National Institutes of Health (NIH). This national clearinghouse of health information helps to direct national research priorities. It is particularly helpful on disorders related to Alzheimer's. 9000 Rockville Pike, Bethesda, MD 20892; telephone: 800-438-4380; TTD: 800-222-4225; www.nih.gov.

New Lifestyles Online. A searchable state-by-state on-line database of Alzheimer's care, assisted-living, and nursing home facilities, with links to each facility. A free paper version covers housing resources in more than forty metropolitan areas. www.newlifestyles.com.

Ronald and Nancy Reagan Research Institute. The institute funds research grants to find the causes of and possible cures for Alzheimer's disease. Contact the National Alzheimer's Association for more information. Telephone: 800-272-3900; www.alz.org/researchers/reaganresearch/over view.htm.

Safe Return Program. Each individual registered in this program, sponsored by the Alzheimer's Association, receives a unique ID number imprinted on a bracelet, making it easier for law enforcement officials and others to identify the wanderer and make sure he is safely returned home. There is a one-time registration fee of $40. Contact the Alzheimer's Association Helpline: 800-660-1993.

SeniorResource.com. Offers information, support, and resources for care partners, including financial advice, humor, and a state-by-state list of resources. P.O. Box 781, Del Mar, CA 92014-0781; telephone: 858-793-7901 or 877-793-7901; fax: 858-792-9080; www.seniorresource.com.

United Seniors Health Cooperative (USHC). Nonprofit national organization committed to education and advocacy for care providers. Publications include *Long Term Care Planning: A Dollar and Sense Guide* and *Medicare Health Plan Choices: Consumer Update* (updated every January). 409 Third St. SW, Suite 200, Washington, DC 20024-3212; telephone: 202-479-6973; www.unitedseniorshealth.org.

Books

Antonangeli, Judy. *Of Two Minds.* Fidelity Press, 1995. Discusses the connection between Down's syndrome and Alzheimer's.

Brawley, Elizabeth C. *Designing for Alzheimer's Disease: Strategies for Creating a Better Care Environment.* John Wiley and Sons, 1997. A thorough approach to designing a therapeutic and safe setting for the Alzheimer's patient.

Brennan, Tim. Through His Eyes: The Collective Works of Tim Brennan. Brennan, diagnosed with Alzheimer's in November 1993, immediately began keeping an on-line journal providing a firsthand patient's perspective. www .nhisgarden.com/his_eyes/page_index.html.

Calkins, Margaret. *Creating Successful Dementia Care Settings,* 4 vols. Health Professions Press, 2000. A holistic and complementary approach to designing or redesigning a dementia-care facility that addresses the physical environment, staff care practices, and residents' needs.

Castleman, Michael, Dolores Gallagher-Thompson, and Matthew Naythons. *There's Still a Person in There: The Complete Guide to Treating and Coping with Alzheimer's.* Berkley, 2000. A practical approach to Alzheimer's disease, with solid information on financial planning and other issues.

Charlap, Dr. Steven S. *Making Sense of Nursing Homes: A Guide for Families.* Age Sense, 2002. Advice on financial issues, emotional support, and nonprofit and governmental resources. To order, call 866-333-5736.

Davies, Helen D., and Michael P. Jensen, *Alzheimer's: The Answers You Need.* Elder Books, 1998. For the newly diagnosed, question-and-answer sections, plus tips for coping, preparing for the future, and ameliorating the personal environment.

De Baggio, Thomas. *Losing My Mind.* Free Press, 2002. One man's inspiring attempt to stay in touch with his world as he battles Alzheimer's disease.

Fazio, Sam, Dorothy Seman, and Jane Stansell. *Rethinking Alzheimer's Care.* Health Professions Press, 1999. Although written for professional caregivers, the book underscores the need to look at the positive aspects of caring for Alzheimer's patients.

Feil, N., and V. Klerk-Rubin. *The Validation Breakthrough: Simple Techniques for Communicating with People with Alzheimer's-Type Dementia.* Health Professions Press, 2002. Simple methods for improving communication.

Glickstein, J. *Therapeutic Interventions in Alzheimer's Disease: A Program of Functional Skills for Activities of Daily Living and Communication.* Aspen Publishers, 1997. A wide range of therapeutic activities designed to stimulate the dementia patient.

Hodgson, Harriet. *Alzheimer's: Finding the Words: A Communication Guide for Those Who Care.* John Wiley and Sons, 1995. A guide for communicating with the Alzheimer's patient plus support tips for the care partner.

Kuhn, Daniel. *Alzheimer's Early Stages: First Steps in Caring and Treatment.* Hunter House, 1999. Addresses the issues many care partners face with a patient in the first stages of the disease.

Landay, David S. *Be Prepared: The Complete Financial, Legal, and Practical Guide for Living with a Life-Challenging Condition.* St. Martin's, 1999. The financial and legal challenges of living with chronic illness.

Mace, Nancy L., and Peter V. Rabins. *The 36-Hour Day.* Johns Hopkins Press, 2001. Newly reprinted, this valuable resource for the family and care partners provides comprehensive information on caring for a person with Alzheimer's disease.

Mahoney, Ellen K., Ladislav Volicer, and Ann C. Hurley. *Management of*

Challenging Behaviors in Dementia. Health Professions Press, 2000. An easy-to-understand presentation of modern scientific understanding of disruptive behavior in people suffering with dementia, with care strategies for nursing and health professionals.

McGowan, Diana Friel. *Living in the Labyrinth: A Personal Journey Through the Maze of Alzheimer's.* Delta, 1994. A first-person account of life with Alzheimer's.

Medina, John J. *What You Need to Know about Alzheimer's.* New Harbinger Publishers, 1999. Explains the biological process of the disease and considers the emotional, material, and coping issues.

National Alzheimer's Association. *Activity Programming for Persons with Dementia: A Sourcebook.* National Alzheimer's Association, 1995. How to help the Alzheimer's patient develop, enhance, and maintain relationships.

———. *Can-Do Activities for Adults with Alzheimer's Disease: Strength-Based Communication and Programming.* National Alzheimer's Association, 2001. Activities to strengthen communication skills. Available from the Benjamin B. Green-Field Library and Resource Center (catalog no. WM 450 E36 2001). Contact the Alzheimer's Association by telephone: 800-272-3900; or fax: 312-335-0214.

———. *Steps to Enhancing Communications: Interacting with Persons with Alzheimer's Disease.* National Alzheimer's Association, 1997. Tips to improve communication between the Alzheimer's patient and care partner. Single copies of the brochure are free. Available from the Benjamin B. Green-Field Library and Resource Center (catalog no. ED310Z). Contact the Alzheimer's Association by telephone: 800-272-3900; or fax: 312-335-0214.

Nissenboim, Sylvia, and Christine Vroman. *The Positive Interaction Program of Activities for People with Alzheimer's Disease.* Health Professions Press, 1998. The benefits of an active life for Alzheimer's patients.

Pierce, Charles. *Hard to Forget.* Random House, 1999. The author faces his own destiny in this memorable trip through familial Alzheimer's with humor and pathos.

Rau, Marie. *Coping with Communication Challenges in Alzheimer's Disease.* Singular Publishing Group, 1993. Improving the communications skills of the patient and care partner.

Ray, B. J. *Alzheimer's Activities: Hundreds of Activities for Men and Women with Alzheimer's Disease and Related Disorders.* Rayve Productions, 2001.

Rose, Larry. *Show Me the Way to Go Home.* Elder Books, 1996. A firsthand account by a man coping with early-onset Alzheimer's.

Schacter, Daniel L. *The Seven Sins of Memory.* Houghton Mifflin, 2001.

How the mind forgets and remembers — a new look at our brains through fascinating stories and scientific findings.

Snyder, Lisa. *Speaking Our Minds: Personal Reflections from Individuals with Alzheimer's.* W. H. Freeman, 1999. Seven Alzheimer's patients discuss their coping strategies, augmented by the author's experiences as a caregiver.

Souren, Liduin, and Emile Franssen. *Broken Connections.* Swets and Zeitlinger, 1994. Elaborates on the different levels of assistance necessary as Alzheimer's progresses.

Strauss, Claudia. *Talking to Alzheimer's: Simple Ways to Connect When You Visit with a Family Member or Friend.* New Harbinger Press, 2002. Advice on getting the most out of visiting a friend or loved one in an extended-care facility.

Visiting Nurses Association of America. *Caregiver's Handbook: A Complete Guide to Home Health Care by the Visiting Nurses Association of America.* DK Publishers, 1998. Designed to help the care partner cope with the patient's emotional and physical needs. An excellent introduction for the home care provider.

Werner, Anne P., and James Firman. *Home Care for Older People: A Consumer's Guide.* United Seniors Health Cooperative, 1994. Provides information and sample worksheets for choosing a home care provider, writing an employment contract, and solving problems related to home care. Large-print format. Available through the United Seniors Health Cooperative, 1331 H St. NW, Washington, DC 20005-4706; telephone: 202-393-6222.

Zgola, Jitka, and Gilbert Ordillon. *Bon Appétit! The Joy of Dining in Long-Term Care.* Health Professions Press, 2001. How to make mealtimes in a long-term-care facility more enjoyable and rewarding for the patient. Much of the information is also applicable to care in the home.

Videos
(Check compatibility with your video machine)

Alzheimer's Disease: Natural Feeding Techniques (one videocassette, 14 minutes). U.S. Veterans' Administration. Helps care partners working with patients who have feeding difficulties. Available from the U.S. Department of Commerce, National Technical Information Service, Springfield, VA 22161; telephone: 703-605-6000; www.ntis.gov/products/pages/caps_alzheimers.asp.

Alzheimer's: Is There Hope? WLIW Productions, originally aired on public television stations on November 1, 2002. Presents the researchers engaged in the scientific exploration of Alzheimer's and offers accounts of care partners. To order a copy, call 800-847-7793 or visit www.wliw.org/productions/alzh.html.

Breakfast Club: Enhancing the Communication Ability of Alzheimer's Patients (one videocassette, 25 minutes). Speech Bin, Vero Beach, FL, 1997. Examines the Breakfast Club Program, a method of easing communication for people with Alzheimer's. Available from the Benjamin B. Green-Field Library and Resource Center (catalog no. WL340 VC #717 1997).

Communicating with Older Adults and People with Dementia (one videocassette, 42 minutes). Assisted Living Best Practices, 1999. How to communicate with the memory-impaired. Experts share their knowledge of agnosia, amnesia, aphasia, apraxia, and attention deficit in persons with dementia. To order, contact Assisted Living, 4101 International Parkway, Carrollton, TX 75007; telephone: 888-578-8394.

Communication, the Heart of the Matter: The Sandwich Generation, Coping with Aging Parents (one videocassette, 20 minutes). Aquarius Health Care, Sherborn, MA, 1999. Communication concerns for care partners and caring for a loved one from a distance. Available from the Benjamin B. Green-Field Library and Resource Center (catalog no. HV 1461 VC #596 1999).

Communication: How to Communicate with Someone Who Has Alzheimer's Disease or Related Dementia (two videocassettes, 58 minutes). Healing Arts Communication, 2001. Covers a range of communication and language techniques useful in such situations as repetitive and difficult questioning, chores, aggression, and more. Available from the Benjamin B. Green-Field Library and Resource Center (catalog no. WV 270 #580 1999).

How to Have a Meaningful Visit with Your Loved One at a Nursing Facility (one videocassette, 38 minutes). Terra Nova Films, Chicago, IL, 1997. For individuals who have recently placed a loved one in a nursing facility, this film is intended to alleviate the guilt, sadness, and discomfort of visiting. Available from the Benjamin B. Green-Field Library and Resource Center (catalog no. WX 27 VC #568 1997).

Interacting with Alzheimer Patients: Tips for Family and Friends: Alzheimer Disease Do's and Don'ts (one videocassette, 20 minutes). Video Press, University of Maryland School of Medicine, Baltimore, MD, 2000. Expert Peter Rabins discusses techniques for interacting with Alzheimer's patients, including distractions, reinforcement, repetition, and independence. Available from the Benjamin B. Green-Field Library and Resource Center (catalog no. WX 27 #720 2000).

Living with Alzheimer's (three-part series on three videocassettes). Long

Island (N.Y.) Alzheimer's Foundation, 2000. Useful information and support for the care partner or health care provider. Nominated for the 2000 Telly Award. To order, contact Long Island Alzheimer's Foundation, 5 Channel Dr., Port Washington, NY 11050; telephone: 866-789-5423; www.liaf.org.

Recognizing and Responding to Emotion in Persons with Dementia (one videocassette, 26 minutes). Philadelphia Geriatric Center, Philadelphia, PA, 1997. People with dementia still have emotions and preferences even though they can no longer express their likes and dislikes. Available from the Benjamin B. Green-Field Library and Resource Center (catalog no. WY 160 VC #488 1997).

Someone I Love Has Alzheimer's (one videocassette, 17 minutes). Fanlight Productions, 1993. Filmed in a support group of children who live with a loved one with Alzheimer's. The children discuss their feelings, share ideas and issues, and offer advice to other children in their situation. Available from the Alzheimer's Association of Massachusetts, 36 Cameron Ave., Cambridge, MA 02140; telephone: 800-548-2111.

STB Forever Young video series. STB Productions. Videos with uninterrupted music to aid in relaxation and recall, designed specifically for Alzheimer's patients. Videos include "A Celebration of the Four Seasons," with Handel's *Water Music;* "Gardens, Blossoms, and Blooms," a virtual walk through a beautiful garden with gentle breezes, waterfall, and singing birds; "Christmas Hearth," a holiday theme with a crackling fire; and "County Fair Memories," featuring ragtime music and the sights, feel, and flavor of an old-time county fair. Other titles also available. To order, contact STB Productions, 71 Rinewalt St., Williamsville, NY 14221; telephone: 716-626-5319; www.stbvideo.com.

Untitled video on communication (one videocassette, 20 minutes). National Alzheimer's Association, Chicago, 1990. Care partners describe their challenges and solutions for communicating with the patient. Ways to help care partners and patients express their thoughts. Available from the Benjamin B. Green-Field Library and Resource Center (catalog no. WM 220 VC #248 1990).

Music and Old-Time Radio

CD Universe. A large selection of nostalgia and oldies' music and spoken-word CDs, audiocassettes, DVDs, and videotapes. www.cduniverse.com.

Radio Spirits. Boxed sets of VHS, CD, and audiocassettes of old radio broadcasts, including Bob Hope, Jack Benny, the Lone Ranger, Nero

Wolfe, the Shadow, and much more. P.O. Box 3107, Wallingford, CT 06492; telephone: 203-265-8044; www.radiospirits.com.

Tower Records. Stores across the country and around the world carry thousands of CDs, LPs, and cassettes of oldies and classics. www.tower records.com.

Wireless Catalog from the NPR Shop (operated by National Public Radio). Audio- and videotapes of classic radio and TV shows. Telephone: 800-669-9999; www.shop.npr.org.

Products

Adaptations by Adrian. Clothing specially designed for the wheelchair-bound. Men's and women's clothing from undergarments to outerwear. P.O. Box 65, San Marcos, CA 92079-0065; telephone: 800-831-2577; www .adrianscloset.com.

AliMed. AliMed Wander Alarm and hundreds of home help aids, including security, kitchen, and bath aids, bedside motion detectors, and bed alarms. 297 High St., Dedham, MA 02026; telephone: 800-225-2610; www.alimed.com.

Allegro Medical Supply. Bathroom security/assistance and other elder-care products, with savings on bulk purchases of incontinence products. Telephone: 800-861-3211; www.allegromedical.com.

Alzheimer's Store. Products for patient and care partner needs, including security, dressing, incontinence aids, and activities, with many stage-specific products. On-line or free print catalog available. Alzheimer's Store Ageless Design, Inc., 12633 159th Ct., North Jupiter, FL 33478-6669; telephone: 800-752-3238; www.alzstore.com.

A-Med Care Center. Incontinence, safety, bathroom, and skin-care products. Many samples available. 800-552-2633; www.a-med.com.

American Ramp Systems. Portable and permanent wheelchair ramps for sale or rent; free in-home evaluations anywhere in the United States. Especially helpful for middle-stage or late-stage patients. 202 West First St., Boston, MA 02127-1110; telephone: 800-649-5215; www.american ramp.com.

Ameriphone. Communication devices, including videophones, enhanced-audio phones, auto-dialing phones, and voice-activated phones. 12082 Western Ave., Garden Grove, CA 92841-2913; telephone: 800-874-3005; TTY: 800-772-2889; www.ameriphone.com.

Assisted Living Store. Home modifications for the elderly and people with disabilities as well as products relating to incontinence, security, bed and bath modification, dining, and dressing. 7687 Hyde Ave., South Cottage Grove, MN 55016; telephone: 888-388-5862; www.assistedliving store.com.

Beyond Barriers. Products for home modification, including bath, toileting, kitchen, and general house use (faucets, auto-flush toilets, grab handles, etc.). Access One, Inc., 25679 Gramford Ave., Wyoming, MN 55092; telephone: 800-561-2223; www.beyondbarriers.com.

Buck and Buck Designs. Fashion wear for people with disabilities, with special items for Alzheimer's patients. Very large selection of men's and women's styles. Buck and Buck, Inc., 3111 27th Ave., South Seattle, WA 98144-6502; telephone: 800-458-0600; www.buckandbuck.com.

Care Medical Equipment. Incontinence and security products, bathroom aids. Free catalog. 1877 NE Seventh Ave., Portland, OR 97212; telephone: 800-443-7091; www.blvd.com/carecatalog.

Care Trak, Inc. Many different kinds of alerts and systems to help prevent wandering or track the wanderer, including GPS positioning devices, waterproof transmitters, and invisible perimeter systems. 1031 Autumn Ridge Rd., Carbondale, IL 62901-9745; telephone: 800-842-4537; www .caretrak.com.

Caregiving Solutions.com. Products for patients in all stages of the disease, ranging from doorknob covers and door entry barriers to bathing/ toileting accessories and gentle personal cleansing products like tearless shampoo. Advice and news about Alzheimer's are offered on the Web site. Alzheimer Solutions, 3122 Knorr St., Philadelphia, PA 19149; telephone: 215-624-2098; www.caregiving-solutions.com.

Clothing Solutions. For women, dresses, muumuus, dusters, two-piece sets, blouses, pants, fleece and other warmer clothing, footwear, sleepwear, and underwear; for men, dressy and casual wear, fleece and warmer clothing, footwear, sleepwear, and underwear, all designed to make dressing easier for the care provider and patient. 1525 West Alton Ave., Santa Ana, CA 92704; telephone: 800-336-2660; www.specialclothing .com.

Colonial Medical Assisted Devices. Door monitors, banner door alarms, exit alerts, knob guards, personal urine alarms, pressure-sensitive alarm mats, and other security devices. 14 Celina Ave. #15, Nashua, NH 03063; telephone: 800-323-6794; colonialmedical.com.

Comfort Clothing. A full line of men's and women's clothing for the special needs of Alzheimer's patients, from underwear to Polartec fleece. Telephone: 888-640-0814; www.comfortclothing.com.

Control Products. Thermostat regulator with auto-call. Telephone: 800-947-9098.

Digital Angel. Electronic tracking devices. With GPS technology, the Alzheimer's patient can be tracked anywhere in the world to within seventy-five feet. The wristband transmitter signals a fall or a dramatic change in temperature around the wearer, and the wanderer alert automatically signals when the wearer goes beyond preset boundaries. South St. Paul, MN; telephone: 866-DGTL-ANGL (348-5264); www.digital angel.net.

Dr. Leonard's. Velcro-closing shoes and other easy-to-wear footwear, plus other home health aids. P.O. Box 7821, Edison, NJ 08818-7821; telephone: 800-785-0880; www.drleonards.com.

Elder Corner. Bathroom aids like full-tub safety mats and tub safety bars, dressing accessories (coiler shoelaces that don't need to be tied), kitchen aids (large-handled flatware), personal care accessories (ergonomically correct bed and back pillows), and more. Telephone: 888-777-1816; www.elder corner.com.

Elder Store. Beamer Video Phone, waterproof sheeting, bed rails, and other elder-care aids and accessories. 920 Park Lane Ct., Alpharetta, GA 30022-2623; telephone: 888-833-8875; www.elderstore.net.

Exclusively Seniors. Home health care products, including bedding protection and incontinence, bathroom safety, back, neck, and foot therapy aids. Telephone: 866-477-7778; www.exclusivelyseniors.com.

Express Medical Supply. Many incontinence products and other medical supplies. On-line or free print catalog available. 218 Seebold, Spur Fenton, MO 63026; telephone: 800-633-2139; www.exmed.net.

Eyes on Elders. Medication dispensers and reminders, fall-detection devices that work even when user is disoriented, unconscious, or otherwise unable to call for help, and remote video-monitoring systems. Featured on MSNBC. VisionAge Technologies, LLC, P.O. Box 231202, Encinitas, CA 92023-1202; telephone: 877-460-5578; www.eyesonelders.com.

Fashions for Special Needs. Adaptive clothing, including wheelchair ponchos, unisex jeans, incontinence clothing, nightwear, wraps, and all-weather gear. 8251 Ridge Rd., RR 4, Welland, ON, Canada L3B 5N7; telephone: 905-384-0741; www.specialneedsclothing.com.

Five Wishes Living Will. This is the most personalized and comprehensive living will, addressing personal, emotional, and spiritual needs as well as medical wishes. It is recognized as a viable document in thirty-five states. Easy to fill out. Aging with Dignity, P.O. Box 1661, Tallahassee, FL 32302; telephone: 888-5WISHES (594-7437); www.agingwithdig nity.org.

Geriatric Resources. Stage-specific products for the care partner and patient, from aromatherapy workbooks to doorstops. Many sensory stimulation products are offered, as well as products designed for professional caregivers. Several catalogs to choose from. Geriatric Resources, Inc., P.O. Box 239, Radium Springs, NM 88054; telephone: 800-359-0390; www.geriatric-resources.com.

Home Delivery Incontinent Supplies. Web-based or mail-order home delivery of a large selection of incontinence products. 9385 Dielman Industrial Dr., Olivette, MO 63132; telephone: 800-2MY-HOME (269-4663); www.hdis.com.

Home Remedies. Automated medication dispensers. Telephone: 800-908-0907.

International Environmental Solutions: Automatic shut-off faucets. 2830 Scherer Dr. N, Suite 310, St. Petersburg, FL 33716; telephone: 800-972-8348; www.ezflo.com.

Internet Wallpaper Store. More than two hundred murals that can be used to camouflage doorways or windows. Telephone: 877-255-0907; www.wallpaperstore.com.

J. C. Penney Special Needs Catalog. Adaptive clothing and home assisting devices. P.O. Box 2021, Milwaukee, WI 53201-2021; telephone: 800-222-6161.

Life at Home. Devices to make the home safe, including wireless and silent wanderer alarms (so the patient isn't frightened), automatic stovetop fire stoppers, carbon monoxide alarms, bathtub grips, doorknob covers, appliance latches, and electronic pill reminders/dispensers. 3630-F Trousdale Dr., Nashville, TN 37204; telephone: 800-653-1923; www.life home.com.

Maddak, Inc., Ableware. Products for independent and assisted living, including bathroom, kitchen, security, communication, tactile/exercise, and therapeutic/recreational aids. 661 Rte. 23, South Wayne, NJ 07470; telephone: 973-628-7600; www.maddak.com.

Maxi Aids. Devices and aids for assisted living and home care, including folding shower chairs, tub and shower mats, no-spill urinals, grab bars and hand grips, toileting aids, and tieless shoelaces. 42 Executive Blvd., Farmingdale, NY 11735; telephone: 800-522-6294; www.maxiaids.com.

MedicAlert. A bracelet or pendant bearing the internationally recognized symbol offers protection for Alzheimer's patients with allergies and other medical problems by alerting any care provider to the wearer's special needs. MedicAlert Foundation International, 2323 Colorado Ave., Turlock, CA 95382; telephone: 800-432-5378; www.medicalert.org.

North Coast Medical Supply. The Functional Solutions catalog features a wide variety of products, including dressing aids, household helpers, adaptive eating utensils, exercise equipment, and transfer devices. 18305

Sutter Blvd., Morgan Hill, CA 95037-2845; telephone: 800-235-7054; www.ncmedical.com.

Personal Touch Health Care Supply. Specialty clothing, including dresses, pants, sweaters and sweatshirts, footwear, and slacks for men and women with incontinence, mobility, and coordination issues. Free shipping on on-line orders of $100 or more. P.O. Box 230321, Brooklyn, NY 11223; telephone: 888-626-1703; www.adaptiveapparel.com.

Pro-Active Eldercare. The themes of the Alzheimer's Survival Kits, which include dozens of activities, range from Springtime to Quilting to Spiritual to Cooking to suit the interests of each Alzheimer's patient. P.O. Box 355, Littleton, MA 01460; telephone: 866-447-0009; fax: 866-447-0008; www.proactiveeldercare.com.

Pyro-Control. Automatic fire-extinguishing system for the stovetop. Telephone: 888-616-7976.

Quilts by Mémère. Handcrafted quilts, bibs, and clothing protectors for adults. www.quiltsbymemere.

Safe and Sound. Safety aids and equipment for seniors, including antiscald valves, large-handled utensils, tub bars and bathtub rails, antislip tub and shower mats, hand-held shower valves, and carbon monoxide alarms. 2490 General Armistead Ave., Suite 202, Norristown, PA 19403; telephone: 610-539-7020; www.123safe.com.

Sammons Preston. Security, bed and bath, home care, adaptive dinnerware, and other aids designed for disabled or cognitively impaired people. Offices in the U.S. and Canada. 4 Sammons Ct., Bolingbrook, IL 60440; telephone: 800-323-5547; www.sammonspreston.com.

Sands Healthcare. Craft project kits. Catalogs include Primelife (for the elderly), Christian Activities, and Judaic Activities. P.O. Box 513, 75 Mill St., Colchester, CT 06415; telephone: 800-243-9232; www.ssww.com.

Security World. Security equipment, including motion detectors, personal alarms, and doorknob alarms. Telephone: 800-669-7328; www.security world.com.

SeniorClix. Adaptive clothing, elder-care products, and the *Sing Along with Barbara* VHS video series, which features seniors singing and interacting in an elder-care setting accompanied on the piano by their exuberant music teacher. 1218 3rd Ave., Suite 500, Seattle, WA 98101; telephone: 1-800-448-5213; www.seniorclix.com.

Seniors, Inc. Adaptive clothing for men and women, including many duster styles, flounces, pantsuits, polo shirts, and jogging suits. 1225 Wagner Dr., P.O. Box 1817, Albertville, AL 35950; telephone: 800-524-4677; www.seniorsinc.com.

Silvert's Elderly Care Clothing. Men's and women's clothing for people with special needs. Free catalog available. Telephone: 1-800-387-7088; www.silverts.com.

Specialty Care Shoppe. Clothing for people with special needs, including those with continence problems, "undressers," those with limited mobility, and Alzheimer's patients in all stages. 16126 E. 161st St. S, Bixby, OK 74008; telephone: 918-366-1208; www.specialtycareshoppe.com.

Stupell Industries. Many styles of faux windows to replace a mirror with a soothing scene. 14 Industrial La., Johnston, RI 02919; telephone: 401-831-5640; www.stupellind.com.

Talon Clothing. Adaptive clothing, including rain gear and outdoor gear such as fleece and water/windproof items, many suited for wheelchair use. 1840 160th St., Suite 247, Surrey, BC, Canada V4A 4X4; www.talonclothing.com.

Telko. Chiming motion detector. Telephone: 800-888-3556.

Trader Joe's. Many finger foods. Stores in eighteen states. Telephone: 800-746-7857; www.traderjoes.com.

Wallpaper Store. Hundreds of murals that can be used to camouflage doors. TandB Decorators, P.O. Box 211, Port Monmouth, NJ 07758; telephone: 800-473-1303; www.thewallpaperstore.com.

WanderCare. Tracking/alert system can track the wanderer from up to a mile away, call the caregiver when the wanderer has strayed, and provide constant updates on the wanderer's location and activity. Telephone: 516-334-7187; www.scorpion-security.com.

Index

accusatory behaviors, 14, 21, 112. *See also* anger; emotional volatility; frustration

acting out, 117–19

activities, enriching
chart of, 142–45
conversational and thinking, 135–36
in daily chores and routines, 130, 136–41
exercises, 130–35
importance of, 127–30
physical, 141–42

activities of daily living (ADL)
defined, 203
daily routines, 130, 136–41
difficulties with, 113
and disease progression, 22–23

AD (Alzheimer's disease) workups, 13–14

adjusting to nursing home, 187–88

ADL. *See* activities of daily living

adult day care, 173–75

advice, from relatives and friends, cautions about, 155–56

afternoon routines, 139

aggressive behavior
as early symptom, warning sign, 14, 21
examples of, 117–19
identifying triggers for, 119–22
sundown syndrome, sundowning, 29, 204–5

alcohol abuse, 15

Alzheimer, Alois, 16

Alzheimer's assisted-living centers, 179, 181–83

Alzheimer's disease. *See also* diagnosis; disease progression
behavior log, 119–22, 203
causes of, 17–18
research, 17–18
workups for, 14–15

Alzheimer's patients
denial by, 21–22
informing of diagnosis, 19, 80
insights, inspiration from, 54–57, 193–99
response of others to, 48–49
talking about the disease with, 49–52
world of, living in, 8, 108–9

amyloid and tau protein deposits, 16

anger
as early symptom, 21–22
how to handle, 112
triggers for, 118–22, 196

Anthony, Jim, 195–96

anti-inflammatory medications, 18

anxiety, fears
addressing constructively, 46, 50–54, 108–9
continual, 123–24
paranoia, hallucinations, 122–23
triggers for, 87–88, 118–22

appearance, grooming, changes in, 4–5, 21

appreciation, expressing, 40–41, 130

Aricept, 18

assisted-living centers, 179, 181–83

autopsy, diagnosis at, 16

Axura (memantine), 18

babying, avoiding, 36, 38

Banging along with Bach exercise, 132

bathing, 85–89. See also daily routines

bathrooms, enhancing visibility, comfort of, 63, 87, 101–4

bedtime, 106–7. See also daily routines

behavior logs, 73, 119–22, 203

behavioral changes
aggressive, angry behaviors, 112, 117–19
concentration problems, 112
decision-making difficulties, 111–12
difficulties with numbers, computation, 114
difficulties with writing, reading, 113–14
as early symptom, 20–22
emotional volatility, 115
evaluating causes for, 109
fantasy worlds, 112–13
frustration, 113
inappropriate behaviors, 115
judgment changes, 113
living in past, 114
loss of inhibition, self-control, 115
memory loss, 110–11
reaction time changes, 114–15
reactions to holidays, 115–16
recognition problems, 111, 115
repetitiveness, 110
task sequencing, 113
time perception, 110
word-finding difficulties, 111

blender beverages, 210–11

body language. See nonverbal communication

bone marrow test, 16

books about Alzheimer's, 221–4

burnout, in care partner, 149–51

busy apron, 203

calm. See also habilitation care model
as goal of habilitator, 53–54
importance of, 7, 118–19
and nonverbal communication, 82–83
and sensory signals, 45–46

care approaches, 33–34. See also habilitation care model

care partner. See also support services
bringing patient into home of, 170–71
burnout symptoms, 149–51
daily routines, suggested structure for, 137–41

defined, 203

eating with patient, importance of, 98

emphasizing patient's skills, 37–39

extra help, relief for, 30–31, 107, 153

and habilitation approach, 33–34, 43–46

handling aggressive, angry behaviors, 118–19

handling patient's sexual needs, 124–26

handling verbal communications, 77–81

listening skills, 49, 130

long-distance care, 158–62

nursing home placement, 186–89

and patient sleeping problems, 104–5

reality orientation approach, 32–33

self-care, tips for, 151–53

share-care, 171–72

support groups for, 156–58

talking with patient about disease, 49–52

care plan
developing, 28–31
and financial planning, 23–24
home care, 163–75
out-of-home care, 176–92
reviewing and evaluating, 47, 176–78

Carrots on the Hat Rack exercise, 134

cars, driving decisions, 24–28

case managers, 172–73

catastrophic reactions, 117–18

celebrations, problems around, 115–16

Celebrex, 18

certified nursing assistants, 167–68

challenging behaviors. *See* behavioral changes

chewing and swallowing problems, 23, 100

childproofing devices, 69–70

choices
handling effectively, 43–44, 111–12
"last word" connection, 81
and self-esteem, 39

cholesterol-lowering drugs, 19

clay, working with, 133

clocks, large-face, 56

closed support groups, 157

clothing. *See also* dressing
choosing, guidelines for, 92–93
sources for, 227–32

color schemes, 63–65

communication
connecting with patient, importance of, 198–99
in habilitation care model, 44–45
handling language difficulties, 77–81
"last word" connection, 81
nonverbal, 7, 81–84

companions, hired, 168

concentration problems, 112

confusion. *See* behavioral changes; perceptual changes

constipation, 104

contrasting visual fields, 64–65, 96, 102–3, 203. *See also* environmental modification

conversation, including patient in, 48–52, 80, 130

COPE self-care, for care partner, 152–53

Counting Backward exercise, 134

crafts and hobbies
    sources of materials, 227–32
    suggested activities, 143
creative approaches
    to bathing, 89
    to dressing, 90–91
    in habilitation care model, 6, 57
Cronin-Golomb, Alice, 63
crying, importance of, 196
cueing, when eating, 98
culturally based support groups, 157

daily care
    bathing, 85–89
    and disease progression, 22–23
    dressing, 89–94
    eating, 94–101
    need for professional care, 23
    routine, importance of, 136–41
    sleeping, 104–7
    toileting, 101–4
daily routines, suggestions for, 137–41
day care centers, 173–75
deafness, assumptions about, 48–49
decision-making, including patient in, 173. *See also* choices; self-esteem
dehydration, 97
dementia, defined, 14
denial
    by friends and family, 4, 50, 155–56
    by patient, 13, 20–22, 24–28
depression, 15
    as trigger for aggressive behaviors, 126
diagnosis
    AD workups, 13–15
    challenges of, 15–16
    early, tests for, 16–18
    and long-term care plans, 186
    risk factors, 17–18
    sharing with friends and family, 6, 55
    sharing with patient, 19, 23–24
    symptom-relieving, delaying products, 18–19
    warning signs, 14
disease progression
    behavioral changes, 22–23
    and care plan, 28–31, 176–78
    and need for out-of-home care, 176–77
disorientation, 14
distractions, eliminating, 63–64
domains, in habilitation model, 41–47
Down's syndrome, 157
dressing, 89–94
Drivers Fifty-Five and Older: Self-Rating Form, 24–28
driving, decisions about, 24–28
drug interactions, 15

early afternoon routine, 139
early diagnosis, importance of, 17, 159
early middle stage, 23
early morning routine, 137
early stage
    behavioral changes, 20–22
    duration, 19
    enrichment exercises, 130–36
    memory loss, 111
    patient and caregiver support groups for, 157–58
    patient's point of view during, 54–57, 193–99
    physical activities, 141
    sexual needs, 124–25
early-onset patients, support groups for, 157

eating
    finger foods, 207–10
    food preferences, respecting, 99–
        100
    food-related enrichment activi-
        ties, 142–43
    and nutritional needs, 97–98
    staples, 206–7
    tips for easier, 95–97
emotional needs
    allowing patient to express, 49
    assessing, reassessing, 29, 46–47
    communication using, 6–7, 45,
        57, 81–84
    supporting throughout daily
        routine, 130
emotional volatility. See also anxi-
    ety; anger; frustration
    how to handle, 115
    as symptom, 14, 15
    triggers for, 119–22, 126
endocrine imbalances, 15
enrichment
    chart of activities, 142–45
    conversational and thinking ac-
        tivities, 135–36
    importance of, 127–30
    mental and cognitive exercises,
        130–35
    physical activities, 141–42
    wall hangings as, 68–69
environmental modification
    bathrooms, 87, 101–4
    color schemes, 63–65
    flooring, 65–66
    furniture, wall hangings, 67–69
    goals of, 62
    interior pathways, marking, 66–
        67, 102
    as management tool, 35–36
    sleeping arrangements, 106–7
evening routines, 139–41

excess disability, 37–38, 203
Exelon, 18
exercises. See also daily routines
    mental and cognitive, 130–36
    physical, 141–42, 151
expectations
    high, maintaining, 104
    realistic, 46
eye contact, 48–49, 81–82, 118

falls, preventing, 65–66
family history, as risk factor, 17–18
family members. See also social
        needs
    cautions about, 154–56
    reconnecting with, 56
    support, help from, 30, 107, 166
    talking with patient about the
        disease, 49–52
fantasy world, living in, 22, 112–13
fears. See anxiety
fencing, for outdoor areas, 72
final stage, 23, 163–64. See also be-
    havioral changes; care plan
financial planning, 23–24
fine motor skills, 23, 204
finger foods, 97, 207–10
fish oils, 19
fish tanks, 68–69
Five Wishes Living Will, 24
flooring, 65–66
Floor Plans exercise, 134–35
focusing, problems with, 22–23, 51–
        52
focusing on what is left. See habili-
    tation care model; strengths
food and nutrition
    eating routines, 95–97
    finger foods, 207–10
    food preferences, respecting, 99–
        100
    food-related activities, 142–43

food and nutrition (*cont.*)
  staples, 206–7
  vitamins, 18
forgetfulness
  fears about, addressing, 51–52
  how to handle, 110–11
  memory-stimulating exercises,
    130–35
  as part of disease process, 20–23
  as warning sign, 12–14
friends. *See also* social needs
  cautions about, 154–56
  staying connected with, 56, 129–
    30
  talking with patient about the
    disease, 50–52
frustration(s). *See also* environmen-
    tal modification
  distractions, 63–64
  during exercises and activities,
    136
  how to handle, 113
  over mirrors, family photo-
    graphs, 67–68
  over speech problems, 77–78, 126
Fun with a Puzzle exercise, 135
functional domain, 43–44. *See also*
    daily routines
functioning, changes in, as warning
    sign, 13–14
furniture
  and enhancing physical domain,
    67–69
  in outdoor environments, 72
  placement of, 70–71

games, 144
gardening, 71
gas stoves, ovens, 70
gates, safety, 69
Geller, Shirley, 197–98
gender-based support groups, 157

genetic predisposition, 16
geriatricians, 159, 204
Ginkgo biloba, 18
glare, eliminating, 63, 68
gliders, 67
grapeseed extract, 18
green tea extract, 18
grooming, appearance, 4–5, 21, 94.
    See also dressing
group home/foster-care setting,
    179, 180

habilitation care model
  bathing, 86–89
  communication domain, 77–84
  components, 33–35
  defined, 7, 204
  development of, 10–11
  domains, 41–47
  dressing, 89–94
  eating, 94–101
  emphasis on strengths, self-
    esteem, 36–41, 85–86
  enriching activities, 127–45
  environmental modification, 35–
    36
  handling behavioral changes,
    108–26
  physical domain, 62–76
  results, 39–40
  and sleep problems, 104–7
  thinking creatively, 6, 75–76,
    89
  toileting, 101–4
  value of, 198–99
habilitator-based home care, 164,
    165–70
habilitator, defined, 204. *See also*
    care partner
hallucinations, paranoia, 53–54. *See
    also* anxiety
Hard to Forget (Pierce), 17

Harris, Sandra, 63
hearing, 45–46. *See also* sound sensitivity
helpers
    evaluating need for, 30–31
    introducing to patient, 166
herbal care products, 18
holidays, problems around, 115–16
home care
    getting extra help, relief, 30–31
    by habilitator, 164, 165–70
    value of, 163–64
home furnishings, specialized, 222–28
home-health aides, 107
home health care agencies
    evaluating, 168–69
    services provided by, 167
housekeepers, 168
humor, importance of, 55, 83–84, 196
hypersexuality, 124–26

images, marking items using, 36, 69
inappropriate behaviors, handling, 81, 115, 117–19, 124–26
incontinence, 63, 103–4
independence
    and environmental modifications, 29, 35, 38–39
    making judgments about, 39–40
infections, 15
inhibition, loss of, 115. *See also* behavioral changes
initiative, loss of, 14
inspiration, from Alzheimer's patients, 193–99
intimacy needs, 29, 124–25
isolation, minimizing, 44, 128–30

judgment problems, 14, 113

labeling household items, 36, 69
language and speech problems
    frustrations around, 77–78, 126
    handling effectively, 78–81
    nonverbal communication, 7, 45, 81–84, 169
    as warning sign, 14
"last word" connection, 81, 111
late afternoon routine, 139
late early stage, behavioral changes, 22
late middle stage, behavioral changes, 23
late morning routine, 138
late (final) stage
    behavioral changes, 23
    chewing and swallowing problems, 100
laughter, importance of, 55, 83–84, 196
laundry, tips on doing, 36
lifespan care, 190–91
lighting, enhancing, 62–63, 102
listening. *See also* nonverbal communication
    to patient, 49, 55–57
    practicing, 130
loneliness, 128–30
long-distance care, 158–62
long-term-care facilities, 204. *See also* nursing homes
lumbar puncture test, 16

Making Items with Clay exercise, 133
mealtime exercise, 131–32
Medicaid, 24, 172
medical decision-making, 24
Medicare, 172
medications
    appropriate use of, 191
    incontinence from, 103

medications (*cont.*)
  monitoring, 109
  for relief, reduction of symp-
    toms, 18–19
  for sleep, 107
memantine (Axura), 18
"memory" cards, 111
memory loss
  fears about, addressing, 51–52
  how to handle, 110–11
  memory-stimulating exercises,
    130–35
  as part of disease process, 20–23
  as warning sign, 12–14
mentally retarded adults, caregivers
  for, 157
metabolic disorders, 15
middle early stage, behavioral
  changes, 22
middle middle stage, behavioral
  changes, 23
middle stage
  duration, 19
  typical behaviors, 176–77
midmorning routine, 137
mirrors, 67–68, 87
misplacing things, as warning sign,
  14. *See also* forgetfulness
Mittelman, Mary, 49
mood changes, as warning sign, 14.
  See also emotional volatility
morning routines, 137–38
motor skills, stimulating, 144–45
moving patient
  closer to care partner, 161
  to nursing home, 186–87
musical activities, 142, 222

naproxen, 18
nasal-passage tissue examination, 16
National Alzheimer's Association
  founding of, 10–11

locating diagnostic facilities, 14
Safe Return program, 56, 204
neighborhood supports, 165–66
neurofibrillary tangles, 16
neuro-psych evaluations, 13–14, 204
nightmares, 106
noise, sound dampening, 72–74.
  See also sound sensitivity
nonverbal communication
  importance of, 169
  sharing emotionally, 7
  tips for enhancing, 81–84
  tone of voice, 45
noontime routine, 138–39
numbers, difficulties with, 114
nursing aides, assistants, 167–68
nursing home
  adjustment to, 187–88
  assessing, factors to consider,
    184–86
  bringing patient to, 186–87
  deciding on need for, 178–79, 183
  financial planning for, 24
  outings from, 145
  reality orientation versus habili-
    tation in, 32–33
nutrition. *See also* eating
  meeting needs, tips for, 97–98
  problems, 15

odors
  changes in perception of, 45
  pleasant, 45–46
  stimulating, 133–34
omega-3 fatty acids, 19
open-ended support groups, 157
optimal independent functional
  level, 39–40, 204
orientation, disorientation, 204. *See
  also* behavioral changes
outbursts, 52–53. *See also* anger;
  emotional volatility

outdoor activities. *See also* daily
  routines
outdoor environments
  safety issues in, 71–72
  urinating in, 101
outings
  ideas for, 143–44
  from nursing home, 145, 188–89
out-of-home care
  assisted-living centers, 181–83
  decisions about, 176–79
  group homes/foster care, 180
  nursing homes, 183–89
  special-care units (SCUs), 189–92
overstimulation, avoiding, 72–73,
  83

pain, and changes in sleep patterns,
  105–6
palliative care, 204
Panella, John, 10
panic reactions, 73, 88
paranoia, hallucinations
  and changing perceptual abili-
    ties, 53–54
  as trigger for aggressive behav-
    iors, 122–23
paranoid behavior, 112
past, living in, 114
paths, outdoor, 71
pathways, interior, marking, 66–67,
  102
patience
  while dressing patient, 93
  importance of, 56, 83
Pecora, Lois, 54, 135–36
perceptual changes. *See also* physical needs
  accommodating, 46, 75–76
  and bathing, 87
  sound sensitivity, 46, 55–56, 72–
    74

as triggers for emotional outbursts, 120–21
visual confusion, 62–65
personality change, as warning sign,
  14
physical exercise, importance of,
  120–21, 141–42
physical aggression, 117–22
physical needs
  assessing, reassessing, 29, 109,
    124–25
  color schemes, 63–65
  flooring, 65–66
  furniture, 67–70
  in habilitation care model, 43
  interior pathways, marking, 66–
    67
  labels, 36
  lighting, 62–63
  noise, sound-dampening, 72–74
  outdoor environments, 71–72
  safety, 7, 61–62, 69–70
  specialty products, 222–28
physicians, 25, 51, 80, 159, 160. *See
  also* care plan; diagnosis
Pierce, Charlie, 17
plan of care. *See* care plan
plaques, 16
portion sizes, 98
praise, value of, 40–41, 104, 130
privacy, time alone
  care partner's need for, 152
  patient's need for, 70–71, 198–
    99
professional care, planning for, 23
progressive dementia
  disease progression, 22–23
  responses to diagnosis, 48–50
Proverbs exercise, 135

questioning patient
  avoiding, 83

questioning patient (*cont.*)
  memory-stimulating exercises, 135–36
  offering choices, 111
questions to ask about support services
  assisted-living centers, 181–82
  home health care agencies, 168–69
  nursing homes, 184–85
  special-care units, 189–91
quiet time, patient's need for, 70–71, 198–99

Raia, Paul, 41, 54, 130–35
reaction time, changes in, 114–15
Reading by Tens exercise, 133
reading problems
  enrichment exercises, 133
  handling effectively, 78–79, 113–14
reality orientation model, 32–33
reasoning, futility of, 86
recognition problems, 111, 115, 125
reflector tape, for marking pathways, 63, 101–2
Reisman, Bernard, 194–95
rejection by patient, learning to handle, 52–54. *See also* anger
relatives. *See* family members
relaxing
  before bedtime, activities for, 140
  by care partner, 151–52, 154
Reminyl, 18
remoteness, withdrawal, 29, 52
repetitive activities, value of, 130. *See also* enrichment
repetitiveness, as symptom, 110
resources. *See also* support services
  books about Alzheimer's, 221–4
  clothing, furnishing, specialty products, 227–232

music, 226–7
organizations, 212–21
specialty products, 227–232
videos, 224–6
respite care, 164–70
rewards, 47
risk factors, 17, 19
routine, daily
  calming effect of, 122
  importance of, 28–29, 43, 130
  and meals, 99
  structuring, 136–41

Safe Return program, 56, 204
safety
  addressing effectively, 65–66, 69–70
  in bathrooms, 88
  concerns about, 30–31, 53–54
  products, sources for, 222–28
saliva test, 16
scolding, avoidance of, 38, 198. *See also* habilitation care model
SCUs. *See* special-care units
selenium, 18
self-control, loss of, 115
self-esteem
  communicating nonverbally, 82–83
  encouraging through listening, 34, 49
  and feeling useful, 36–37
  finding ways to enhance, 7–8
  and food preferences, 97, 99–100
  in habilitation care model, 45, 47–49, 198
  praise, 41
  and public speaking, 193–94
  tips for encouraging, 55–57
sensory domain. *See also* perceptual changes
  addressing sensory loss, 45–46

sensory stimulation exercises, 130–35
sound sensitivity, 72–74
services. See resources; support services
"Seven-Minute Screen," 16
sexual behavior, sexual needs, 124–26
share-care, 171–72, 204
short-term-memory loss. See memory loss
silence, allowing, 198–99
Silverio, Elaine, 54
skills, remaining, focusing on, 7, 8, 36–37, 85–89, 194–99. See also habilitation care model
sleeping, 104–7. See also bedtime
sloppiness, as early symptom, 21
smell, sense of
    changes in, 45
    stimulating, exercise for, 133–34
"sniff" test, 16
social needs
    assessing, reassessing, 29–30
    dining activities, 98–99
    enriching activities, value of, 127–30
    furniture arrangements for, 70–71
    in habilitation care model, 44
soothing activities
    at bath time, 88–89
    before bedtime, 106–7
sound sensitivity, 46, 55, 72–74
special-care units (SCUs)
    assessing, 189–92
    defined, 179, 204–5
    habilitation care model in, 9
special moments, savoring, 161–62
speech and language problems
    frustrations around, 77–78, 126
    handling effectively, 78–81

and nonverbal communication, 7, 45, 81–84, 169
    as warning sign, 14
spiritual needs
    activities for addressing, 143
    identifying, 29
staples, food, 206–7
statins, 19
Stimulating the Sense of Smell exercise, 133–34
Stimulating the Senses exercise, 132
stores, using familiar, 111
strengths, focusing on, 7, 8, 36–37, 85–89, 142, 194–99. See also habilitation care model
stress. See also anxiety; frustration
    in care partner, 149–51, 154
    minimizing, in habilitation model, 41
sundown syndrome, sundowning, 29, 204–5
support groups, 15
    for care partners, 126
    for patients, 54–57, 156–58
support organizations, 212–21
support services. See also resources
    assisted-living centers, 181–83
    home care, 159–61, 164–69
    group homes/foster care, 180
    nursing homes, 183–89
    special-care units (SCUs), 189–92
swallowing problems, 23, 100
symptoms
    early, 14, 20–22
    products to relieve, delay, 18–19

task-sequencing difficulties, 113
temperature-taking, 109
time
    care partner's need for, 152–54
    patient's changing perceptions of, 110

time of day, as trigger for aggressive behaviors, 121
toileting, 101–4. *See also* bathing; bathrooms
tone of voice, 45. *See also* communication
Touch and Tell exercise, 131
touch lamps, 102
touch-based activities, 143
trauma, 15
triggers, for emotional outbursts
  anxiety, 123–24
  depression, 126
  during exercises and activities, 136
  identifying through behavior logs, 119–22
  paranoia, hallucinations, 122–23
  sexual feelings, 124–26

understanding, versus speaking, 79

verbal casserole, 204–5
verbal skills, stimulating, 144

videos about Alzheimer's, 224–26
visiting nurses, 159–60, 167
visual enhancements. *See* perceptual changes: accommodating; physical needs
visual skills, activities for stimulating, 144
vitamins, 18

wall hangings, 67–69
warning signs, early symptoms, 14, 20–22
What Time Is It? exercise, 132
What's the Main Idea? exercise, 131
Which One Is Different? exercise, 132–33
withdrawal, 29, 52
word-finding difficulties, 14, 22, 111. *See also* conversation; speech and language problems
writing, difficulties with, 78–79, 113–14

Vermilion books are available from all good bookshops or by ordering direct on 01624 677237. Or visit our website at *www.randomhouse.co.uk*